AF471232

LUCY + JORGE ORTA
LIGHT WORKS

black dog publishing
london uk

CONTENTS

5 JAMES PUTMAN
Language of LIGHT

9 GABRIELLA SALGADO
Printing with LIGHT

20 LIGHT WORKS

22 IMPRINTS ON THE ANDES 1992
52 RITES AND SACRIFICES 1992
56 LEÇONS TÉNÈBRES 1991
62 POÈME INFOGRAPHIQUE 1991
68 POÈME INFOGRAPHIQUE II 1991
72 POÈME INFOGRAPHIQUE III 1991
78 LIGHT OF STONE 1993
94 SACRED LIGHT 1994
102 THE CRY FROM THE EARTH 1994
118 WOVEN LIGHT 1995
134 PATHS OF LIGHT 1995
140 LIGHT MESSENGER 1995
156 VIA CRUCIS 1996
168 CROSSROADS 1996
174 OPERA.tion LIFE NEXUS Act IV 2000
176 NEXO CORAZÓN Act V 2001
180 OPERA.tion LIFE NEXUS Act IV 2001
184 OPERA.tion LIFE NEXUS Act VIII 2002
192 OPERA.tion LIFE NEXUS Act IX 2003
202 LILLE LIGHTS 2003–2004
208 CASA ABIERTA 2006
214 LIGHTS ON TAMPA 2006
224 BRASILIA EM LUZ 2009

230 BIOGRAPHY
231 BIOGRAPHIES OF CONTRIBUTORS
232 LUCY+JORGE ORTA CURRICULUM VITAE
235 ACKNOWLEDGEMENTS
236 BIBLIOGRAPHY

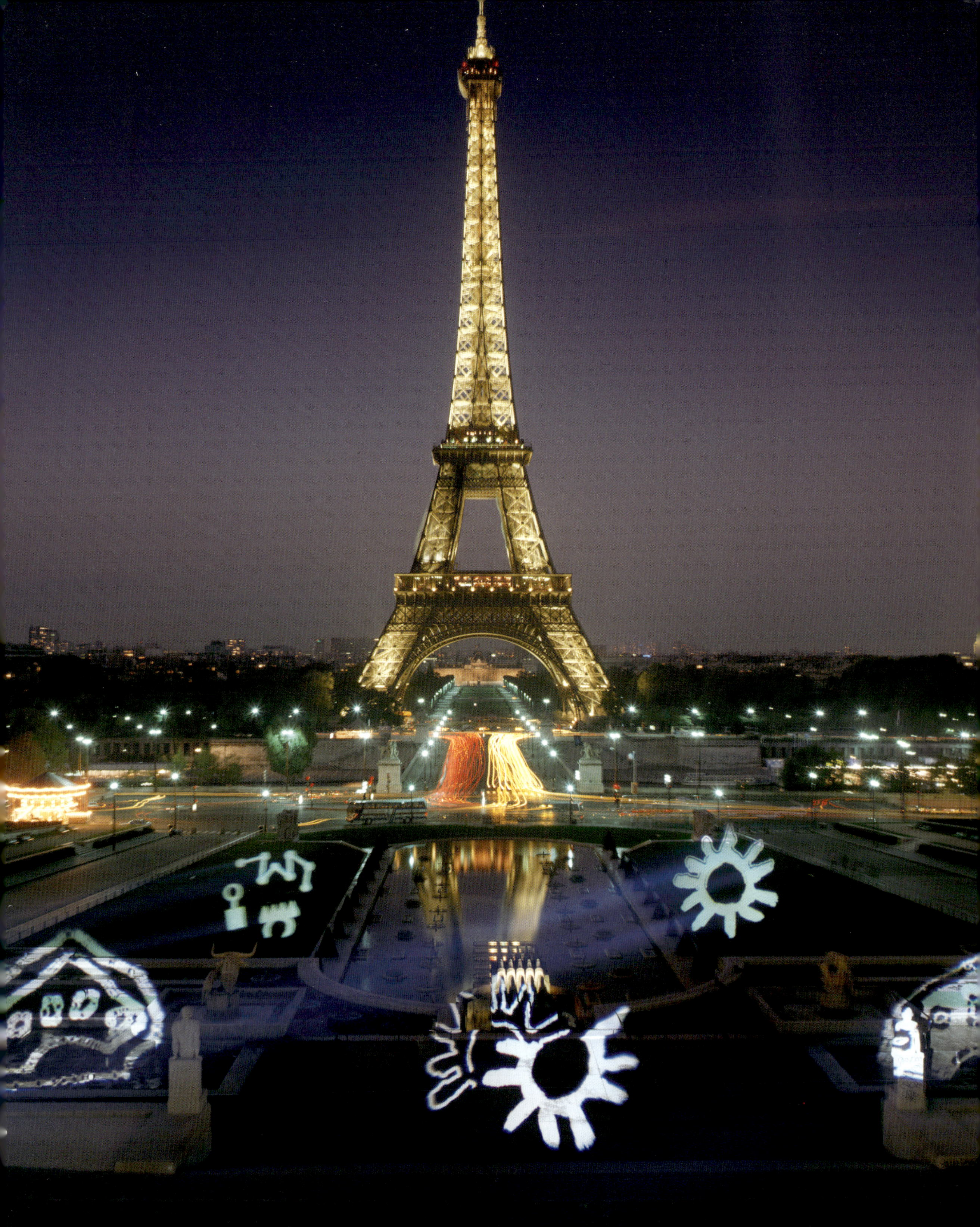

JAMES PUTMAN

Language of LIGHT

Everything we see is a product of, and is affected by, the nature of light. Since the beginning of time, it has been a vital part of our lives and continues to have a great impact on art. As a form of energy that our sense of sight can detect, light also forms the basis of our perception of the primary colours, which artists have traditionally used when mixing pigment. It is the chosen medium for Studio Orta's Light Works where vast projectors act as 'brushes' to paint the landscape with it. The central visual component of Light Works is a codified system of thousands of graphic marks and signs called the planetary alphabet. This vast ongoing lexicon consists of representational and conceptual elements, drawn from diverse regions and cultures of the world both past and present. Linked to collective memory, it is a composite fusion of cultural, sacred, mythical and social elements. The alphabet is political in that it contests the notion of national identity in favour of a global vocabulary that aspires to communicate universal meaning. The signs comprise of individual pictograms of anthropomorphic shapes that aim to mirror our social reality. Besides personal artist statements, the signs and marks allude to familiar and obscure symbols, glyphs, pictograms and icons from biblical, hermetic and other mystical traditions. There's also frequent reference to archaeological material like the signs used in ancient writing systems such as Chinese pictograms or Mayan and Egyptian hieroglyphs that represent different objects, actions, sound or ideas.

The signs have their roots in circles, triangles, arrows, dots, suns, crosses, squares and other geometric shapes which are synthesised to create a pictographic, seemingly animated language of light. Some of the signs also resemble the ancient markings and carvings on stone called "petroglyphs". These tend to incorporate the five most universal shapes—the circle, the cross, the triangle, the spiral and the square. It is claimed that some of these prehistoric drawings and paintings with abstract non-figurative patterns, such as zigzags, wavy lines, dots, grids and arabesques result from the vision of people undergoing trance. This may have a relationship with shamanistic rituals or be purely schematic with narrative functions. Pictograms are still in use as the main medium of written communication in some non-literate Third World cultures. Because of their graphical nature and fairly realistic style they are also common in contemporary urban life as simple, pictorial, representational symbols where they are widely used to indicate services in public areas. In the same way the planetary alphabet is intended as a form of global communication that transcends linguistic and cultural boundaries.

The alphabet is an ever-evolving system to represent inherently human archetypical signs. This has parallels with CG Jung's proposal that some symbols are 'archetypes' since they have a universal range of meaning across individual and cultural

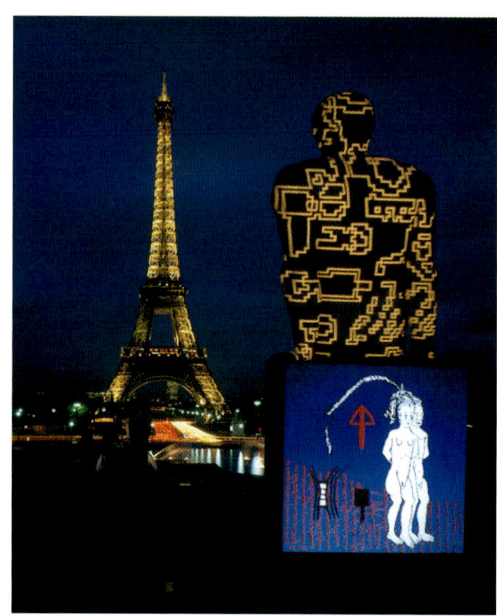
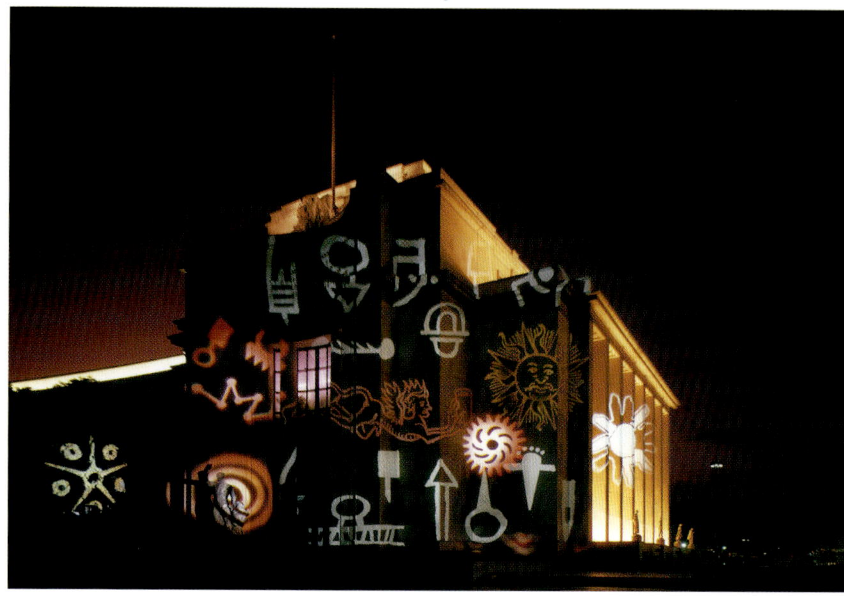

Rive des Amériques, 1992
Musée de l'Homme Paris, France
Commemorating the 500-year anniversary of the "Encounter of two Worlds"

borders. When we view signs or symbols, their meanings and associations are naturally and unavoidably there. We acquire universal associations all through our life, and usually without being aware that we are acquiring them. The planetary alphabet includes signs that will have personal, cultural, and universal associations for the viewer conveying many unpredictable layers of meaning to a diverse audience. Rooted in drawing practice it is both personal and archetypical. According to Jorge Orta the alphabet comprises in part "contextual signs and images of a collective memory". Each project has provided the opportunity to create a multitude of new signs assisted by the advances in computer technology and digital manipulation since the early 1990s. The ongoing alphabet has been organised into a number of specific categories: Ideogram Signs, Objects Signs, Meta-social Signs, Textual Signs and Sound Signs.

For each project the methodology involves a process of intensive research into the history and the present locale of the individual sites in order to develop the signs. *Imprints on the Andes* at Macchu Pichu and *Rives des Amériques* in Paris, 1992, had elements of Inca hieroglyphs and incorporated aspects of the present day indigenous culture. It included extensive studies of ancient Peru petroglyphs, Inca illustrations and reports of the Spanish conquest by local people both past and present on exhibit in the Musée des Beaux-Arts in Chartres. For *The Cry of the Earth*, 1994, the Aso volcano project, Kyushu, Japan, the research process involved the sketching of the source imagery on paper scrolls in calligraphic ink. The designs of natural forms like leaves, shells and stones were projected as abstracted ideograms, providing an intuitive sign system originating in nature.

The signs used in *Woven Light*, 1995, at Cappadocia were inspired by motifs found in traditional Turkish rugs, which were emblematic of the collective memory of the troglodyte villages. *Sacred Light*, 1994, celebrating Chartres Cathedral's 800th anniversary, included signs based on crosses and other Christian iconography and the signatures of the stonemasons who originally built it.

The signs are usually projected onto immense locations in places of natural beauty or cultural significance using the so-called "image cannons" invented by French engineer, Léon Miquel. Presentation to mass-audiences relates to Jorge Orta's notion of *Citizen Art* and his first innovative public actions in Rosario, Argentina from the late 1970s. Here he staged projections in public spaces using the latest technologies such as carrousel slide projectors or video monitors in front of large audiences. This was during the military dictatorship (1976–1983) when public gatherings for art performances were forbidden as they were viewed as potentially subversive. In resistance to the government art censorship, like some other South American artists, who used Mail Art and performance such as Eugenio Dittborn or Edgardo Vigo, Orta's practice broadened from painting to include a non-object based alternative form of visual communication. Light Works subsequently evolved as an ongoing practice with a mission to communicate with a wider public rather than a specialist art audience. Light Works are anti-materialistic and outreach to a vast audience on their own terrain beyond the confines of the insular, elitist system of gallery-based contemporary art.

Although the planetary alphabet is present in Jorge Orta's formative solo works it continues to feature in major projects done in collaboration with his partner Lucy with whom he founded Studio Orta in Paris in 1991. The following year they worked together on *Imprints on the Andes*, which is probably the most quintessential example of Light Works, due both to its conceptual impact and technical complexity. The project included an arduous expedition with heavy equipment across the Andes mountain range, to reach Machu Picchu which is one of the most impressive pre-Columbian archaeological sites. It involved projecting the signs from the planetary alphabet on to the sacred mountains surrounding the ancient ruins before two hundred thousand spectators. The event coincided with the official celebrations of the 500th anniversary of the discovery of the Americas. However in the local context this project represented a symbolic act of resistance from the indigenous inhabitants of America as a challenge to the official celebration of the discovery of America by Christopher Columbus.

Imprints on the Andes was also staged to coincide with the traditional Inca festival of the sun or *Inti Raymi*, to mark the winter solstice of the Southern Hemisphere. This was the most important and spectacular annual festivity carried out by the Incas who believed they were descendants of the sun. Nowadays it is held on 24 June in Saqsaywaman, a fortress built by the Incas in the sixteenth century to resist the invasion of the Spanish *conquistadores*. It comprises a ceremony with the crowning of the Inca king who is actually an ordinary citizen chosen among the people to be the leader of the solar year. Hundreds participate wearing historical Inca costumes, and during the ceremony the incarnation of the Sun God delivers a speech containing guidance for the times ahead to the assembled multitude. *Imprints on the Andes* was therefore able to communicate with the local spectators and revitalise their ancient traditions. Although they were generally unable to read and write they were familiar with some of the signs and pictograms that related to their own culture, which were projected over their sacred mountains.

The site or landscape onto which the signs are projected becomes an integral part of each project although the Light Works should not be confused with Land Art. Their intention is more anthropological than visual, driven by conservation and environmental concerns involving a complex fusion of cosmology, collective memory, social experiences and popular beliefs. Some of the most effective projects have involved sites that have a sacred significance such as Machu Picchu, Cappadocia and Chartres Cathedral. They add an important dimension to *Light Works* because they are interwoven with peoples' beliefs, traditions, religions and rituals. Besides being used for worship, prayers and sacrificial offerings to deities, many sacred places were once sites for seeking oracular wisdom or spiritual purification. They also symbolise a kind of world axis since some of them are built on ley lines that are believed to give them psychic energy. Sacred places can often retain an aura of sanctity simply because our senses can react in the same ways as they did in our ancient forebears. They provoke a sense of the spiritual within us now as then, because even though the way our minds work may differ from our ancestors, we share common psychological impressions. Some inborn need to experience place in such meaningful ways could explain why so many of us are attracted to powerful sacred sites of antiquity steeped in the mythic power and imagery of our ancestors. And yet they are deemed sacred not only through the physical characteristics of their locations but also because of the mentality that perceives them as sacred.

By temporarily illuminating the landscape Light Works can reawaken a lost sense of spirituality in the spectators and offer them an opportunity to reflect on mankind's origin and ongoing existence with an awareness of the unbounded universe. They may prompt quite complex questions by means of an alternate history where the landscape resonates with narratives of collective memory and personal experiences. Light Works facilitate a kind of psychogeography with a placement of memory through association with forgotten language, names, stories, myths and rituals. They reference the past through the planetary alphabet of signs where buildings and landscape are rendered contemporary through a synthesis of past and present civilisation. Light Works embrace Studio Orta's ongoing mission to establish connections between mankind and nature, linking the historical context of the site with a collective consciousness thereby creating a powerful fusion of self, space and time.

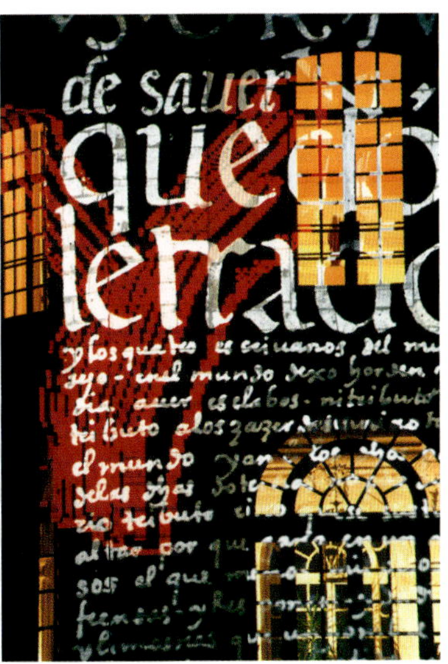

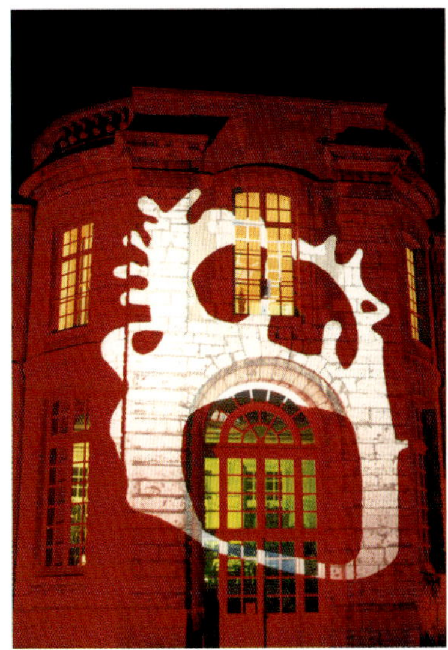

L'Art des Incas, 1992
Musée des Beaux-Arts Chartes, France
Opening of the exhibition The Art of the Incas

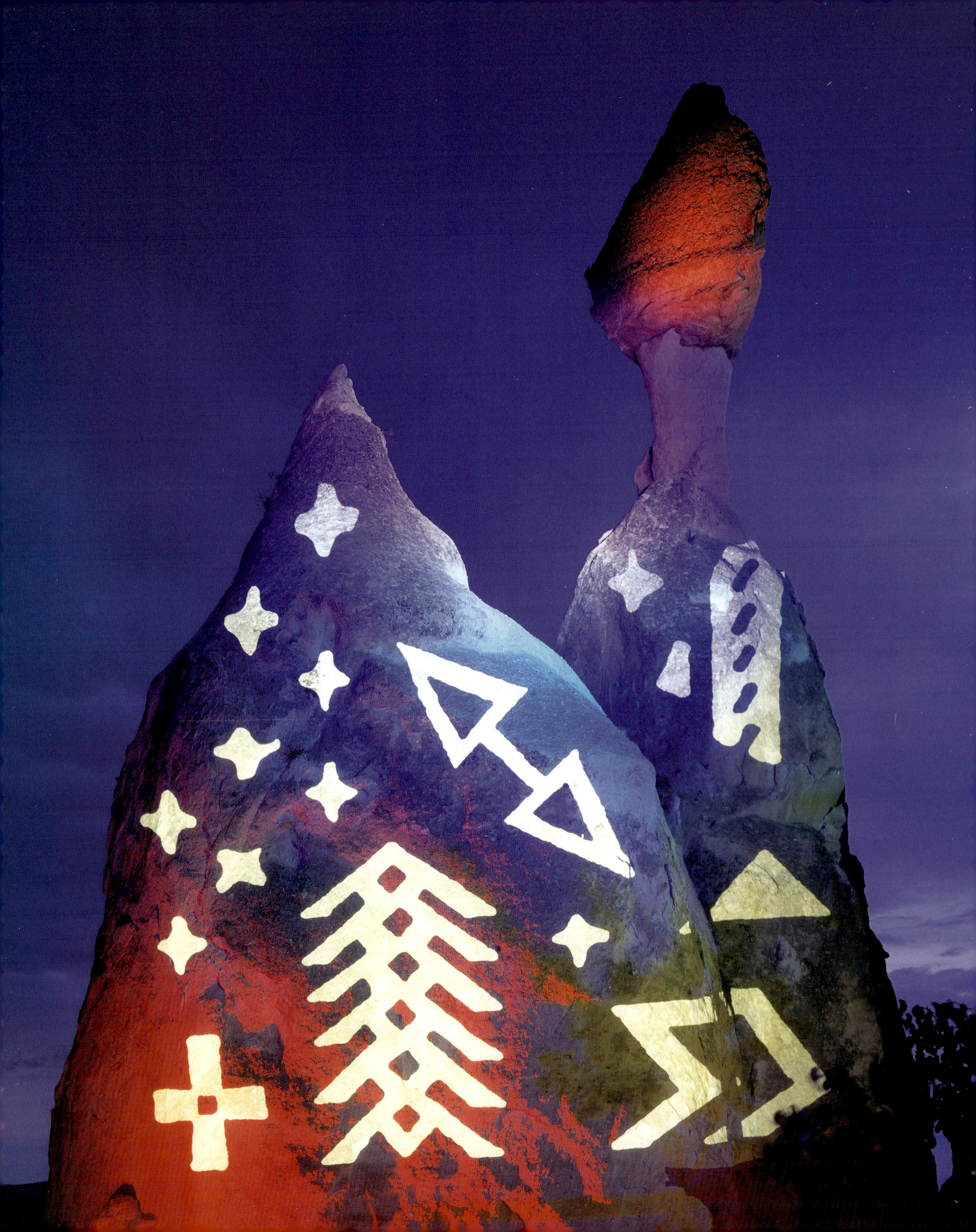

GABRIELLA SALGADO

Printing with LIGHT

In 1946, Argentine artist Gyula Kosice made the first light-based sculpture, a simple form made of neon, years before the widespread use of the material by American and European Minimalist artists.[1] However, the recognition of this groundbreaking artwork as pioneering in the use of electric light is notably recent. The history of twentieth century art as known in Western countries seems to disregard key moments of innovation in art-making that blossomed in the rest of the world, producing dynamic currents and breakthroughs. Gyula Kosice's theoretical approach to art was based in an experimental use of materials and processes including water, light and mechanical movement; but also contributed to expanding the realm of art from the confined space of galleries and museums to the streets through actions and interventions in the 1940s.

Madí's emancipatory premises were to be explored and developed further by artists in Argentina, Brazil and Venezuela from the 1950s to the 1970s, fostering various material and philosophical breakthroughs such as Brazilian *Neoconcretismo*, the Kinetic art movement in Venezuela and *Tucumán Arde* and the Experimental Art Week in Rosario, Argentina. These initiatives were echoing the concerns of European and American artists such as those associated with Fluxus who in the same period were investigating indeterminacy, questioning authorship and including chance elements in their work.

In Latin America one of the artists who embraced an art to be completed by the experience of the viewer was Argentine artist Julio Le Parc, born in 1928 in the Andean province of Mendoza. In 1942, when he was still an adolescent, Le Parc moved with his family to Buenos Aires, where he studied at the Manuel Belgrano Art School under the tutelage of Rosario-born Lucio Fontana. By that time Fontana was in the process of formulating his groundbreaking "White Manifesto", while sharing his ideas on Spatialism with his students, whom as Le Parc recalled, where made responsible for signing the manifesto.[2] In it, Fontana advocated for an art made with the help of scientists, whose research should be directed "...towards the discovery of the luminous and malleable substances and the sound-producing instruments which will make possible the development of tetra dimensional art."[3]

In an attempt to materialise these principles—already explored by artists like László Moholy-Nagy in the early 1920s—Fontana developed a series of experimental works in the 1950s, which incorporated filters for light projections and movement from television emissions. [4] Le Parc became interested in the investigation of light as material. But in parallel to his formal discoveries, the social intention of his practice manifested in a particularly acute interest in activating the viewer through mechanical devises. Le Parc's highly poetic light structures are constructed by means of very basic technologies, principally mechanical and electrical, that he applied to create his kinetic sculptures. But most significantly, these developments were accompanied by a theoretical reflection on the role of art in social relations. After his formative years, Le Parc obtained a grant from the French Cultural Services, which allowed him to travel to Paris in 1958, where he still resides. In Paris he met Vasarely, Vantongerloo, Morellet and the French dealer Denise René and in 1960 became one of the founders of the *Groupe de la Recherche d'Art Visuel* (GRAV).[5] The group, formed by the artists, Sobrino, Yvaral, Morellet, Stein and García Rossi, proposed collective strategies devised to delegate the creative act to the viewer/participant, a concept of much currency in contemporary art today. The principle of stimulating the creative force within humans—later enunciated by Beuys in his legendary "Everybody is an artist" mantra—became a deep preoccupation for the group that advocated that art play a wider, more active role in society.[6] Alongside Le Parc's investigation of light with mechanical means Venezuelan artists Carlos Cruz-Diez and Alejandro Soto, also based in Paris and exhibiting at Galerie Denise René, sustained a production of paintings, reliefs and sculptural installations that led to the flourishing of Kineticism in the 1960s.

The acknowledgement of such a continuum of experimental art practices is fundamental to contextualise Jorge Orta's trajectory, his interest in light, his understanding of the link between images and content and his emphasis on the role of art as a vehicle of communication.

Born in Rosario, Argentina in 1953 Jorge Orta began his career in painting and printmaking, after graduating from the Faculty of Fine Arts and the Faculty of Architecture of the Universidad Nacional de Rosario in 1979 and 1980. In response to the censorship established by the Argentine military regime that ruled from 1976 to 1983 his practice expanded to include non-objectual alternative forms of visual communication, such as Mail Art and performance, widely practiced throughout South America in the 1970s as strategies of resistance.[7] From this formative period of experimentation until the realisation of his first light-based large-scale public artwork in 1991 in Paris, Orta embarked on the investigation of the possibilities of using images in public space. This impulse was driven by an acute sense of the ethical dimension of art, a commitment that has shaped his artistic endeavours through to the present.

The Light Works that became a trademark of his practice are anchored in drawing and the elaboration of a sign-based

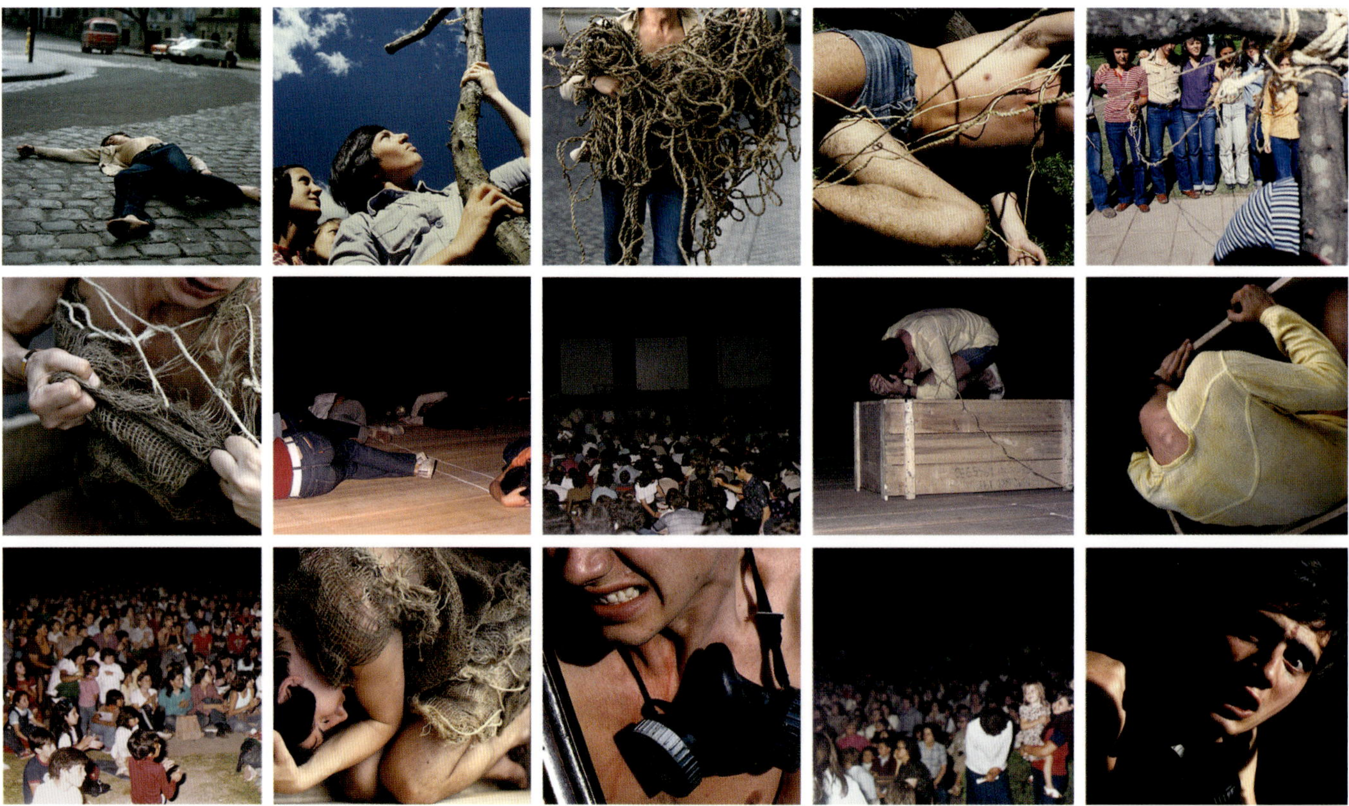

Transcurso Vital, 1978
Performance in front of 2,000 spectators
Plaza Vicene Lopez y Planes, Rosario, Argentina

conceptual structure: a planetary alphabet that Orta started devising in 1974.

The alphabet encompassed formal and conceptual elements common to a diversity of cultures and was initially composed of a family of signs named *makos*—a term coined by the artist—with the purpose of serving the communication of codified meaning. The *makos* consisted of anthropomorphic shapes that mirrored social reality, including individual pictograms congregated as human groups: an iconographic Latin American community built by the imagination. Formally, the *makos* inhabit a visual space that exists between the representation of the human form and language signs. The alphabet was conceived as a means to represent inherently human archetypes and it referenced symbols, pictograms, and a varied repertoire of archaeological material. A permanently evolving system made of thousands of signs, the alphabet is politically complex as it somehow abolishes concepts of national identity in favour of a global vocabulary, a widely accepted concept in the twenty-first century, but certainly less common in the mid-1970s. The creation of the planetary alphabet became pivotal in Orta's visual language: it is present in his works made as a solo artist and continues to feature in the works made in collaboration with his partner Lucy with whom he founded Studio Orta in Paris in 1992. But most importantly, the planetary alphabet is at the core of the visual makeup of the Light Works to which we devote this essay.

Public art in the era of terror

In 1978 Jorge Orta had begun creating public interventions in his city of birth, Rosario, with the aim to bridge the gap with a wider public beyond the specialist audiences of art. Taking the form of Mail Art, performance, and projections in public spaces using the basic early image technologies such as slide projectors, these works predate the Light Works he made in Europe, which helped him achieve international recognition.

The first work of the series was *Transcurso Vital (Life Path)* in 1978, which can be considered the precursor of all the Light Works and was presented in a public square in Orta's Rosario neighbourhood, Fishertown. *Transcurso Vital* employed 16 Kodak carrousel projectors synchronised to back project images on eight screens placed in a semi-circle. The projections were screened in sequence blending into each other: a simple strategy to create a cinematic effect while a performance was simultaneously presented on a stage. *Transcurso Vital* is described by the artist as "a personal and collective path, a conviction communicated visually through a set of Christian symbols—the cross, blood, and the lifeline represented by a rope". The work employed the most sophisticated technologies available at the time to project images drawn from Christian iconography in a public space, becoming a work of political resistance. A 2,000 strong audience saw it at a time when the

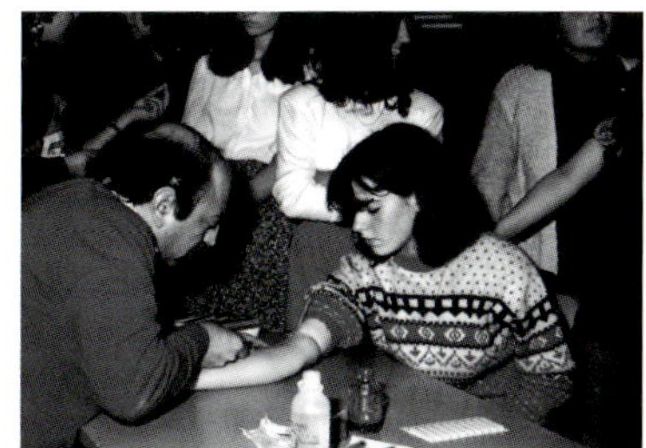
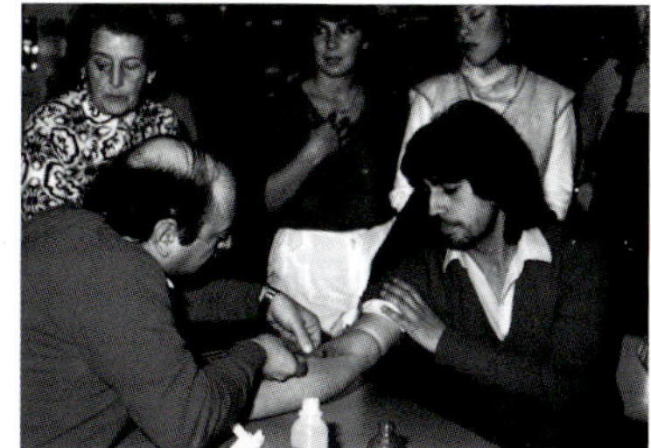
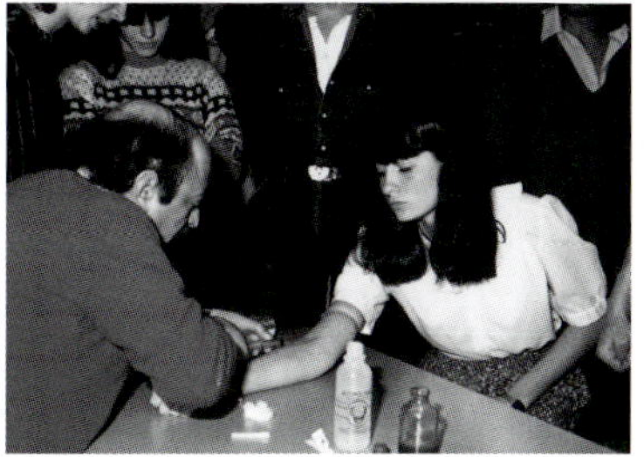
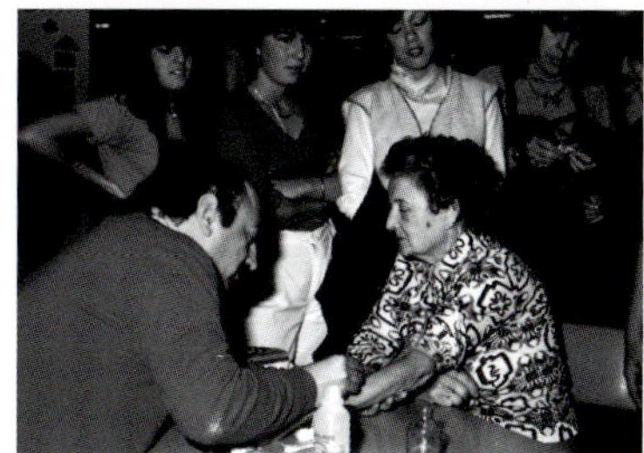

Fusión de Sangre Latinoamericana, 1984
Performance
Bernardino Rivadavia centro culturel Rosario, Argentina

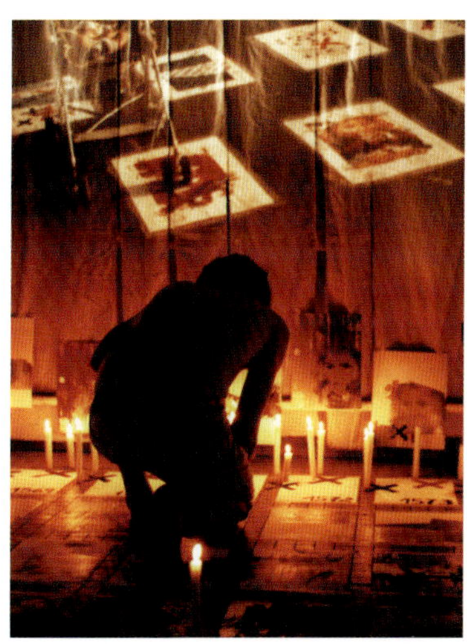

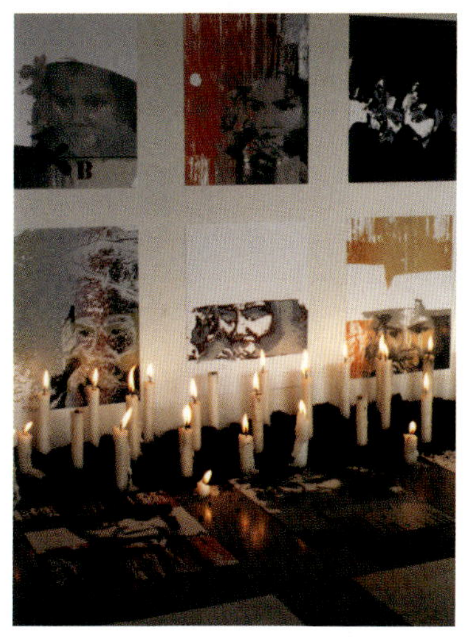

Resbalar sobre la Sangre, 1985
Performance
La Sorbonne Paris, France

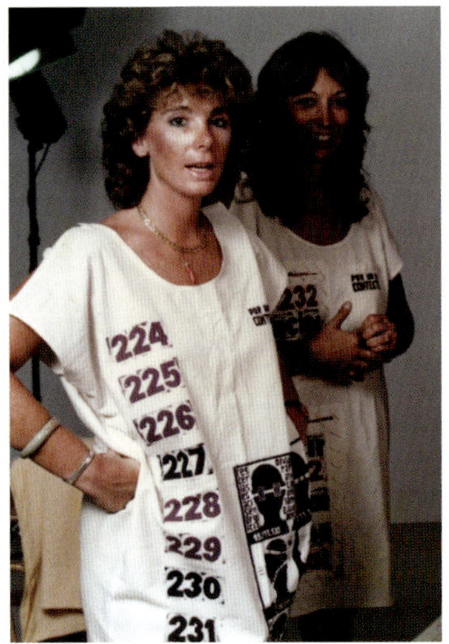

Arte Portable, 1983
Street catwalk
Calle Córdoba de Rosario, Argentina

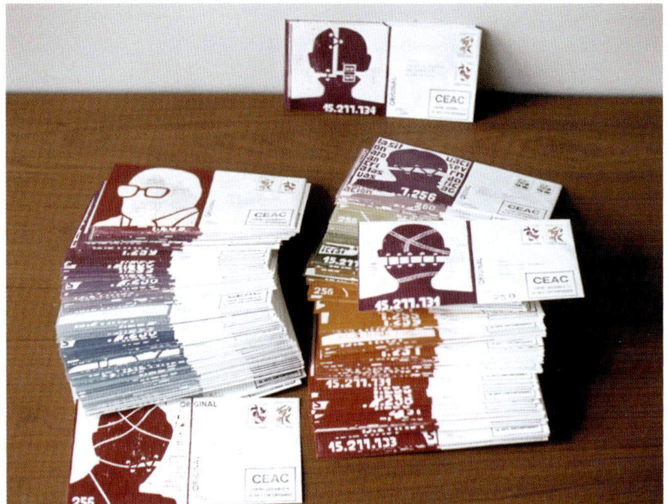

Arte Correo, 1980-1984
Mail Art
Rosario, Argentina

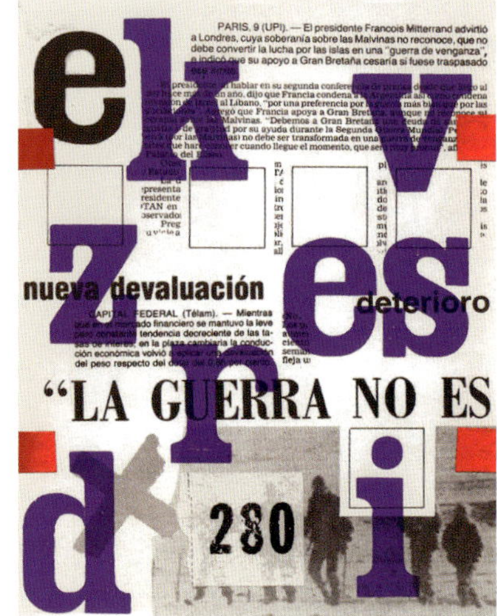

law strictly prohibited public gatherings, as a curfew limited to three the number of people who might gather in the streets at night. The event steered clear of repression due to the support of Father Libio Gorza, a progressive priest who promoted it as a church-based action. From this point onwards, Jorge Orta made public spaces the favourite arena for the realisation and display of his art. At this time, he also introduced Video Art in Rosario by setting up the first video lab, and his work *Crónica Gráphica* (*Graphic Cronicle*) was selected to represent Argentina in the 1982 edition of the Paris Biennale by critic Guillermo Whitelow.

Orta's second public projection, *Testigos Blancos* (*White Witnesses*), also took place in a Rosario square in 1982. It consisted of an impromptu installation of handmade crosses built with old clothes and puppets disposed around a central bonfire. The performance took the public and the authorities by surprise. Given the time-based and ephemeral nature of such work, the gathering of remnants became crucial. Orta recorded the action on video, as well as making a number of wooden boxes to contain collected ashes, soil and fragments of the sculptural elements. The reliquary nature of the boxes, with glass fronts allowing for closer inspection of the contents, translated into sculptures that evoked the tragic pressures of an historical moment.

During the following years and prior to his departure from Argentina in 1984, Jorge Orta continued exhibiting prints, woodcuts, engravings and paintings in galleries such as the Buonarroti Gallery and the Galería Krass in Rosario and making public installations and performative actions outside the gallery space. In *Arte Portable* (*Wearable Art*), of 1983, he employed the format of a fashion show to display politically charged images silkscreened on garments designed by stylist Graciela Vrecht. By showing the works on models' bodies, the controversial imagery printed on the dresses took on the appearance of innocent *prêt a porter*. This single event precedes the public works made with garments that Jorge Orta collaborated on with his partner Lucy, a trained fashion designer, whose main philosophy is based on the use of the body as a vehicle for communication of social and political issues.

Mail Art: an art from the base upward

In the late seventies, alongside artists Clemente Padín in Uruguay, Damaso Orgaz in Venezuela, Edgardo Vigo and Graciela Marx in Argentina, Orta joined a network strategy for communication and distribution of ideas through Mail Art that proliferated throughout Latin America. They believed in "an art from the base upward, without artists", which embraced a critique of society, politics and the very conservative and commercial face of the art world.[8]

Mail Art was one of the main modes of widespread distribution of visual arts in the 1970s and early 1980s, and was eagerly employed in Latin America. In the context of political repression, it served artists to create ubiquitous platforms to disseminate messages otherwise blocked by State controlled circuits such as the printed media. Orta was no exception: at that time he also conceived conceptual works encompassing *Concierto por Teléfono* (*Telephone Concert*)—a music recording distributed by arbitrarily choosing numbers from the phone book to defy social isolation and the lack of interest in culture—and *El Globero* (*The Balloon Seller*) which consisted of costumes made with helium filled balloons containing written messages that were freely released in the air. The works were made collectively, transgressing the isolation promoted by the regime and the fear of persecution. For some of these projects he worked in collaboration with

Edgardo Vigo, one of the strongest figures of conceptualism in Argentina. With Vigo and other international artists Orta participated in the creation of rubber stamps editions to print images for distribution via the postal services. In 1984 Orta organised the First International Mail Art Seminar of at the Centro Cultural Bernardino Rivadavia in Rosario and founded, with Uruguayan artist Clemente Padín, the Latin American Association of Mail Art.

The dissemination strategies employed in these initiatives are clear precursors of current global projects made for the internet. The images that Orta produced at the time included children's faces symbolising social injustice; tied hands and feet, remnants of bodies, making reference to the disappearances in Argentina Such iconography, its use of colour and graphic composition is constant in Orta's works to date. Paramount in his practice is that although materials and techniques might have evolved through time, the concepts and the ethical intentions of the imagery are a continuum which spans from the early years in Argentina to the latest works of Studio Orta made in collaboration with his partner, Lucy, and an increasing number of project associates.

Among the most remarkable works of Orta's Argentine period is a participative printmaking project held at Galeria Miró, Rosario, in 1981. *Grabado en Cinta Continua (Continuous Print Roll)* consisted of a printing carousel with two hundred images engraved on a roll, which allowed participants to print and cut off individual fragments and appropriate an original art work. Once printed, the images could be taken away as if they were freshly baked bread rolls from the oven. The event was framed by a highly politicised text attacking the economic system of the art market and the fetish value of art objects. An excerpt reads: "to counterbalance the degradation in the investors market imposed by the work of art through the distribution of the multi edition of print works. To abolish the fetish value of the object, the participatory action (... consists of) a physical intervention to produce a unique work that will dissolve by means of the public will... those interested in 'acquiring' a work will have to cut it off the roll." This action reminds other iconic examples of artists attempts to promote a democratic consumption of art, such as Felix Gonzalez Torres' free editions of prints and candies piled up in galleries and offered to the public, and Victor Grippo's clay oven to bake bread for the public, dismantled by the police in a Buenos Aires public square in 1973.

Light Works selected chronology

The last piece Orta made in Argentina was while teaching at the Rosario Faculty of Arts in 1984. *Fusión de Sangre Latinoamericana (Latin American blood fusion)* was a performative action consisting of the drawing of blood from the participants to the International Mail Art Seminar at the Bernardino Rivadavia Cultural Center. The blood of all seminar delegates was mixed and incorporated

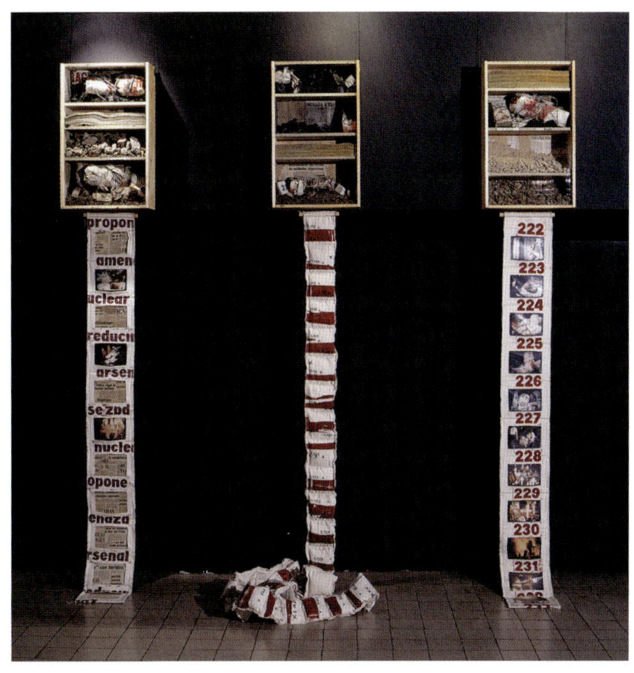

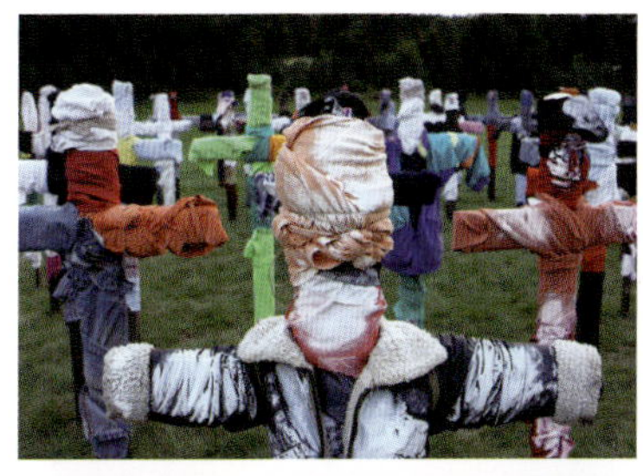

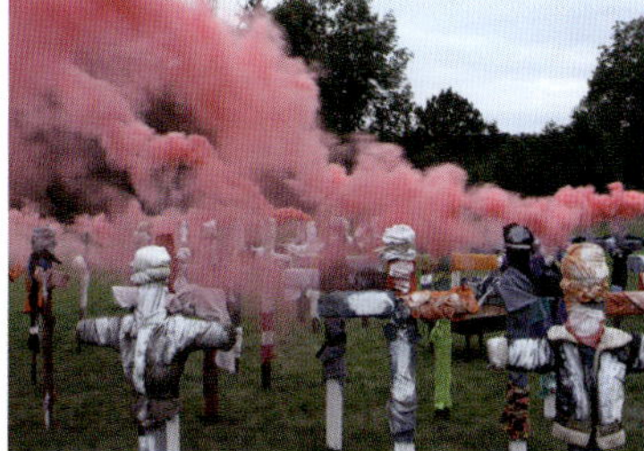

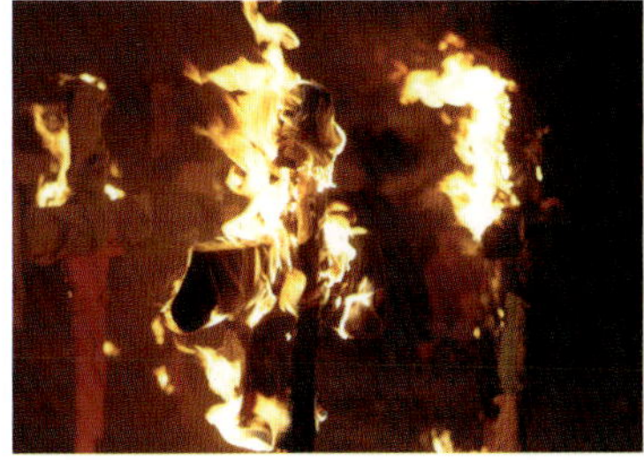

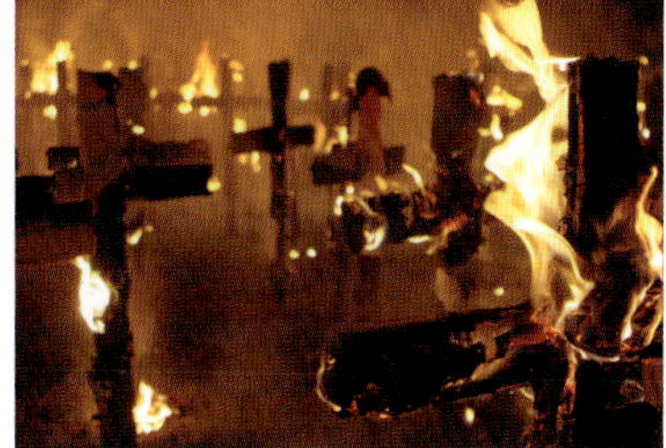

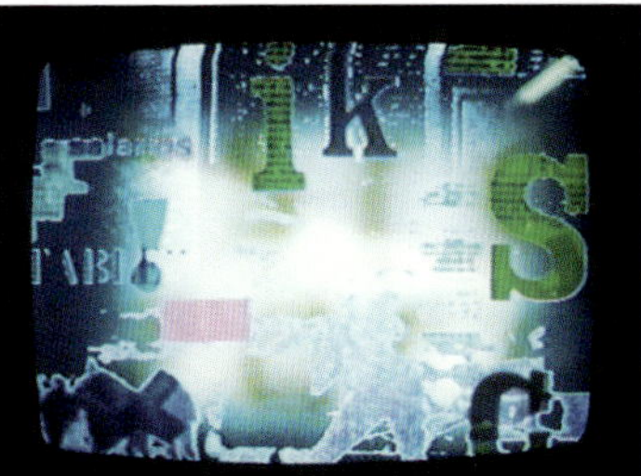

Relicarios, 1982
Ash, remains of Testigos performance, fragments of newspapers, photographs, textiles
170 x 170 x 40 cm
Centre de Arte y Comunicación, Buenos Aires

Testigos, 1982–2008
Public installation
Plaza Santa Cruz Rosario, Argentina

Crónica Gráphica, 1982
Video performance
XII Biennale de Paris, France / Bernardino Rivadavia centro culturel, Rosario, Argentina

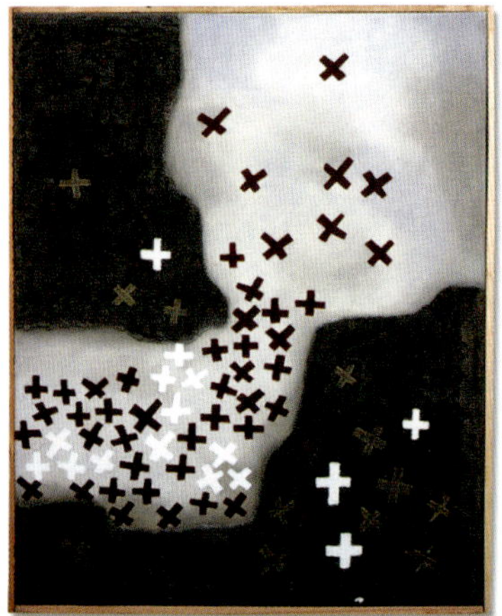

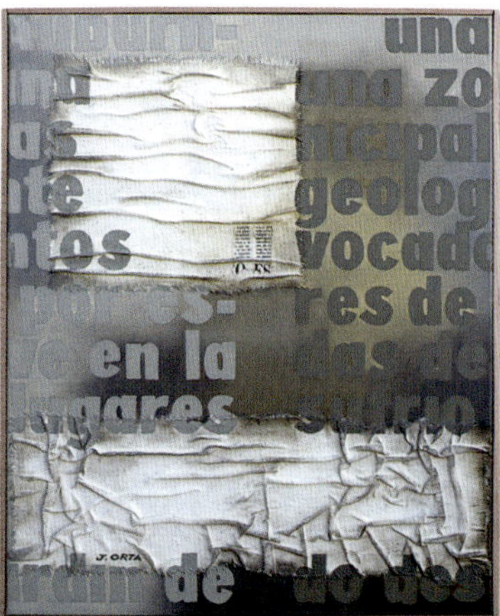

Pinturas Contextuales, 1976–1980
Mixed media
40 x 30 cm

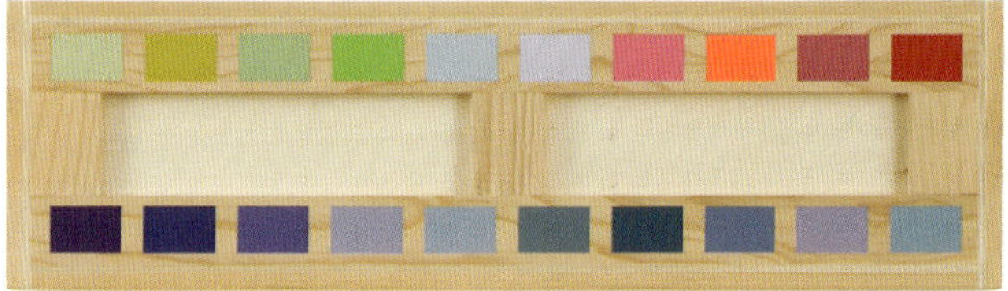

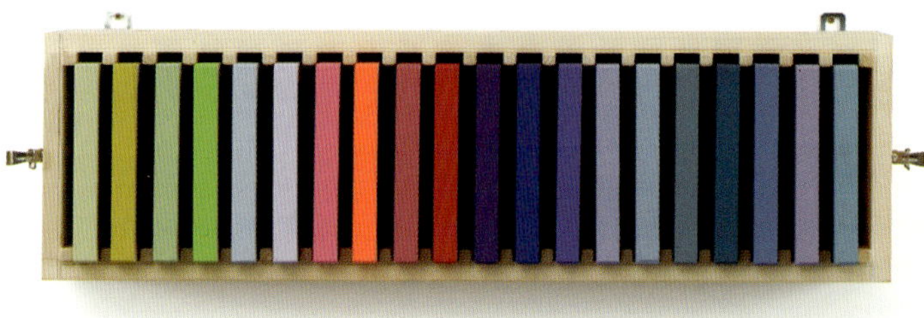

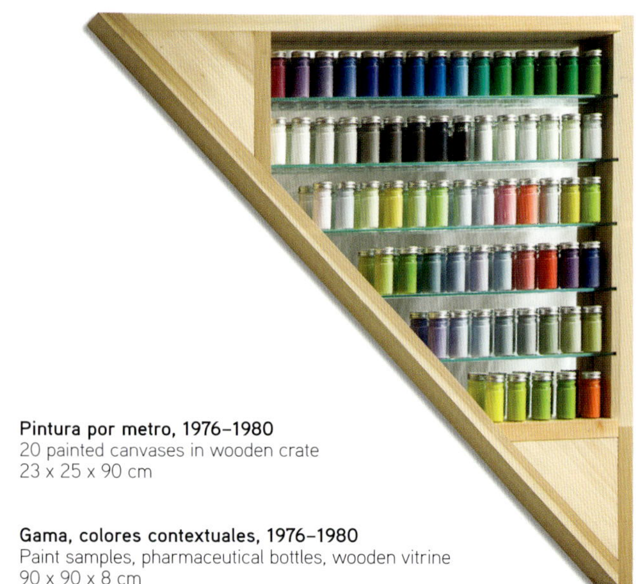

Pintura por metro, 1976–1980
20 painted canvases in wooden crate
23 x 25 x 90 cm

Gama, colores contextuales, 1976–1980
Paint samples, pharmaceutical bottles, wooden vitrine
90 x 90 x 8 cm

into an artwork as a symbolic ritual of brotherhood in the face of the indifference of Latin American people to their closest neighbours and as an energetic tribute to life. As a result of the piece Orta was reprimanded by the Faculty management who considered the action inappropriate by an acting professor. Frustrated and exhausted by the lack of imagination of the newly installed democratic government, and prompted by a French government grant, Jorge Orta decided to leave Argentina to arrive in Paris in 1984.

With the emergence of the Paris-based FIAC (Foire Internationale d'Art Contemporain) art fair, the articulation of the French art market helped to emphasise commercial and individual production, particularly painting. In this environment, not favourable to the production of immaterial actions, Orta was faced with the difficulty of continuing his experimental work done in Argentina. This circumstance, however, prompted him to explore the possibility of employing light to express his interest in public art in the new environment. At that time he began researching for a PhD at La Sorbonne University and becoming simultaneously involved in the production of the PAE 2500 *image canons* developed by the light engineer Léon Miquel, which helped him focus on the exploration of the use of light as a prime material for the production of large-scale works. The technique that he invented for projection of large-scale long-distance light beams was to use heat resistant image projection plates that were famously pioneered by Jean-Michel Jarre in Houston, Texas in 1986 during his international tour of light and sound mega concerts. Orta's silkscreen print studio in the Quai de Seine was the laboratory where he developed the procedure to print epoxy-based enamel images onto ceramic glass—which could withstand the high temperatures of the PAE's concentrated light beams. The PAE 2500 projectors have a light output of 2,500–5,000 watts each and can project images up to 5,000 square metres over a distance of hundreds of metres.

But in 1991 disaster struck Jorge Orta with the sudden burning of his newly renovated warehouse studio, on Canal de l'Ourc near La Villette district. This marked the beginning of a period of scarcity and prompted a change of direction in his career. With the studio—also his home—all his possessions burned down, including his entire art production, the automatic silkscreen machines, personal records, his library and his photo and video archives. In the midst of a new global economic crisis prompted by the fist Gulf War and faced with a lack of materials, references and working space, Orta began the reconstruction of a fundamental part of his artistic endeavour by resorting to the planetary alphabet in a small temporary studio in Rue Brancion. At the same time, he met English born artist Lucy Jenkinson with whom he began to develop art projects in association. The encounter meant a shift in Jorge's practice.

After ten years of waiting Jorge Orta was finally able to employ the PAE image cannon for his own research purposes and began using it as a 'paintbrush', painting with light in public spaces. His first large-scale light projection was *Poème Infographique*, produced in 1991 for the Georges Pompidou Centre in Paris in the context of the "Rencontres d'Art Electronique". The artist developed images that would decompose and metamorphose in dialogue with the industrial and hard edge architecture of Renzo Piano and Richard Rogers' building. During a period when Macintosh was developing software to produce the first computer generated images, Orta's images for *Poème Infographique* were hand-drawn in the studio, digitised using the first computer-aided design programmes and then silkscreen printed onto the ceramic glass plates.

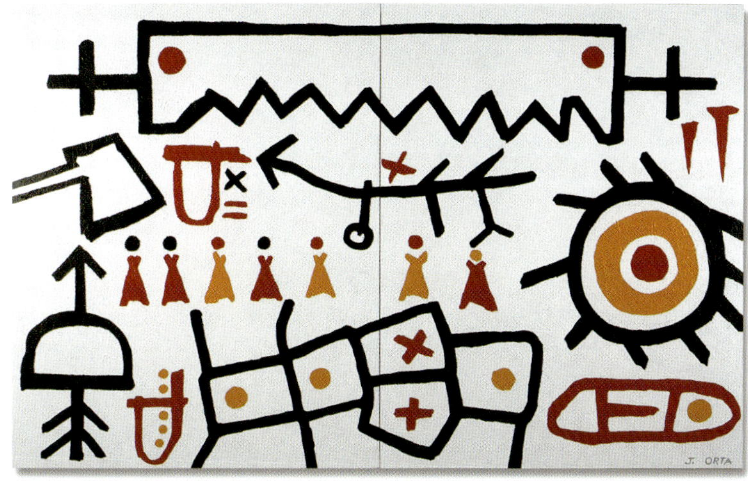

Imprints on the Andes, 1992

Following a second light projection series in 1992 at the Palais de Tokyo in Paris and the Chartres Museum, Jorge and Lucy alongside Claude Namer embarked in the most ambitious and emblematic *Light Work: Imprints on the Andes* a work in chapters that began in the millenary city of Cuzco, Peru, site of the Inca Empire. The project included an expedition across the Andes Mountain range, *Sacsayhuamán*—the Inca fortress—culminating in the magnificent Machu Pichu citadel, one of the most impressive archaeological enclaves of pre-Columbian America. During the projections Orta's symbols bathed with their colourful gleam the ancient sacred mountains and temples before the eyes of two-hundred thousand people, as a symbolic counter-celebration of the 500th anniversary of the discovery of the Americas in 1492. *Imprints on the Andes* remains the beacon piece of all Light Works made by Lucy+Jorge Orta, due both to its conceptual impact and technical complexity.

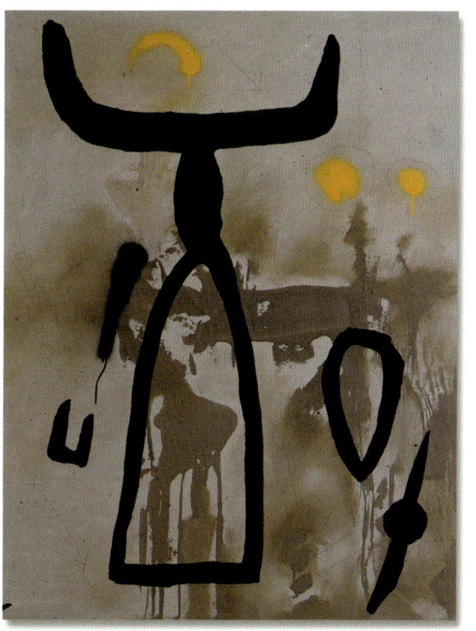

Alfabeto planetario, 1990
Acrylic on canvas
146 x 228 cm

X Escuardra equinoccial, vapor de piedra, P.N., 1990
Acrylic on canvas
130 x 90 cm

The local context for this monumental work was the celebration in Peru of Indigenous America, organised by aboriginal communities to challenge the commemoration of the discovery of America by Columbus as an act of resistance. The event, a reunion of the Inca with 200,000 indigenous people in the day of *Inti Raymi* marked the beginning of winter and the raising of the Pleiades in the southern skies.[9] During *Inti Raymi* the people of the Andes enthrone their leader, the Inca, in a large ceremony held at the Inca fortress—the pukara—of *Sacsayhuamán* a place of high historical connotations as it was built in the sixteenth century by the Inca Manko to resist the invasion of the Spanish *conquistadores*.[10] In spite of the establishment of Catholicism as the official religion and the secular tendencies of the political classes, the ancestral law of the Inca is maintained year after year, as a display of the people's own sense of democracy.

From a logistic viewpoint the preparation of the sequence of projections entailed numerous difficulties and risks. The socio-

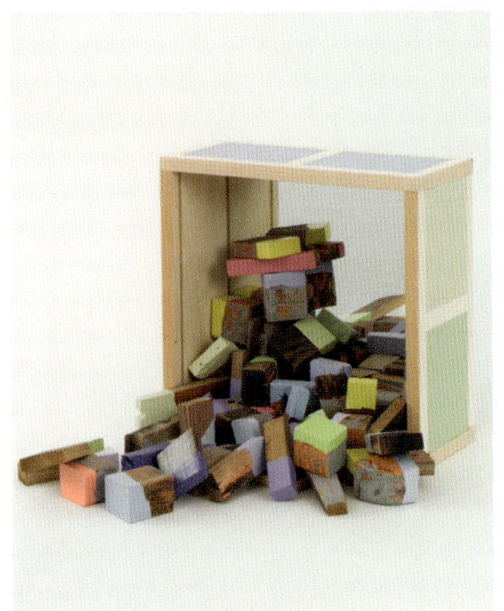

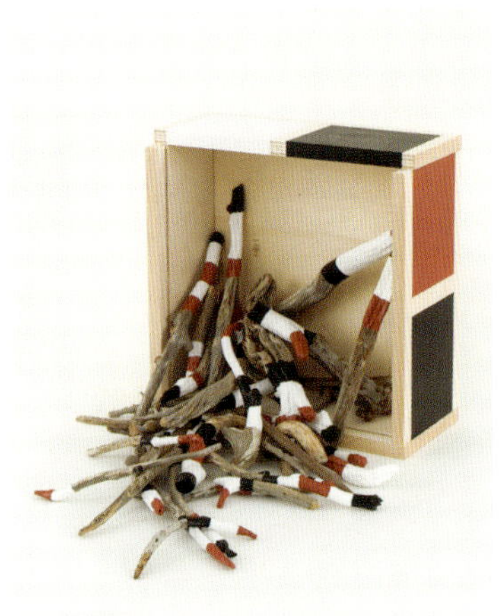

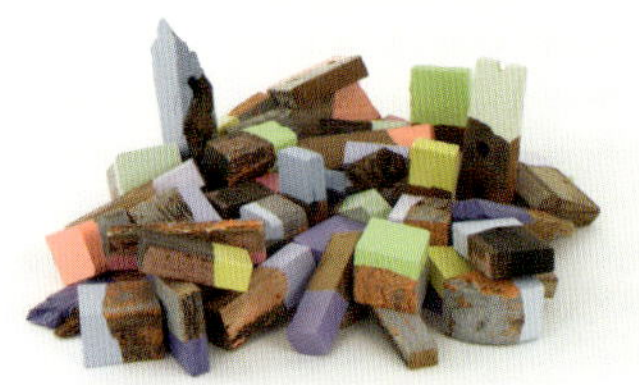

Poema naufragado, 1981
Remains of boat, drift wood, acrylic Gamas paint
30 x 30 x 10 cm

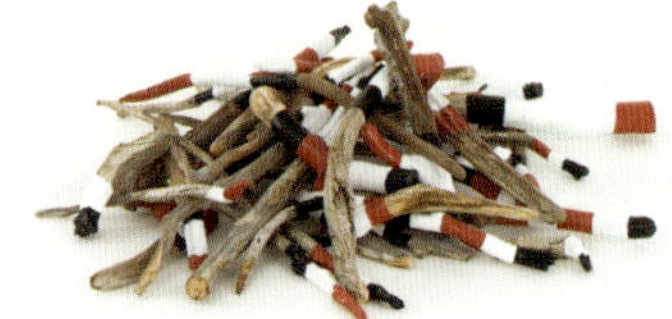

Poema erosionado, 1981
Branches, acrylic Gamas paint
30 x 30 x 10 cm

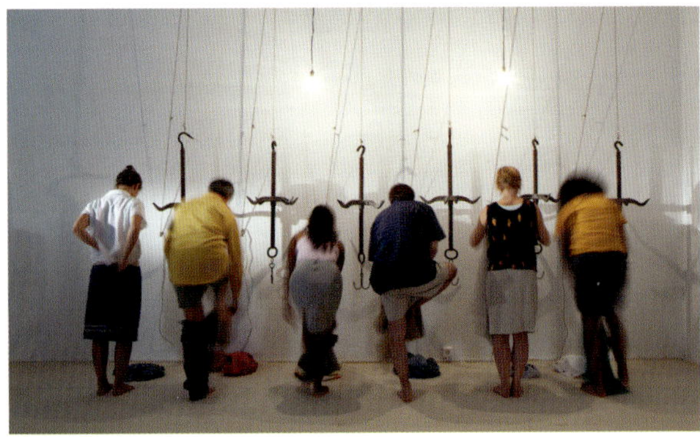

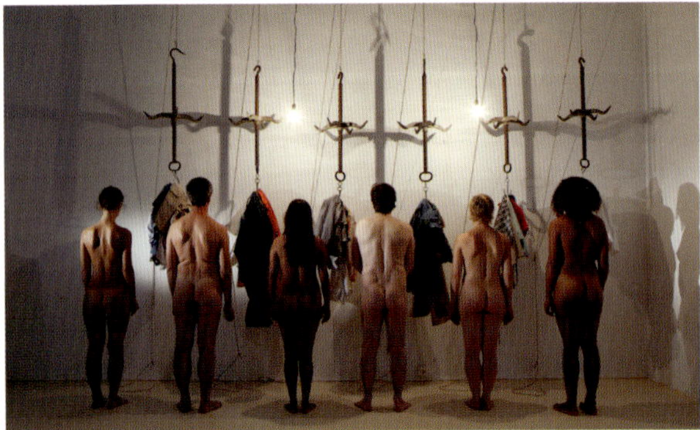

De-espalda, 1982–2009
Video performance with meat hooks

political climate of President Alberto Fujimori's Peru was tense due to the presence of guerrilla groups in the country and the recent coup d'état. A week before the expedition was scheduled to depart France, the entire team of technicians resigned due to safety issues posed by the state of emergency, which led to the need to assemble another team in a matter of days. Once in Lima, remaining defiant of official advice, the Ortas set out to Cuzco in an operation that might have seemed out of Werner Herzog's epic film *Fitzcarraldo*. With the help of traditional Andean carriers the team transported the heavy equipment, consisting of projection canons and oversize electricity generators—which amounted to one tonne in weight—through narrow mountain paths from the city of Cuzco to Machu Picchu, relaying entirely on manpower.

Imprints on the Andes remains the Orta's most emblematic *Light Work* despite being the most technically challenging and financially costly. It is also their favourite because of the ideological and emotional impact the work had for both artists and audiences. The images, partly extracted from *The Book of the Inca*—a visual compendium of the massacres and tortures suffered by the Incas in the hands of the Spanish *conquistadores*—ran their mythical power over the spectacular mountain range.at over 3,000 metres above sea level. Despite the work being shown in isolated sites, an intelligently devised press campaign led to a considerable coverage, notably in the French newspaper *Le Figaro*, which proudly announced it as "a French expedition". This naturally helped the project by making it an international piece of news, followed by headlines in major newspapers and glossy magazines across the world. However, in Machu Picchu the projections acquired a different meaning: although mainly illiterate, the Andean audiences of the work could readily identify with the use of signs and pictograms already present in their iconographic tradition. The codified language made of symbols projected over their sacred mountains connected the local audiences to their past and present condition without mediation. Furthermore, the projection was enriched by local traditions in the framework of *Inti Raymi*. During the festival, the Inca reproduce ancient costumes made of gold by employing metallic paper to reflect the sun and thus represent their God—*Inti*. For the crowning of the Inca, an ordinary citizen is chosen among the people to be the leader of the solar year. Upon the ceremony, he delivers a speech containing guidance for the times ahead to a crowd of thousands.

The main achievement of *Imprints on the Andes* was undoubtedly that the artists' work could, in this environment, revitalise energies and expressions through the values attributed to materials in an alchemic ritual. The clear relation between materials, symbol and its representation made by the audiences in Machu Picchu was a true revelation to Lucy and Jorge. The reception of this piece of contemporary art was clearly more inclusive than if presented to an art educated European public who would have needed interpretative tools to de-codify its meaning.

The Cry from the Earth, 1994

Following the international media attention of *Imprints on the Andes*, Lucy+Jorge Orta were invited to produce a similar piece in Japan, by the Asahi television company. *The Cry from the Earth*, sponsored by NEC, was part of a larger commission of artists including Cai Guo-Qiang, to create unique works, using innovative technologies and of a large-scale that would be broadcast on Japanese television during the peak viewing time on New Year's evening.

Preparations for the work included a several week expedition trek across Japan, visiting sites as remote as the Okinwa islands, the sacred temples of Kyoto, and the Hiroshima Peace Memorial, to source natural and man-made symbols that would form the iconographic basis of the *Light Work*. As a constant methodology, the symbols for each project are sourced from the history and the particular natural environment or anthropological imprints of each site. In Japan, the chosen location was the largest volcano in activity in the world. The crater of Mount Aso volcano is several kilometres wide and visitors to the volcano range are forced to shelter against the eruptions and the intermittent sulphurous rain in 'volcano bunkers'. The research process involved the sketching of the source imagery on paper scrolls in calligraphic ink. The designs of natural forms like leaves, shells and stones unfolded into abstracted ideograms, providing a new sign system generated by and combination of intuition and constructive methodology, and originated in nature. The resulting ideograms were added to the planetary alphabet that Jorge began in the early 1970s.

The distinctive quality of the *The Cry from the Earth* is that for the first time the Light Works correlated sound and image. Using the UPIC computer music system invented by Iannis Xenakis in 1950 and built in the French CEMAMU research centre in 1976, the artists' recorded sounds of the eruptions and volcanic activity were transformed into images, likewise the hand-drawn pictograms could become sounds. Hence, their musical notation is linked intrinsically to the morphology of images, and *vice versa*. Developed in six months, the Aso project also involved the latest in NEC technology, including filming from radio controlled helicopters. However, despite the availability of means, the projections had to be cancelled three times due to the instability of the volcano. When finally underway, the stunning effect of the projections over the sulphur clouds managed to strike a chord in the country's imagination as they related conceptually to Hiroshima and Nagasaki. Coinciding with the 50th anniversary of the bombings, the imagery recalled the emissions of the nuclear explosions when broadcasted to 30 million Japanese homes. Moreover, the allusion to atomic power was made more poignant by Chirac's controversial announcement of the re-launching of the atomic tests in the Pacific region.

This luminographic work, alongside those made later for the cathedrals, one ancient and one contemporary *Chartres, Sacred Light*, 1994, and *Evry, Crossroads*, 1996, employed the graphic writing of music. Orta's generation of sound from visual elements takes inspiration from the electro-acoustic experimental music of the 1950s and 60s, which explored the writing of scores based on codified imagery.[11] According to a notation system designed by the artist, instruments—both electro-acoustic and analogue—play the codified images, which result in the generation of coloured light filters and sound effects determined by a strict numbering system and time code. As a matrix of the Light Works, the Orta notation scores became hand printed limited editions and sometimes unique works that act as mementos of how the works were conceived and executed.

Light Messenger and *Woven Light*, 1995

Jorge Orta's lifetime work was honoured at the XLVI Venice Biennale of 1995, where he was invited to represent Argentina with his piece *Light Messenger*. Given that Argentina had lost its national pavilion during the 1980s due to the lack of interest in contemporary art at the time of the dictatorship, Jorge was left with little opportunity to exhibit work, and so for this occasion he created a spectacular Light Works for the Venetian Palaces and churches, from a Venetian cargo boat navigating the Grand Canal. The event lasted three nights, employing ephemeral light graffiti including drawings from workshops conducted by Lucy+Jorge Orta with underprivileged communities in South America and homeless youth groups in France. Using water as a support to reflect images, the angle of projection changed. The coloured lights projected from the surface of the water onto the building transmitted the vibrating effect from the movement of the waves, mirroring the canal's activities onto the architecture. As the festivities of the Biennale inauguration were taking place inside the palaces, the giant graffiti imprinted themselves momentarily onto the gleeful faces, ironically printing them momentarily with images produced by those excluded from the system. Parallel to the evening's Light Works, Lucy Orta conducted one of her iconic *Nexus Architecture* interventions.[12] Rallying support from the architecture students at the University Iuav of Venice, the human chain linked through the bright yellow and purple suits snaked the Biennale circuit, both communicating through distributed tracts and images, signs and texts silkscreen-printed onto the garments duplicating those of the projections. Devoid of a fixed place to demonstrate their work, the artists invaded the public space, strategically deploying all means of communication.

But in the mid-1990s Studio Orta's ongoing interest in art's relation to social communication and the artists' view of their role as a mediator reached a break point. The work the *The Cry from the Earth* for the Mount Aso volcano highlighted the incapacity of individual artists to effectively provide a clear concept at such a gigantic scale. Furthermore, the great input needed in such processes, with a personal involvement of a minimum of six months to up to two years made it all too time consuming. This brought about a deep enquiry into the contradictory nature of the Light Works, which had a tendency to be concentrated in locations with greater financial resources, with the wish to create works with minimum resources and a greater investment on content to reach more disadvantaged audiences. The realisation that the large-scale, several thousand dollar projects were distorting the nature of their interest in participation and the challenging of notions of authorship, led the artists to devote the next ten years to a collaborative global project: *The Gift—Life Nexus*.

From Light to Life

The Gift—Life Nexus, began in 1996 as a multidisciplinary project that expanded to 45 cities in a decade. With *Life Nexus* Studio Orta began to build a discourse of solidarity and raise awareness on organ donation with the symbol of the heart at its core, as an accessible referent. The project involved collaborations with scientists, philosophers and medical doctors as well as musicians, visual artists, ceramicists, choreographers, dancers and ordinary citizens. Conceptually, it proclaimed respect for life and formally it was constructed as an Opera in acts, giving birth to a number of related participatory projects that acted as fragments of a larger corpus to be shaped through time. The roots of *Life Nexus* are in the viral methodologies that artists in Rosario and the rest of South America were proclaiming in the 1970s and 80s. The model was established as self-financed, low cost and large impact projects done with the progressive addition of people and participation from different artists, collectives and individuals without the support of the gallery system. The principal output consisted of mountains of hearts, hand sculpted or cast in different materials by hundreds of participants in locations around Europe, North and South America employing materials representative of those cultures. Without a focus on the place of art in the global economy, the chapters of *Life Nexus* constituted small-scale initiatives that would become the cogs of a larger wheel.

OPERA.tion Life Nexus, act VI—Battement des Grands Jours, 2001
Palais de Tau / Reims Cathedral, France

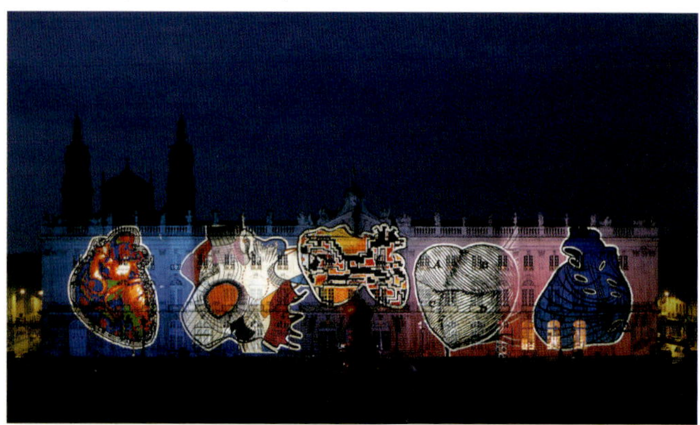

At the same time, the studio continued to create and produce one or two Light Works a year, but they became less central to Lucy+Jorge's practice, or they involved collaborations which stimulated or led to new participative works.

On the occasion of *OPERA.tion Nexo Corazón, act V*, a *Light Work* in Mexico City was produced in 2001. This work involved a series of workshops with communities living and working around the city centre district, where crime is at its highest density. To create the imagery for the projections Lucy+Jorge worked with street children, prostitutes, vendors and street painters —namely the infamous Vichis family of *ex-voto* painters—prior to the project, and took back the drawings and paintings to their Paris studio to be re-worked into image projection plates. They also collaborated closely with composer Pierre Henry, to create a music score and urban soundscape for the central plaza of Mexico City, where thousands of Mexicans gathered for the evening events.

For *OPERA.tion Life Nexus, act VIII* in the Saint Eustache Les Halles district of Paris, 2002, the luminographic work to celebrate the city's autumn music festival included the collaboration with composer and musician Simon Stockhausen, who played live on a stage suspended on scaffolding on the church while the moving projections glided over the facade and musicians.

OPERA.tion Life Nexus, act IX, Nancy, 2003, was one of the most participative Light Works. Conceived to mark the World Transplant Games it was generated by three complementary projects. First, the engagement of tens of thousands of students from 88 schools and their families to create a code of ethics for organ donation. This led to the production of drawings that were transformed into iconographic images for a Light Works projected on the buildings surrounding Stanislas Square. The third element was a sculpture made of bronze hearts sited at the Place de la République, which constitutes a perennial testimony of Lucy+Jorge's time-based interventions and community work.

In these instances, the Light Works became a cog in the wheel: a means to giving wider visibility to a larger idea rather than focusing on the final product of the projection itself.

Founding Utopia: *Escuela 21*

In 1997 Studio Orta was invited to participate in the Medellin Biennale, Colombia, to produce a work for the opening event. Due to the scarce resources available, the artists proposed the making and exhibition of clay hearts, but the curators were adamant that their participation includes a large-scale, "full impact" *Light Work*. But the Biennale did not count on resources

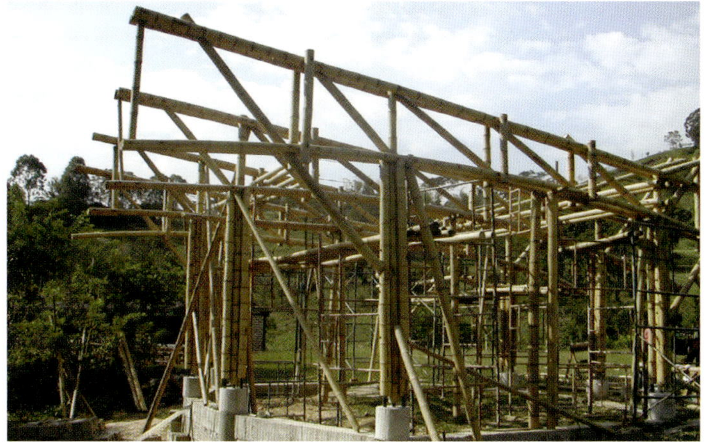

Escuela 21, 1997–2002
Construction of rural school in Palmichal, Medellín, Colombia
Collaboration with architect Juan David Chavez

Rive des Amériques, 1992
Musée de l'homme Paris, France

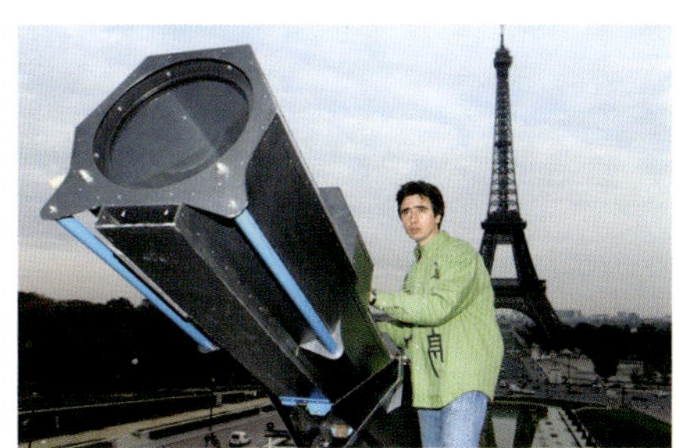

to produce such works. Given that the only available resource was the media, the artists decided to employ radio and TV networks during one week of the Biennale to talk to audiences about the work that they could not realise. In the given airtime, Jorge Orta would talk about the social dynamic of participation in art projects to move society from the base up. His newborn idea, *Escuela 21* was used as an example of a cooperative enterprise that would aim to provide basic services, such as school buildings, in deprived areas. Thanks to the media campaign, after the opening event university students, professors, architects and activists offered their help to continue working in collaboration. Coordinated by the local architect Juan David Chávez the group made possible the renovation and building of the first school in Palmichal. From that humble start, *Escuela 21* continues as an ongoing project designed to support education through cooperative fundraising by building schools in remote areas of South America.

Since the end of the first part of *The Gift—Life Nexus,* undertaken from 1996 to 2006, Lucy+Jorge's most recent works have focused on global issues. Encompassing food and water shortages, migration and borders, climate change and biodiversity, their more recent works address the commonality of contemporary concerns, which defy localised approaches. In light of these developments, it becomes highly meaningful to look at the political complexity of the planetary alphabet when considering Lucy+ Jorge Orta's recent work on Antarctica presented at the Hangar Bicocca, Milan in April 2008 and Galleria Continua/Le Moulin, Paris in June 2008. The work employs a repertoire of universal symbols and the flags of all nations to represent humankind and sites them in a geographical space without borders.

Through their focus on the concepts of migration, food and water wastage, the imminence of climate change or the need to conserve our natural environment, Studio Orta navigates a distinctive artistic path, where the ethic and the aesthetic inherent in art and life have no borders.

1. Gyula Kosice was founding member of Movimiento Madí in Buenos Aires in 1944.
2. Julio Le Parc in conversation with the author in Zurich on June 4, 2005.
3. Fontana, Lucio, White Manifesto: We are Continuing the Evolution of Art, Buenos Aires, 1946
4. In 1922 László Moholy-Nagy employed light and sound in his 'Licht-Raum Modulator' sculpture
5. Nicknamed La Papesse de l'Art Abstrait, Denise René was committed to the promotion of abstract art since the 1940s. A decade later she helped launch Kineticism through her gallery.
6. Through the 1960s, GRAV articulated a thorough theoretical corpus in the form of manifestos among which the seminal No More Mystifications written in 1961 and distributed in the form of pamphlets in the Paris Biennale that same year. The manifesto defined with great clarity the main concerns of the group: ..."We want to develop in the spectator a powerful ability to perceive and take action. A spectator aware of his power to take action and tired of so many abuses and mystifications will he be able to create the true 'revolution in art'. He will put into practice the slogans:

   It is forbidden not to participate
   It is forbidden not to touch
   It is forbidden not to break."

7. The years of the last military dictatorship in Argentina (1976–1983) when State terrorism was responsible for the disappearance and illegal detention of over thirty thousand citizens.
8. Orta, Jorge in interview with Janna Graham, Discussion: Participation, Becoming, Action. Lucy+Jorge Orta, an introduction to collaborative practices. Pattern Book, Black Dog Publishing, Ed. By Paula Orrell
9. Andean people's festival of the sun in June 24th, marking the beginning of the winter solstice.
10. Andean eagle in Quechua language.
11. Musical graphic notation—symbols first began to appear in the works of avant-garde composers such as Karlheinz Stockhausen and Krzysztof Penderecki, as well as the works of experimental composers such as John Cage and Earle Brown.
12. Nexus Architecture interventions, are a symbolic action consisting of a chain of particpants wearing overalls created by the artist and joined through a series of fabric tubes and zippers, representing the social link.

LIGHT WORKS

IMPRINTS ON THE ANDES

1992

The Andes Mountain Range

To cut a knife
Simply with a flower
And to offer it like a flower
To one who knows how to see

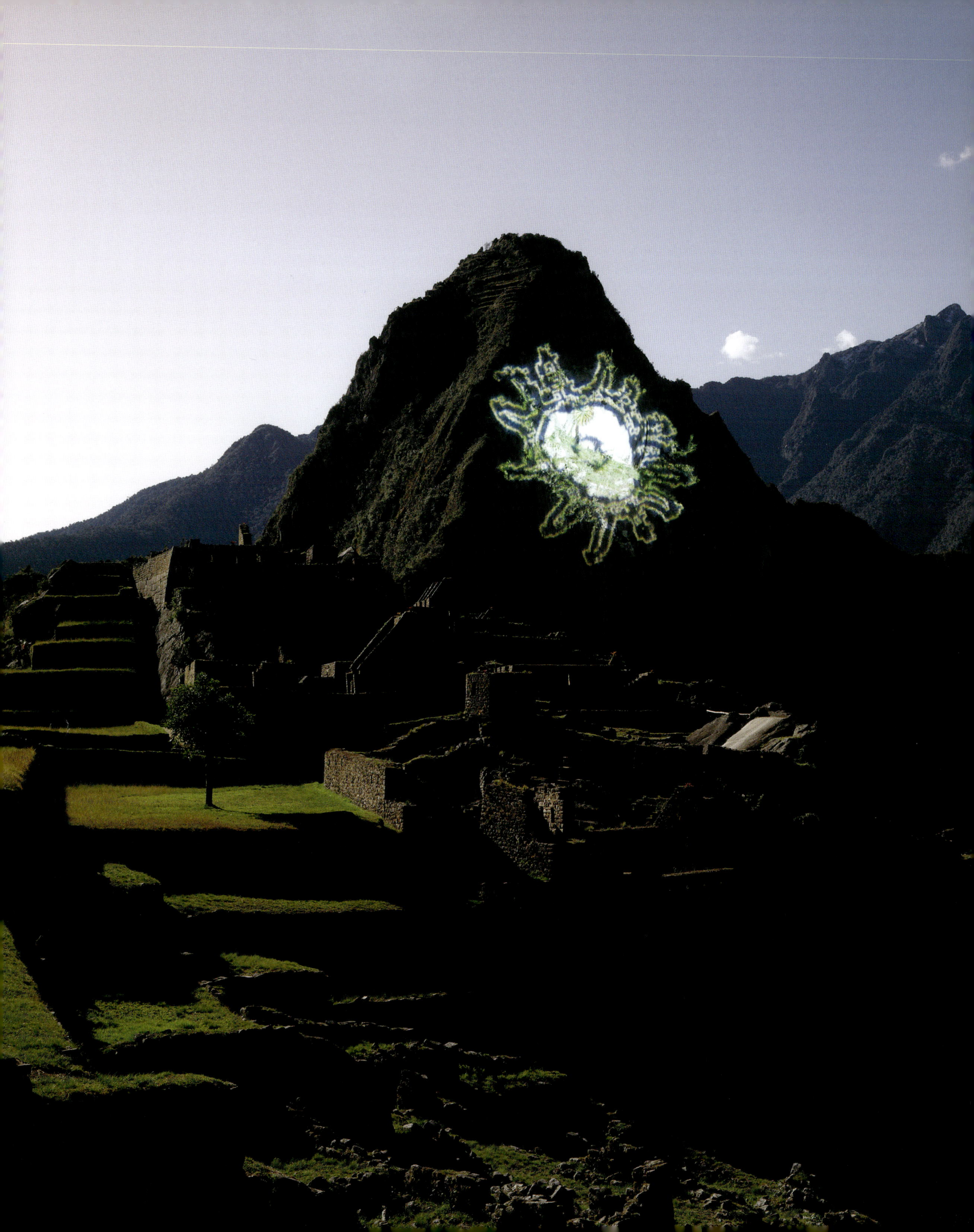

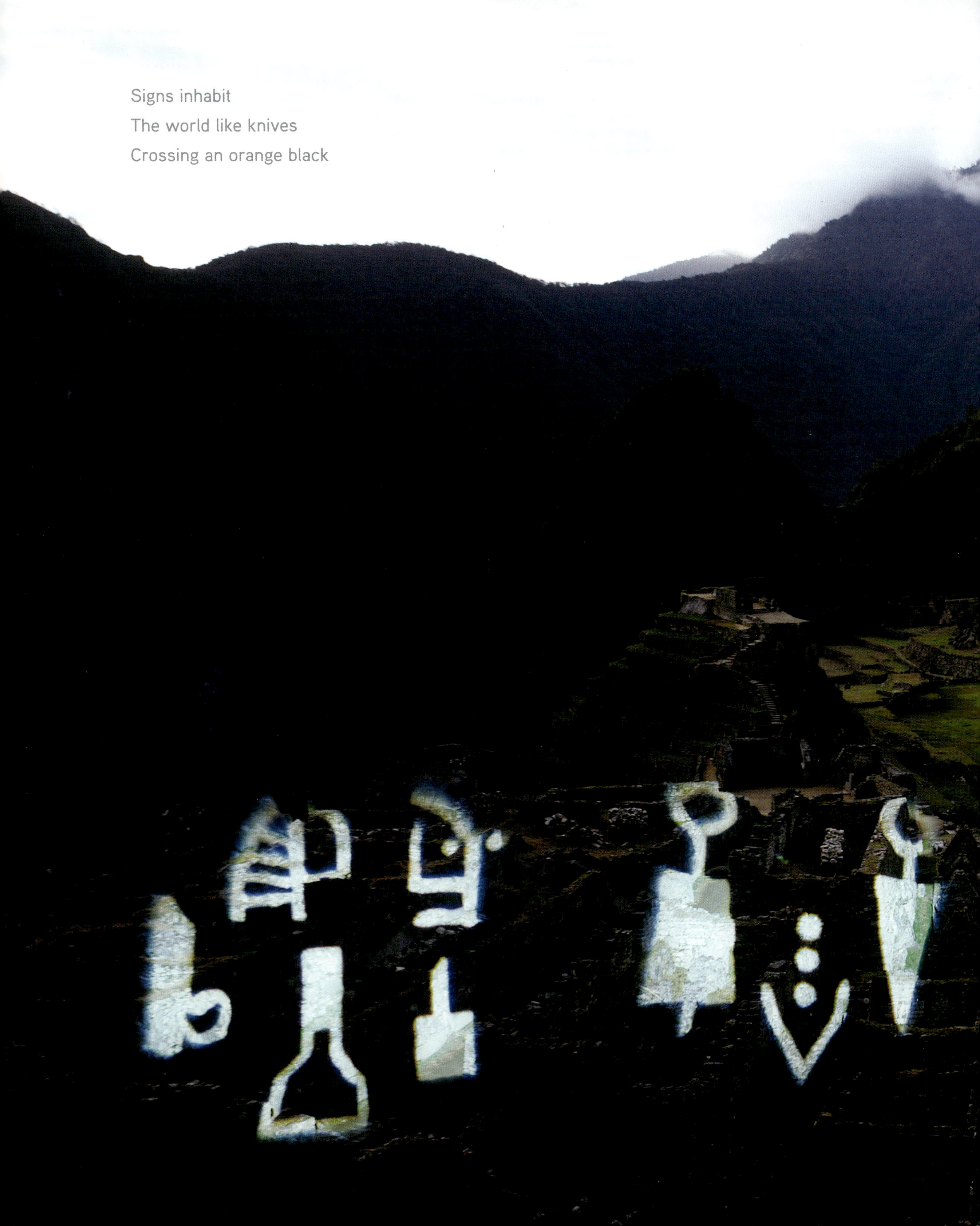

Signs inhabit
The world like knives
Crossing an orange black

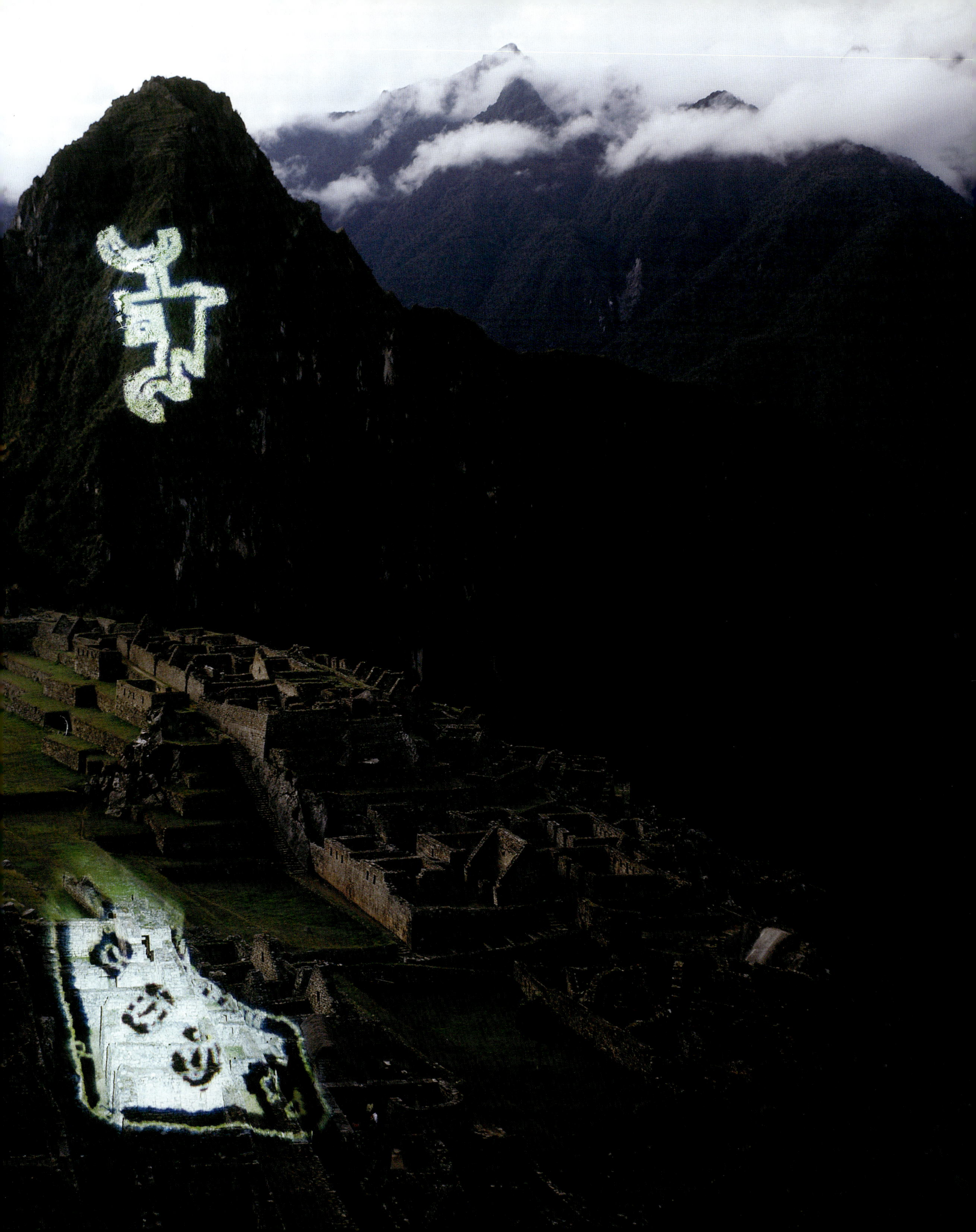

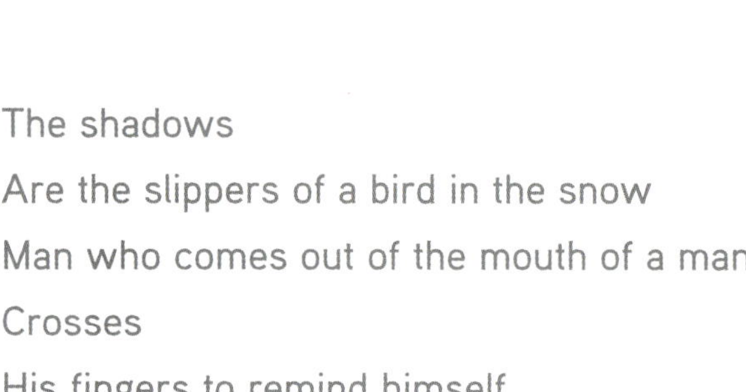

The shadows
Are the slippers of a bird in the snow
Man who comes out of the mouth of a man
Crosses
His fingers to remind himself

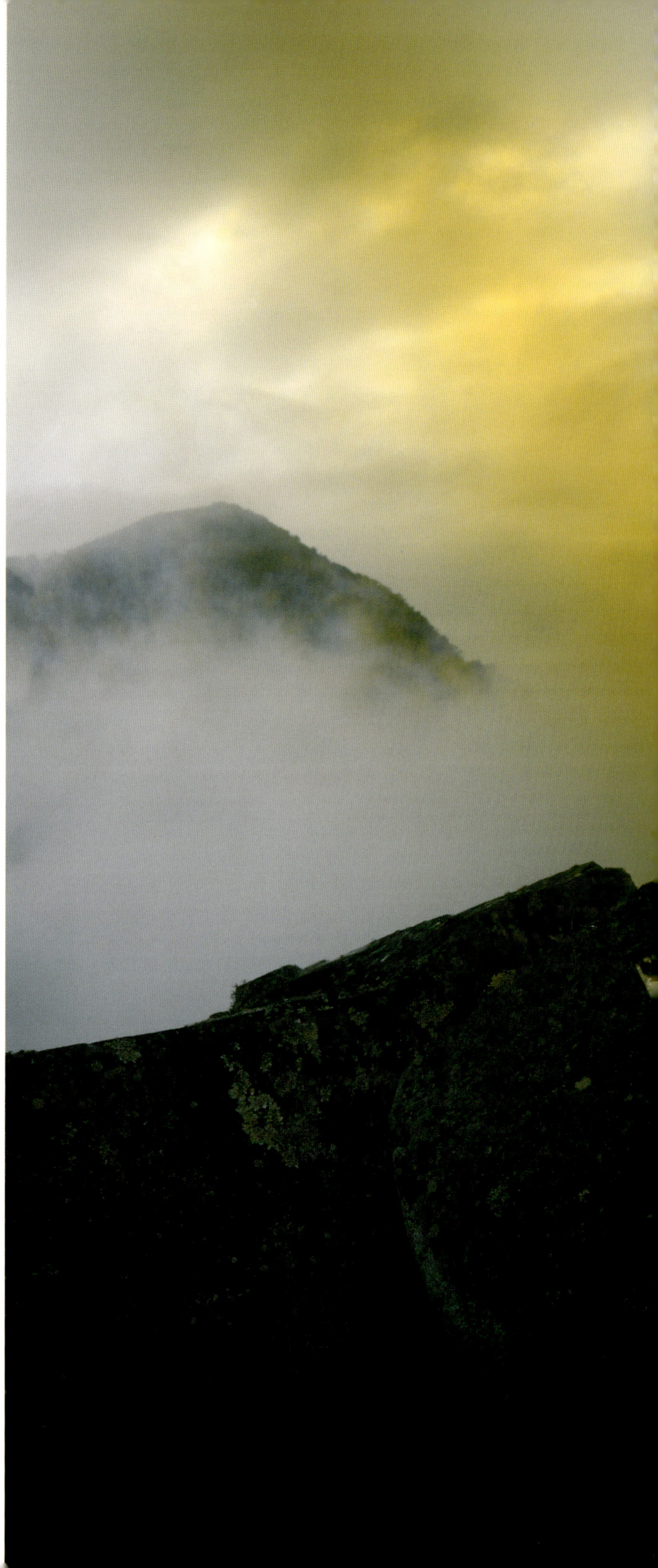

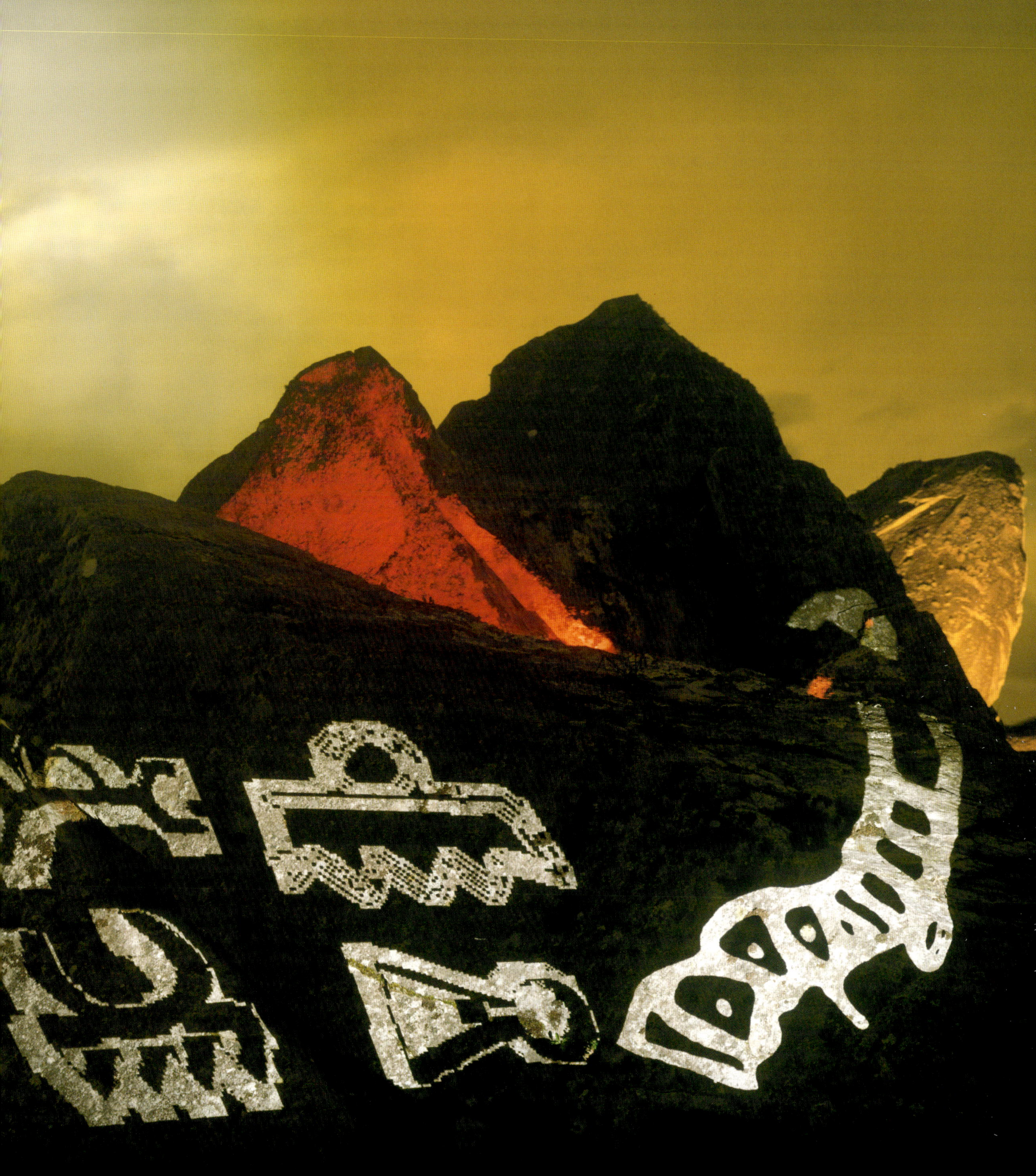

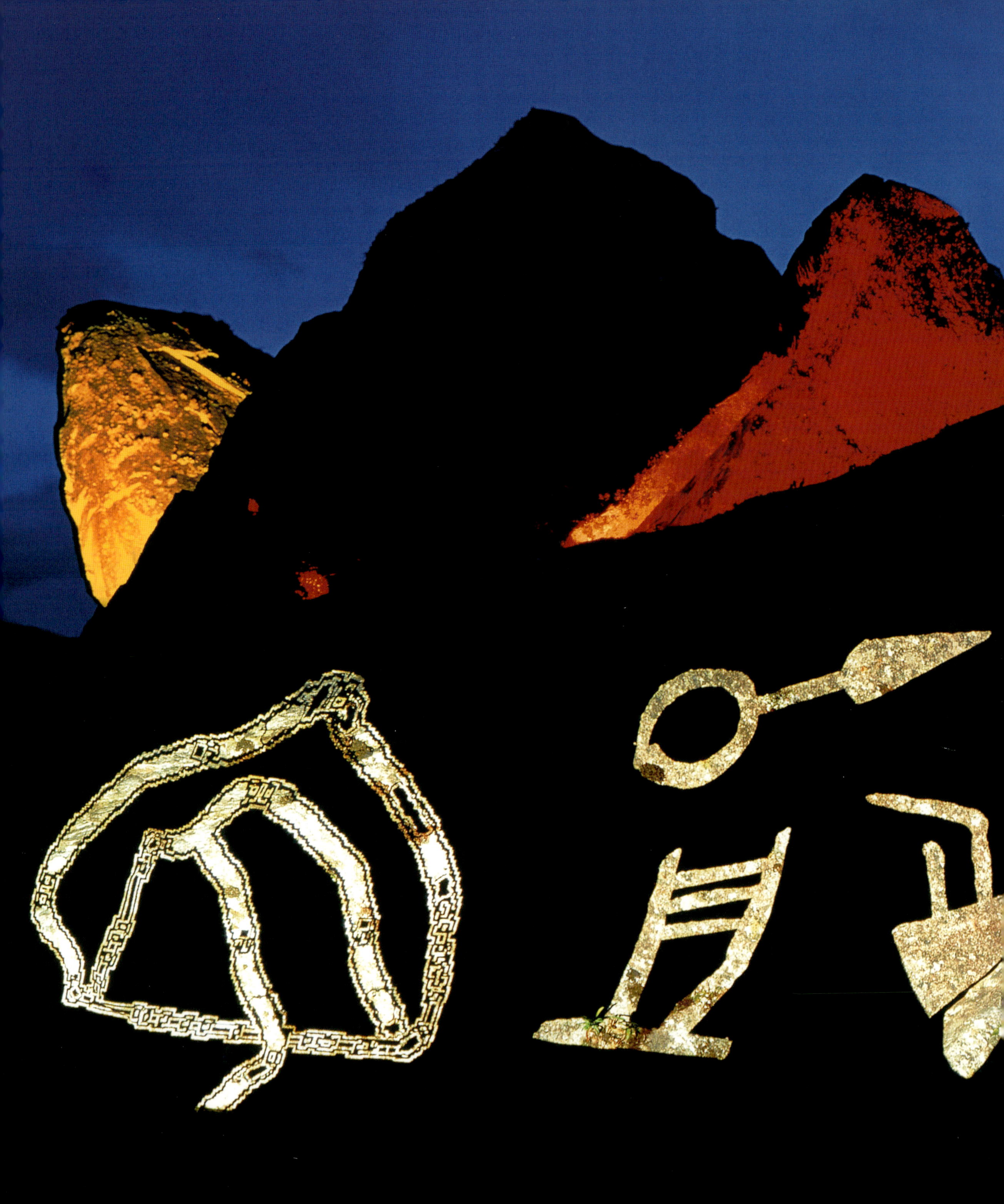

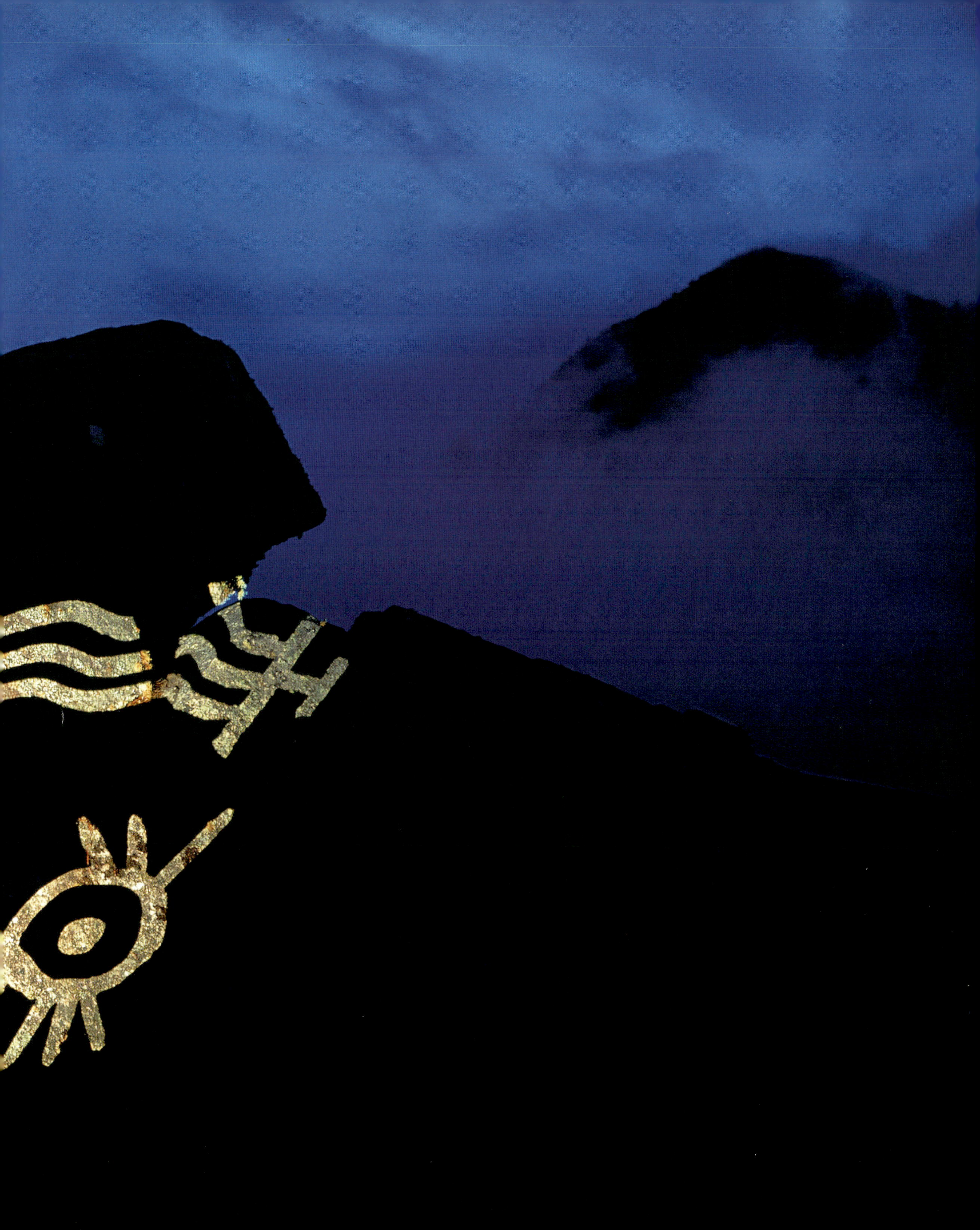

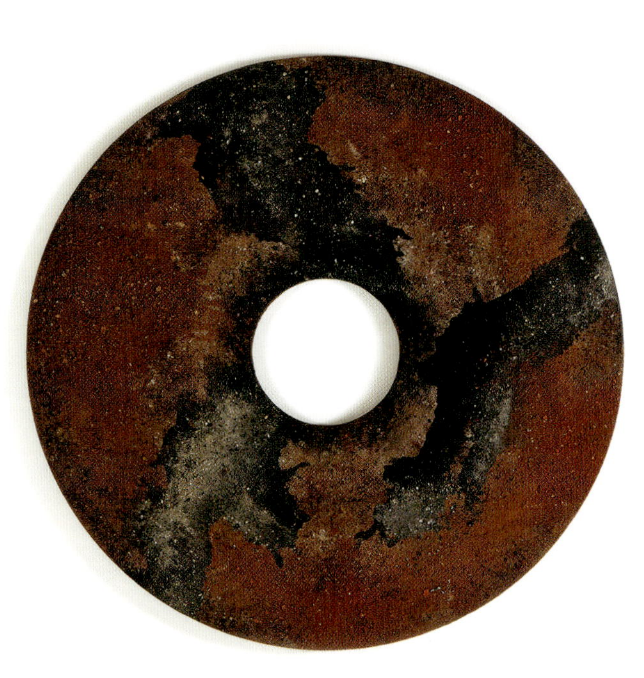

Destino Esperanza, 1996
Wood, earth, volcanic ash, minerals, neon
80 x 80 x 7 cm
Courtesy of Galería el Museo, Bogotá, Colombia

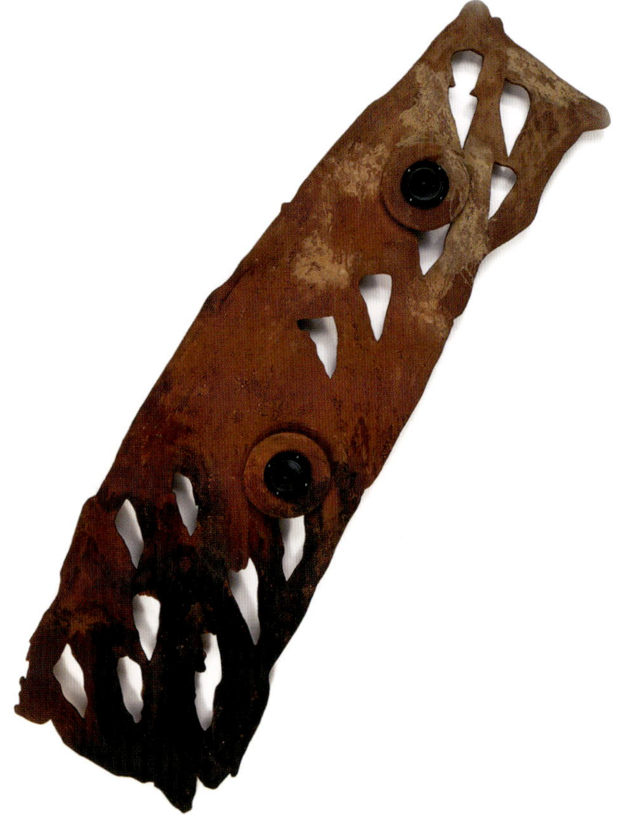

Networks of Dust, 1995
Wood, earth, volcanic ash, minerals, neon, loud speakers
222 x 70 x 9 cm

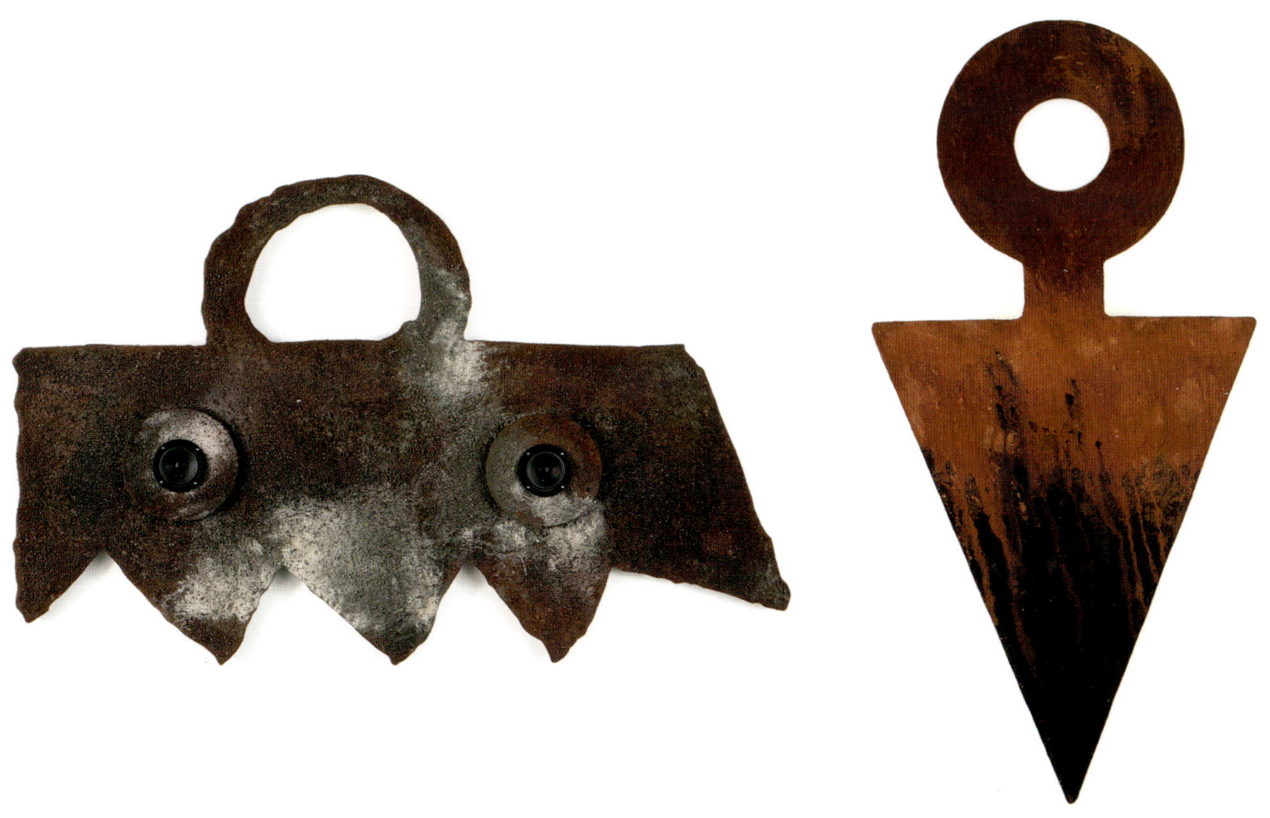

XXXIX Dentadura Nevada, trueno frìo, P.N., 1995
Wood, earth, volcanic ash, minerals, neon, loud speakers
110 x 180 x 9 cm

Tùnica triangular, pollen de piedra, P.N., 1995
Wood, earth, volcanic ash, minerals, neon, loud speakers
190 x 100 x 9 cm
Courtesy of Catherine Pettigas, London

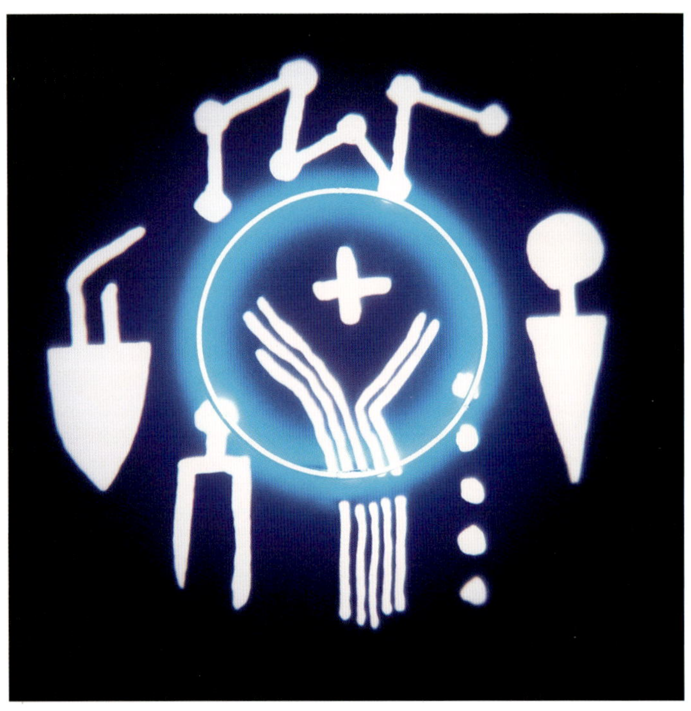

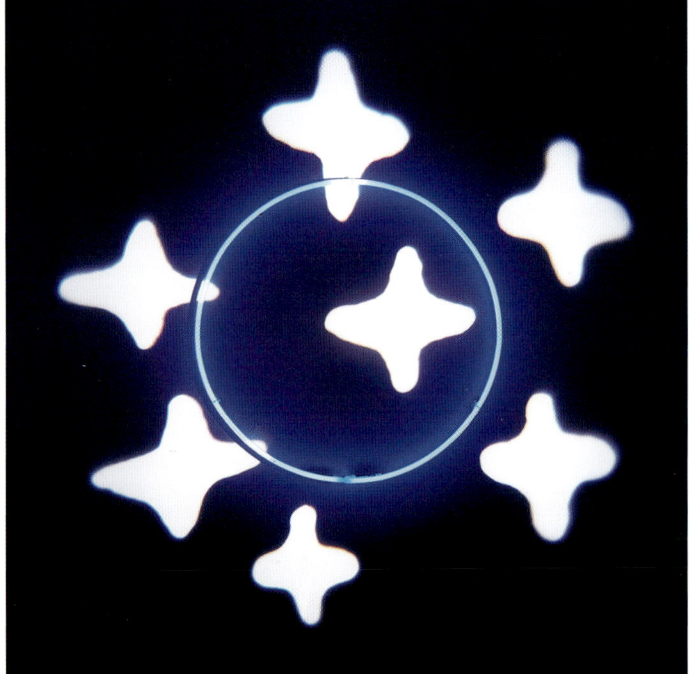

XIII Madrépora del tempo sumergido, P.N., 1996
Neon, light projector, gobo
Approx. 120 x 120 cm

Croix Cardinale, 1996
Neon, light projector, gobo,
Approx. 120 x 120 cm

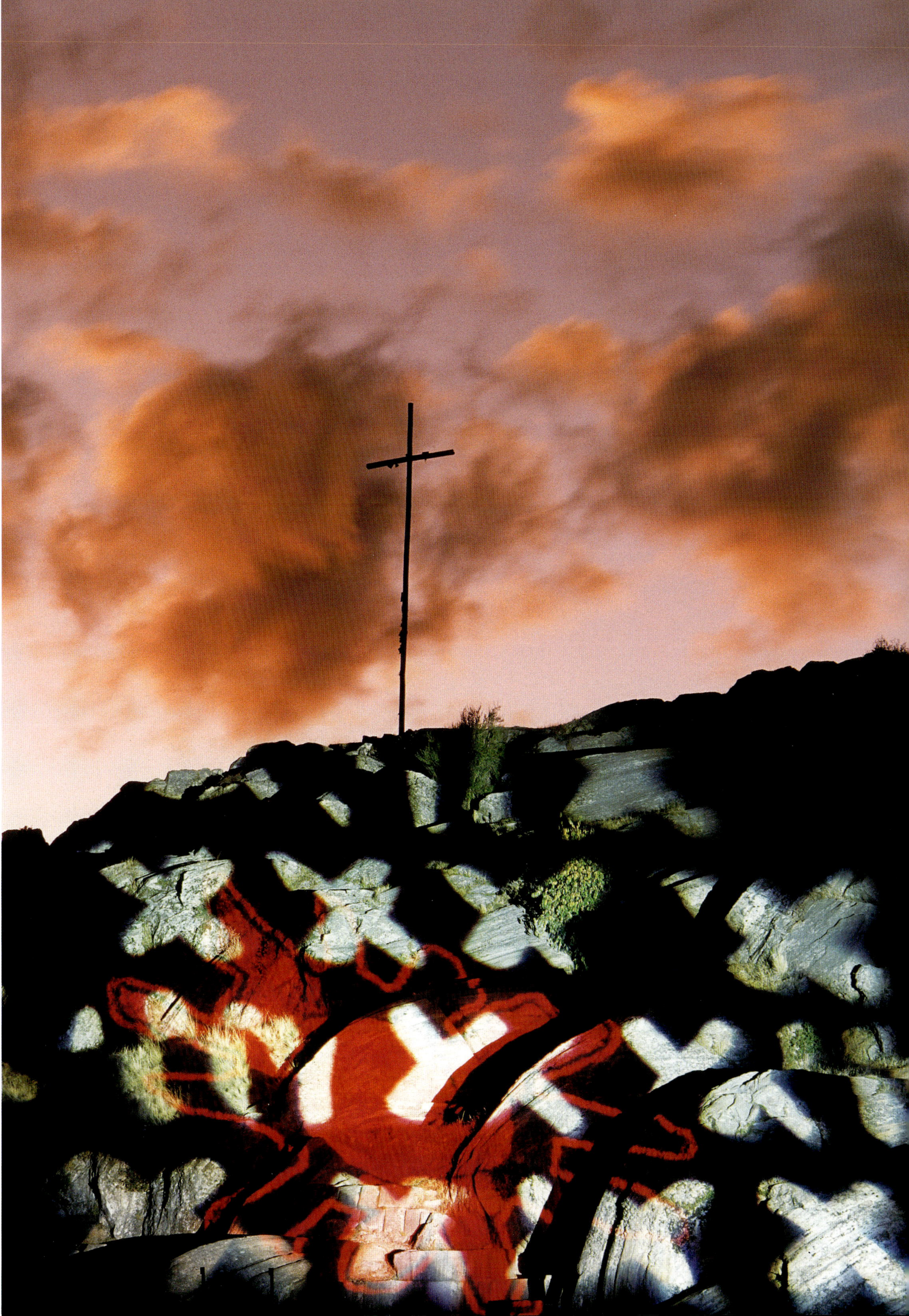

The face captures a bone with its fingers
And blows into it like a flute
To wake up the right hand
Who slaps death

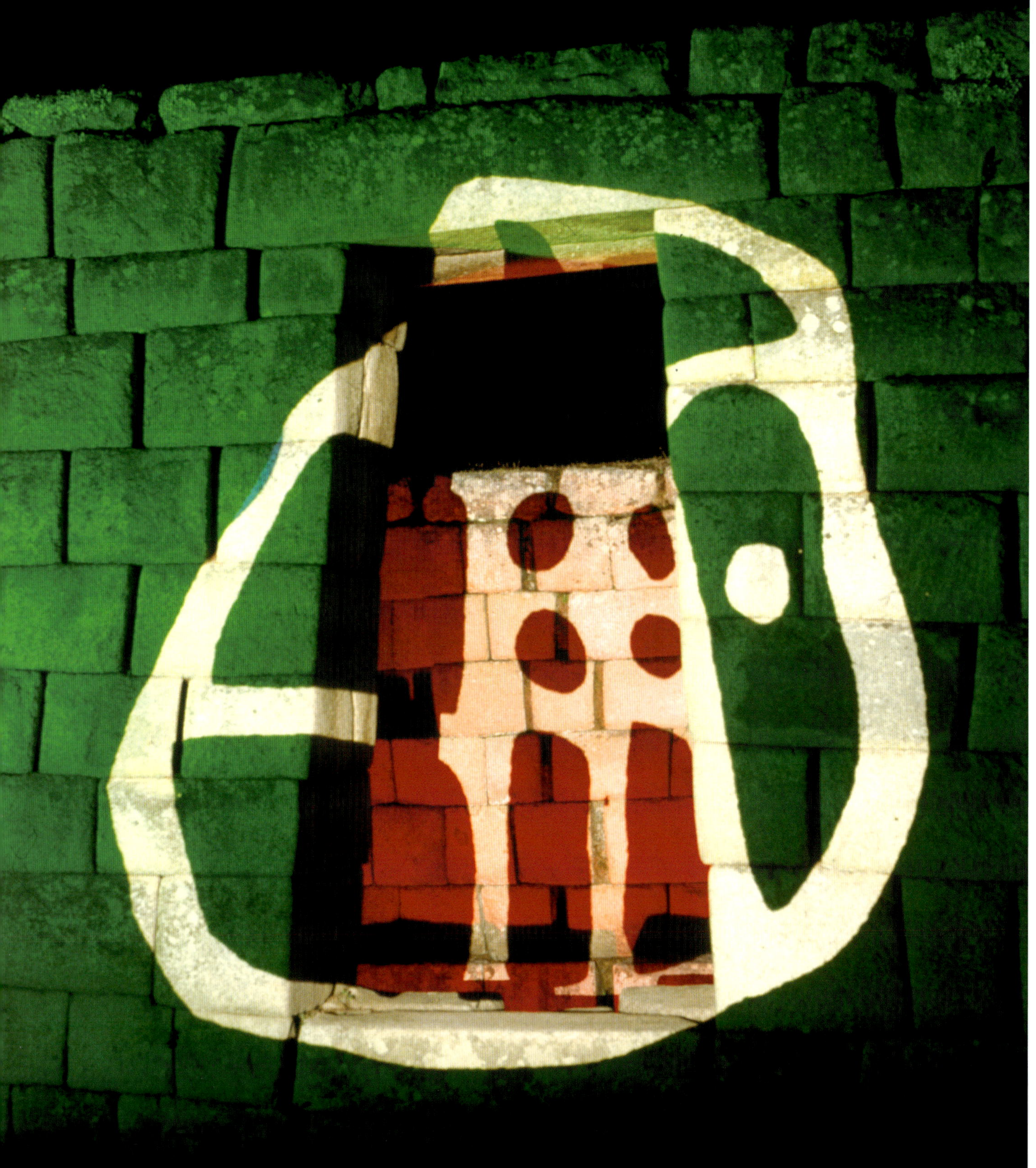

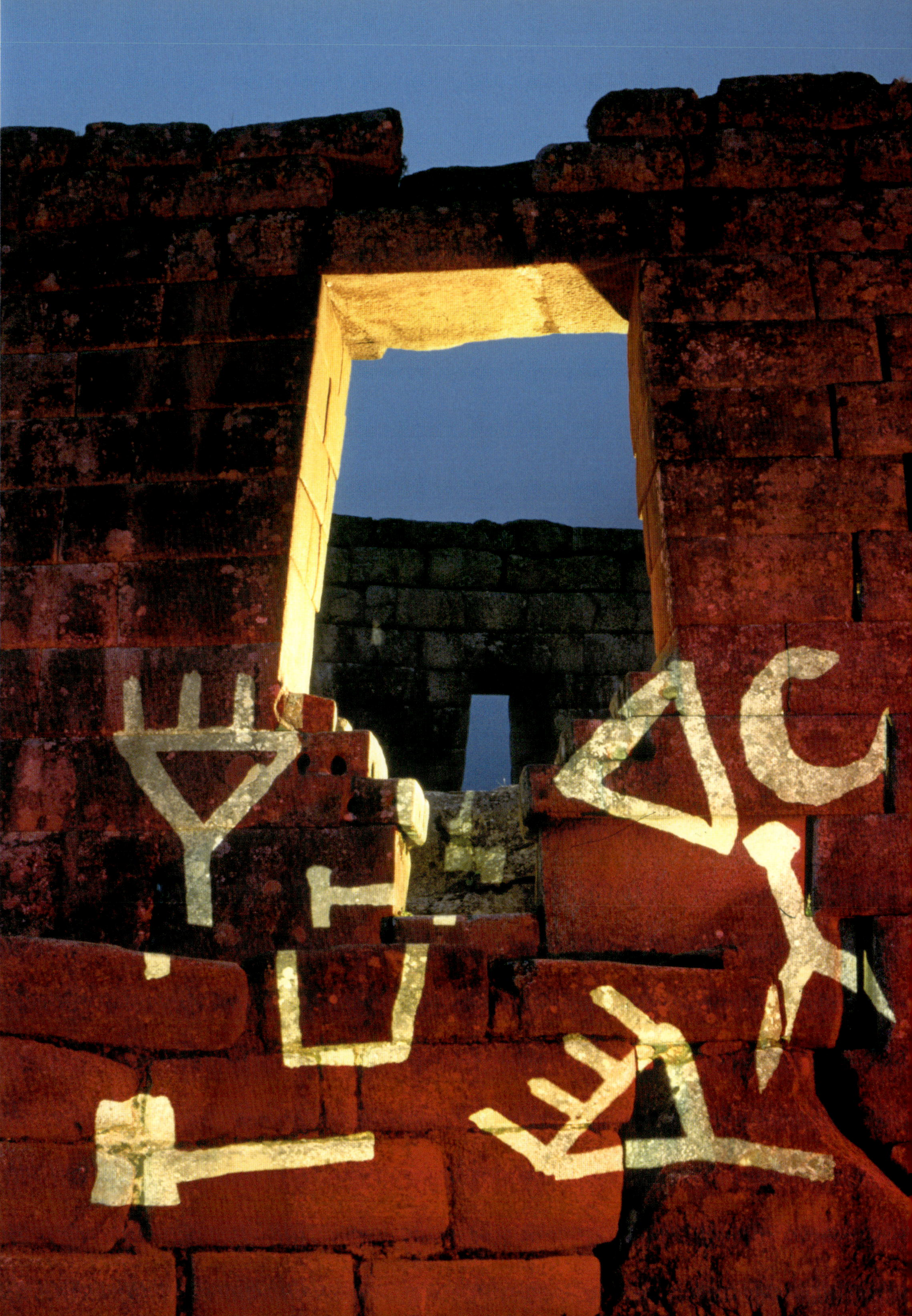

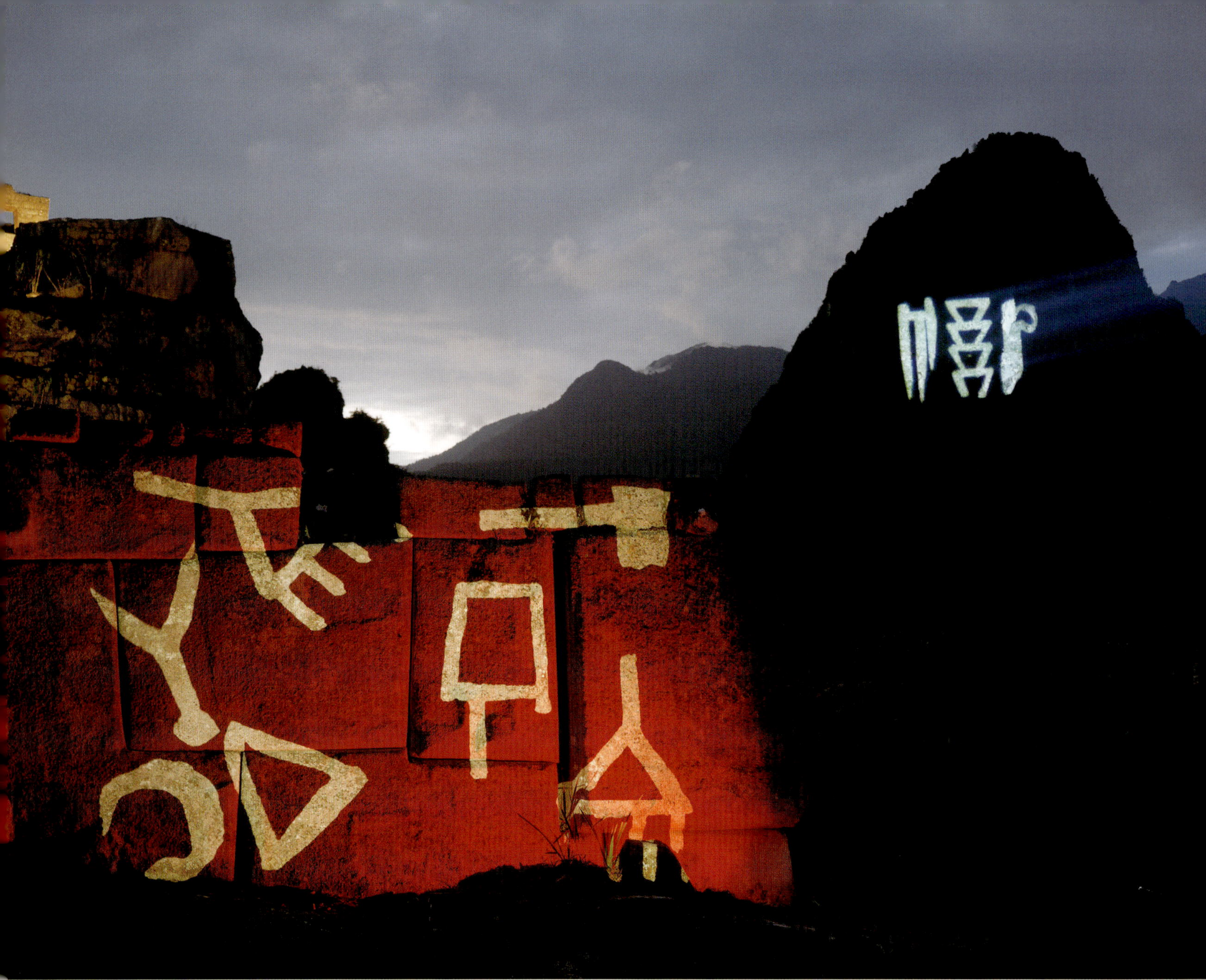

Gods speak without speaking
And drop their key rings
Which no longer open the door locks
That they had erected on the mountains

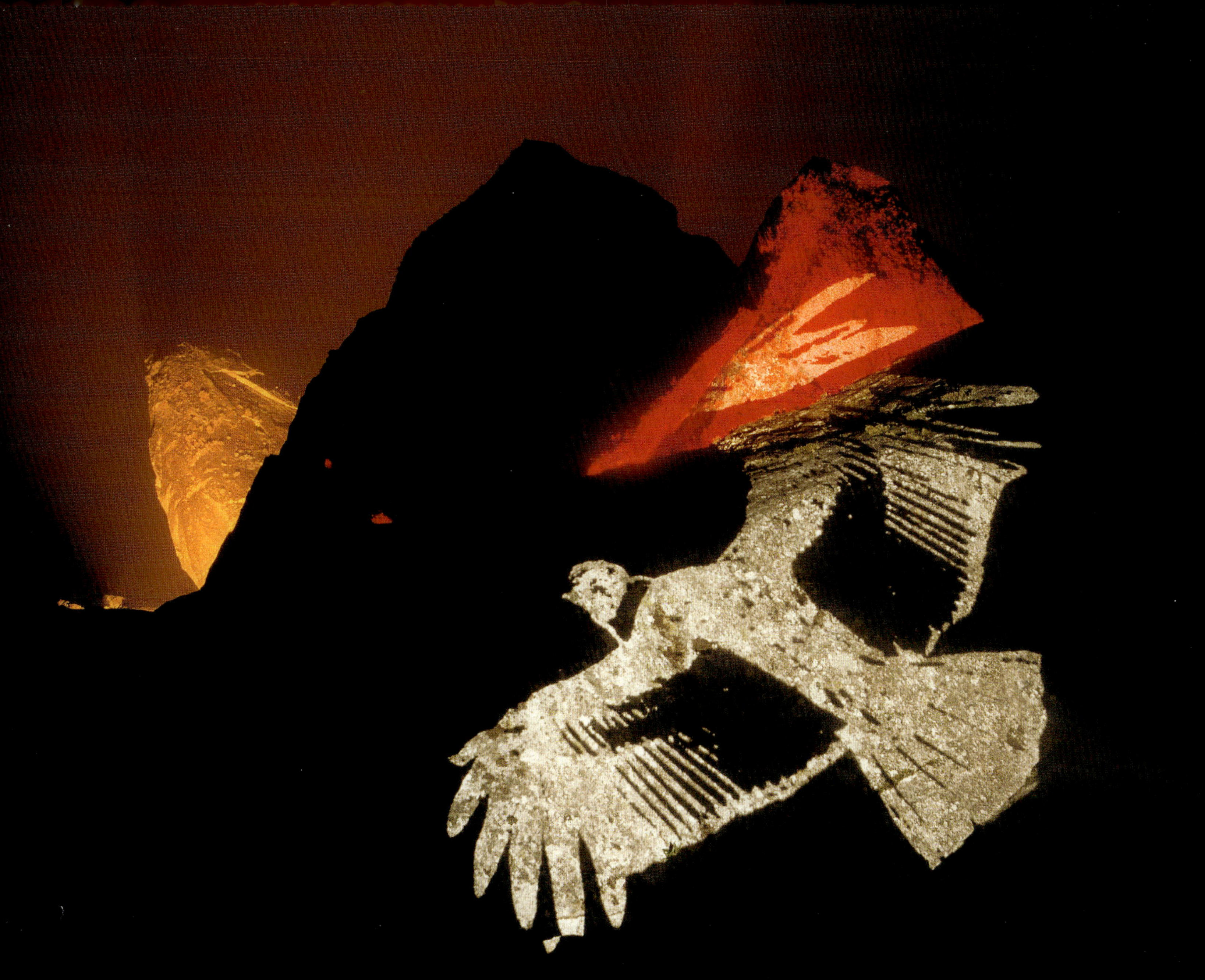

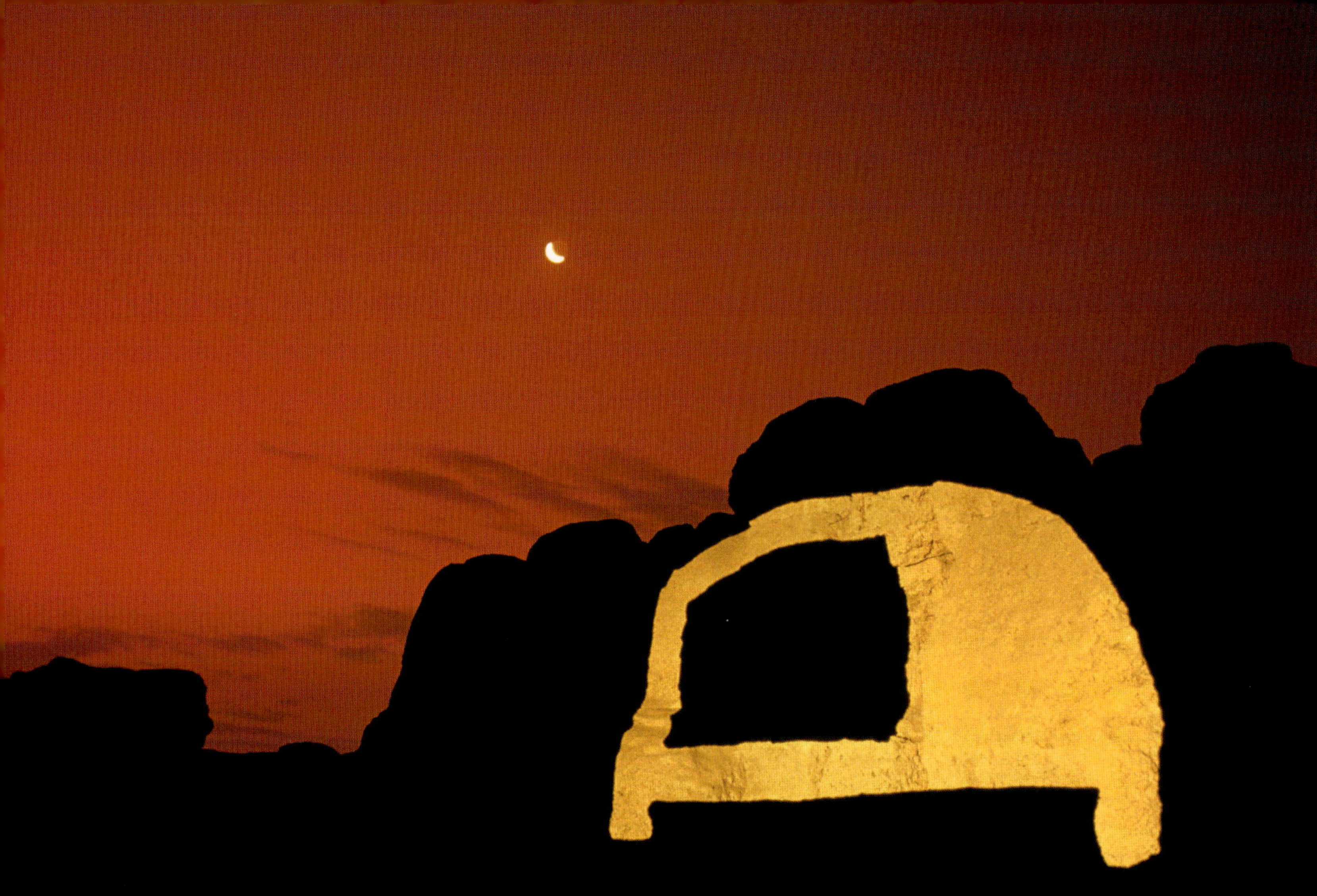

Like a glass of water
Which would be open at the side
And that should be drunk with the head bent
Kissing a woman

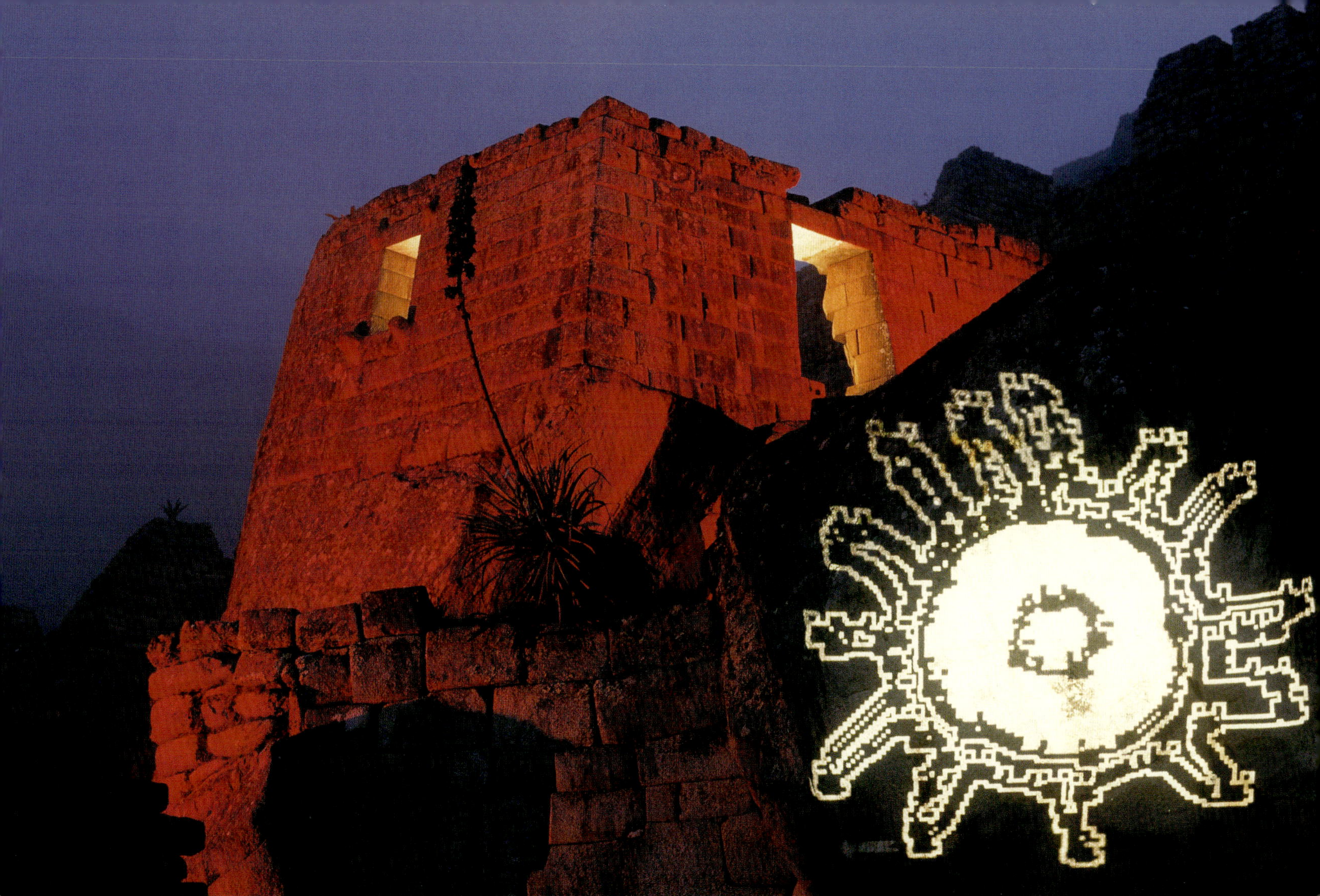

Because man wishes to hold the cold sun in his hands
From where the sun watches from the sky
Because man establishes his difference
On the slice of mirror which cuts the sky
Into two suns

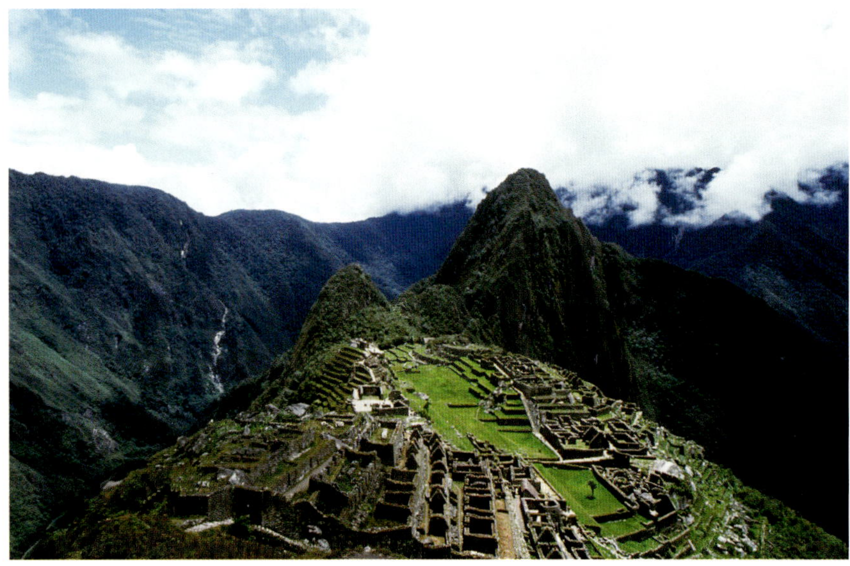

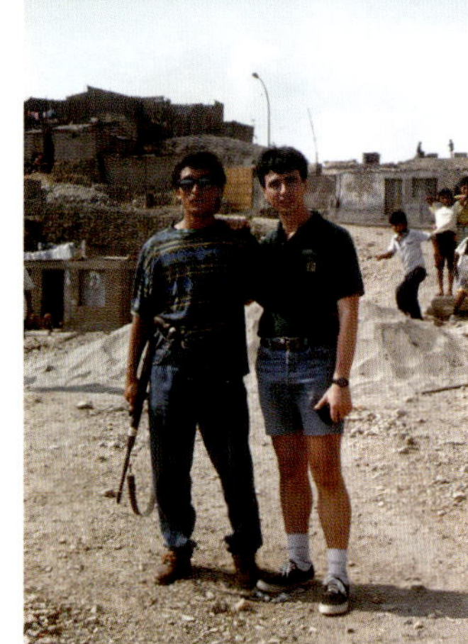

Marking the 500th anniversary of the discovery of the American continent by Christopher Columbus, *Imprints on the Andes* along the Inca trail was carried out during a treacherous five-week expedition across the Peruvian cordilleras. The Light Works coincided with a the capturing of Abimael Guzmán, the leader of the Sendero Luminoso (Shining Path), a Maoist guerrilla organisation in Peru, and a wave of violent attacks surged. The aid promised by the French Embassy in Lima to realise the work was reduced and the French team had to abandon, leaving Lucy+Jorge Orta and associate Claude Namer to mount the expedition with a new inexperienced crew and an armed guard.

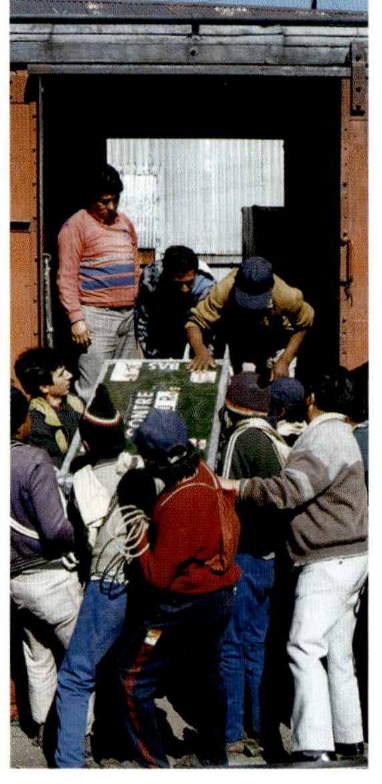

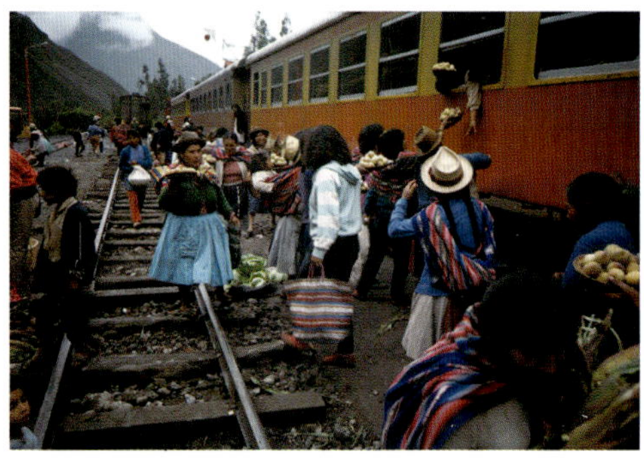

The date set for the Light Works *Imprints on the Andes*, was highly symbolic as it marked the most important gathering of over one hundred thousand people in Cuzco, the historic centre of the Inca Empire, to celebrate the Inti Rymi (Festival of the Sun). The PAE image projectors transported from France, arrived just in time for the public event on 24 June, the day when the Inca ceremonial events begin with an invocation by the Sapa Inca in the Qorikancha ruins, in front of the Santo Domingo church, which is built over the ancient Temple of the Sun. At 8:30pm the Light Works projections commenced on the Cuzco Cathedral, gliding over the baroque facades of Plaza de Armas and onto the surrounding hills, in front of the awe-inspired audience of hundreds and thousands. The combination of the advanced technology projectors with their powerful light beams, the universal motifs and the symbolic occasion, made for a truly unique and highly emotional event for the spectators, which surpassed the expectations of the artists.

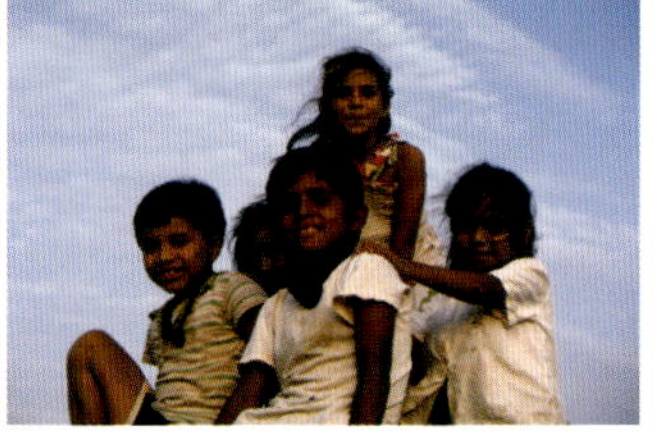

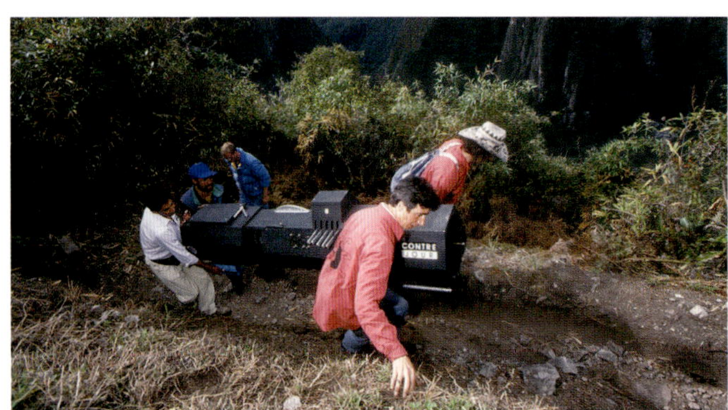

After the Inca celebrations Lucy+Jorge Orta followed the cortège to the ancient fortress of Sacsayhuamán, in the hills above Cuzco. Here the crew worked for several nights until the early hours of the morning before sunrise in the ruins with a petrol generator, in freezing conditions and at the breathless altitude of 3,700 metres. The PAE projectors have a light output of 2,500–5,000 watts each and can project mobile images up to 5,000 square metres from a distance up to 1,000 metres. These mighty light-

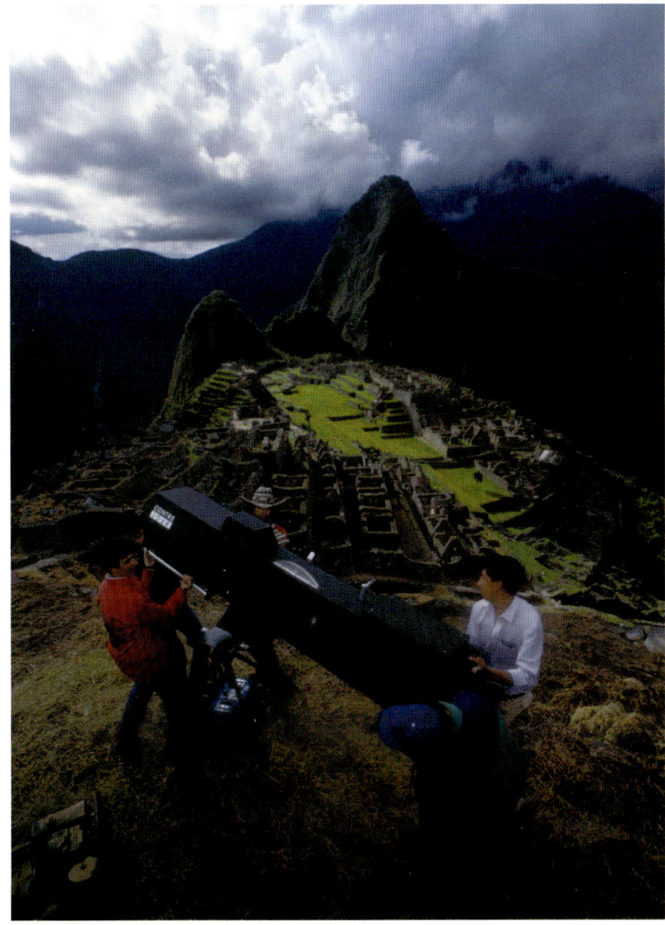

paintbrushes are perfectly adapted to the artists' large scale image projections as each of the massive hand-carved limestone blocks that make up the impressive Inca fortress can weigh up to 200 tonnes.

After the exhausting nights in the ruins of Sacsayhuamán, further light experiments continued in the Inca ruins of Tampu-Machay: the ancient water source which served the city of Cuzco, a sacred site based on the cult of water. The Inca architecture incorporates the natural topography of the stony ground around the source, which comes from the ground, creating a perfect harmony between man and nature. Gusilluchayoc: a snake's head appears at the entrance of the temple of the moon and its body inside symbolising the link between the interior and exterior world. At certain times in the year a hole in the ceiling of the temple is lit by moonlight for rites, sacrifices and offerings to the gods. After, another night of projections and a performance in Qenko the PAE image projectors were loaded into the cargo wagon at Cuzco station for the spectacular train journey along the Sacred Valley to the ancient ruins of Machu Picchu.

The train to Machu Picchu descends 2,000 metres into the Sacred Valley with dramatic views of the Urubamba River canyon at the foothills of the deep green Andes with their snow-covered caps. The crew off-loaded the 1, 200 kilogrammes of equipment at the Aguas Caliente station for the treacherous lorry drive back up the hairpin bend tracks to the entrance of the Inca citadel. Once inside the ruins the projection equipment and petrol generators were carried on foot to the sacred locations throughout Machu Picchu. Camping amongst the silent ruins from 27 June to 4 July, the crew worked in the bitter cold from dusk until dawn to paint the ancient stone walls, temples and surrounding peaks with light signs: fours hours for two minutes of video, one hour for three minutes of 35mm film and all night long for just two photographs to record *Imprints on the Andes*.

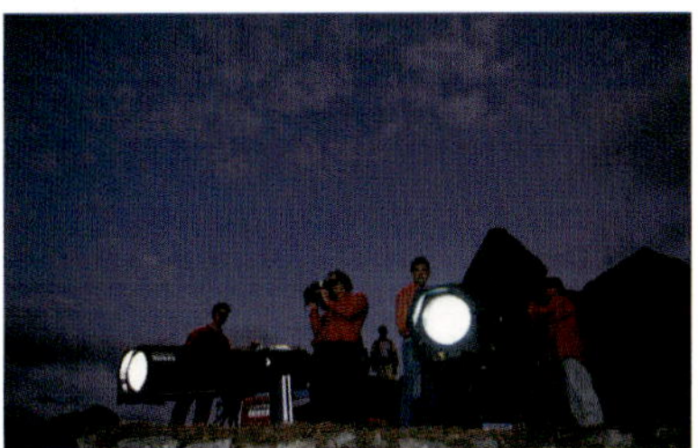

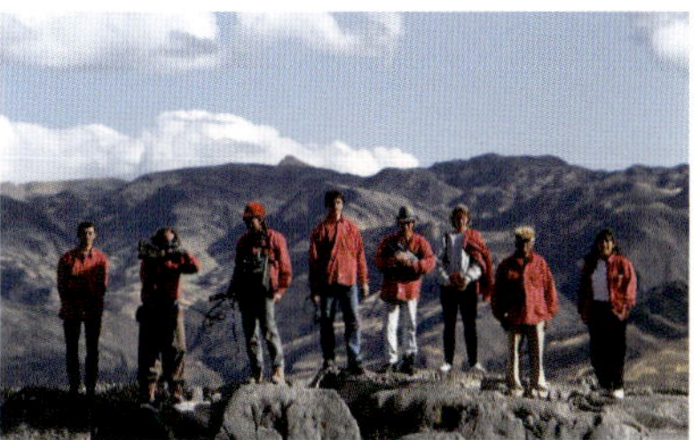

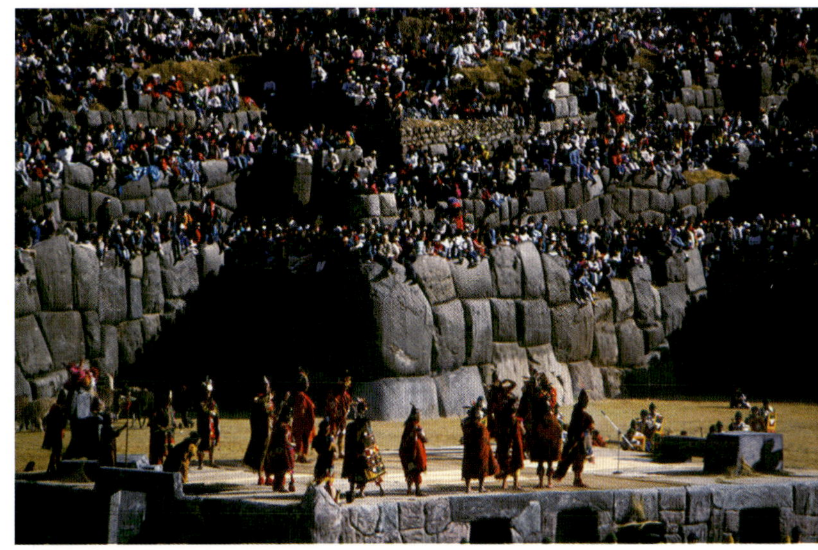

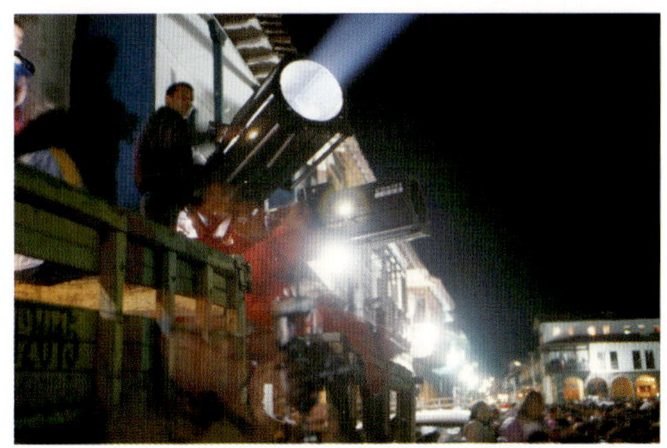

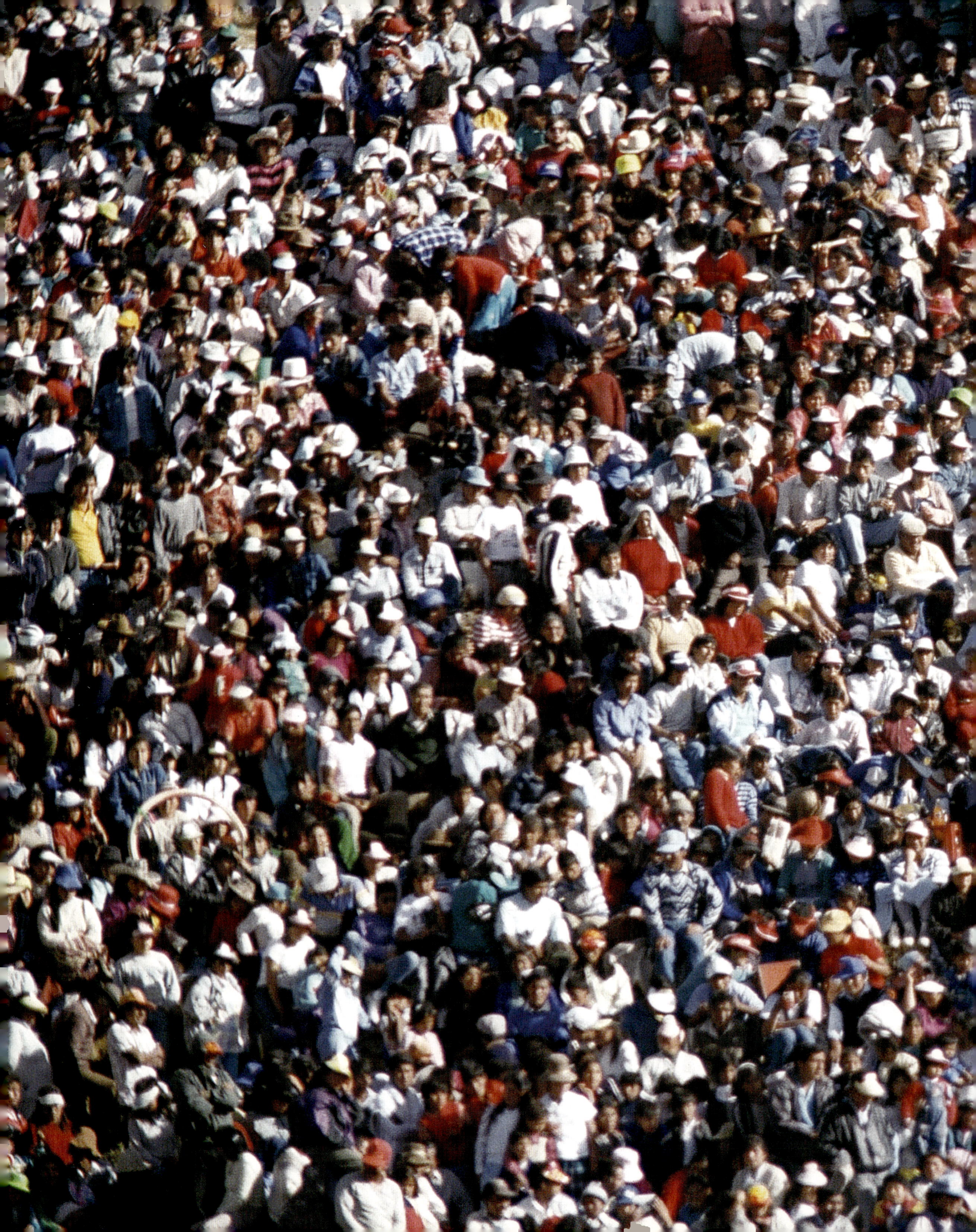

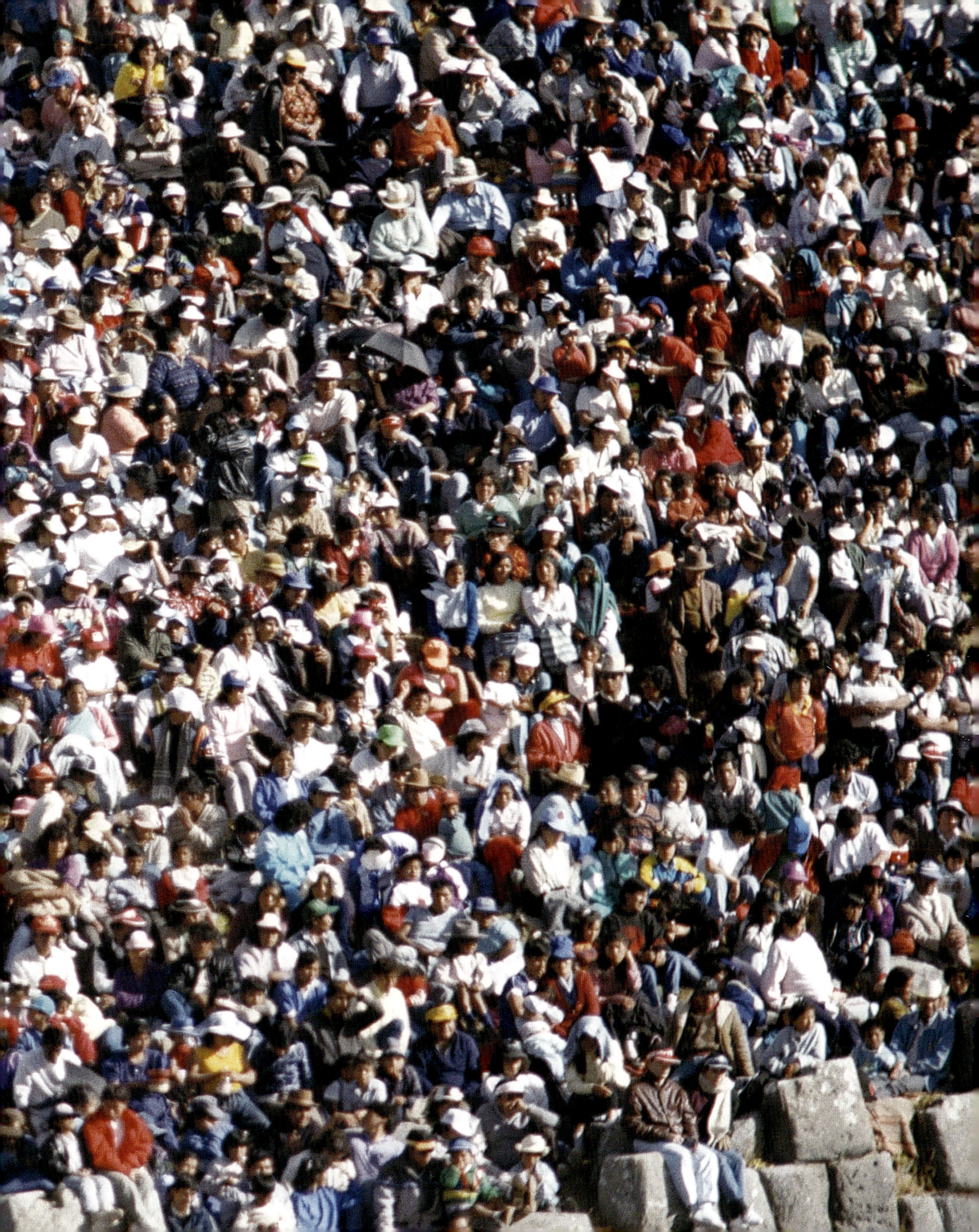

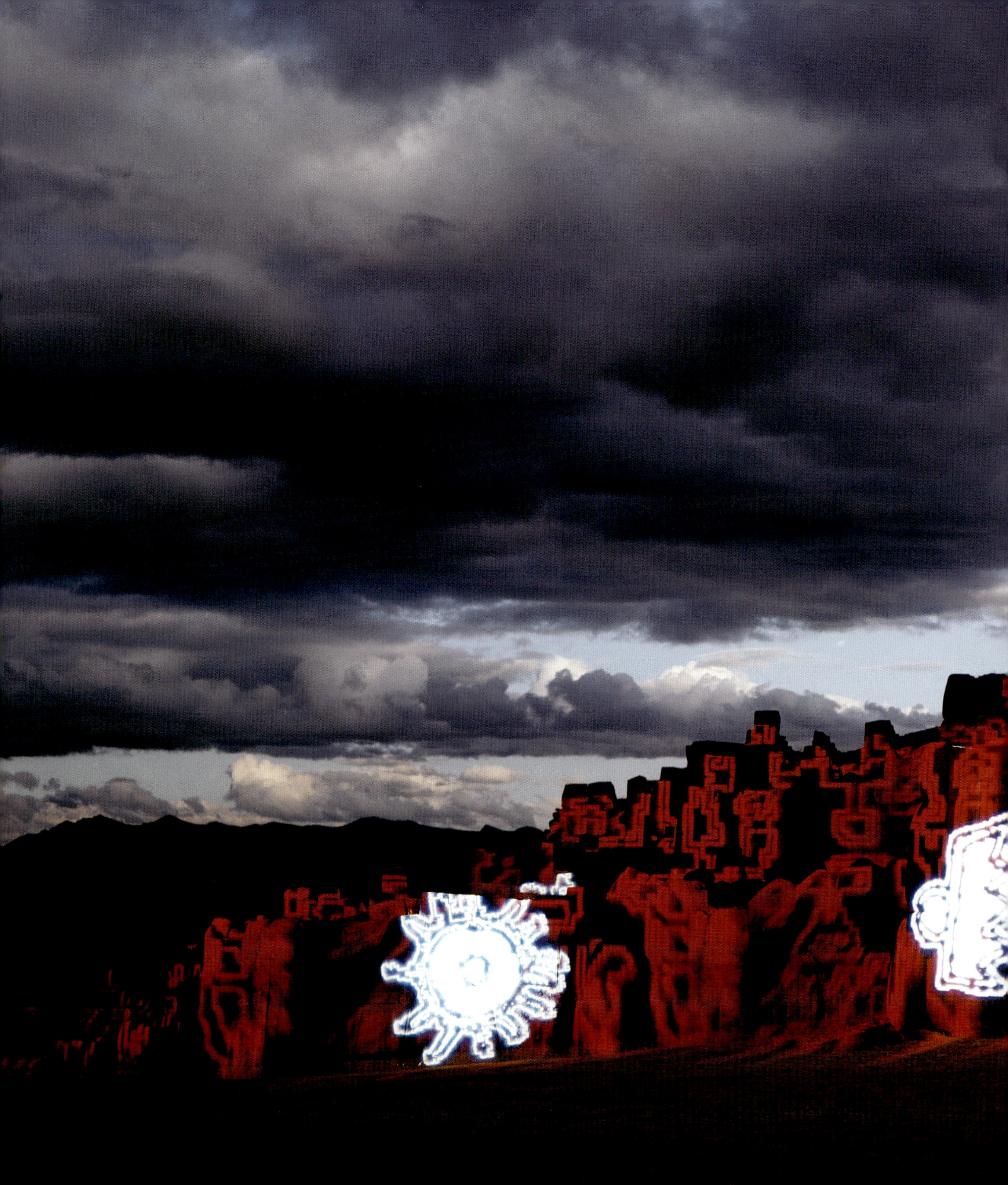

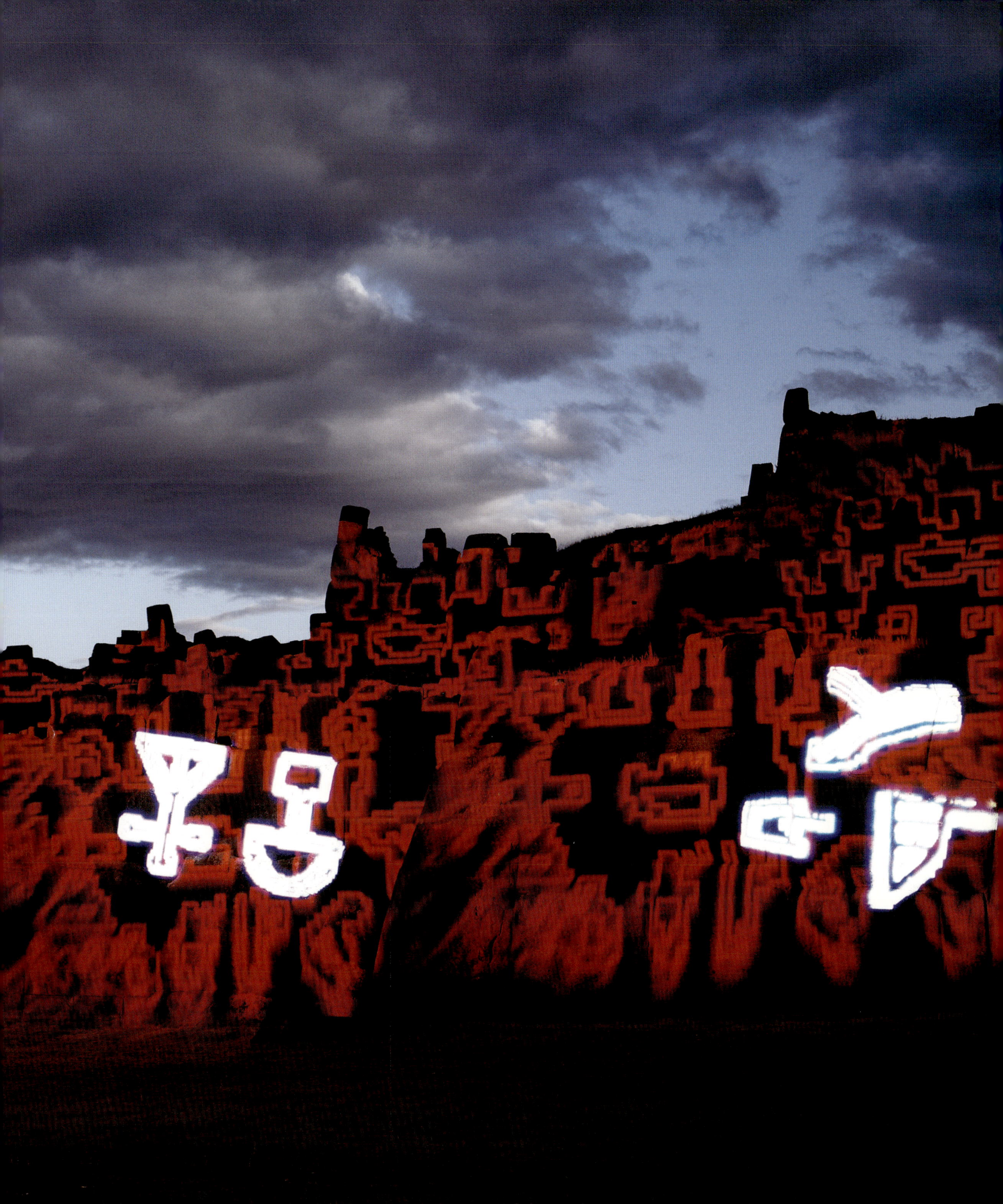

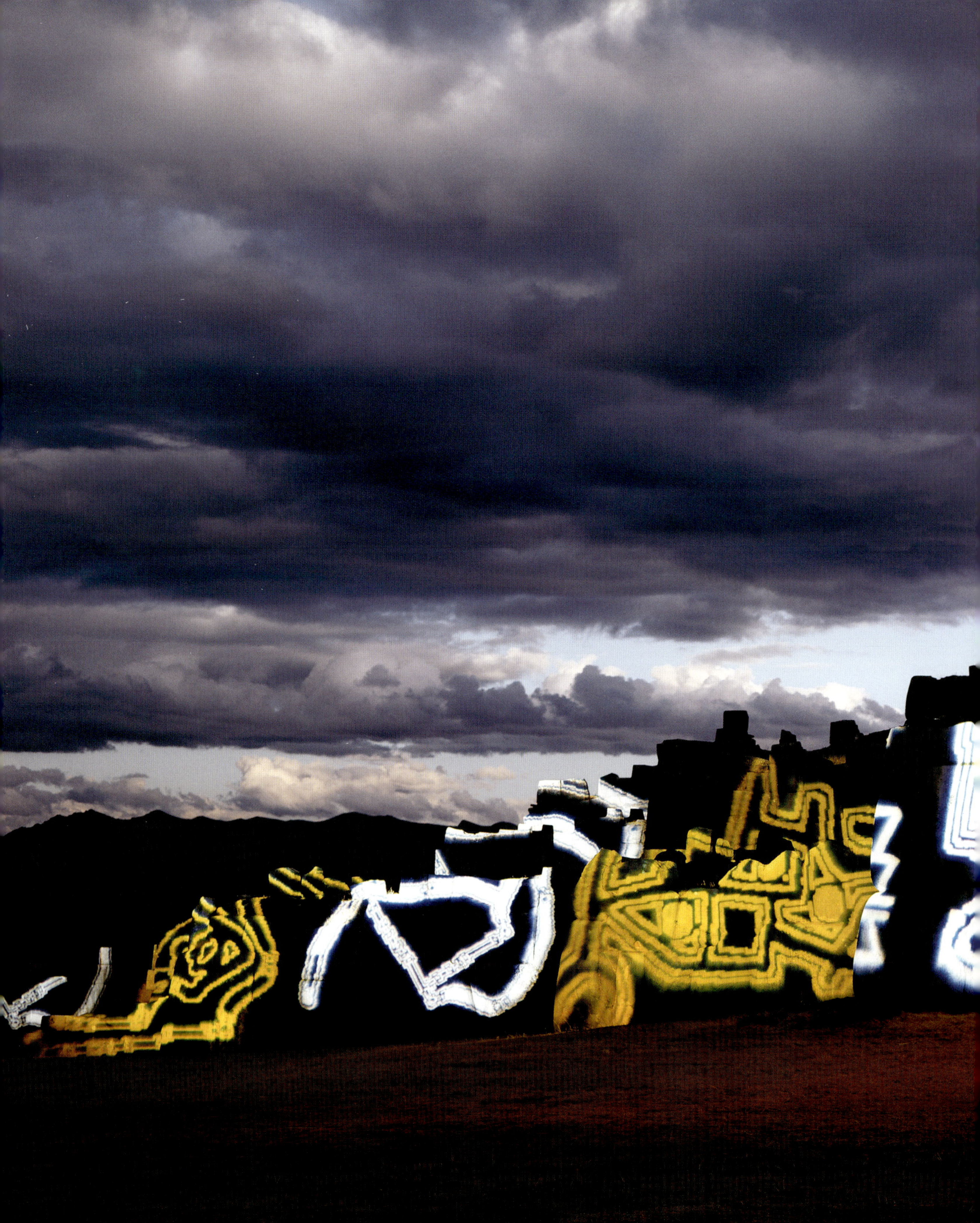

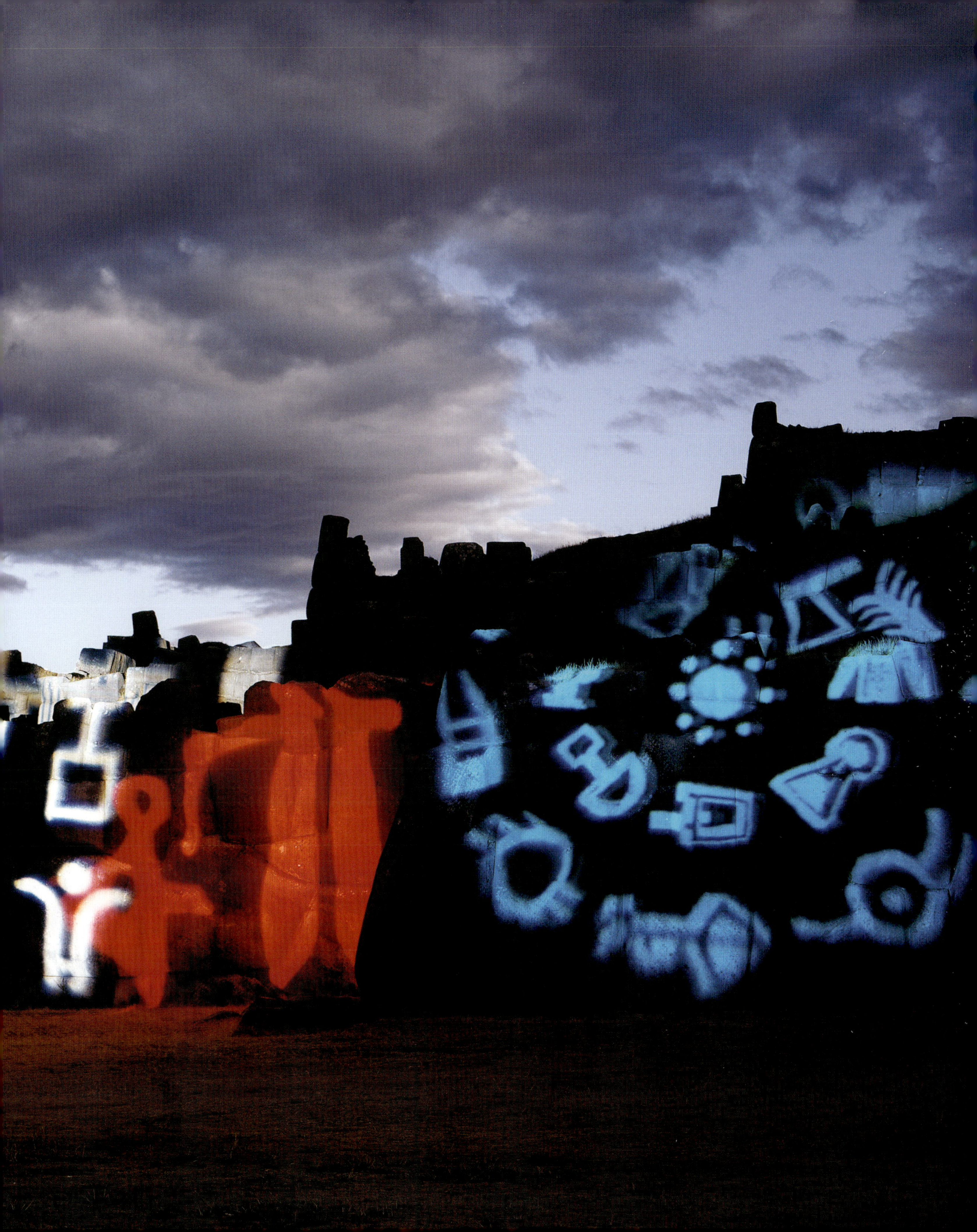

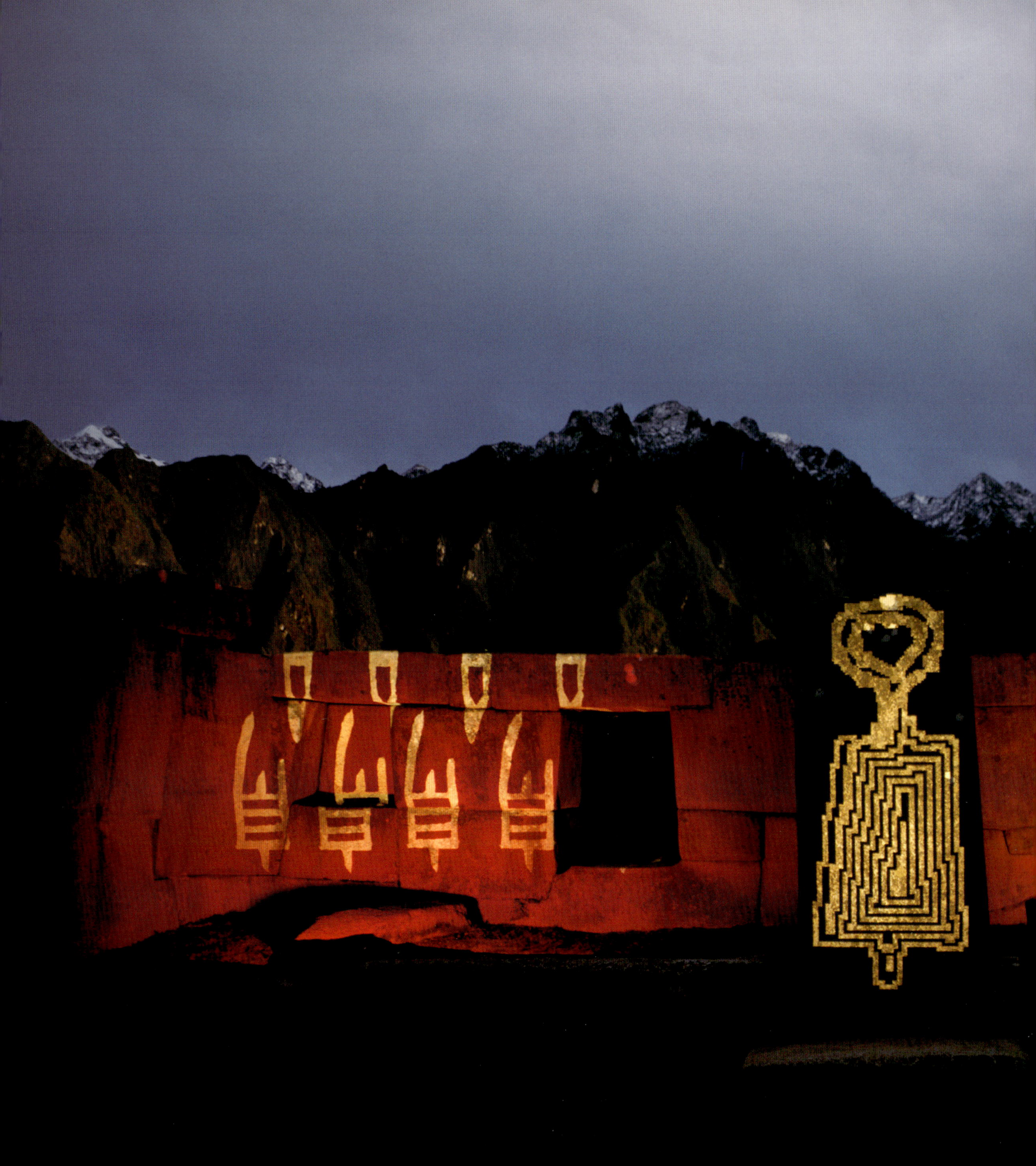

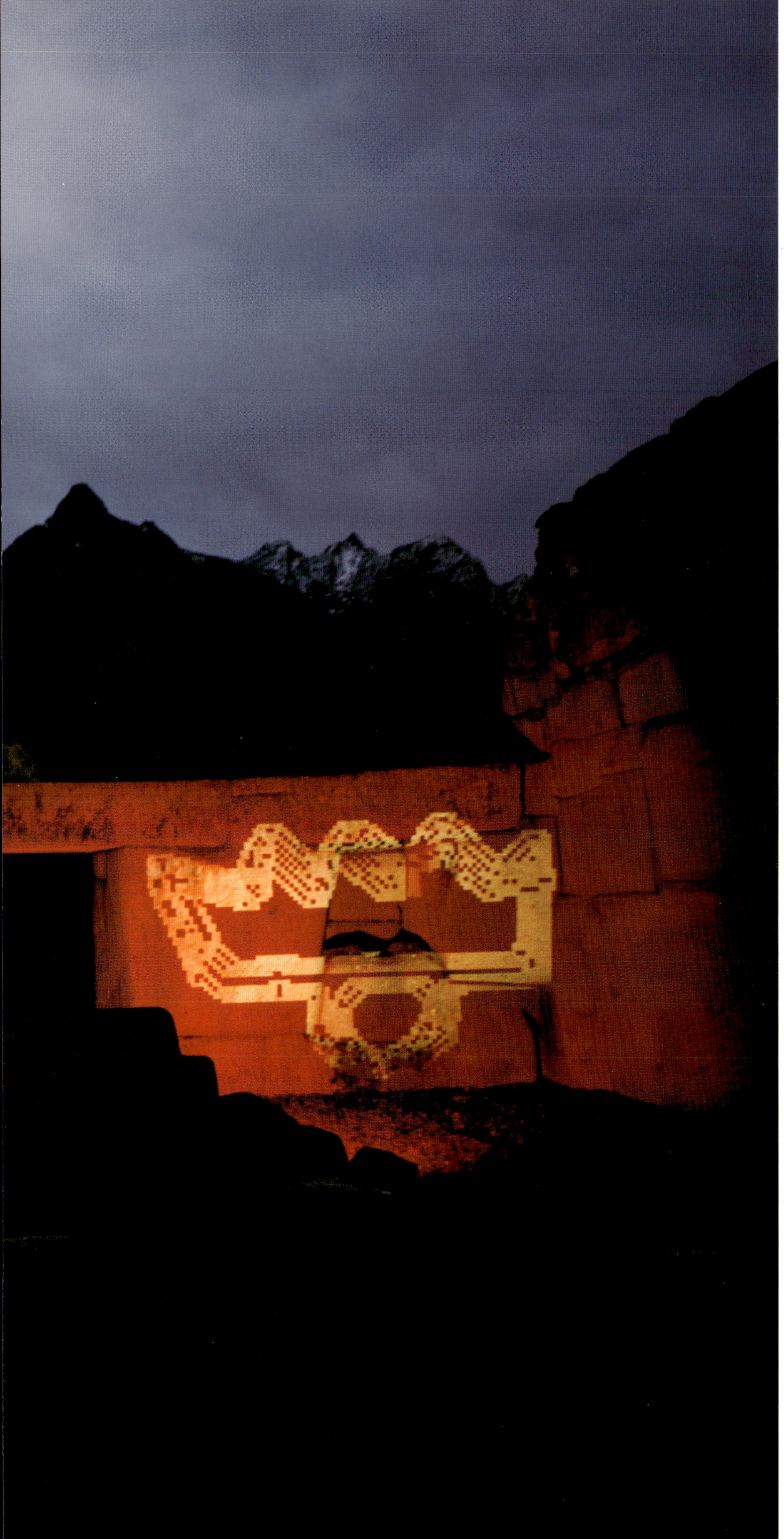

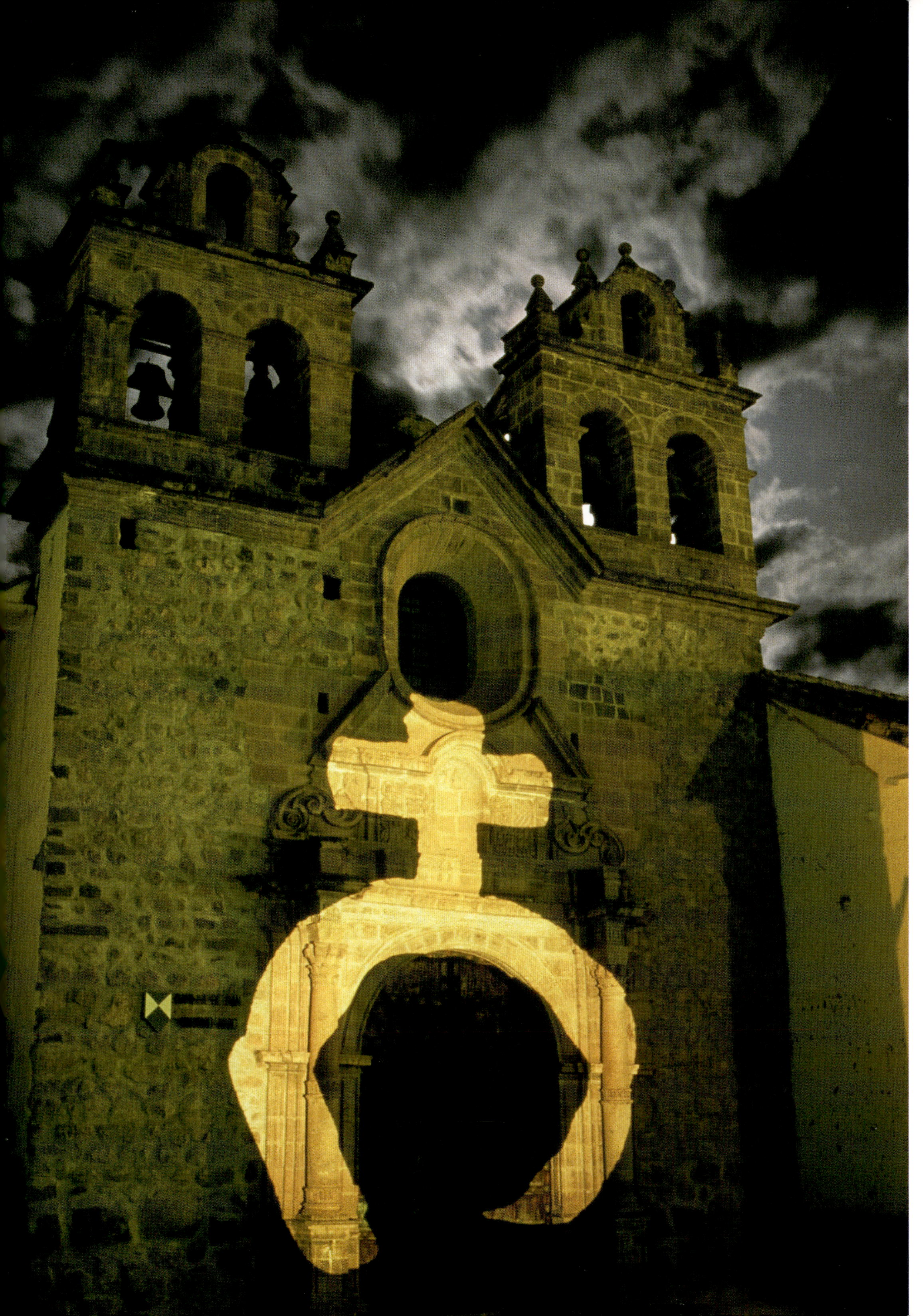

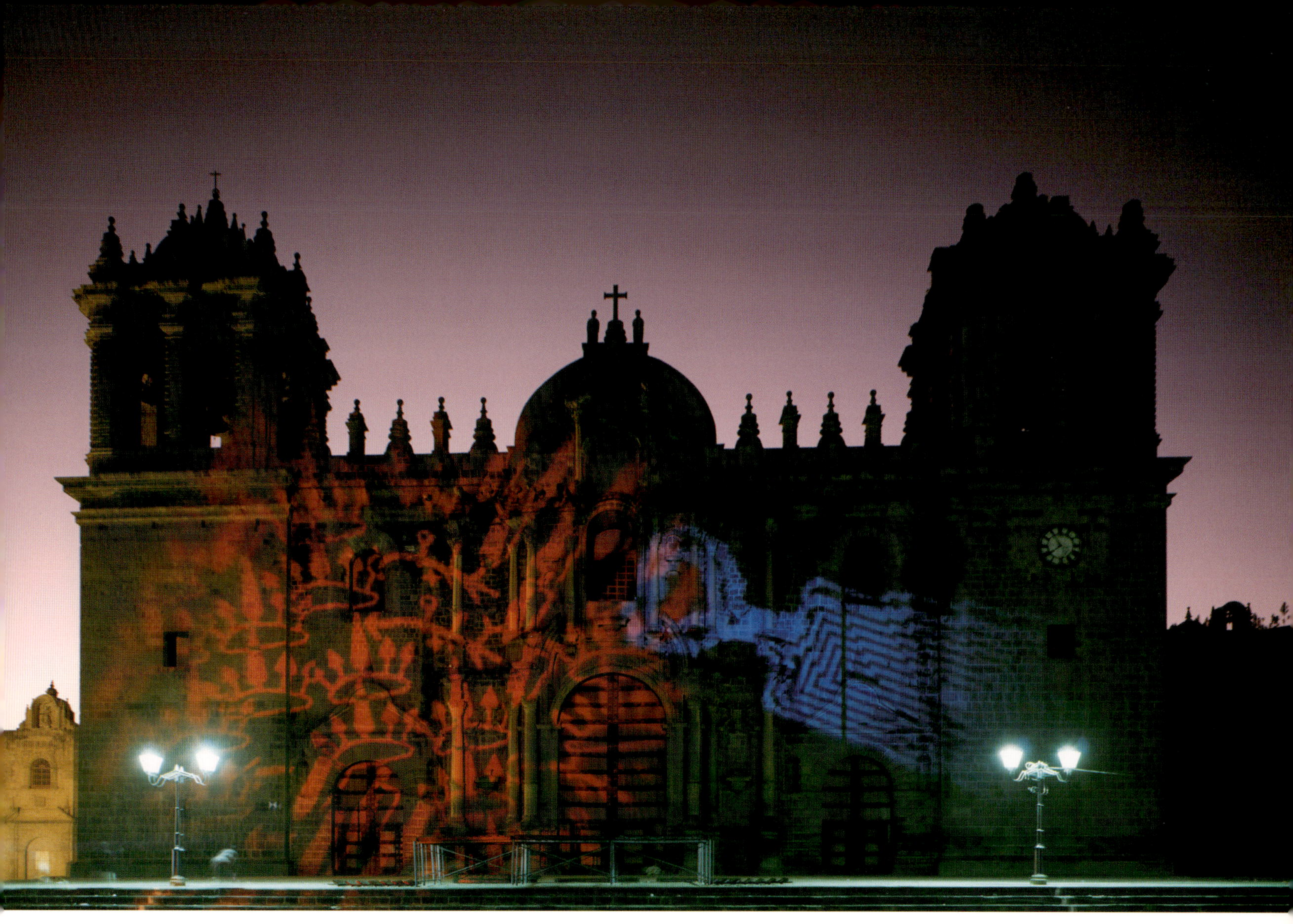

The sign is upside down
In its cross and sole a twisted hoof
Against the doorstep

Serge Pey

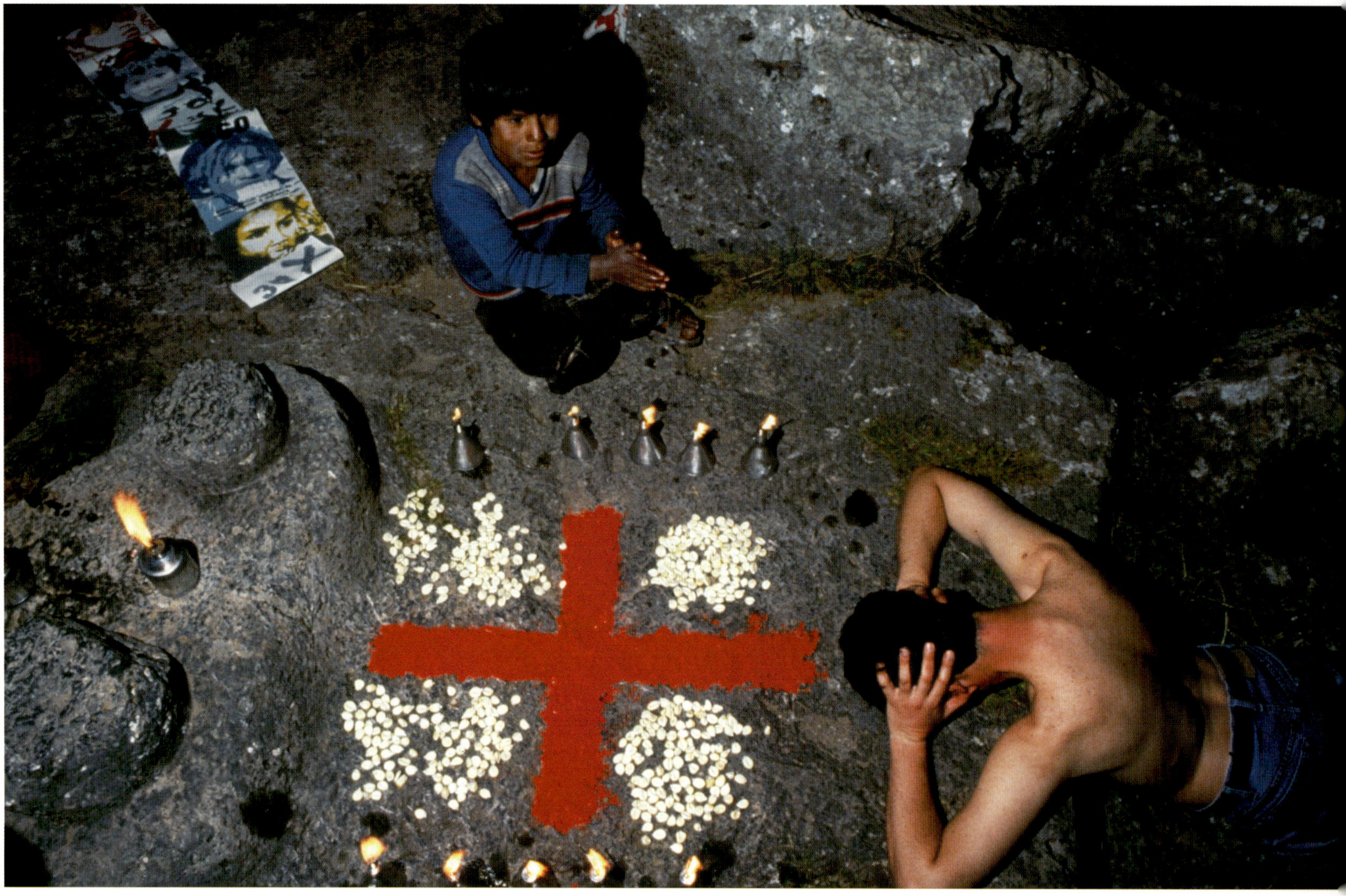

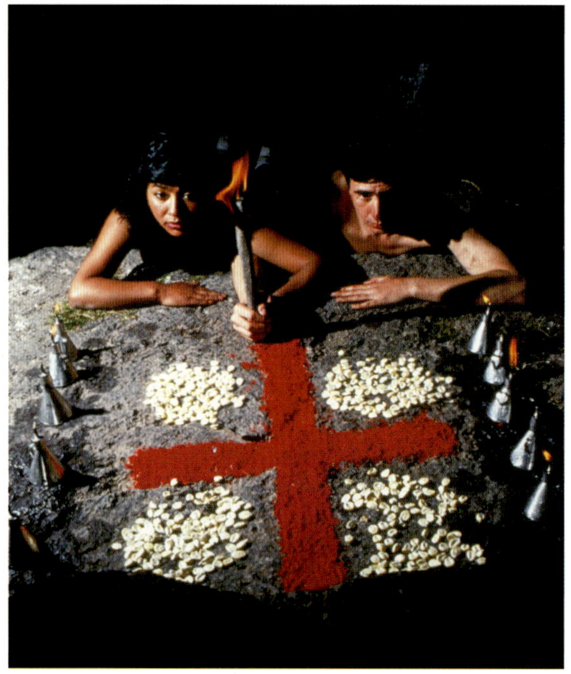

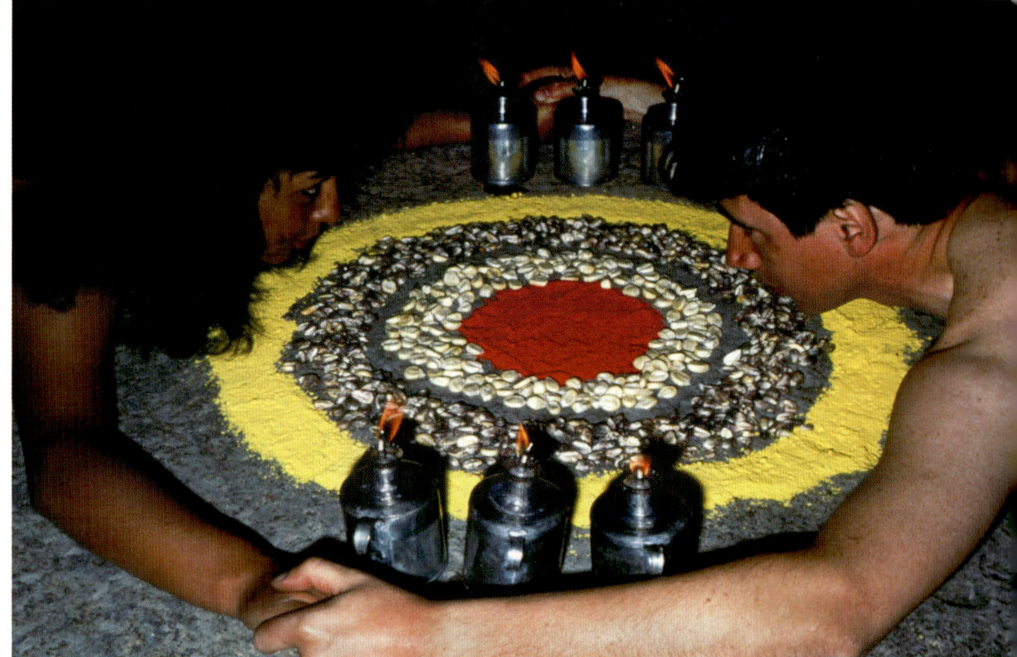

RITES AND SACRIFICES

Performance, Qenko, Peru 1992

Reflecting on the 500th anniversary of the discovery of the Americas during their expedition along the Inca trail, the artists chose the ritual site of Qenko, northwest of Cusco for an spontaneous performance. It was believed that the Incas worshiped the Sun and the Moon here and in the zigzag shape carved into the rock was said to have flowed the holy water, chicha (corn beer) or blood during sacrifices. The Orta's ritual performance evokes the sacrifice and the destruction of this culture either through barbaric acts or ignorance. Assembled around the Intihuatana with its two stone sundials, are the naked bodies, dispossessed, and recreating a magical-ritualistic rite during the winter solstice.

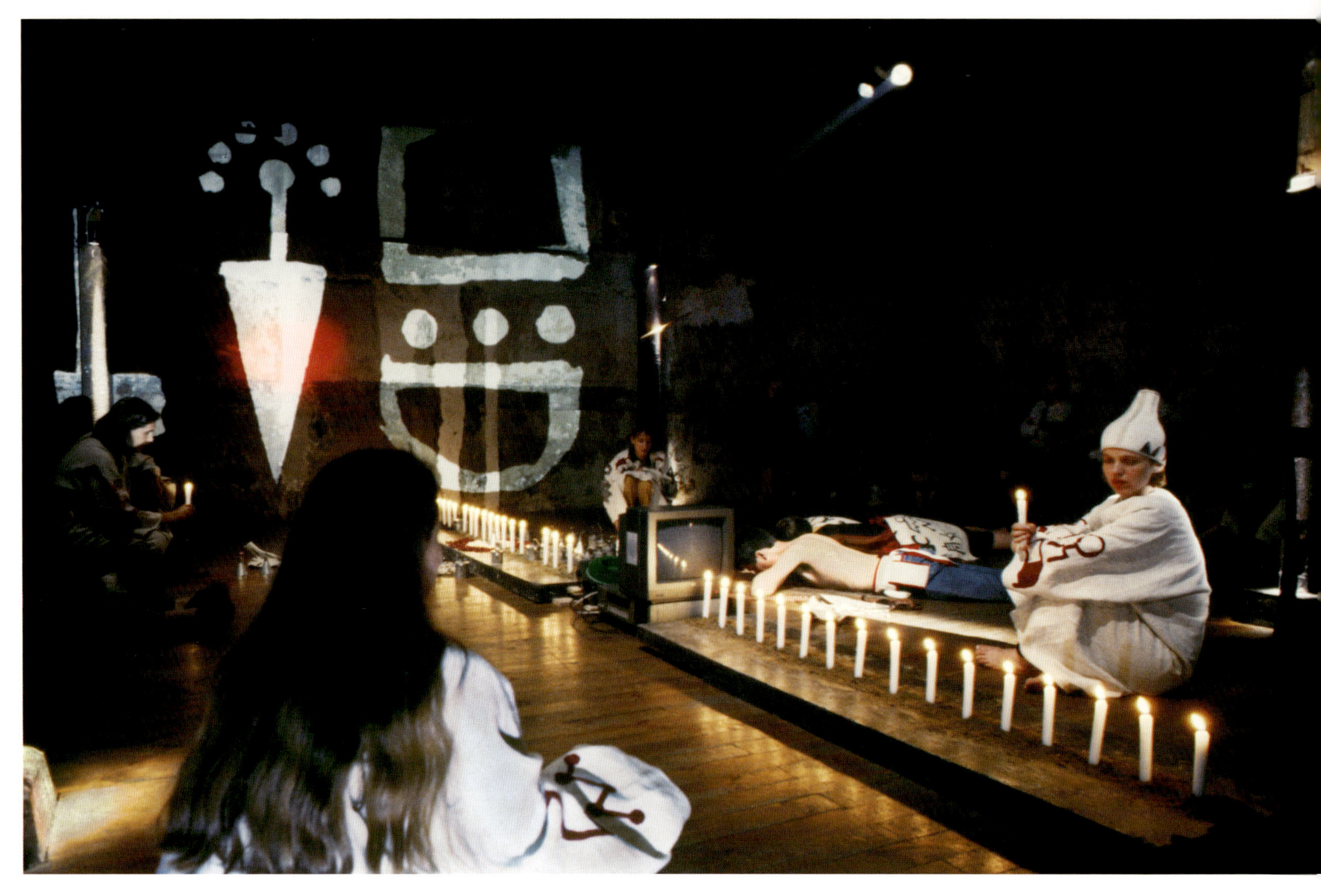

Terre, 1992
Performance, Galerie Procréart, Paris, France

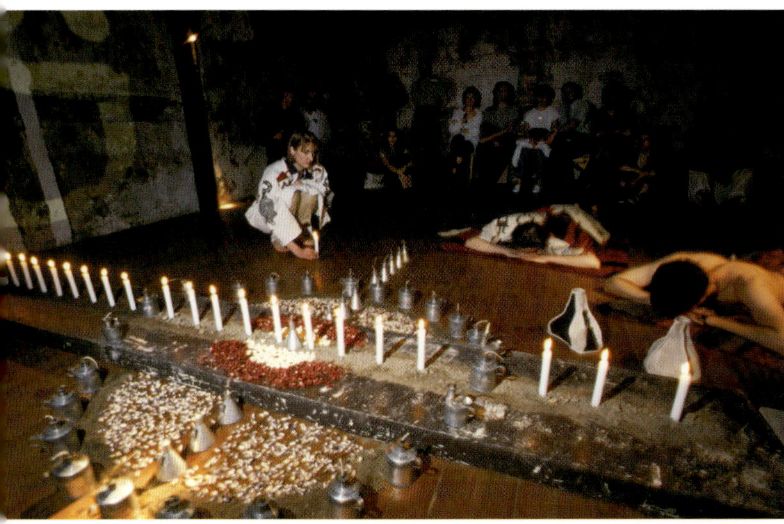

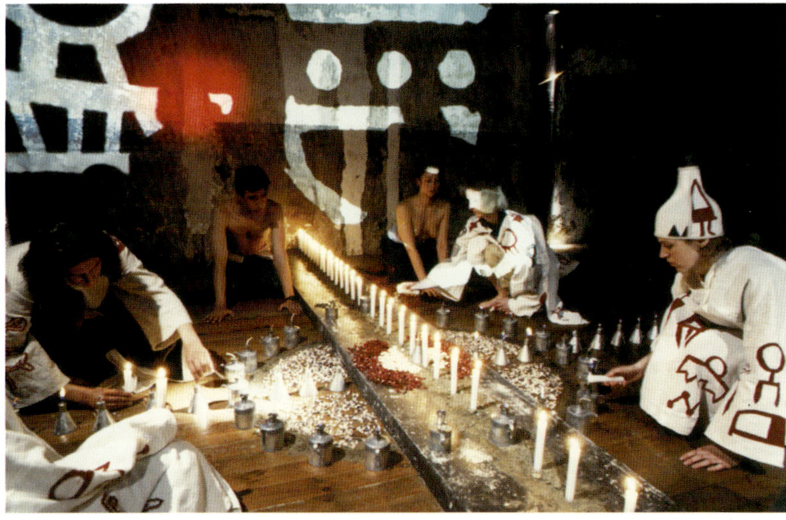

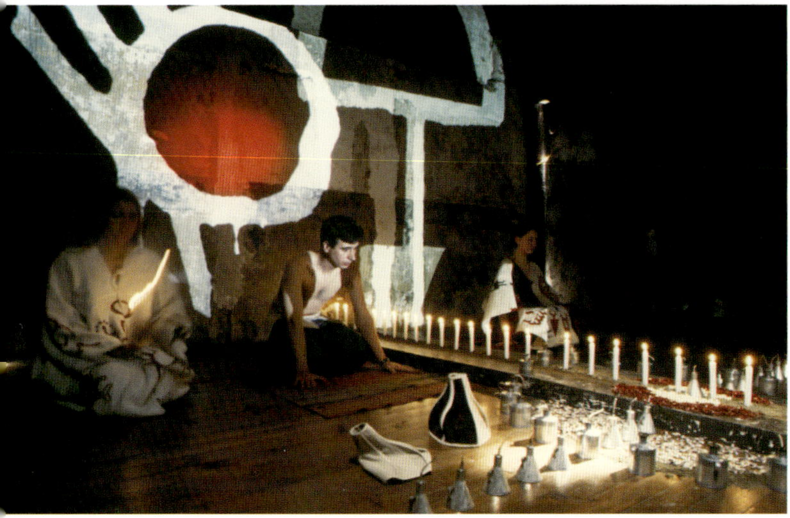

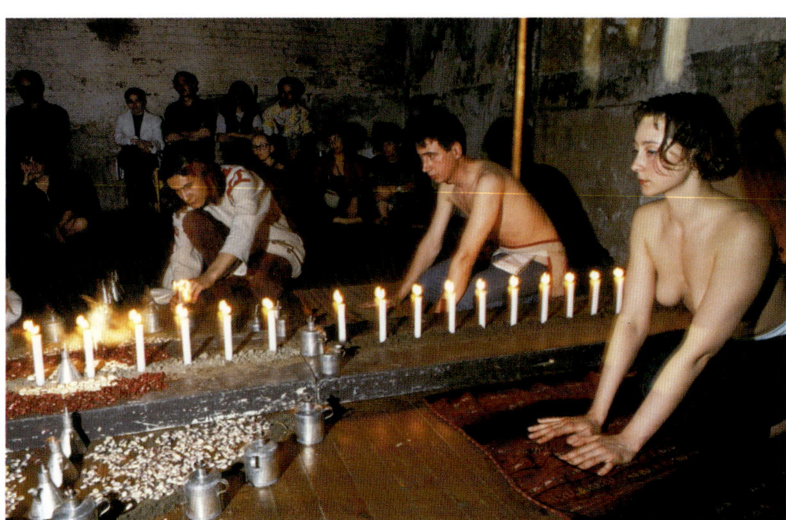

LEÇONS TÉNÈBRES

Basilique de Neuvy-Saint-Sépulchre, France

1991

Leçons Ténèbres is first Light Works to be created by Lucy+Jorge in France. Coinciding with Holy Week, this ephemeral work celebrates the work of baroque composer Giuseppe Domenico Scarletti. A vocal concert and light projections were staged inside the basilica now one of the UNESCO World Heritage sites of the pilgrimage routes of Santiago de Compostela in France.

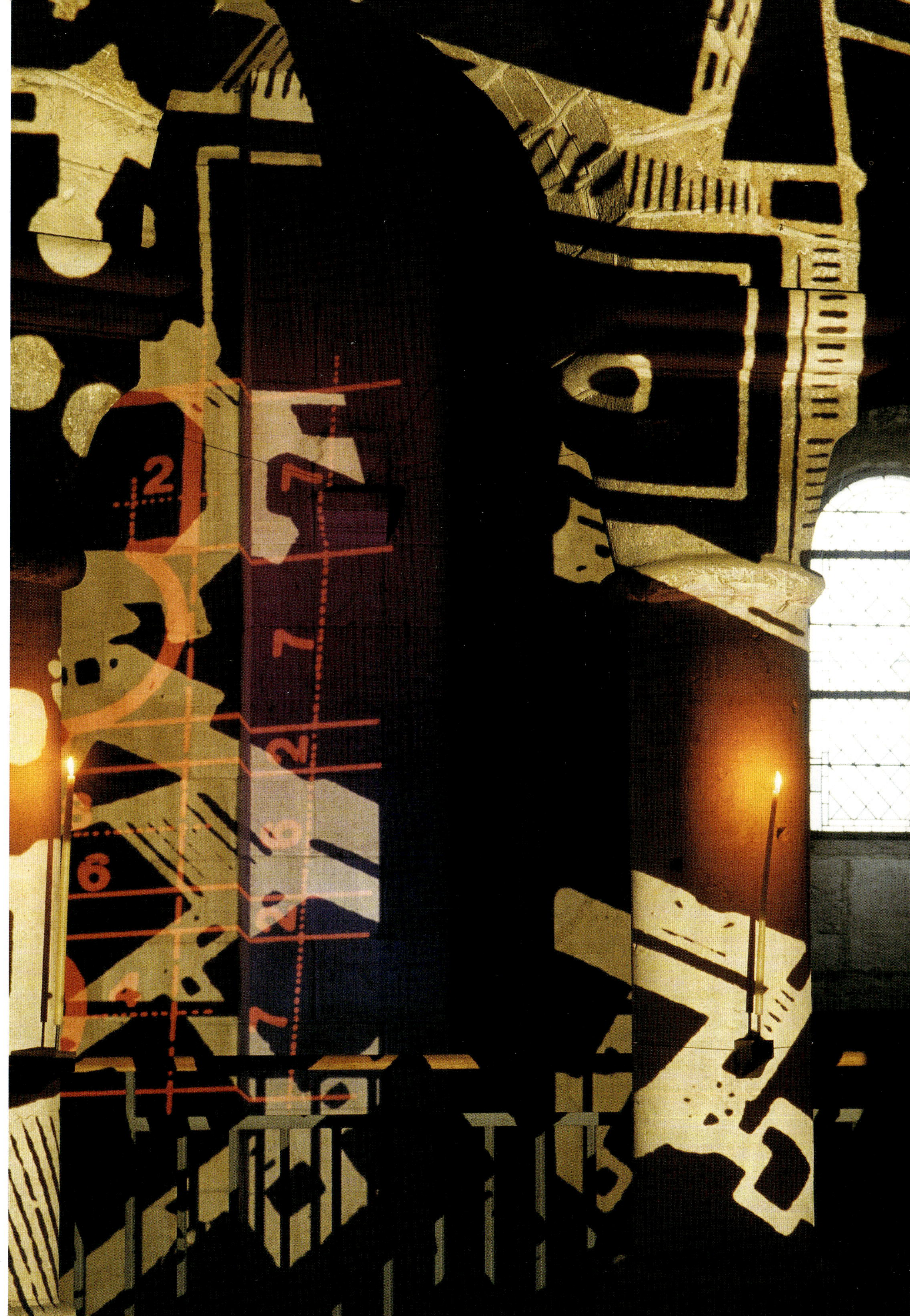

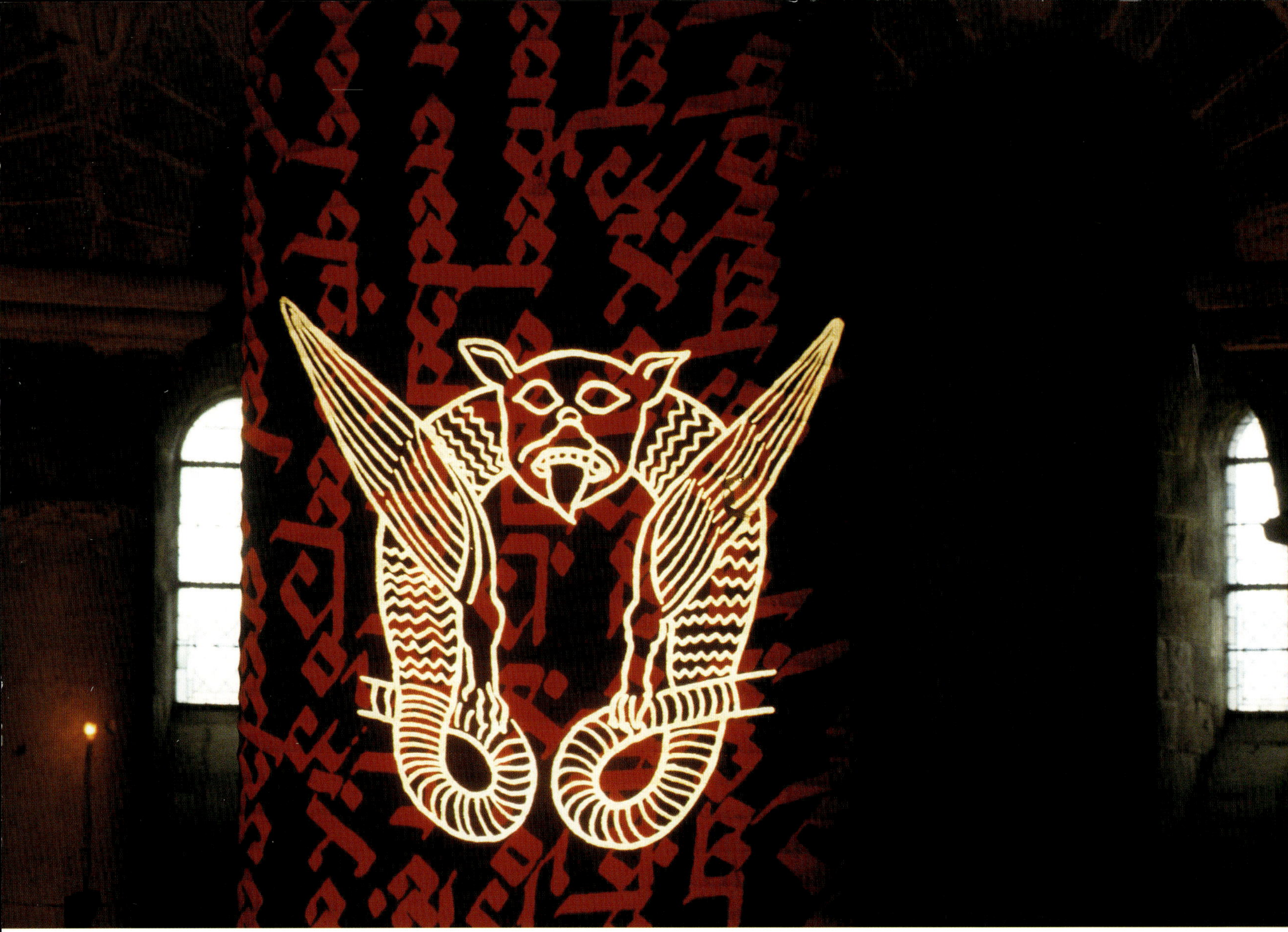

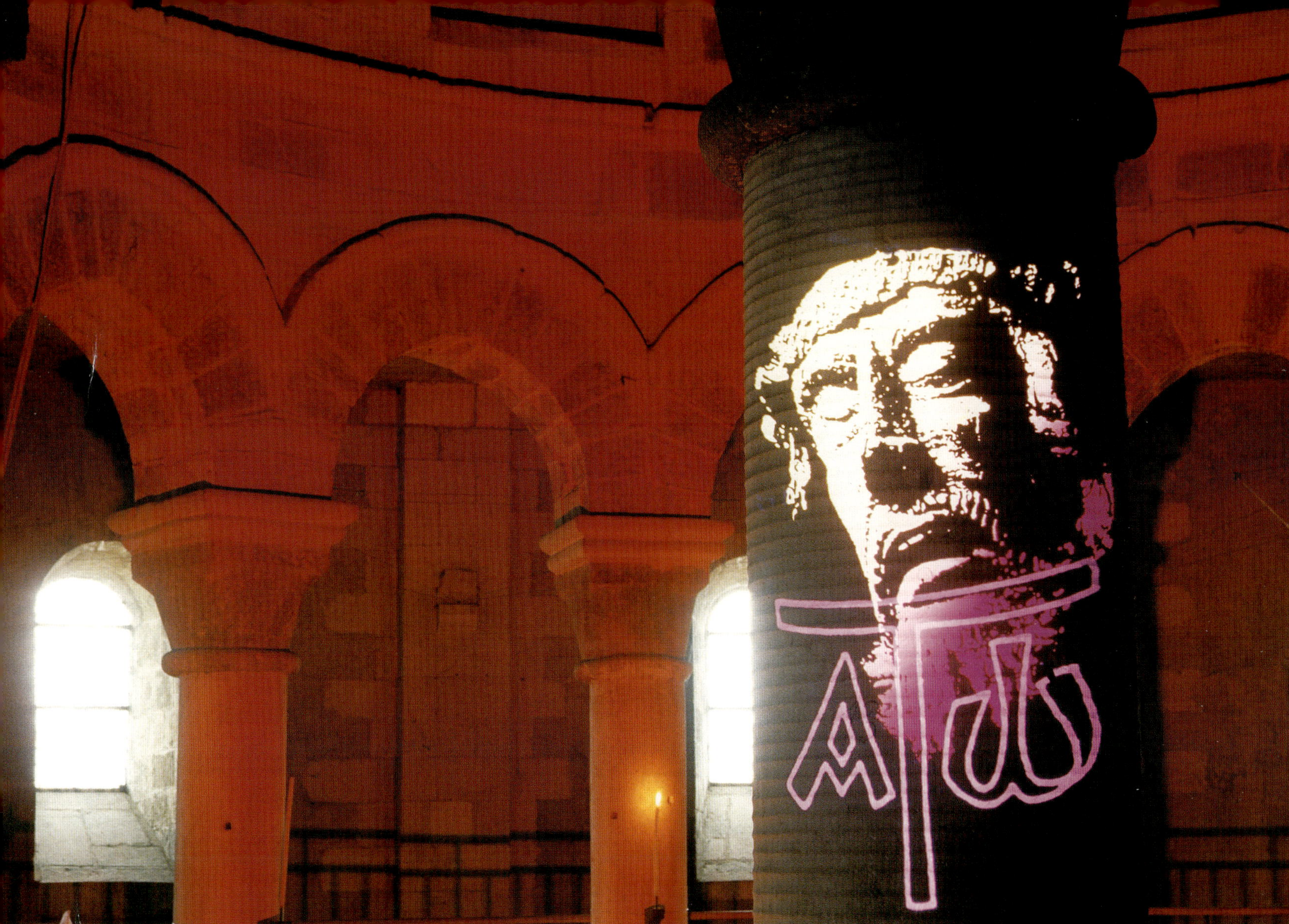

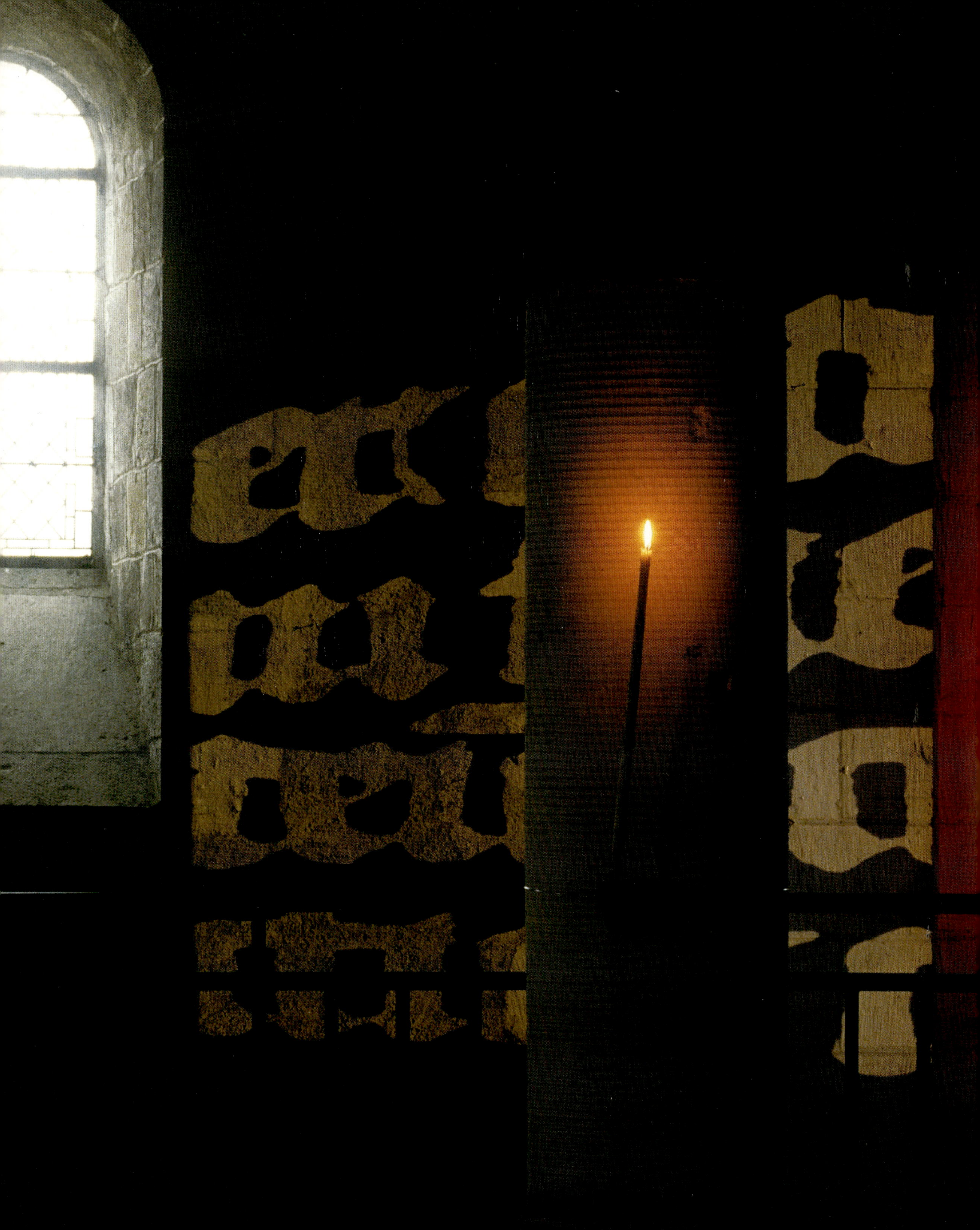

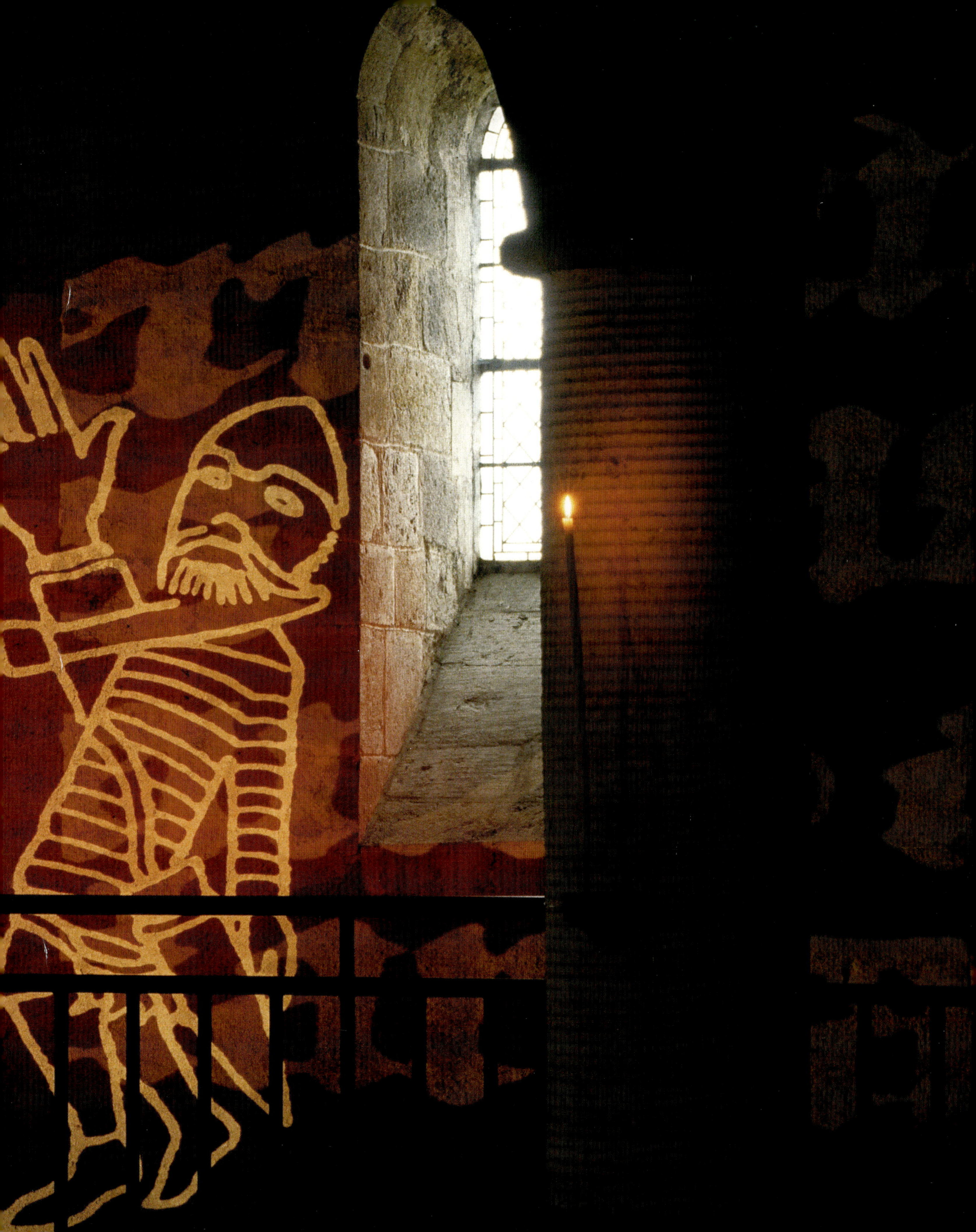

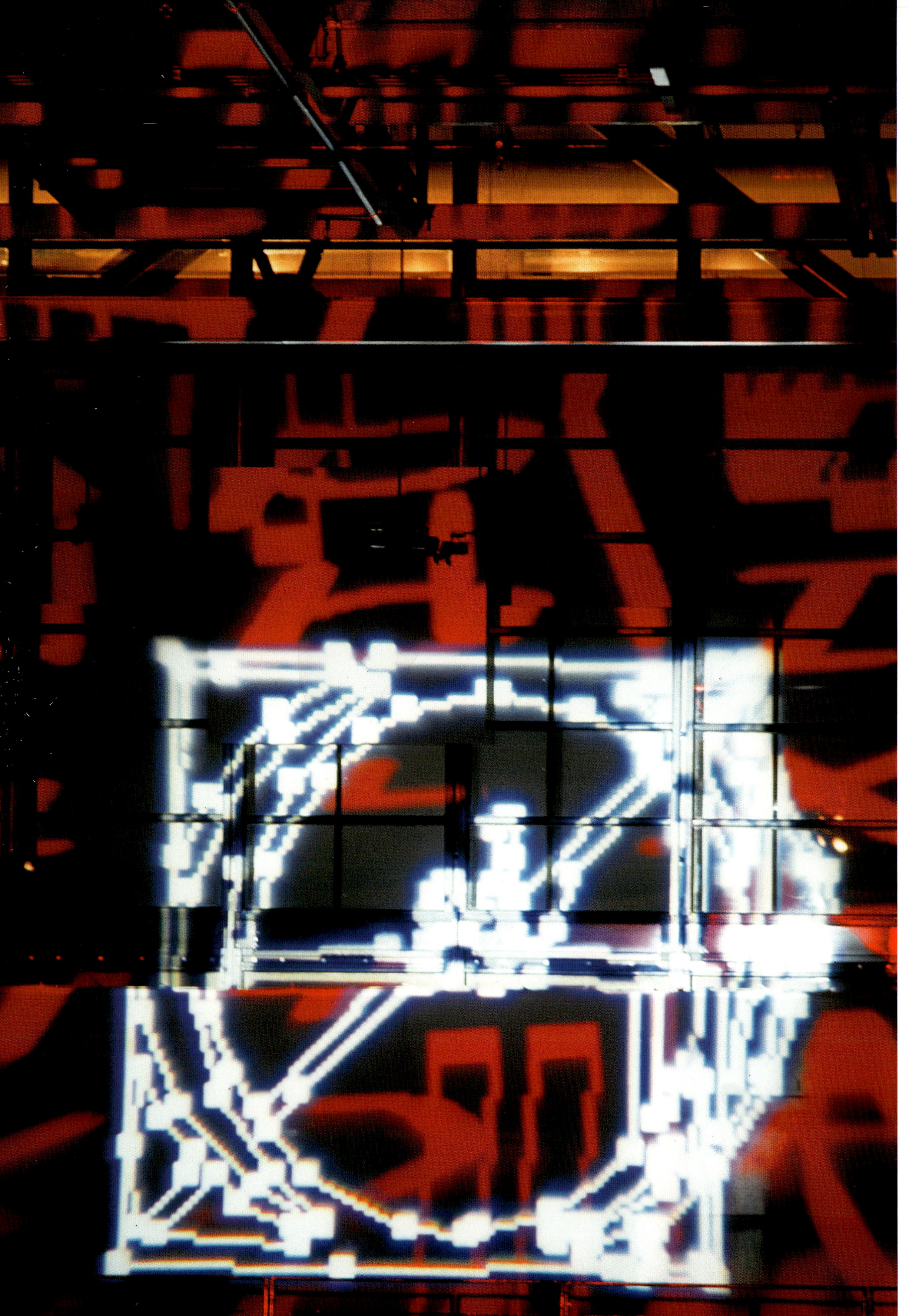

The digital poem projected inside the Pompidou Centre, is the first example of the artists use of digital imagery commissioned by the French digital arts festival, Art 3000. Working with the artists, French typographer Eric Paillet has digitalised a family of Jorge Orta's early signs and the resulting computerised language intermingles with the skeletal frame of Richard Rogers and Renzo Piano's spatial architecture.

POÈME INFOGRAPHIQUE

Centre Georges Pompidou, Paris, France

1991

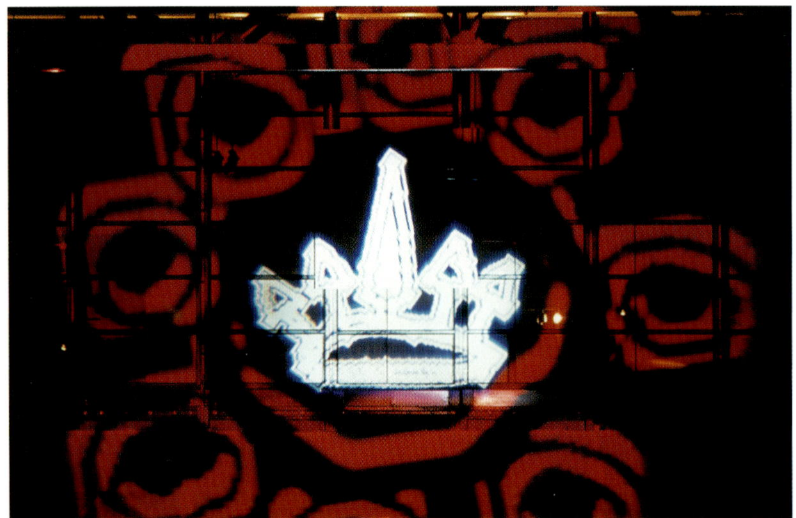

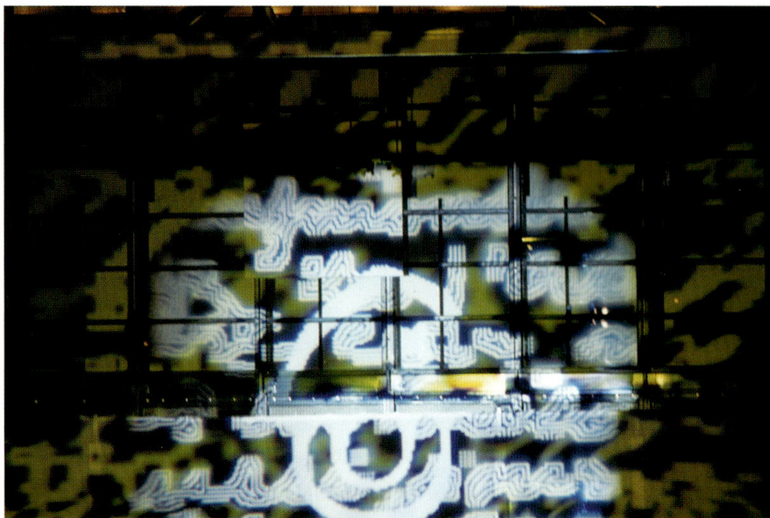

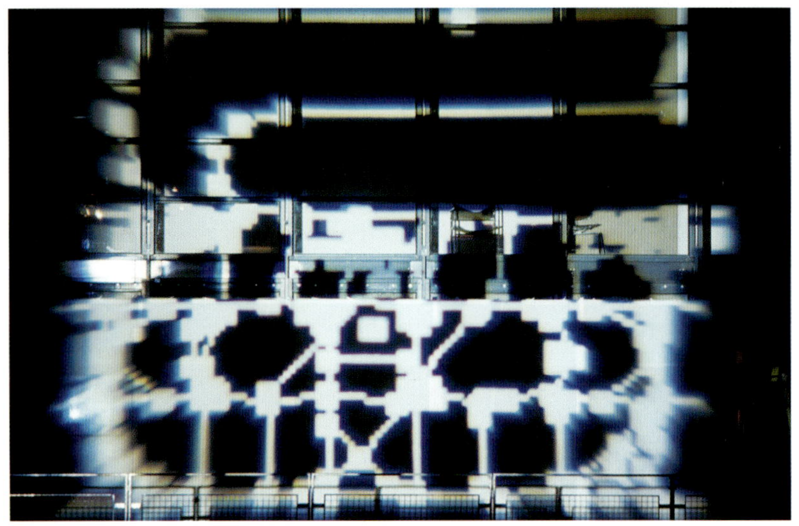

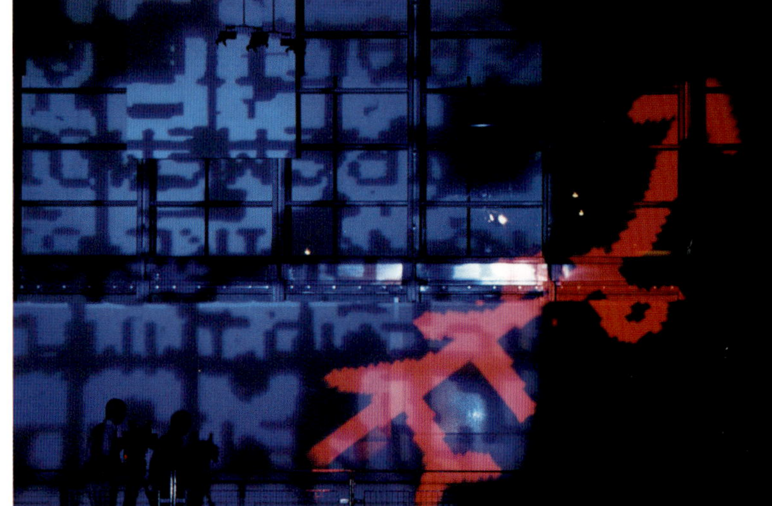

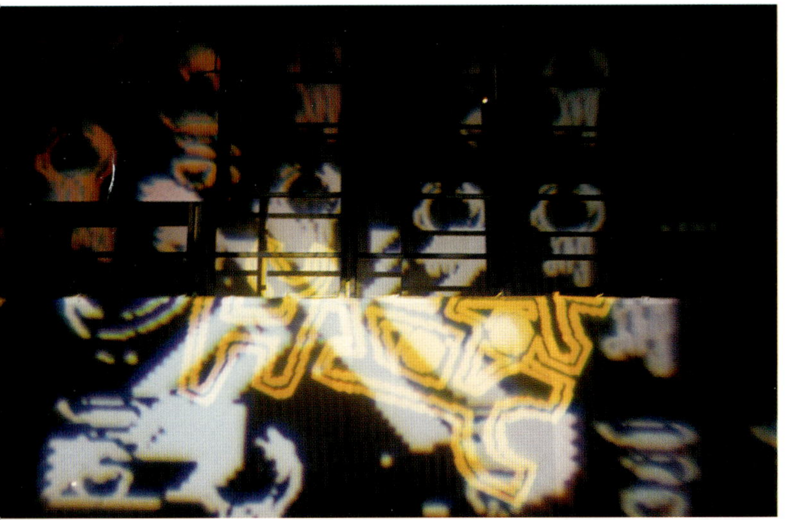
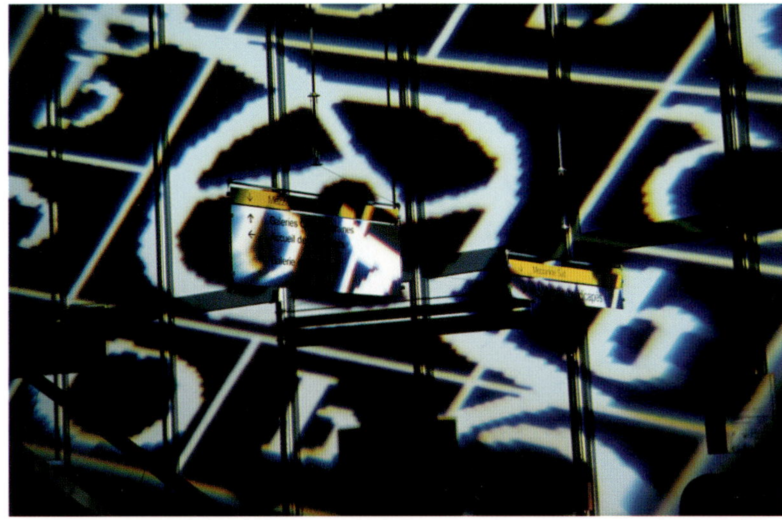
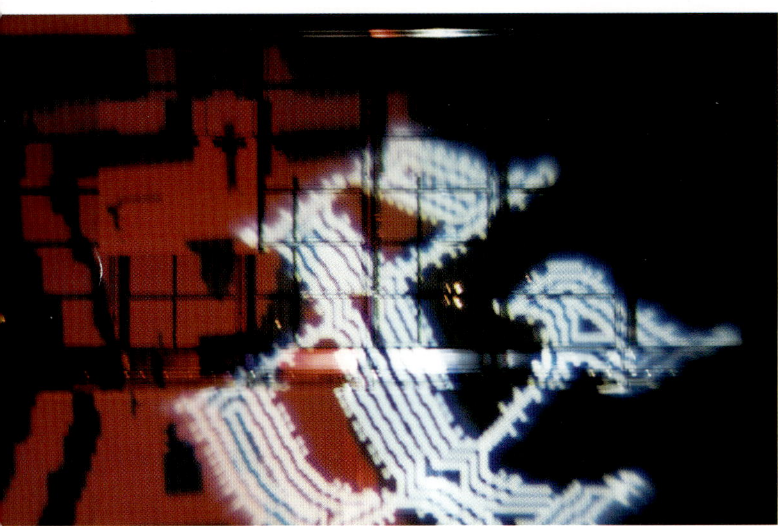
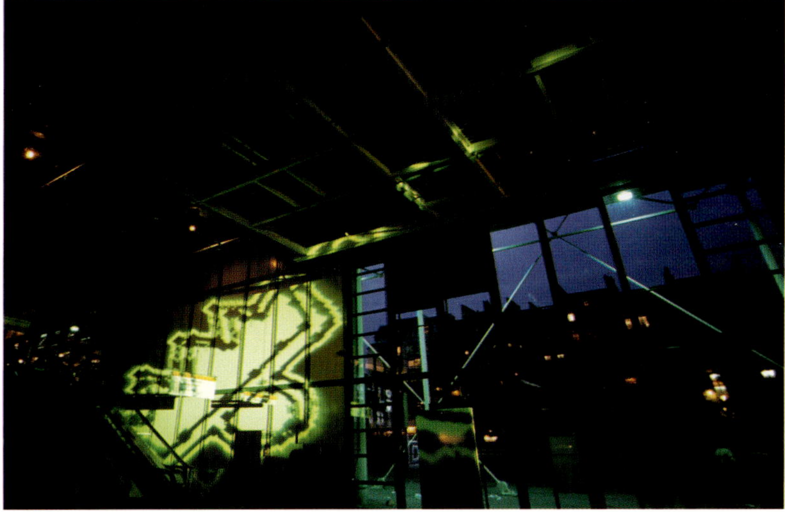

It is my belief that exciting things happen when a variety of overlapping activities designed for all people—the old and the young, the blue and white collar, the local inhabitant and the visitor, different activities for different occasions—meet in a flexible environment, opening up the possibility of interaction outside the confines of institutional limits. When this takes place, deprived areas welcome dynamic places for those who live, work and visit; places where all can participate, rather than less or more beautiful ghettos. RICHARD ROGERS

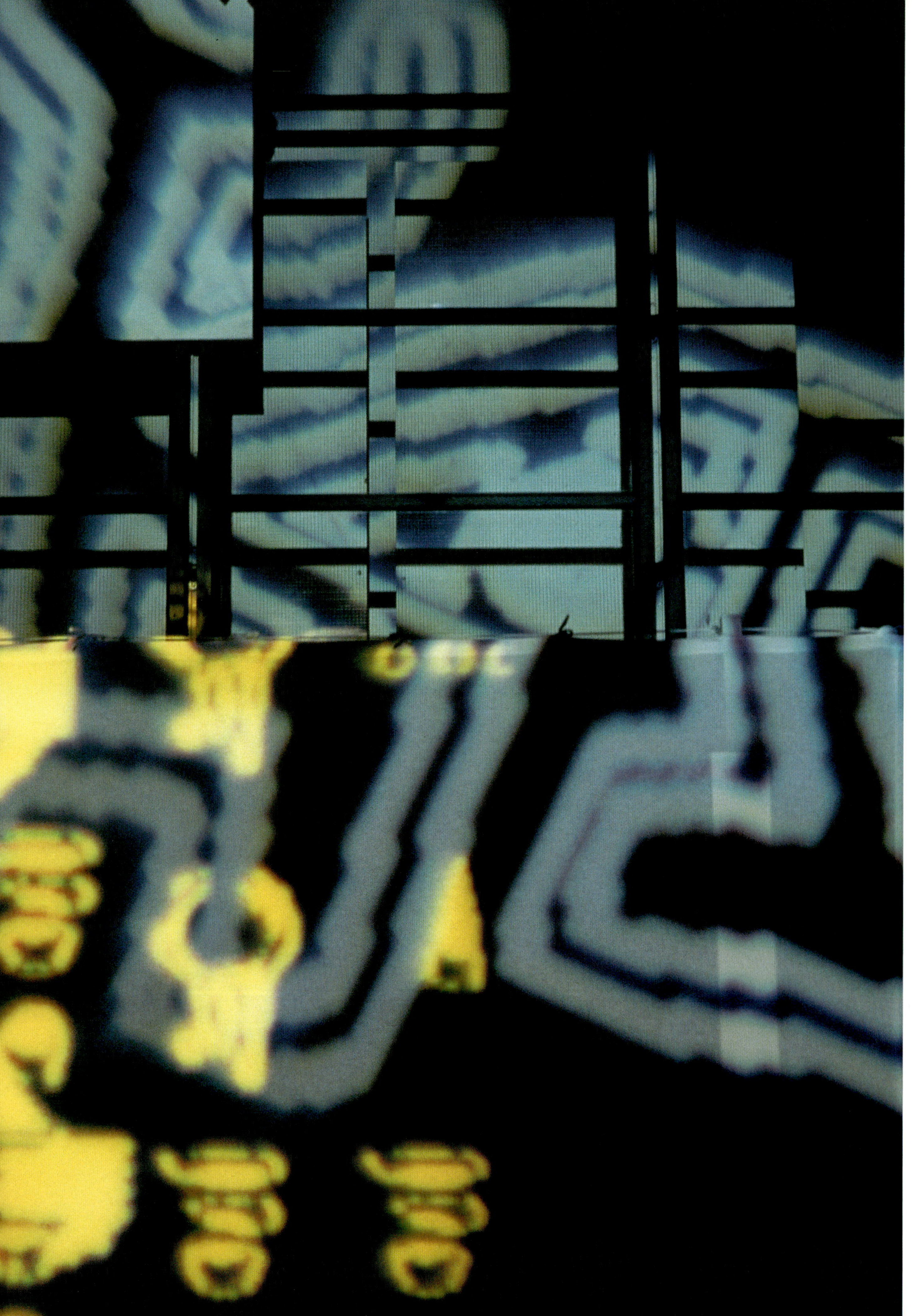

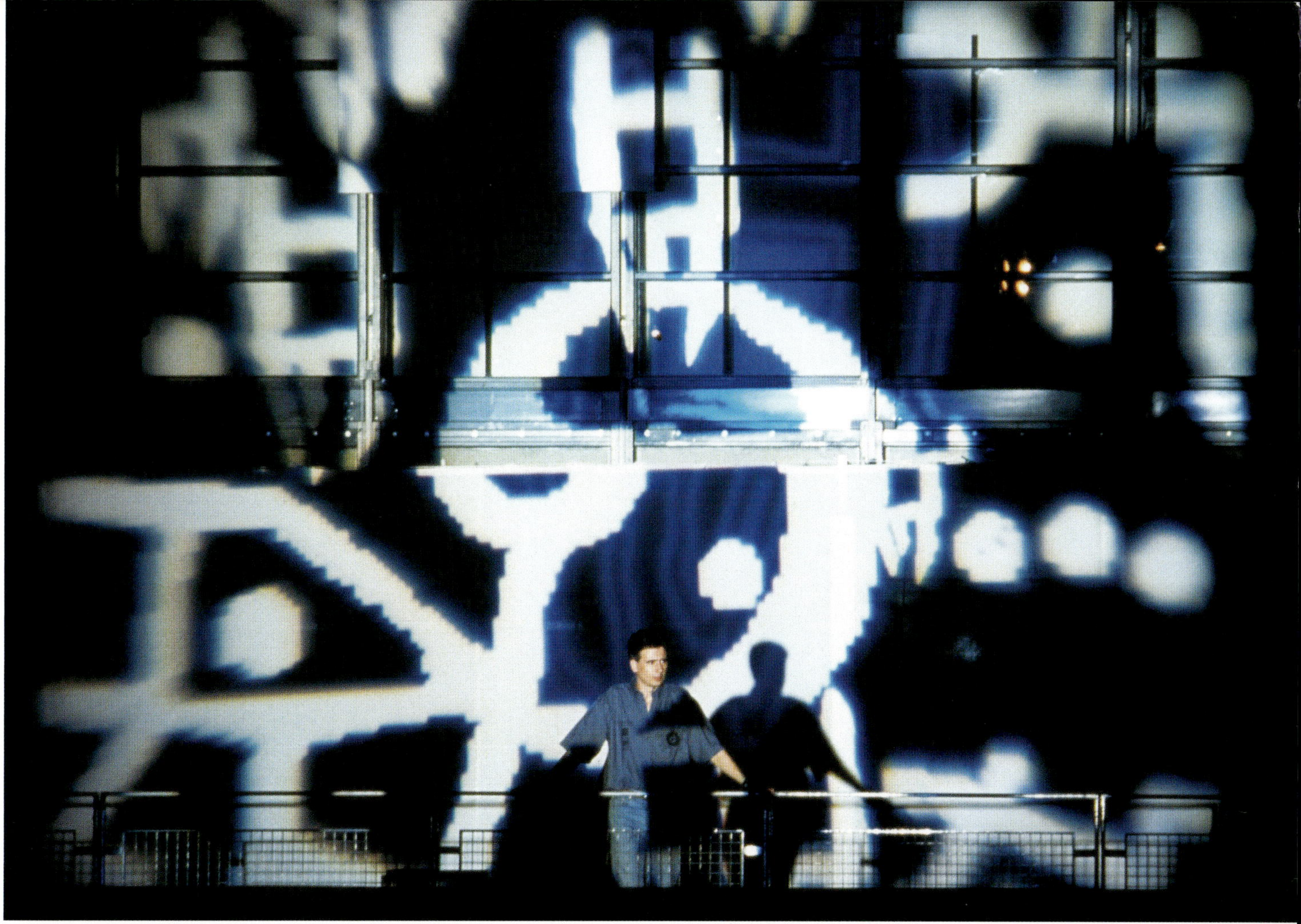

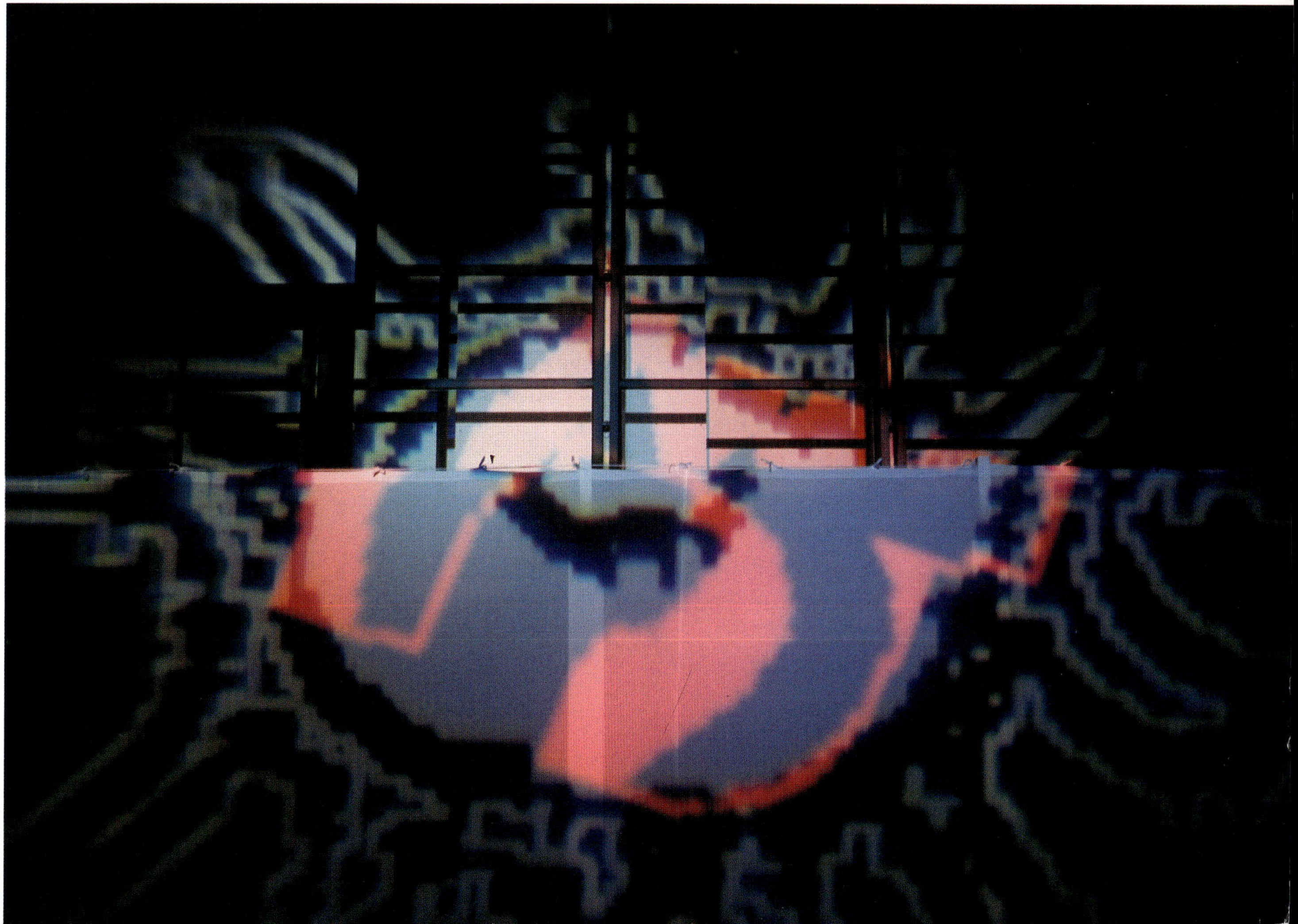

1992

POÈME INFOGRAPHIQUE II

Art 3000, Jouy-en-Josas, France

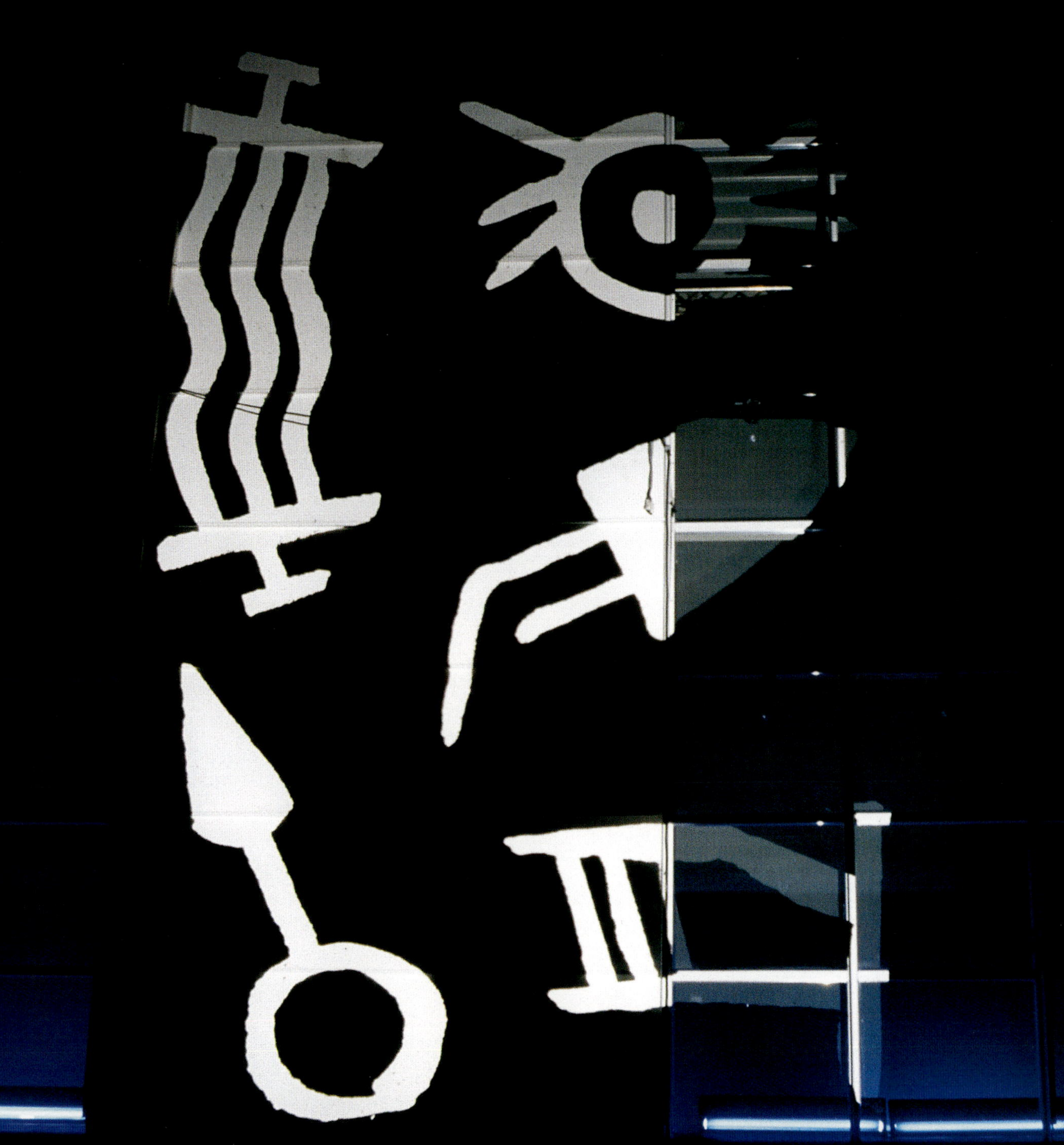

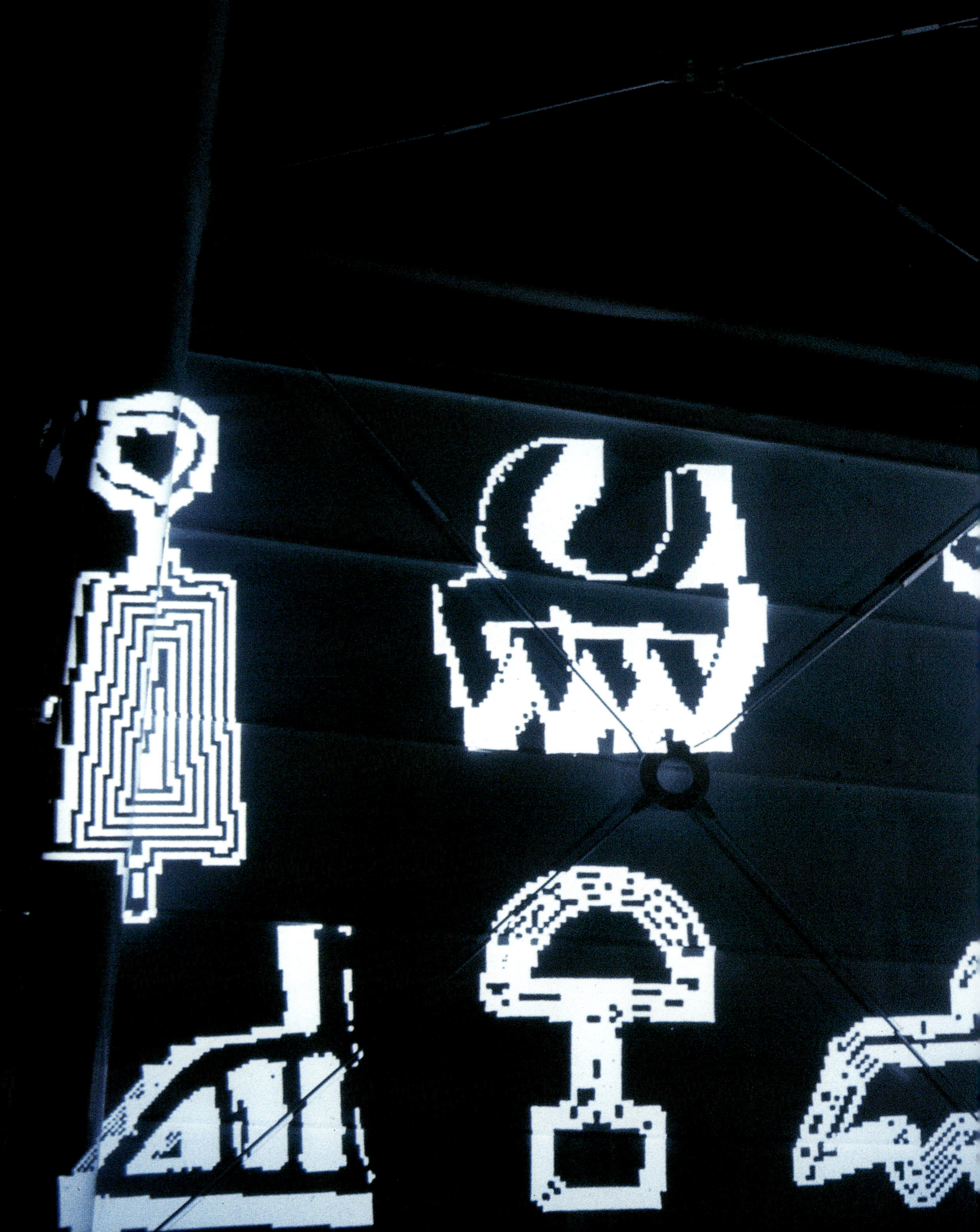

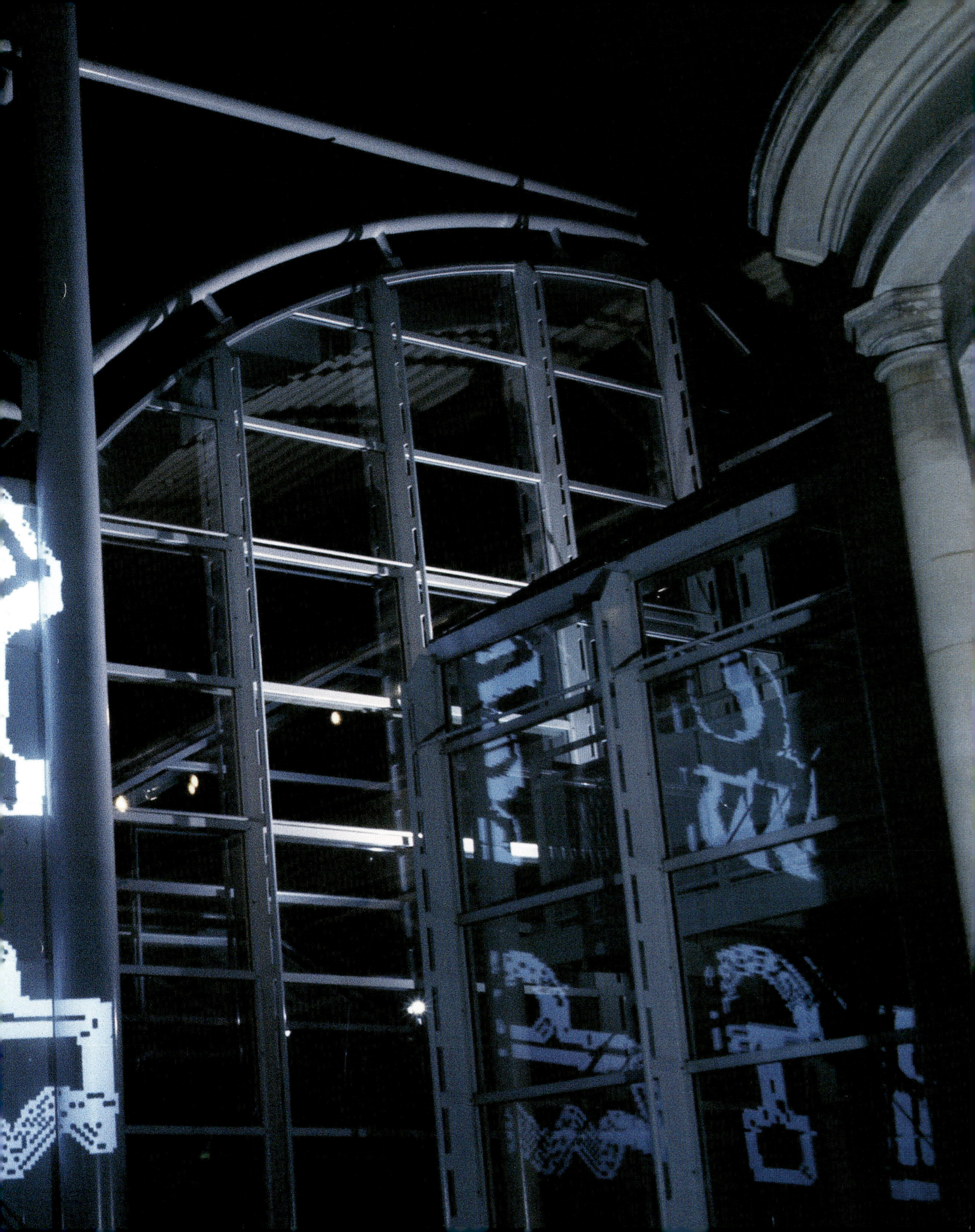

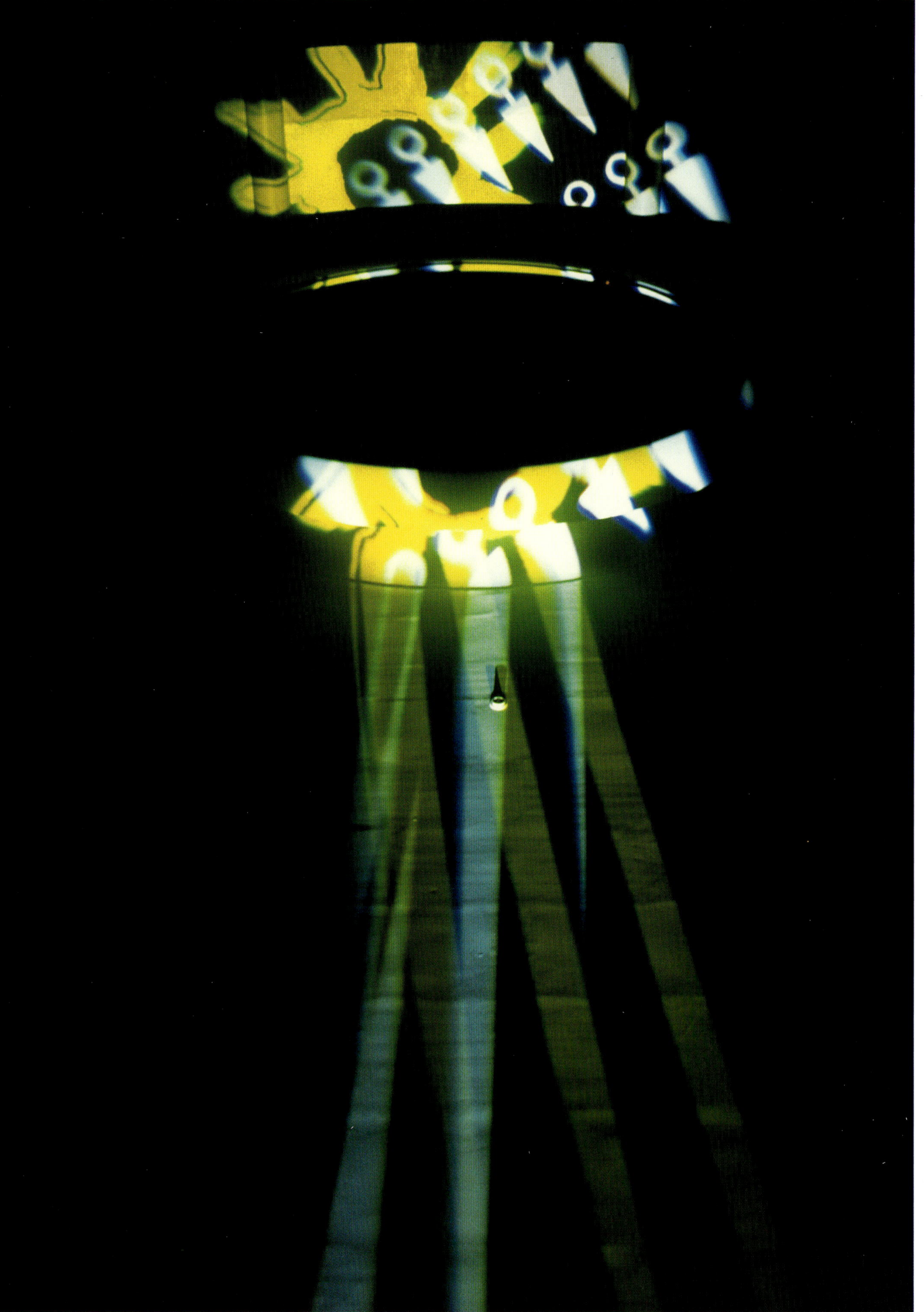

POÈME INFOGRAPHIQUE III

Palais de Tokyo, Paris, France

1992

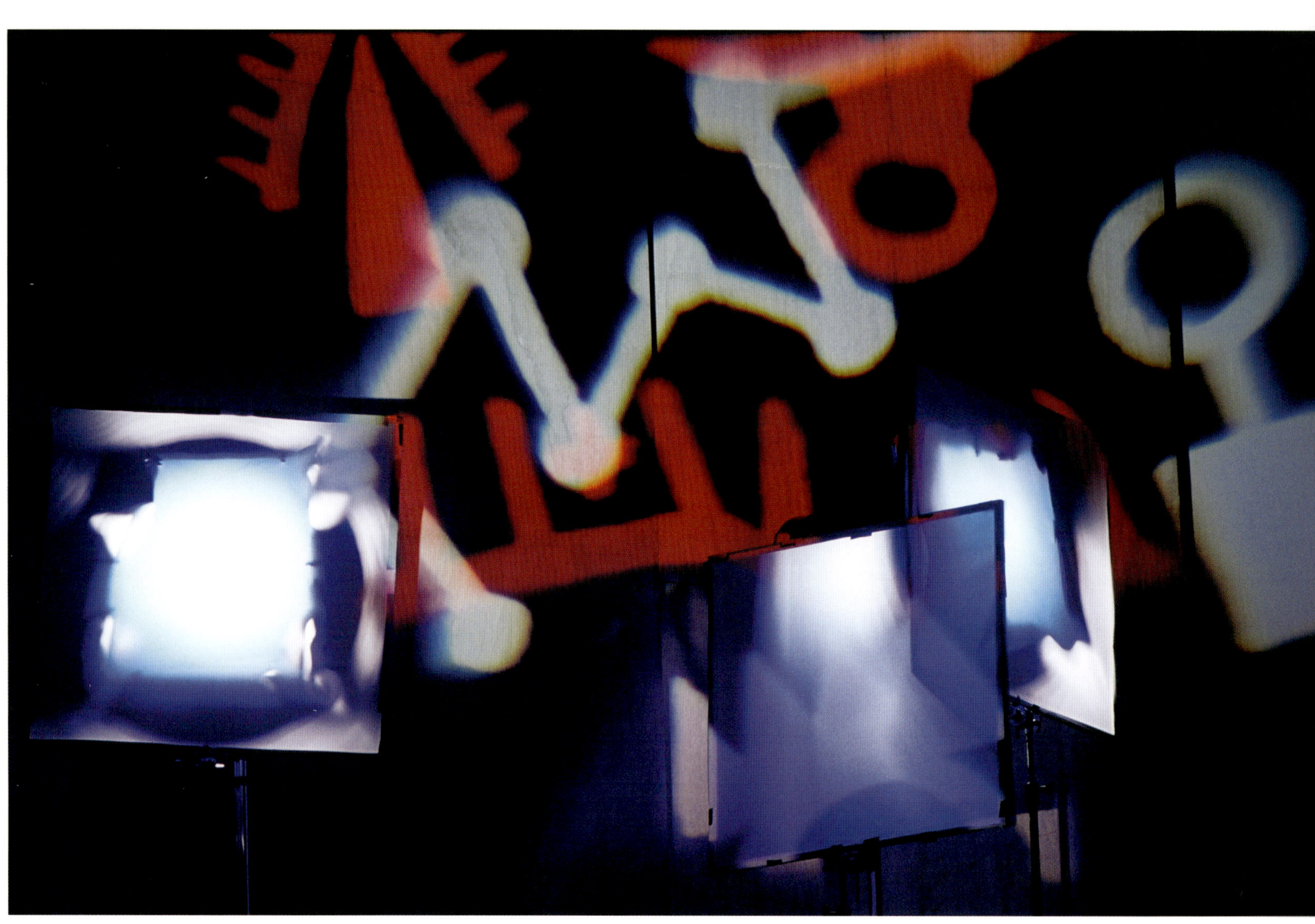

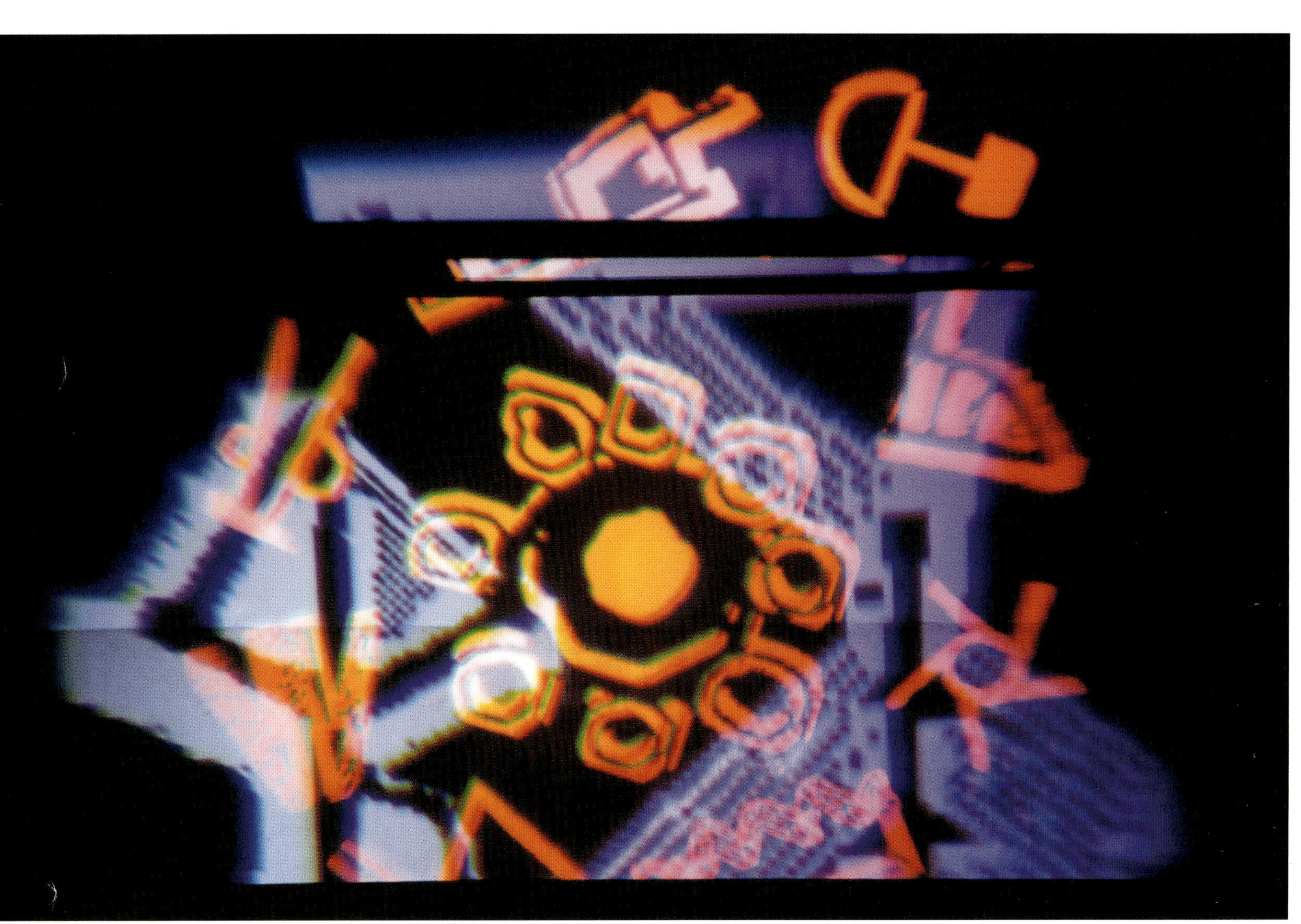

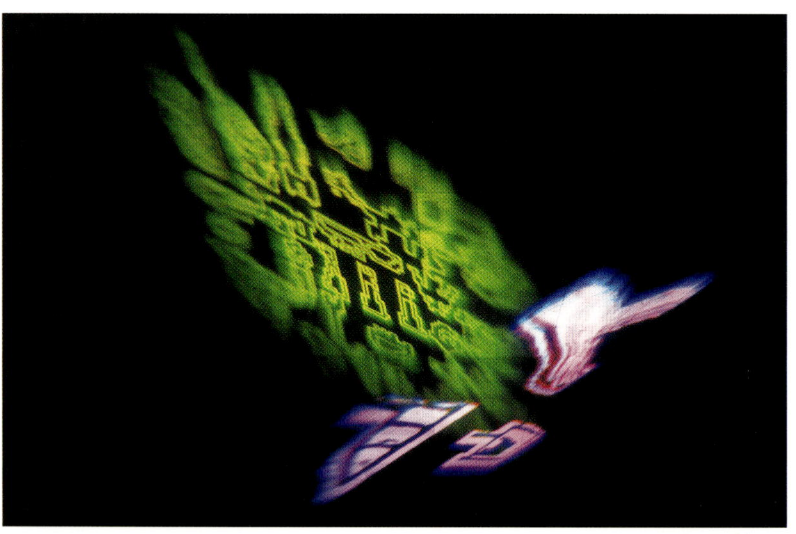

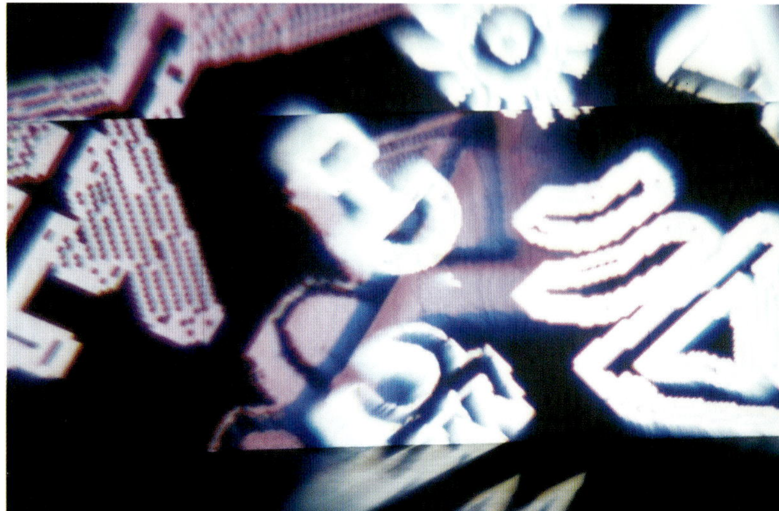

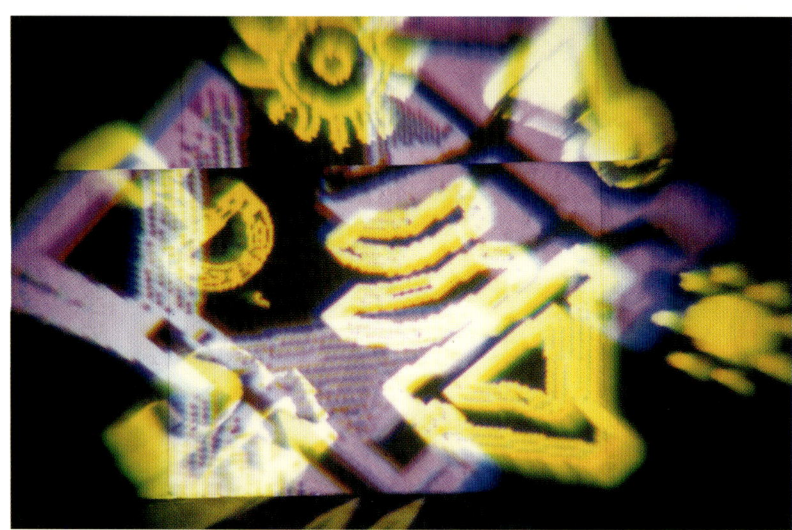

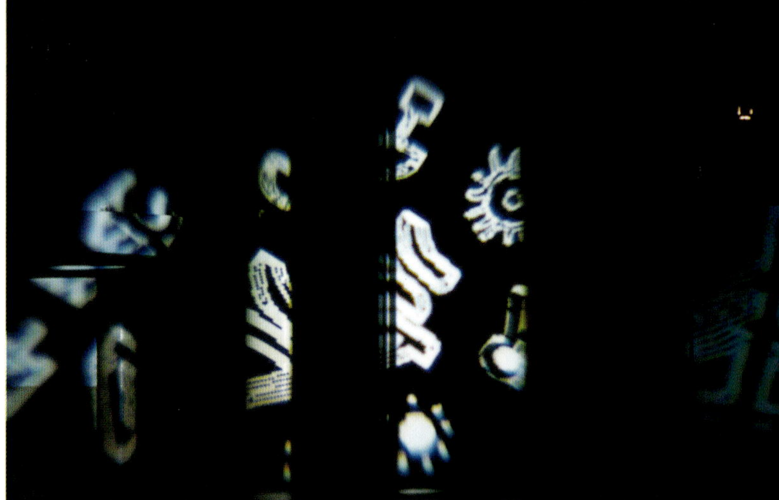

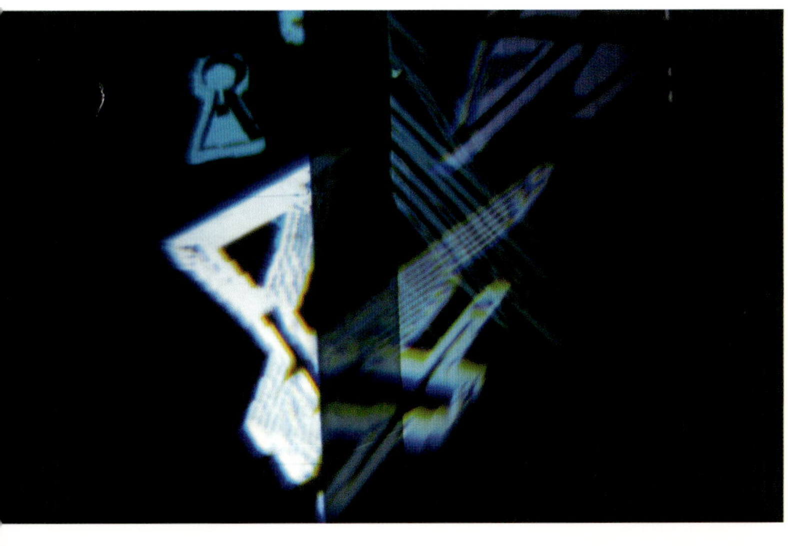
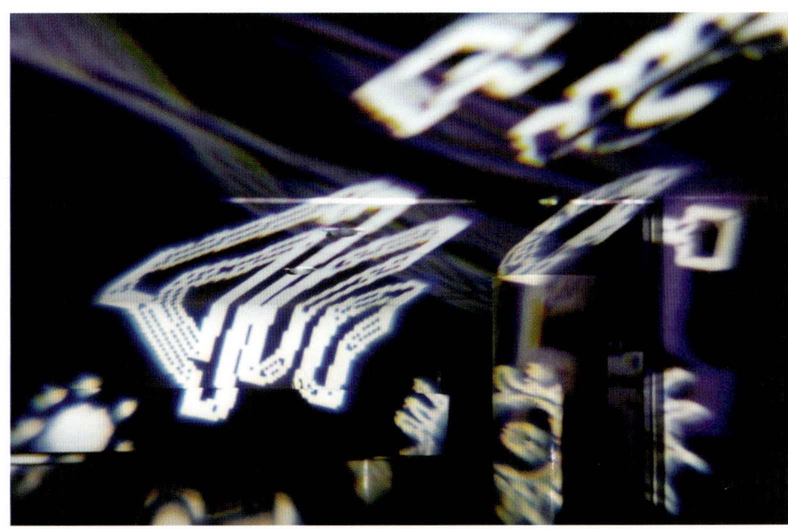
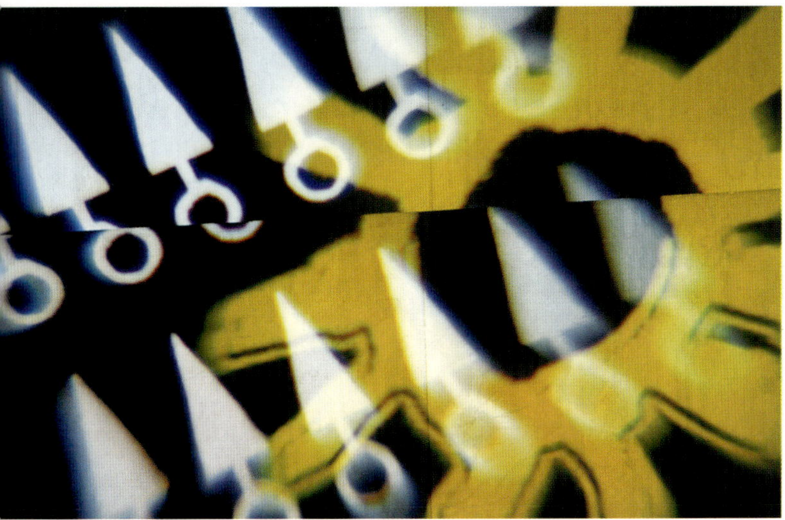
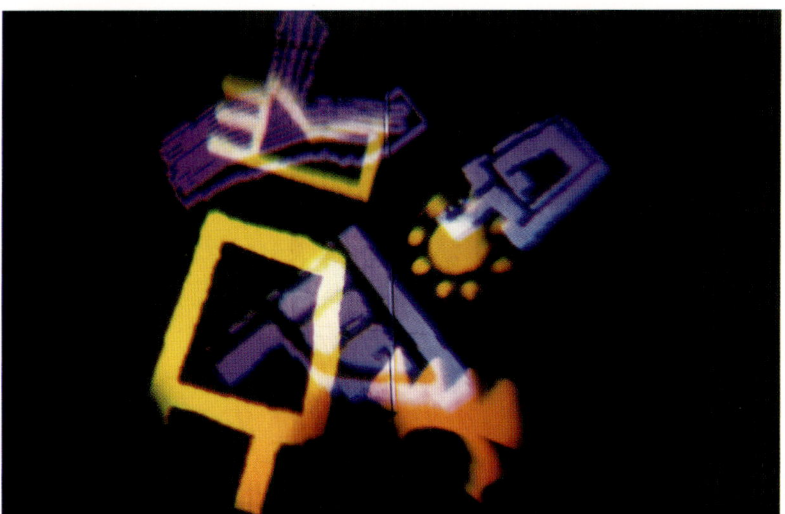

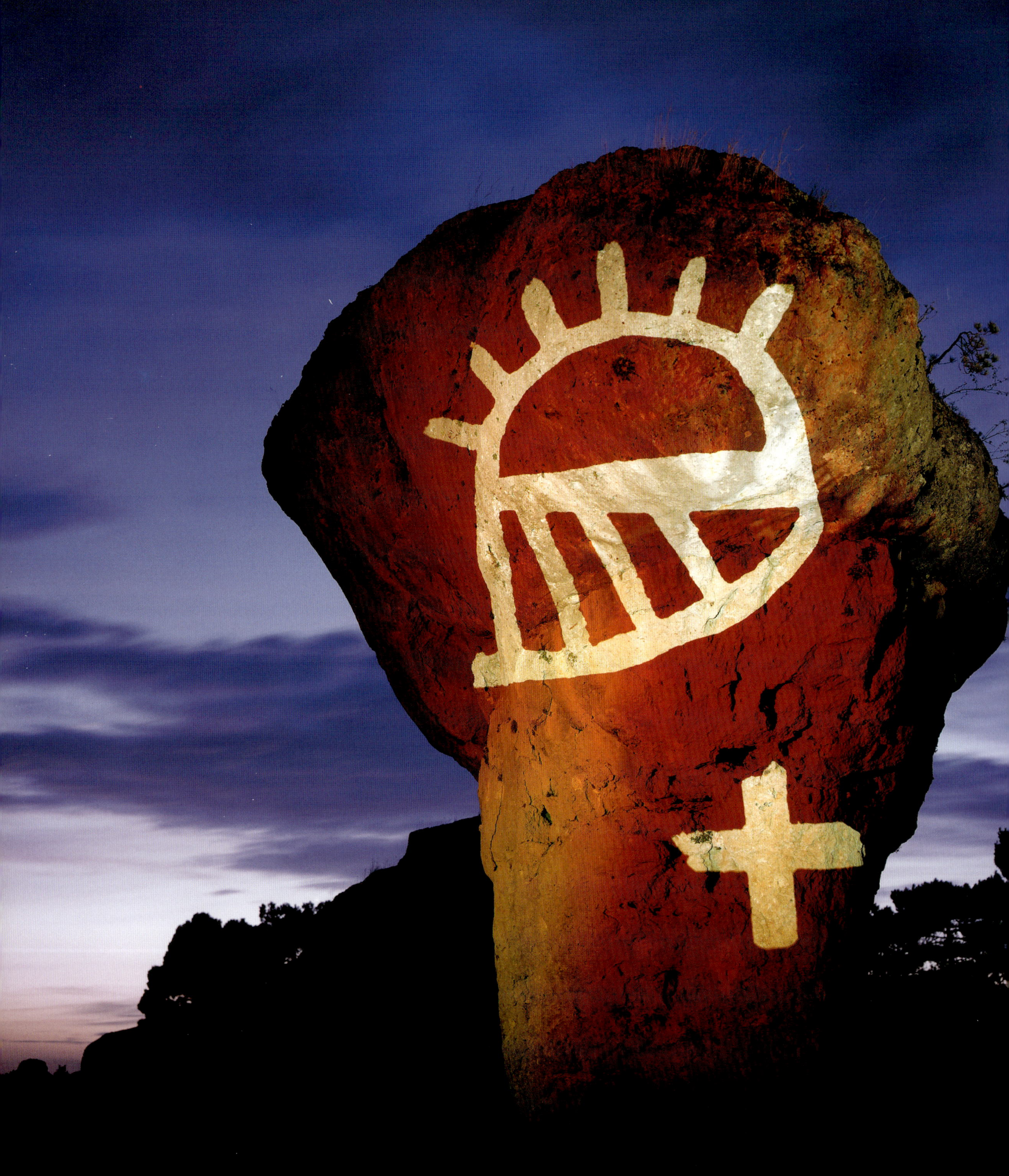

1993

LIGHT OF STONE

Castille-La Manche, Cuenca, Spain

Commissioned by the Banesto Cultural Foundation, *Light of Stone* is made up of a two-part expedition with the PAE light projectors in the region of Castille-La Manche in Spain. The first experimentation took place in Cuenca, the capital of the province and a UNESCO World Heritage site. Cuenca, the 'eagles nest', is located across a steep spur, whose slopes descend into deep gorges of the Júcar and Huécar rivers. The fifteenth century hanging houses built over a rock above the Huecar River Gorge formed an impressive backdrop for a series of 22, 20,000 metre square light murals. The visual iconography is derived from hand drawings conducted in the anthropological museum in the city. The PAE 2500 light projectors positioned across the canyon can project images up to 5,000 square metres and over a distance up to 1,000 metres.

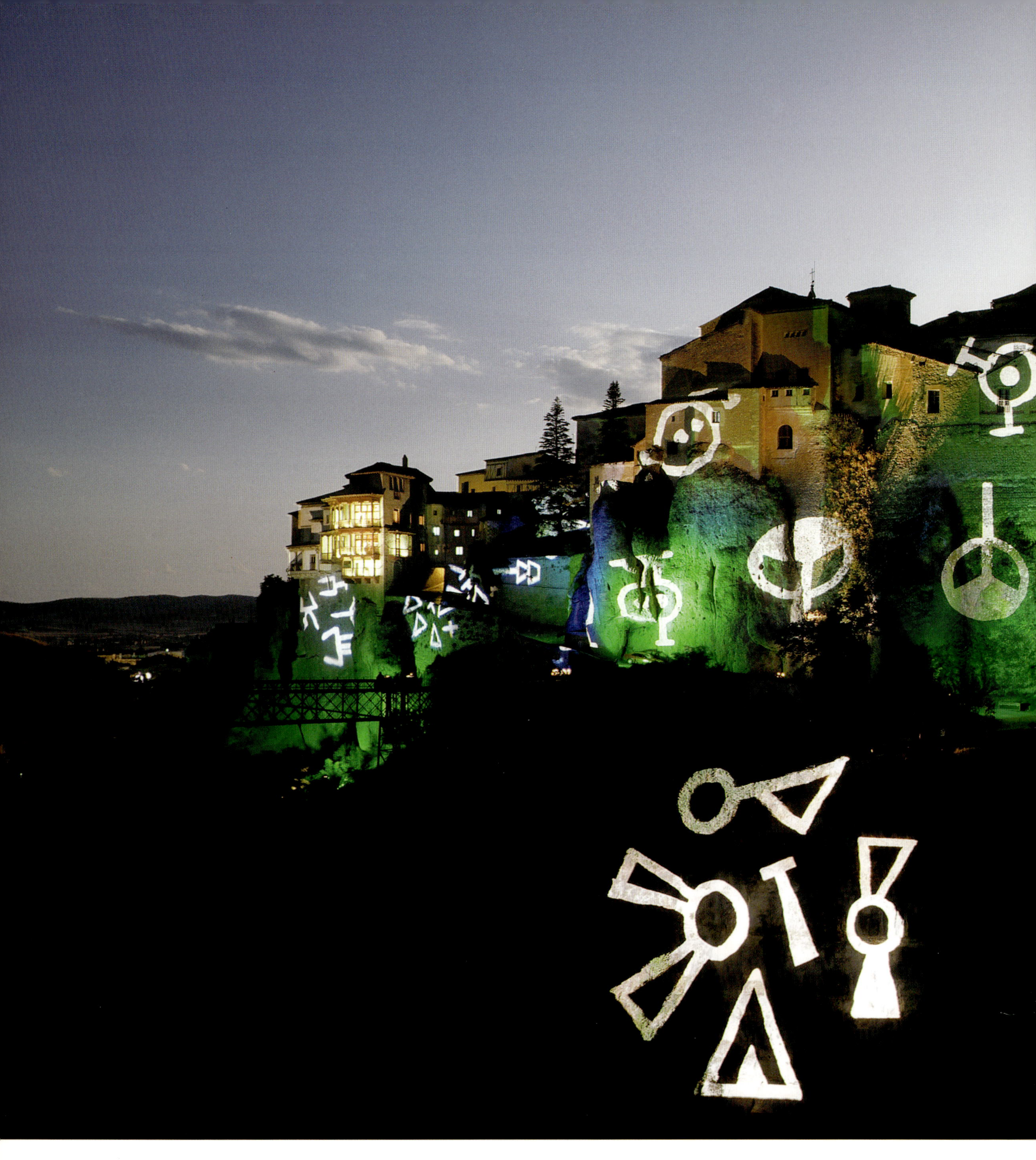

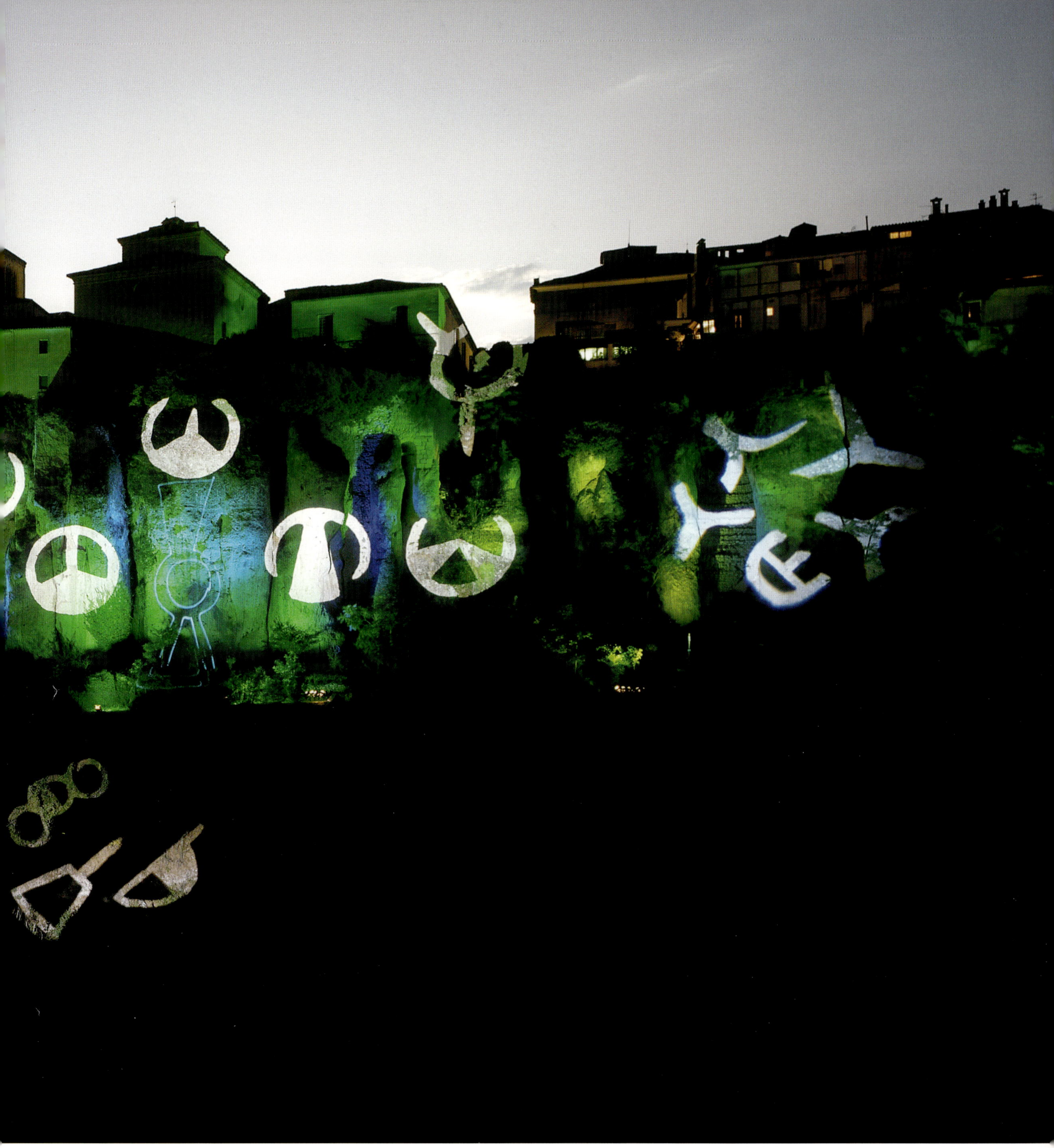

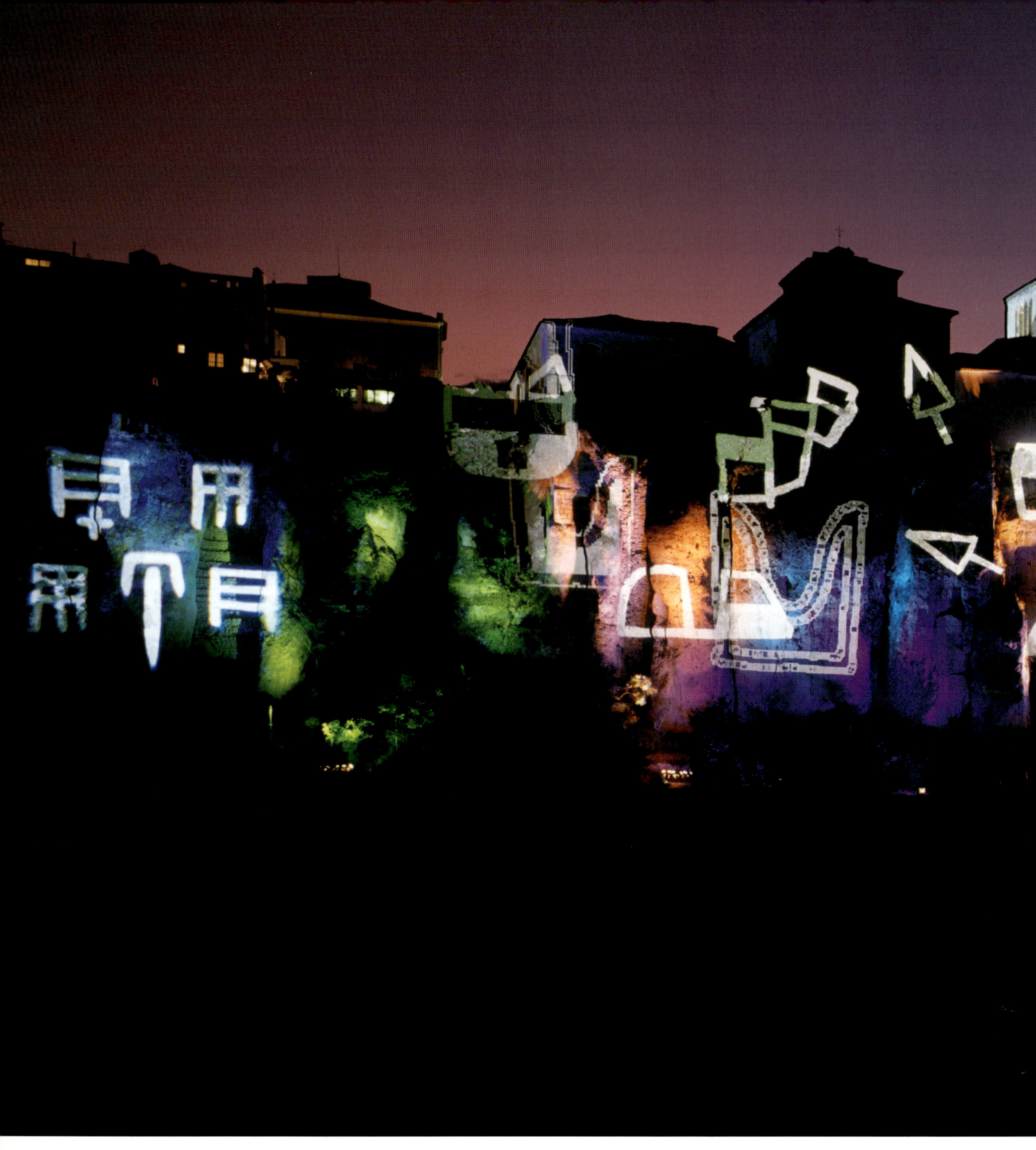

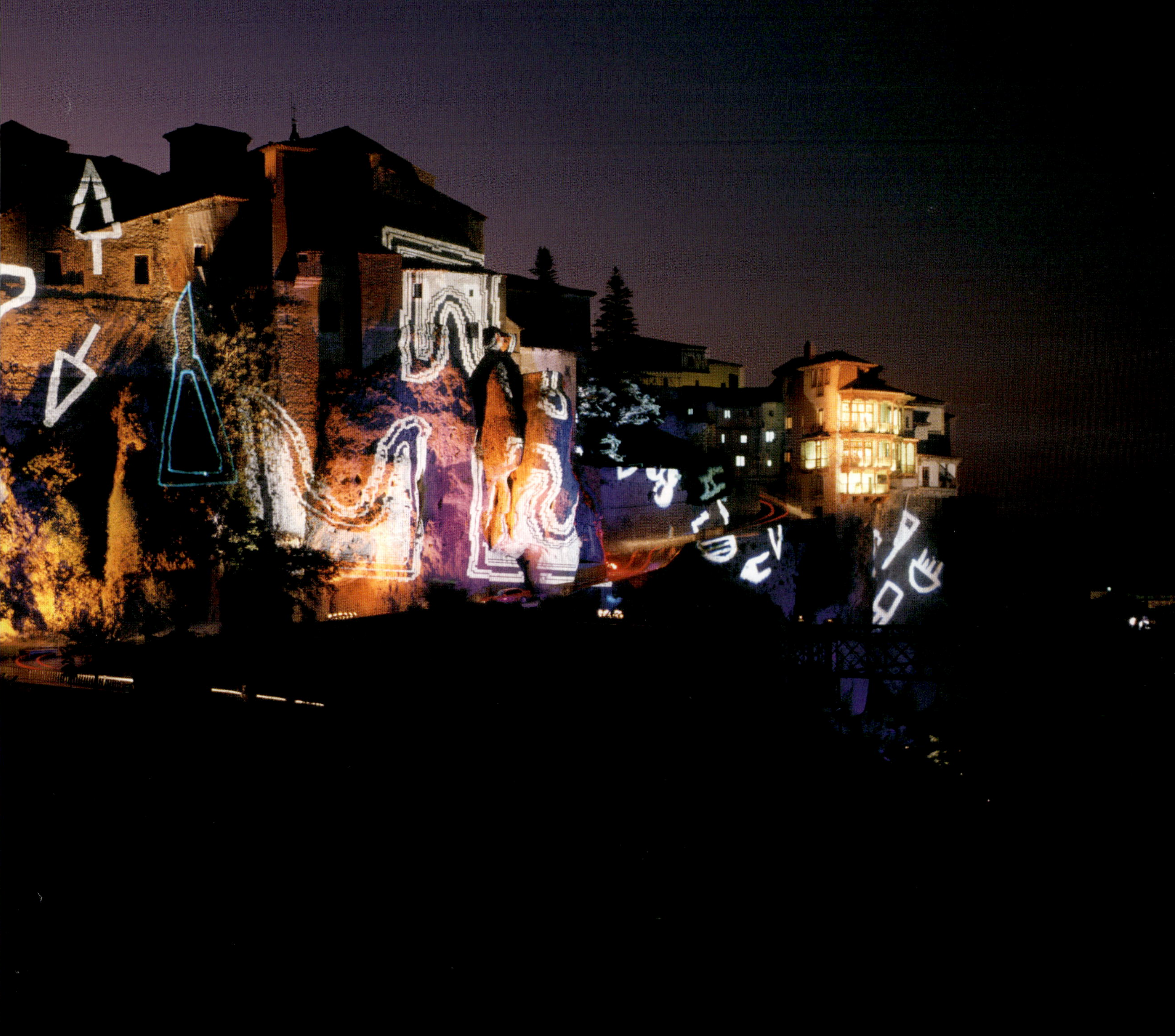

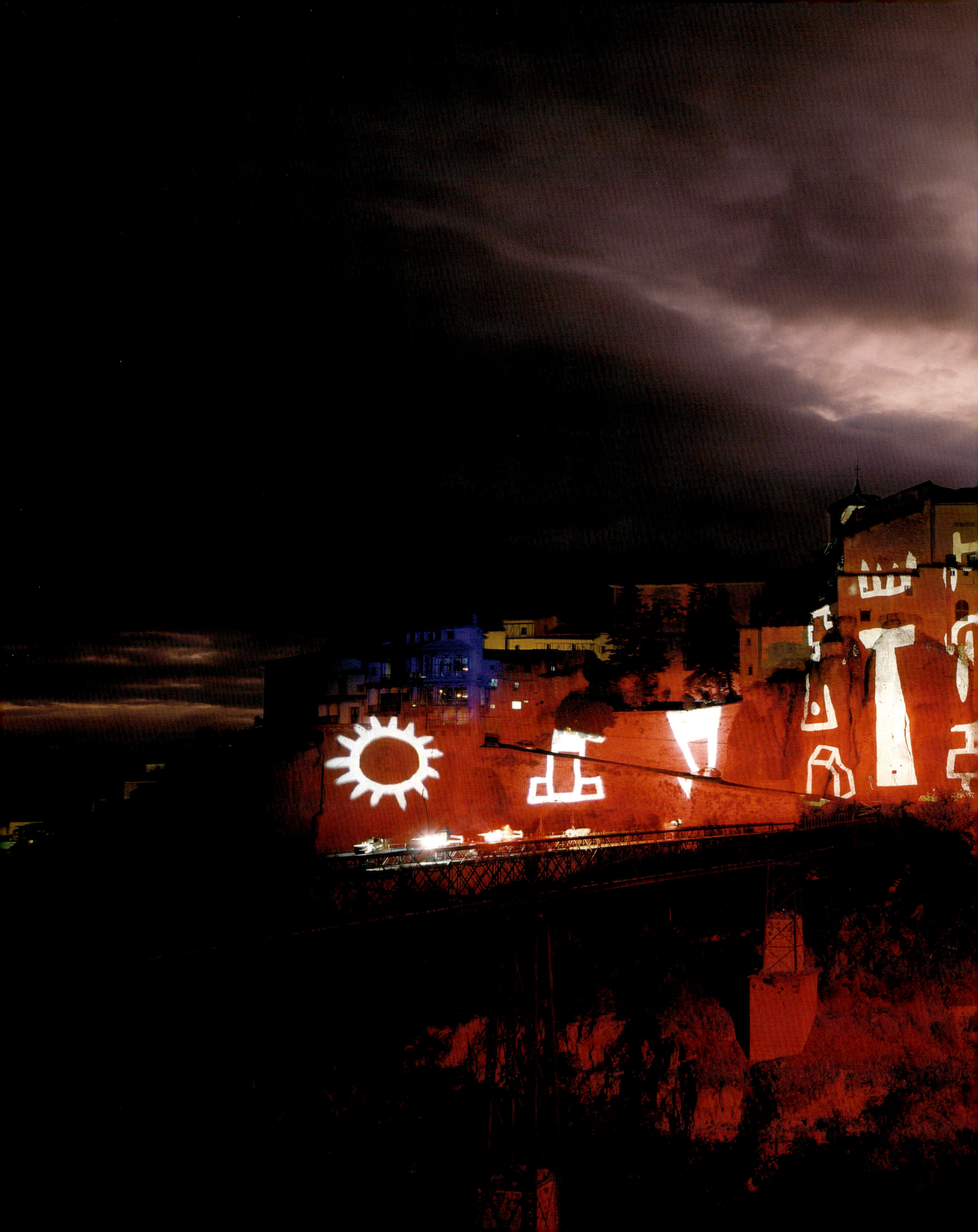

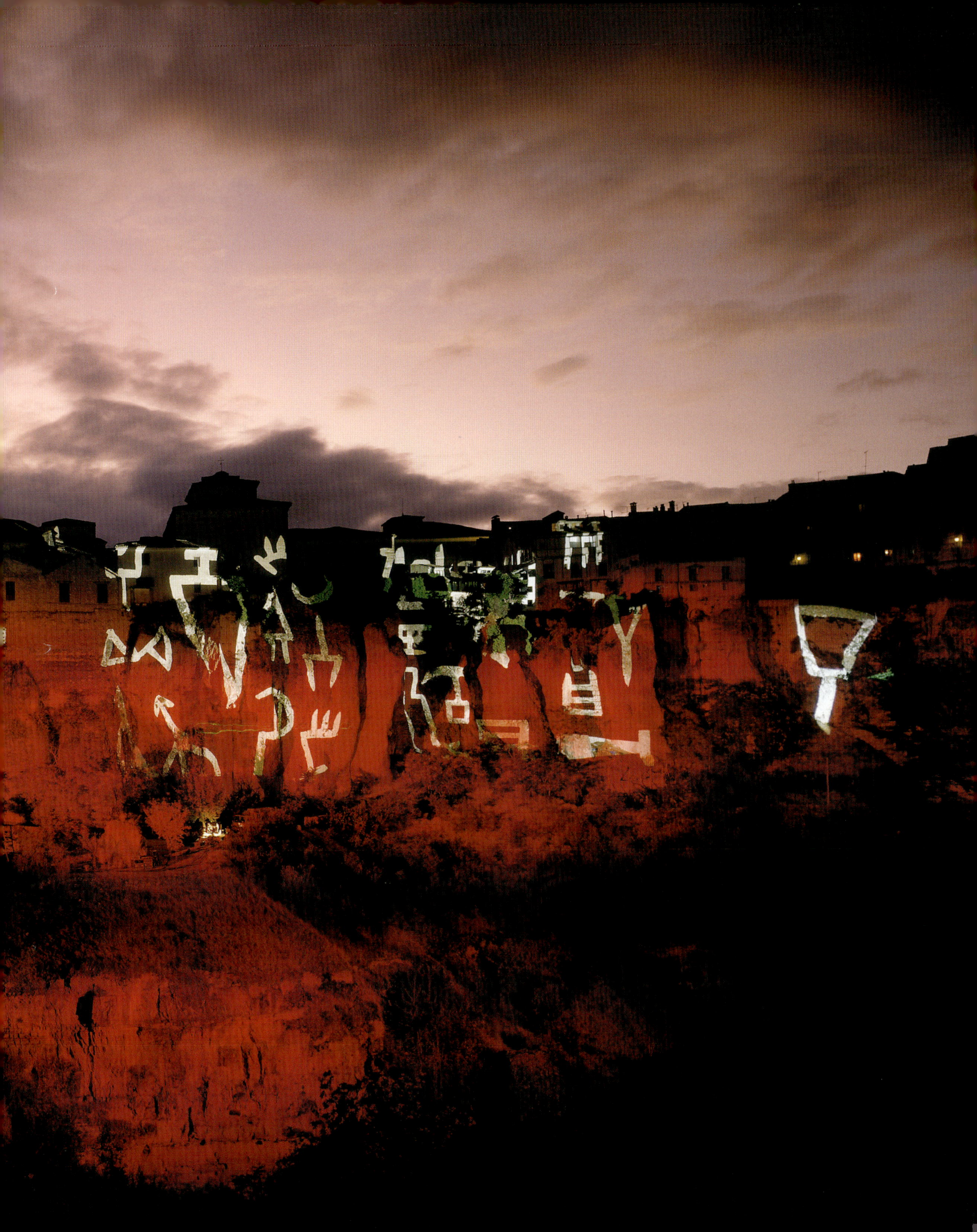

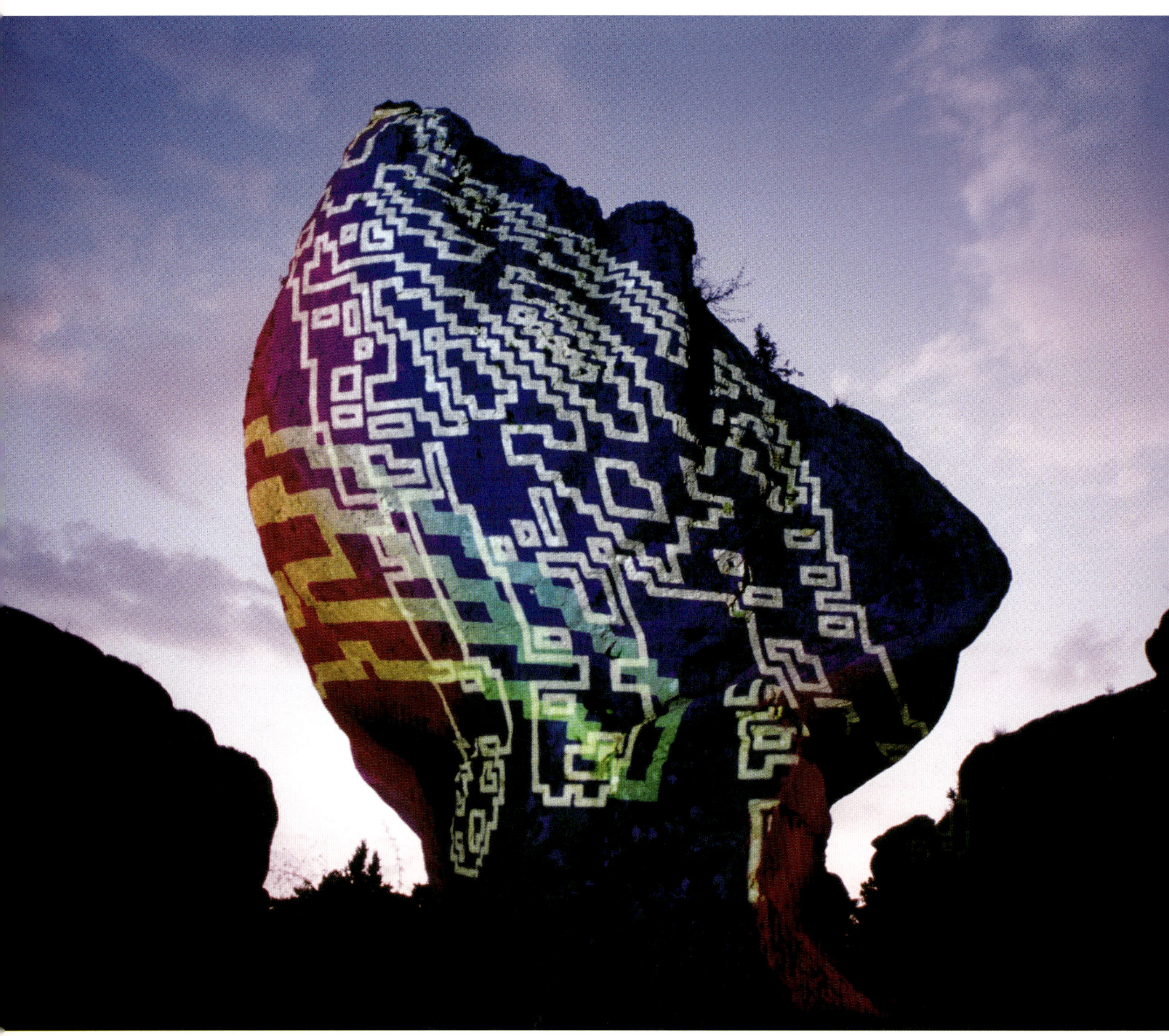

The second *Light of Stone* experiment to take place in the Castille-La Manche region was in the Cuidad Encadada (Enchanted City), an unusual geological site near of the city of Cuenca, where the erosive forces of weather and the waters of the Júcar River have formed the limestone into distinctive shapes. The fantastical rock formations, the composition of the different minerals in the stone and the effects of the coloured light filters created a mystical series of ephemeral sculptures.

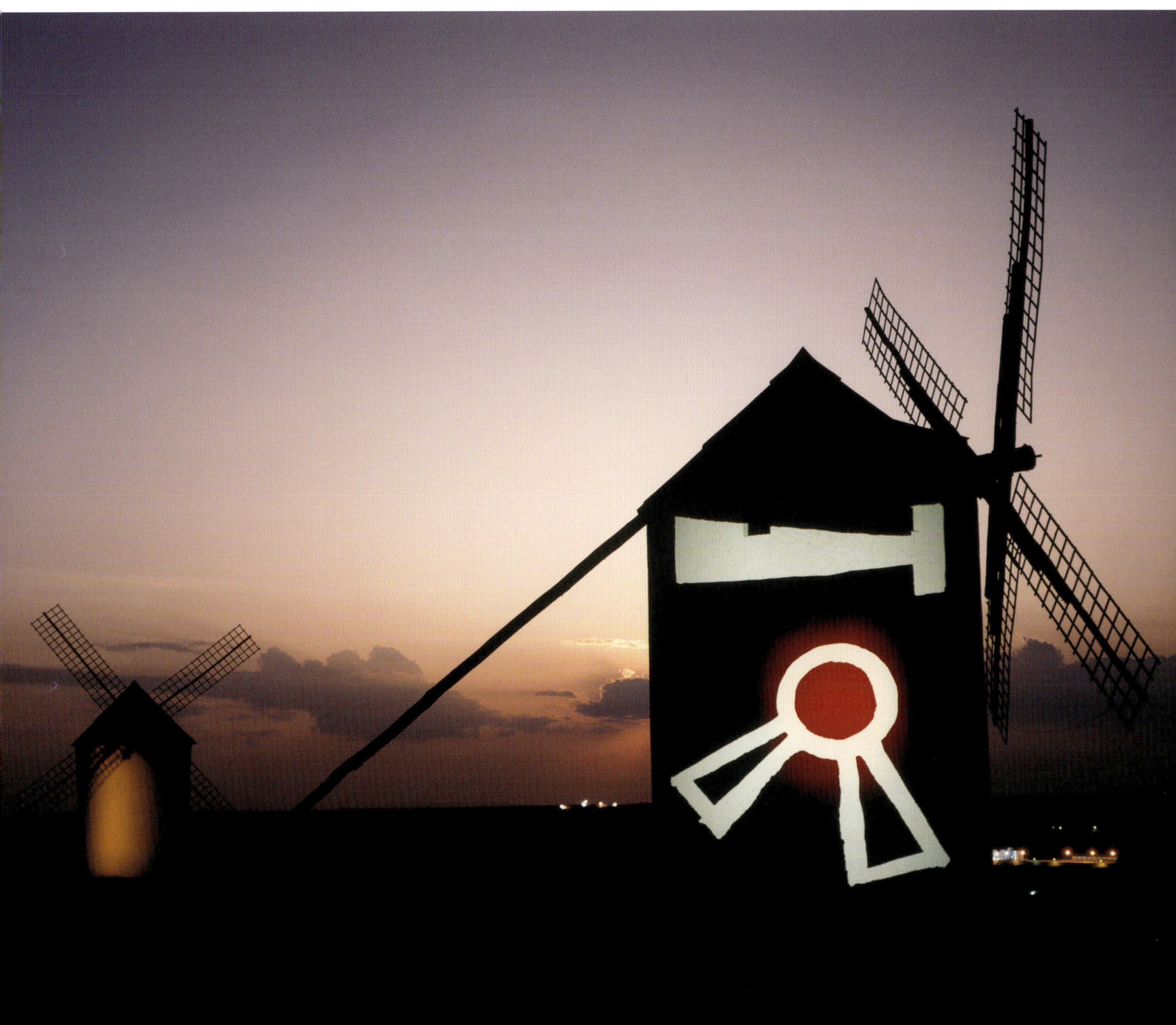

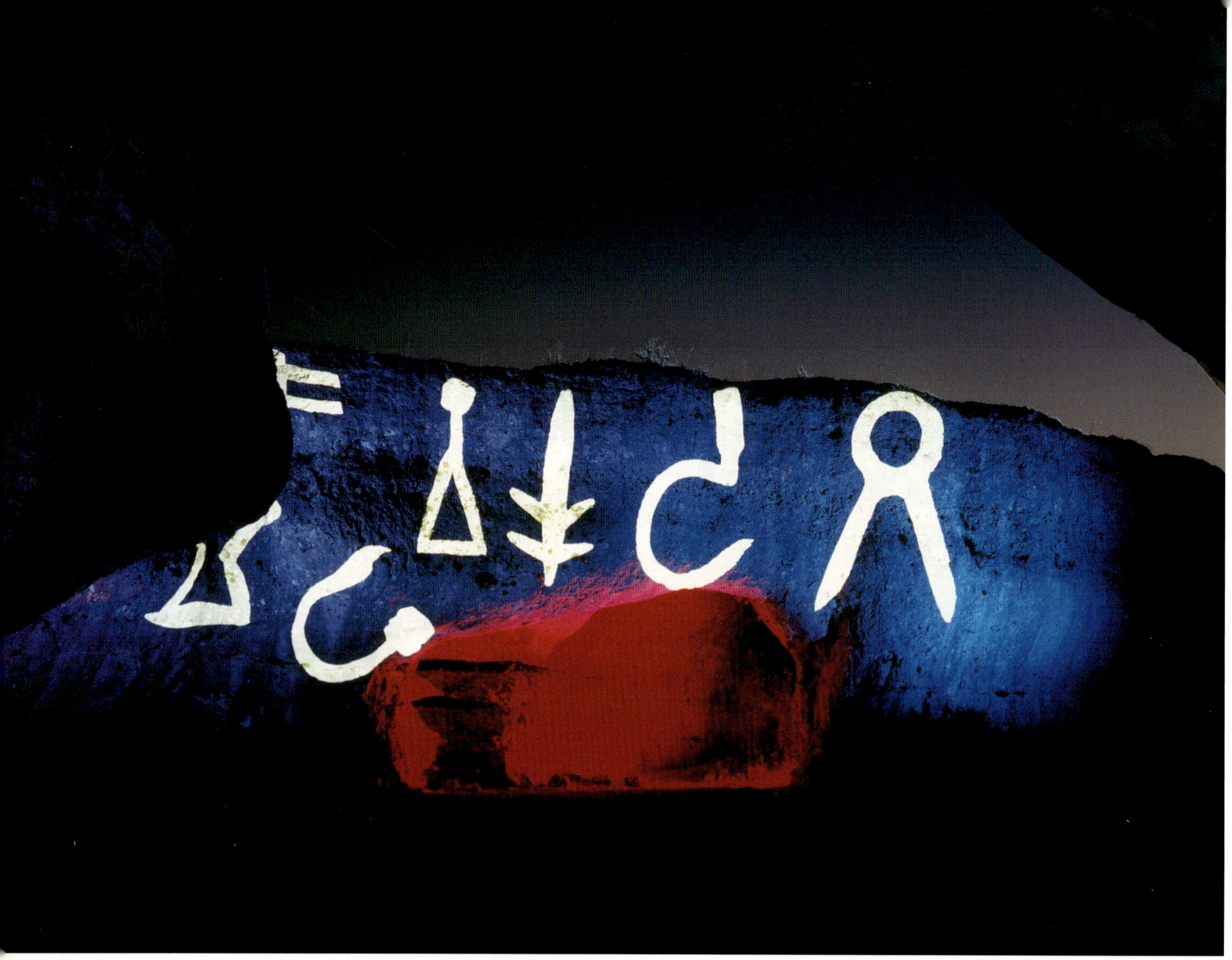

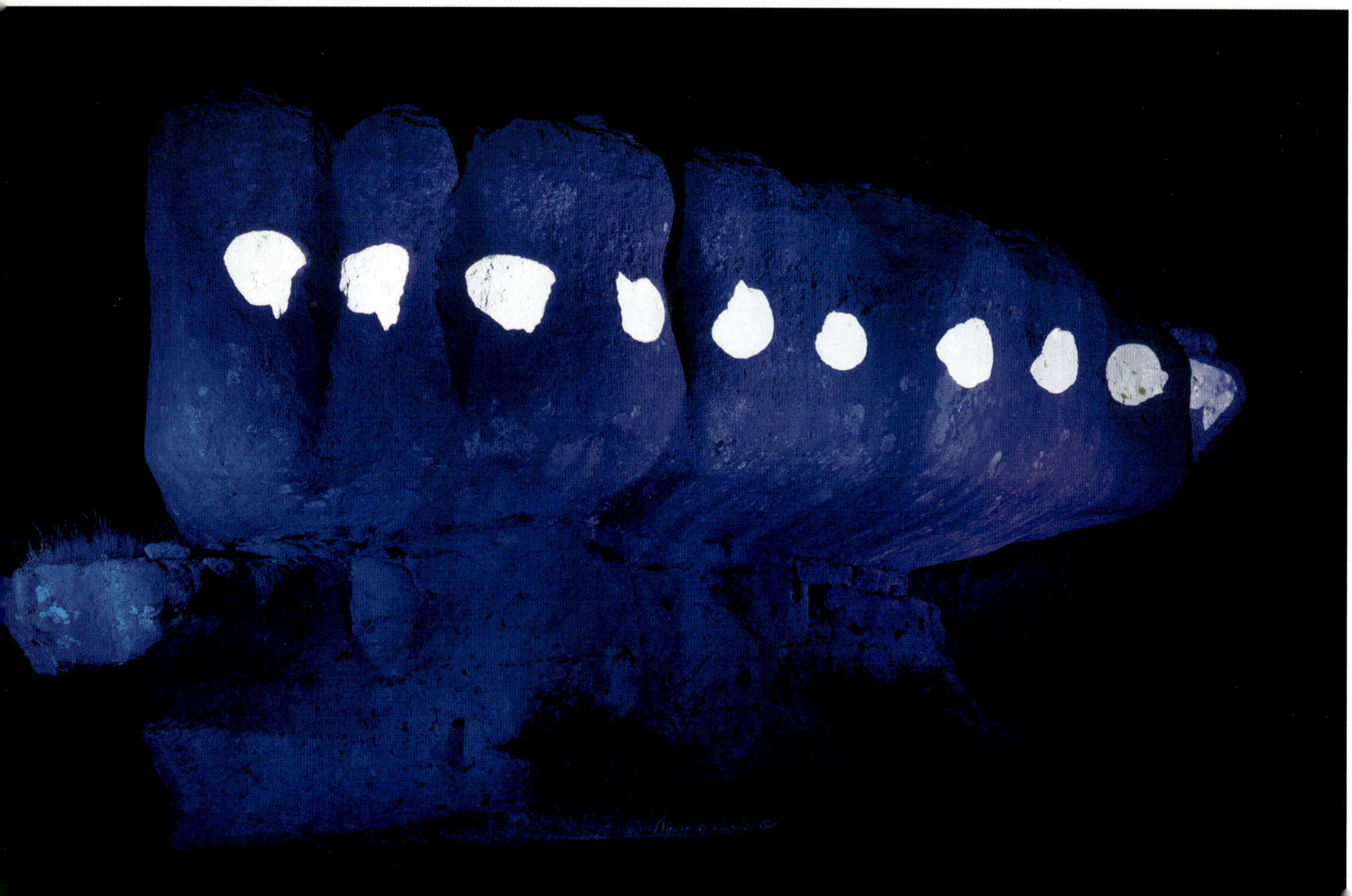

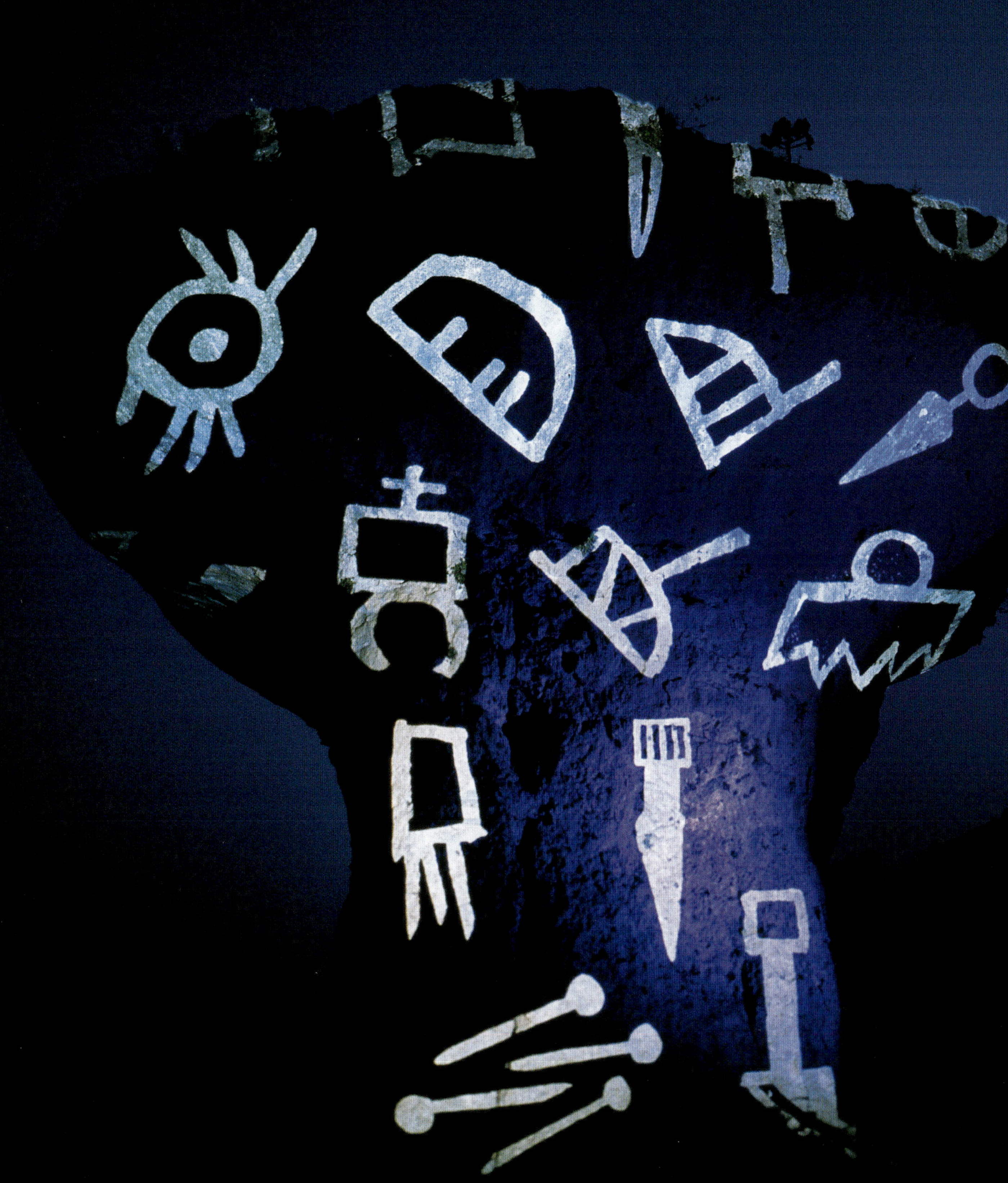

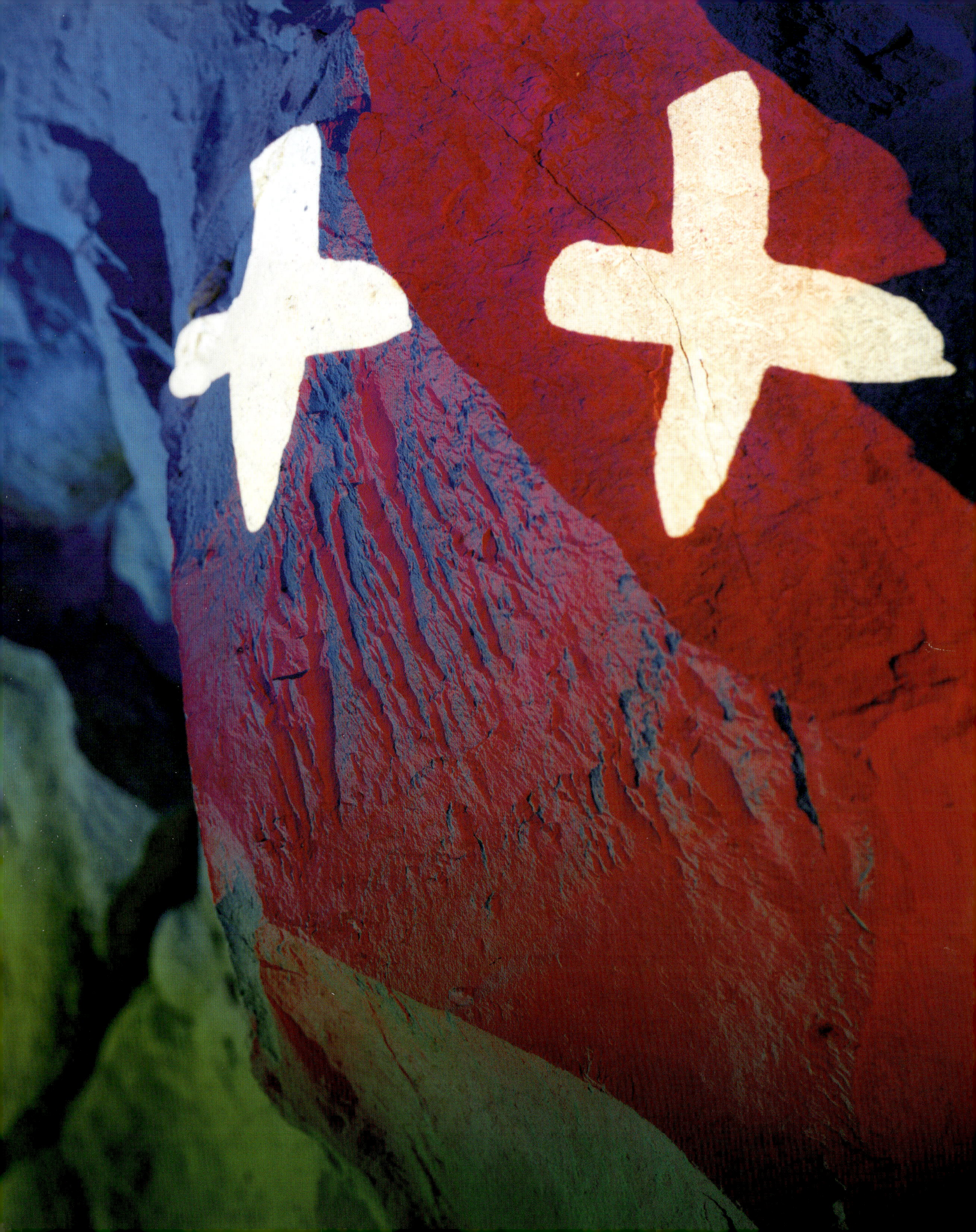

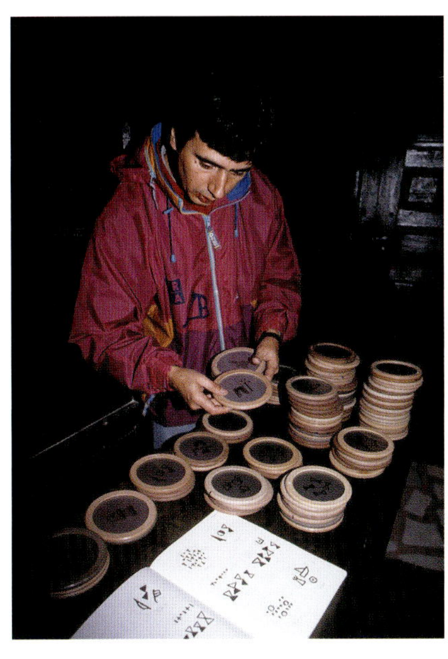

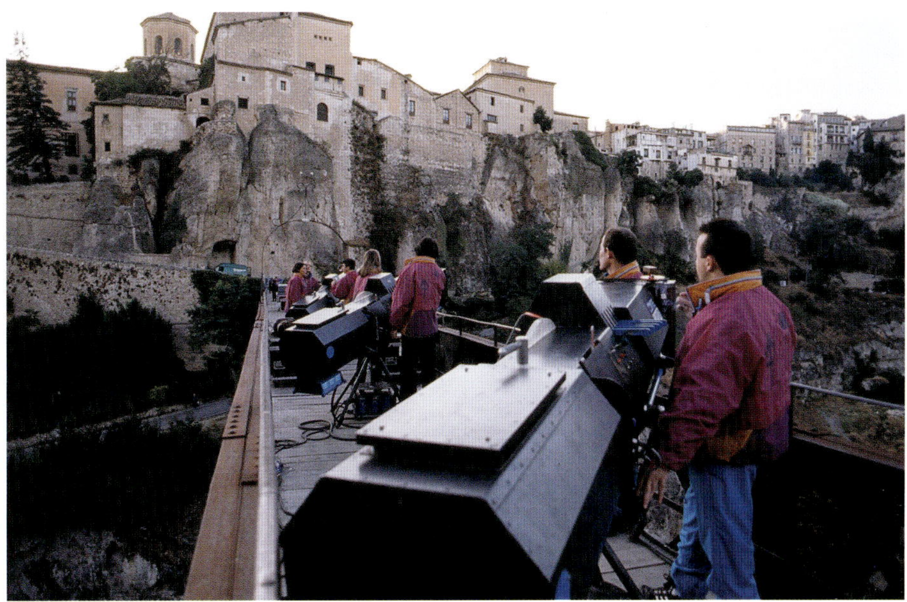

Cuenca. How did you like how drop by drop
the water carved this city in the pines?
Did you see dreams, faces and roads, the signs
and walls of pain where gale-winds whip and chop?
Did you absorb blue slopes made of the broken
moon which the Júcar soaks with glass and trills?
And were your fingers kissed by florid buckhorn
Playing its crown of love on rocky hills?
Did you remember me when you were climbing
up to the silence suffered by the snake,
a prisoner of crickets and black sighs?
In lucid air did you observe a shining
dahlia of joys and pains, coming awake,
Sent by my heart with fire into your thighs?

Francisco de Quevedo, translated by Willis Barnstone

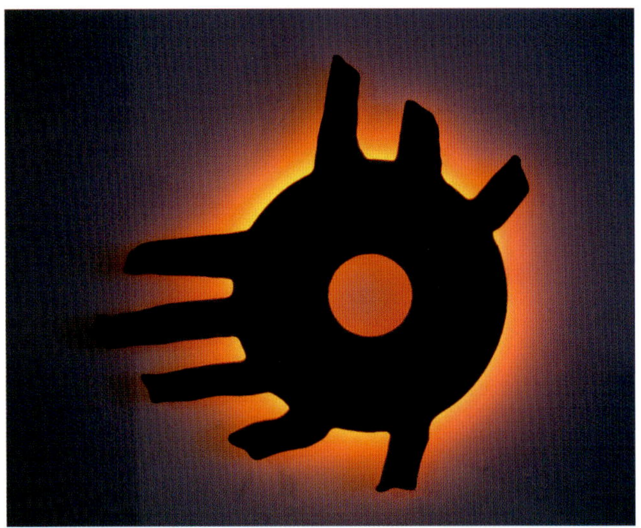

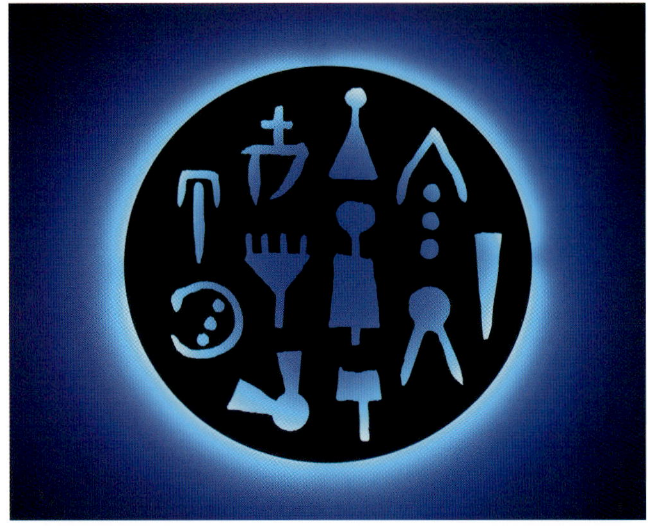

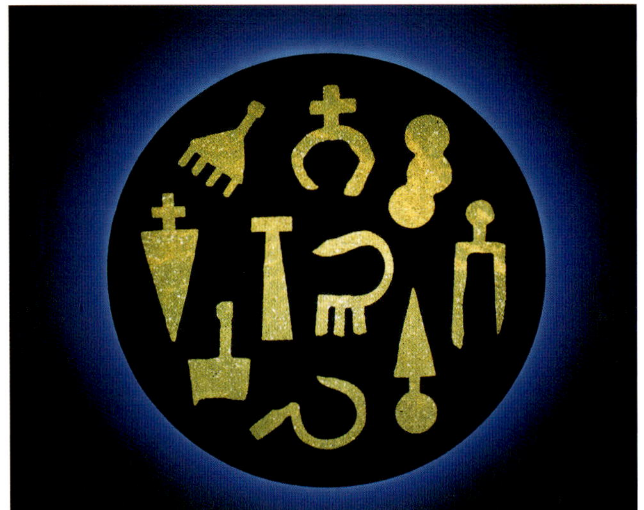

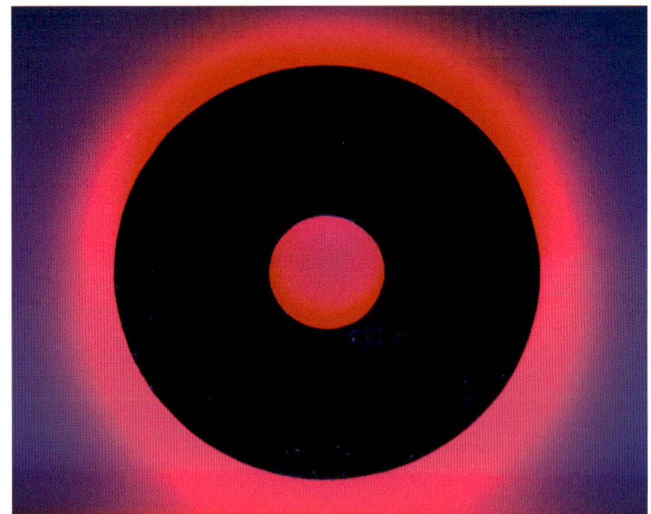

IV Proyección solar, 1997
Wood, earth, volcanic ash, minerals, neon
120 x 120 x 7 cm
Courtesy of Galería el Museo, Bogotá, Colombia

The Cry from the Earth, 1994
Wood, earth, volcanic ash, minerals, light projector, neon
150 x 150 x 10 cm

The Cry from the Earth, 1994
Laser cut steel, neon
120 x 120 x 10 cm

XIV Factor humano, 1996
Wood, earth, volcanic ash, minerals, neon
120 x 120 x 7 cm
Courtesy of Galería el Museo, Bogotá, Colombia

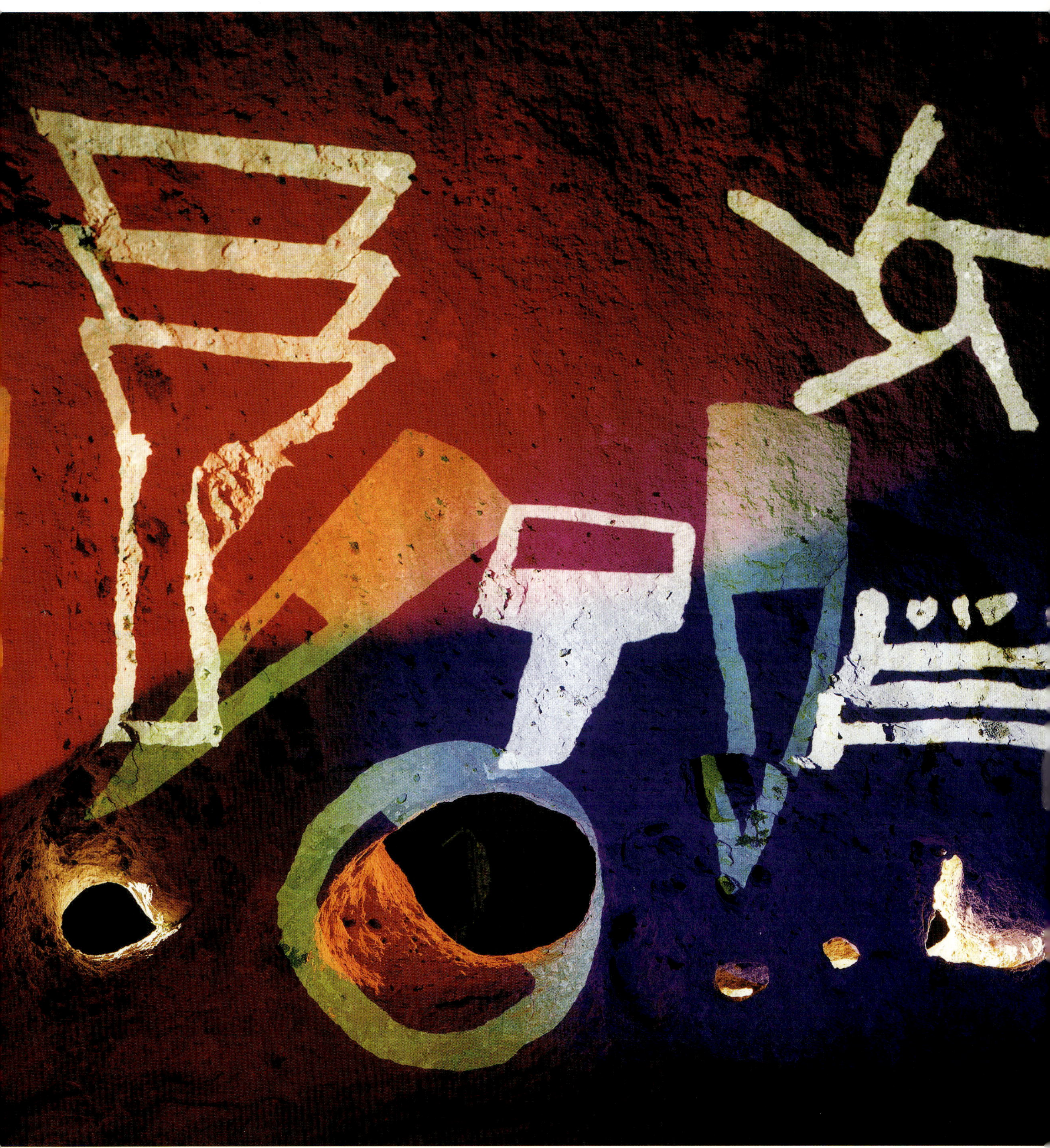

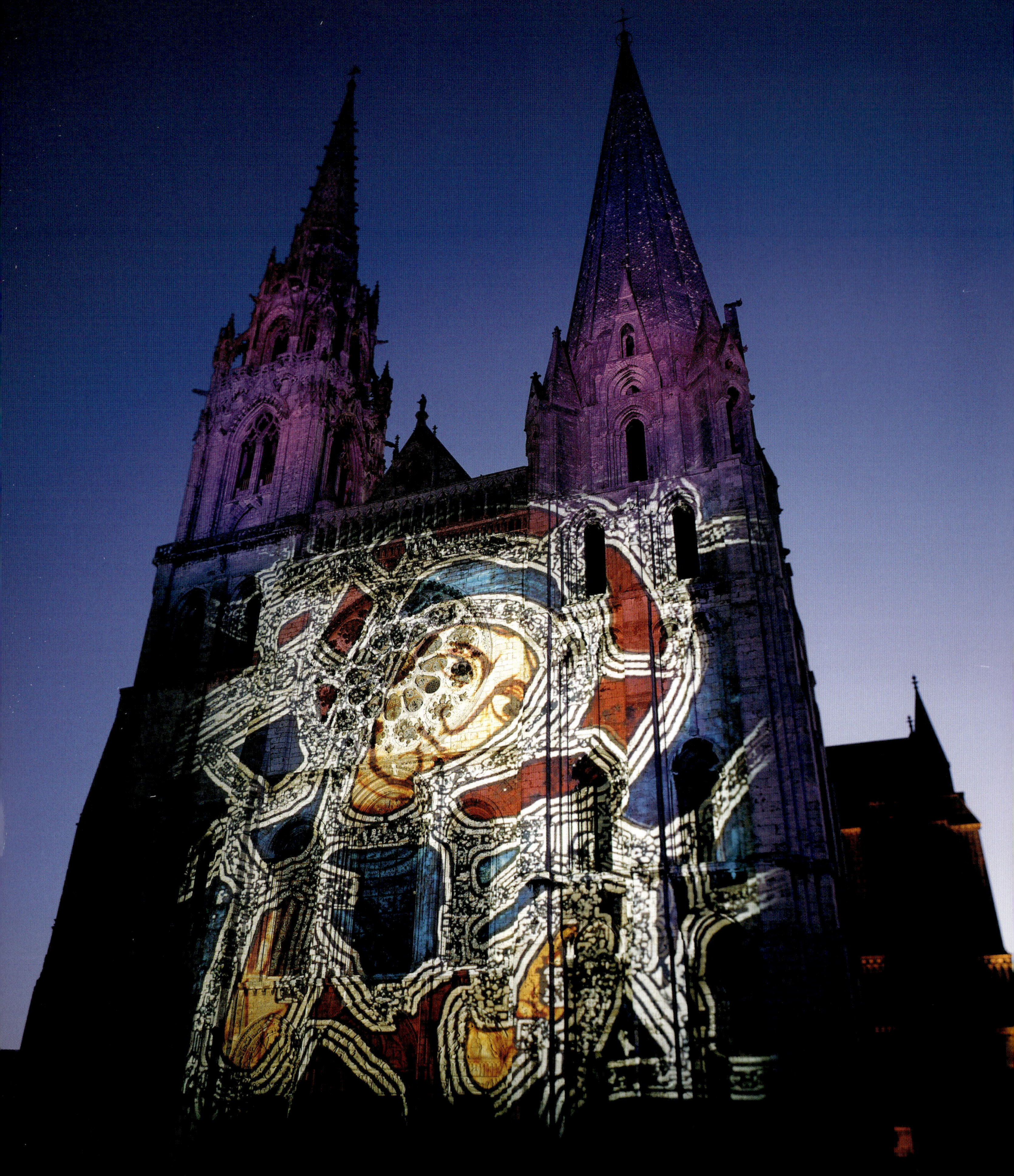

SACRED LIGHT

Cathédrale de Chartres, France

1994

To celebrate the 800th anniversary of Chartres Cathedral the artists derived the iconography for *Sacred Light* from the history of the construction of the Cathedral. For the public showing they collaborated with master organist Odile Jutten to create an immersive visual-acoustic experience. On the night of the projections, the graphic score was projected onto the three facades of the Cathedral simultaneously, while the organist correlated her gestures with the images and the organ music was diffused live into the public space creating an intimate bond between the sacred interior and profound exterior space.

Establishing a link between the past and the present, Jorge Orta worked with the stained glass artisans to create a series of leaded stained glass projection plates. The result of the luminosity of the colours was remarkable once the light transposed the metallic salt coloured glass is refracted against the ancient stones. The signs and pictograms are in fact the signatures of the forgotten stonemasons as well as the famous labyrinth, which fills the nave of the Cathedral. Around 300 men are said to have carved and assembled the Cathedral leaving traces of their workmanship engraved into the masonry and architectural features. The labyrinth design, 13 metres in diameter, was built around 1200 and used as a repentance ritual site, where pilgrims could meander on a searching journey with the hope of becoming closer to God.

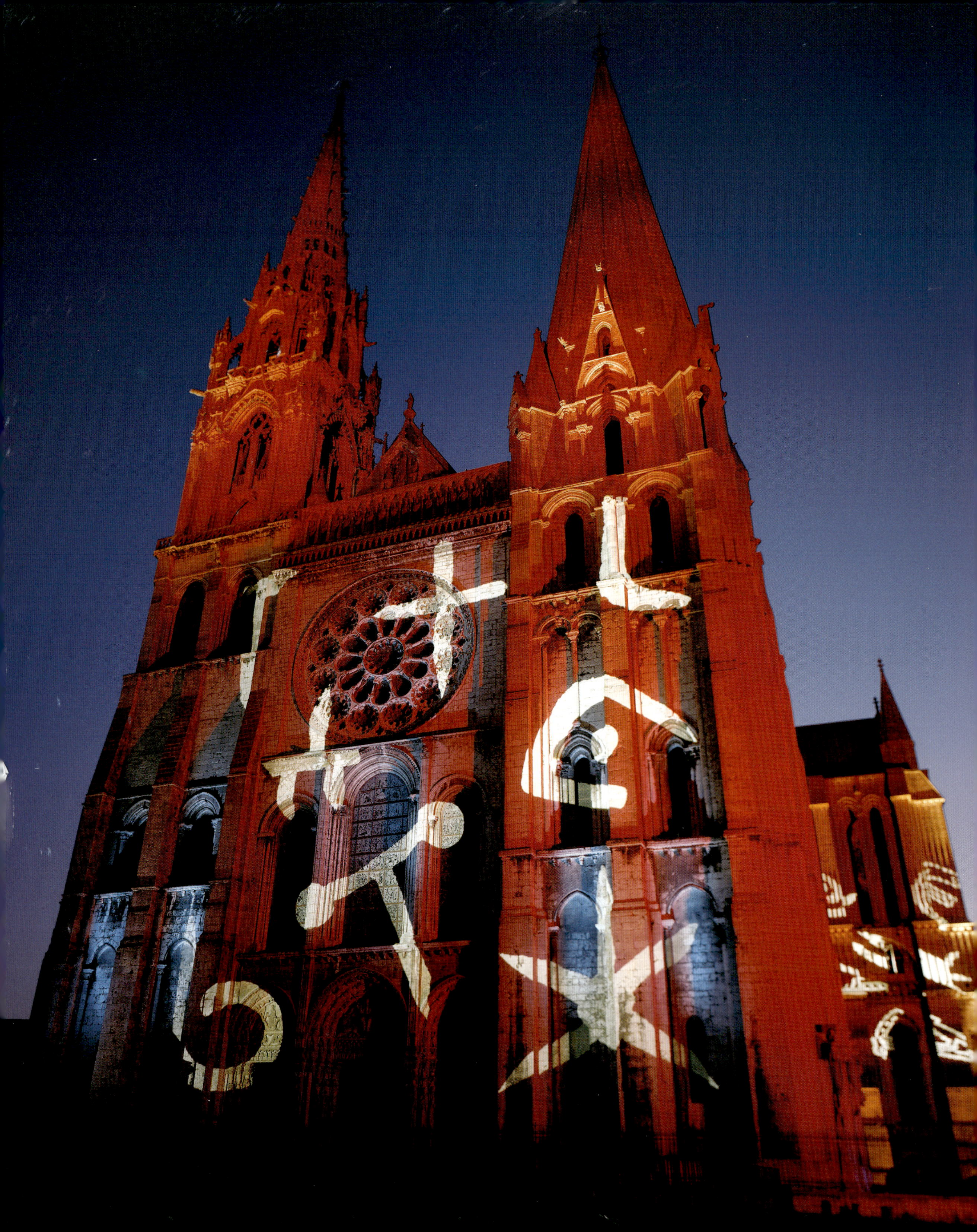

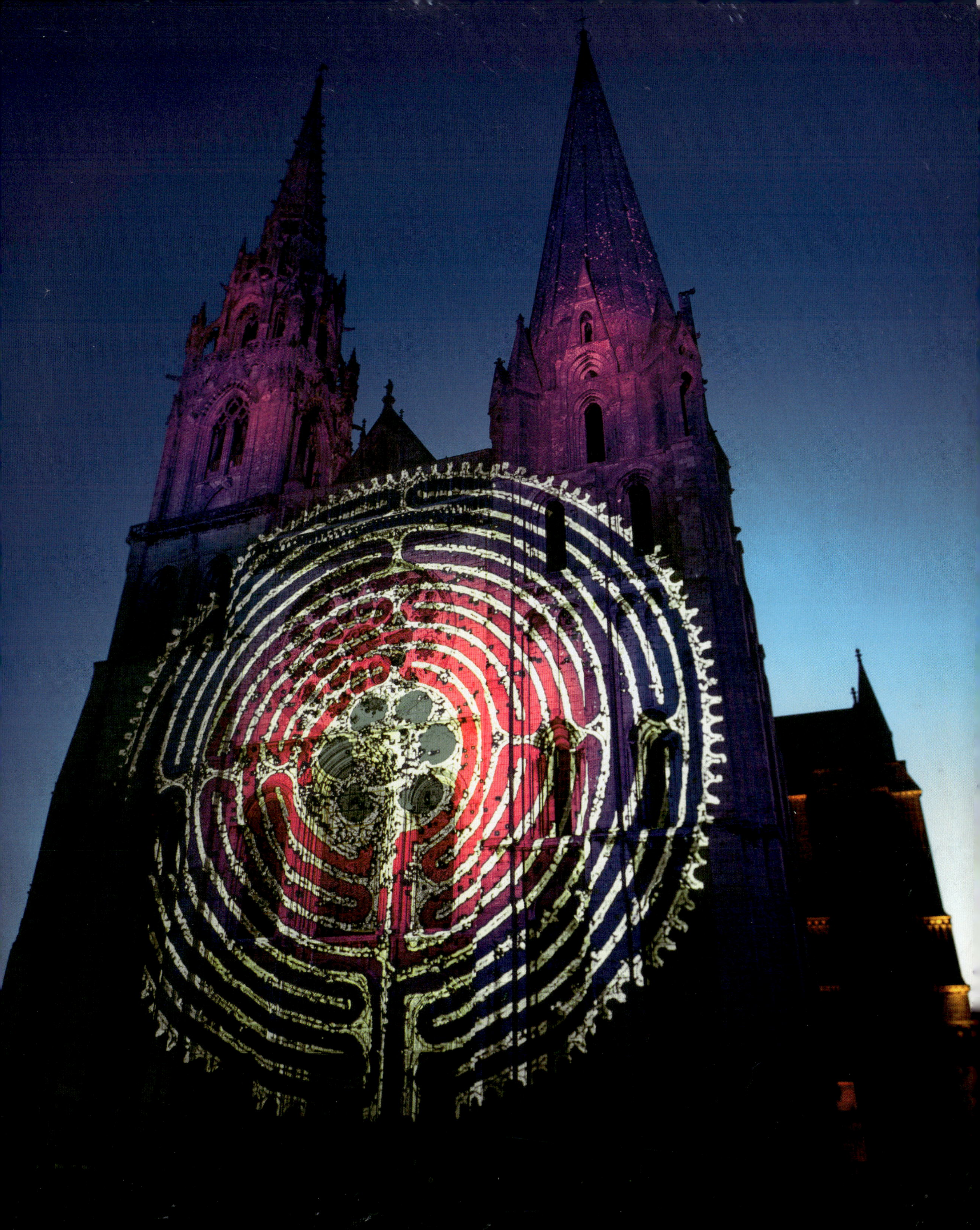

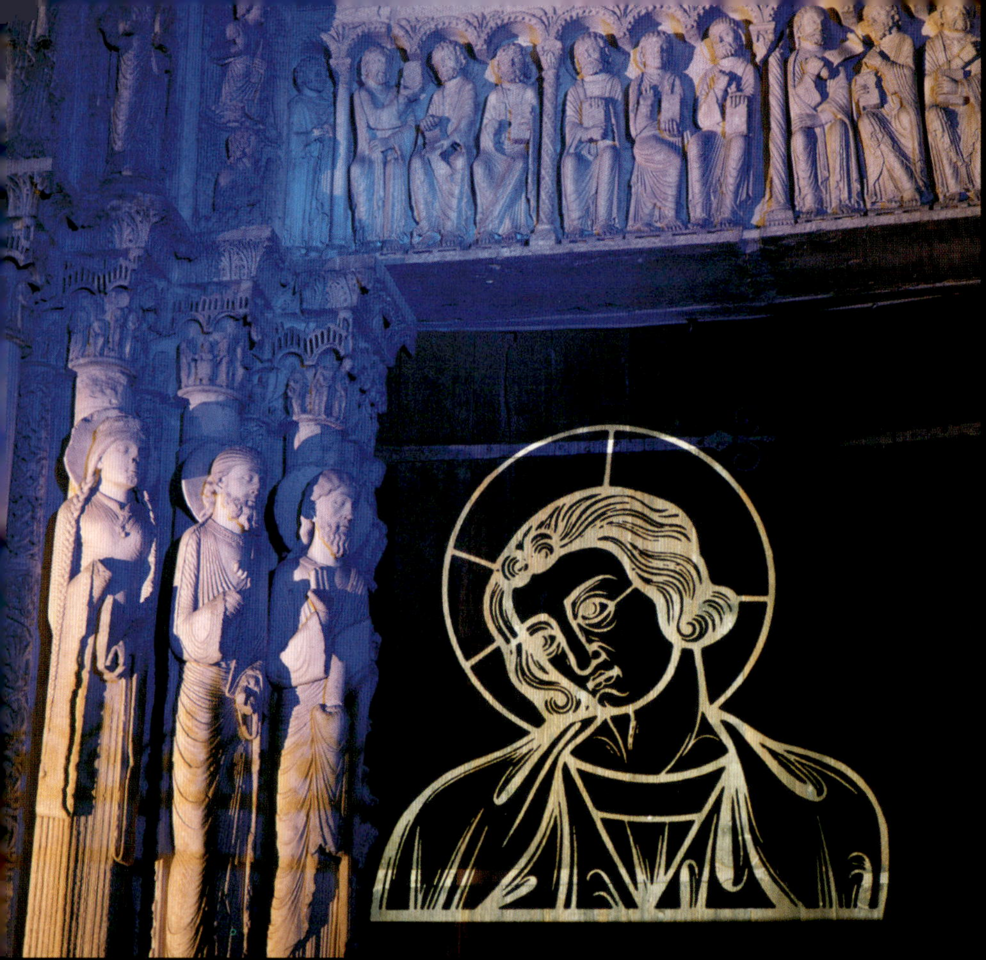

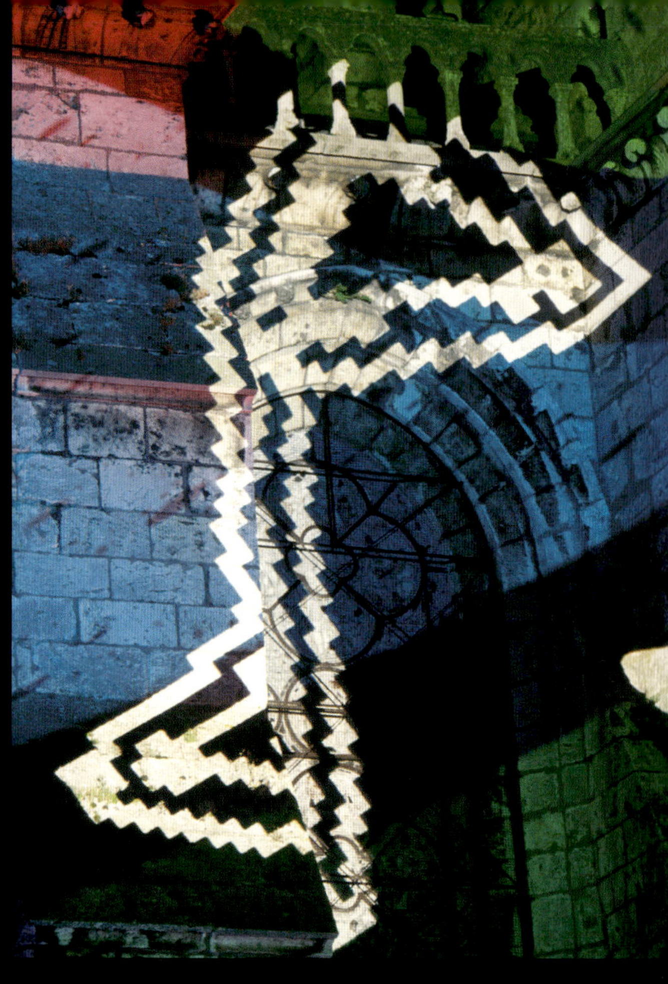

At a time when the churches and cathedrals were painted, tympanums, colonnades, gables, spires and statues were rich with colour. Red, blue, yellow enhanced the sacred and helped understand the meaning of these great stone works. The dimension of this polychrome technique, imagined by the cathedral masters has since been forgotten. Orta's Light Works concert bring an added dimension to the architecture of the Middle Ages, closer to the reality than we think. ALAIN ERLANDE-BRANDENBURG

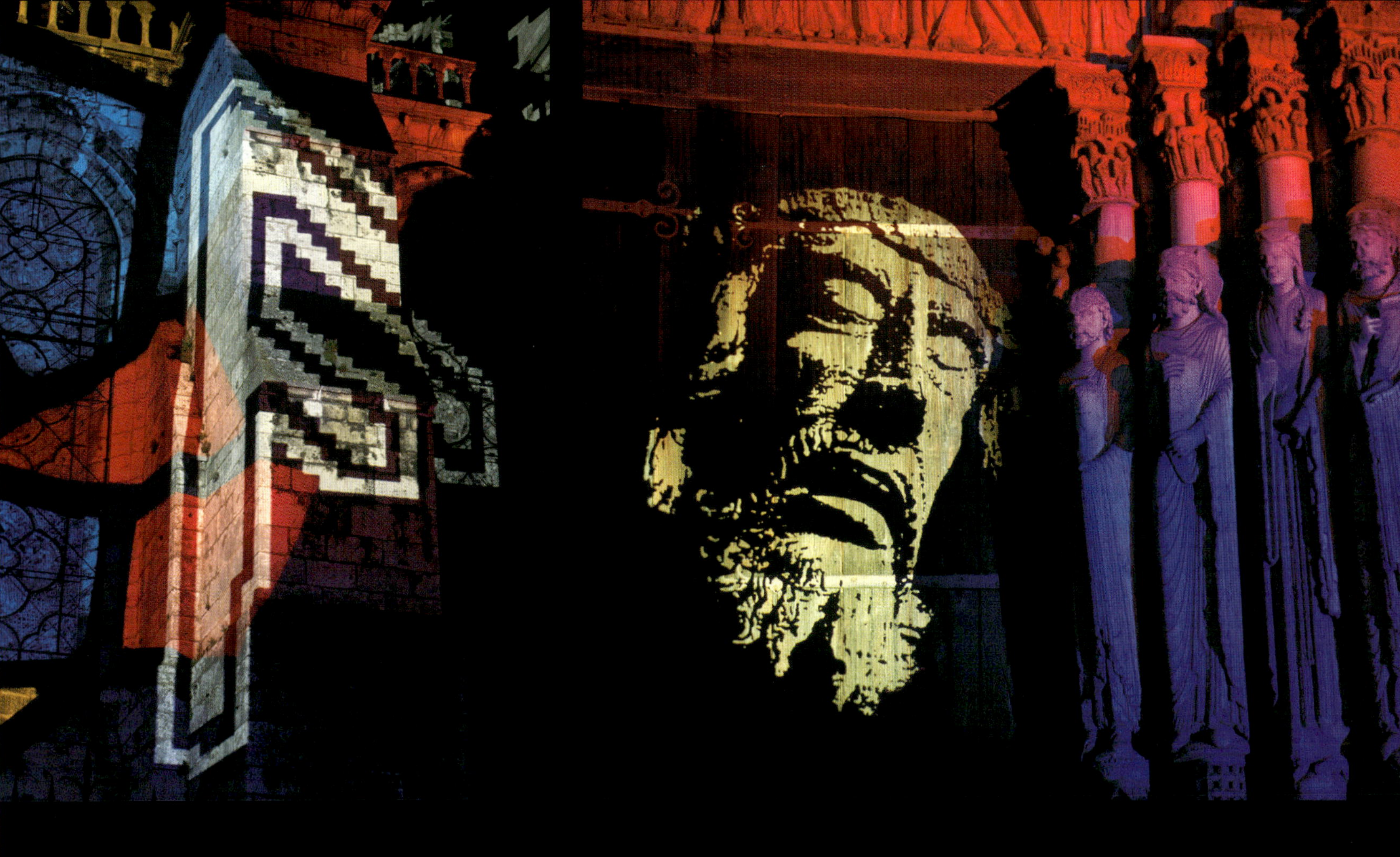

The natural cycle of light filtered by the stained glass—following the rhythm of day and night, distorting the images, making them appear and disappear as the sun's rays cross the sky, changing with the seasons—is a great inspiration. The cathedral is a whole world of colours, a giant exploding kaleidoscope. Jorge Orta

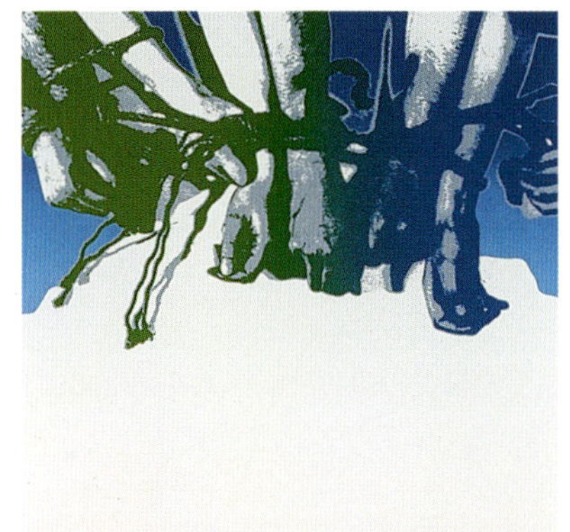

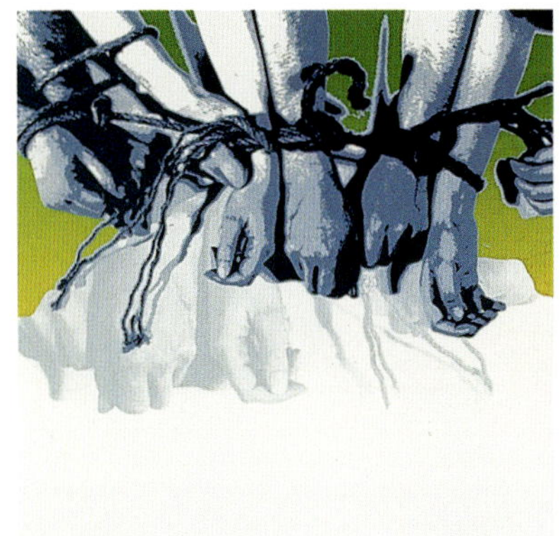

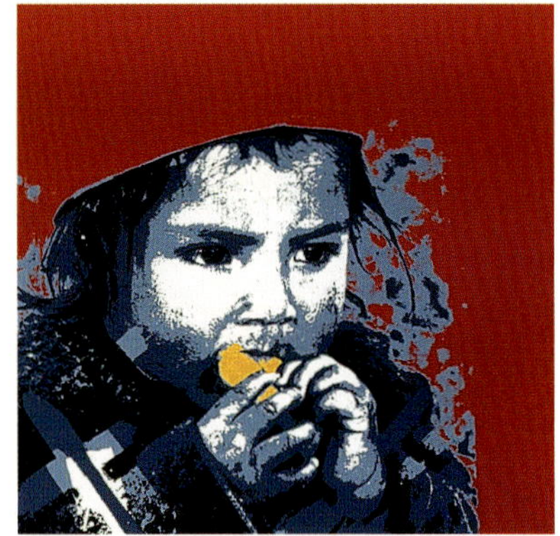

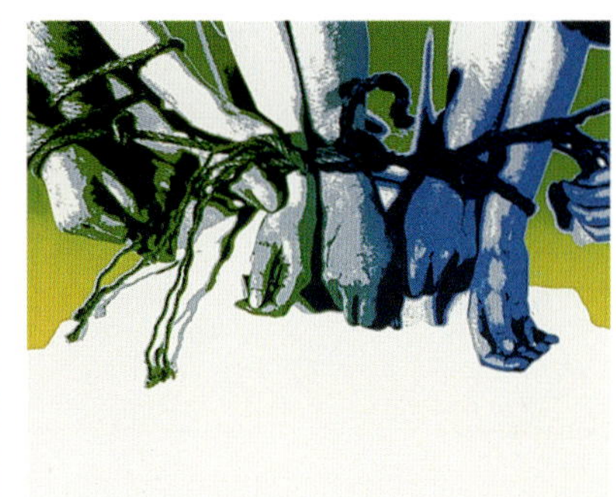

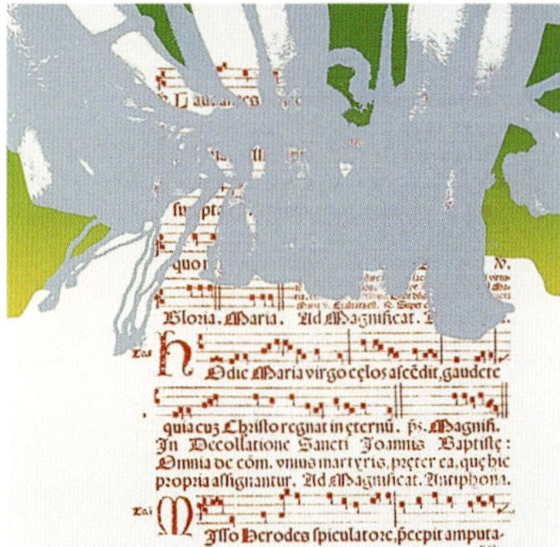

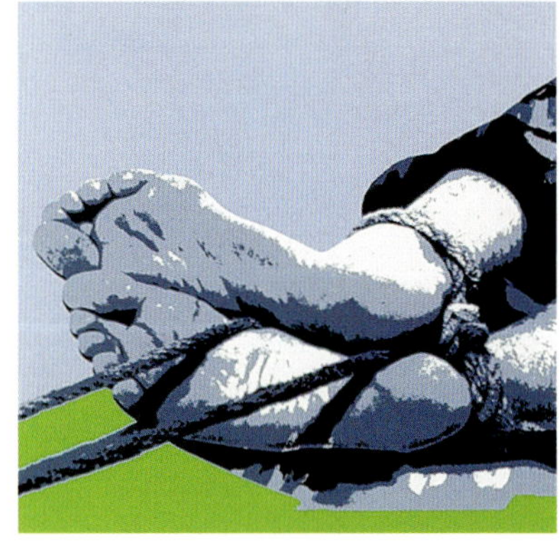

Cruz del sur I, 1987
Silkscreen print on paper
215 x 160 cm

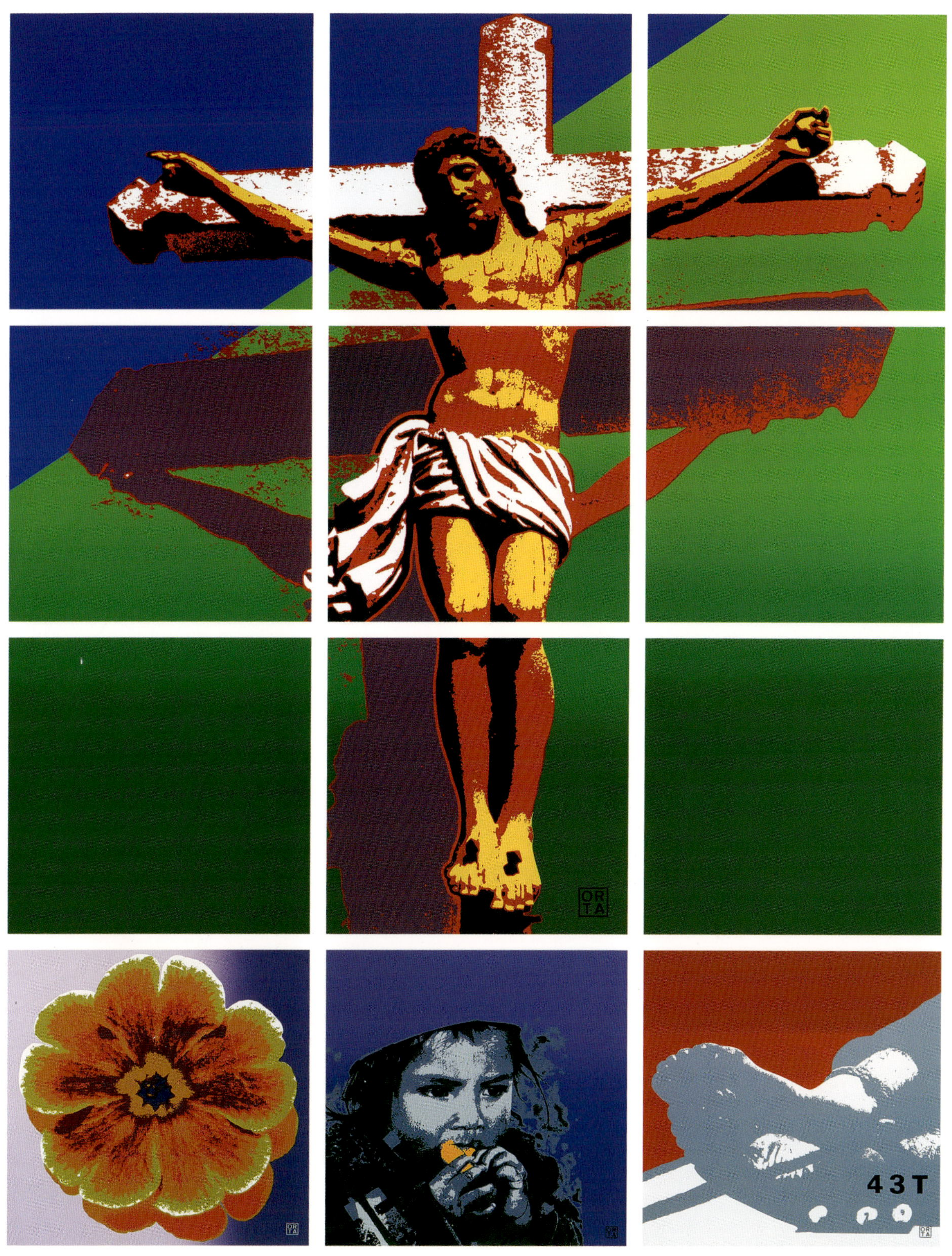

Cruz del sur II, 1988
Silkscreen print on paper
125 x 160 cm

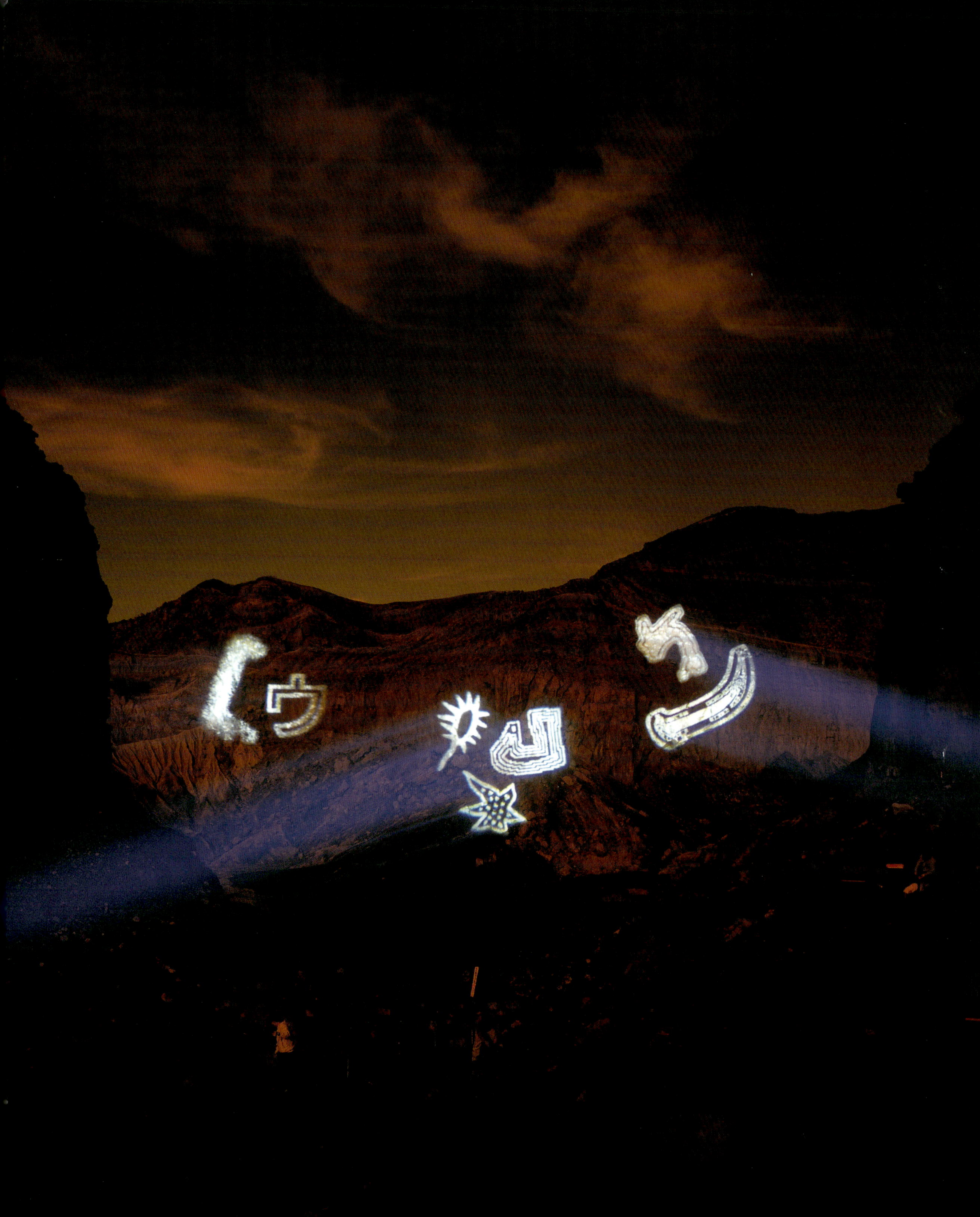

THE CRY FROM THE EARTH

1994

Mount Aso volcano, Kyushu, Japan

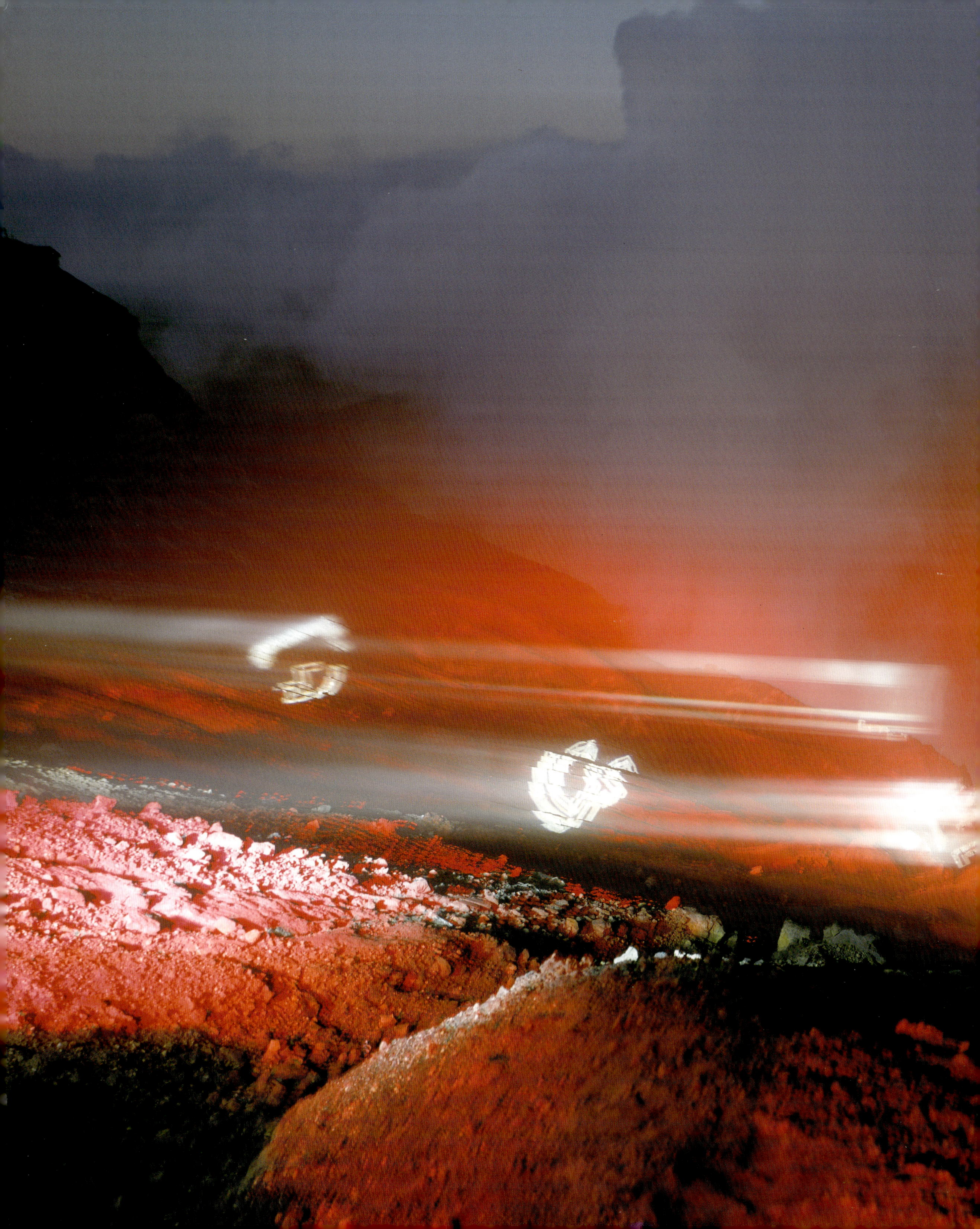

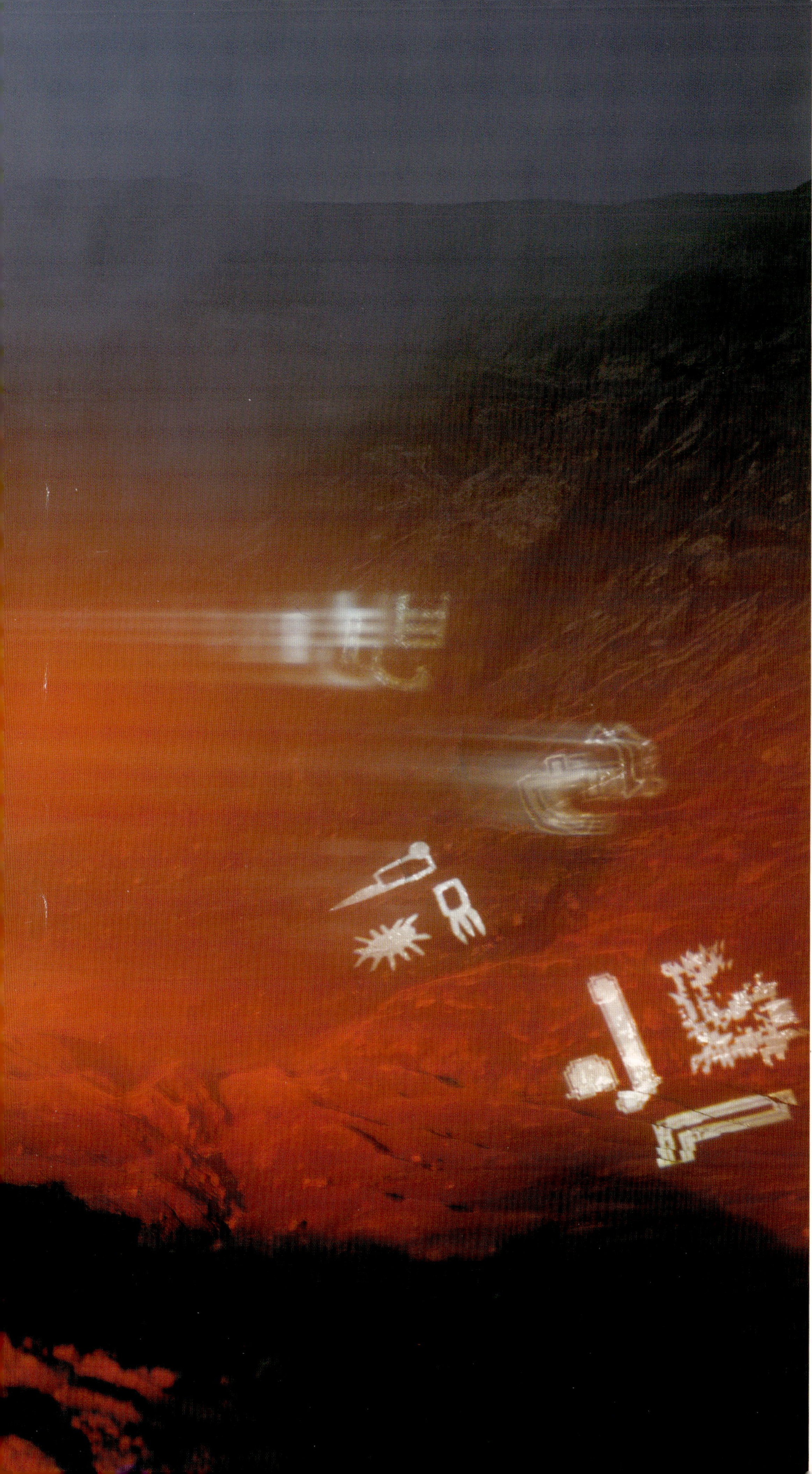

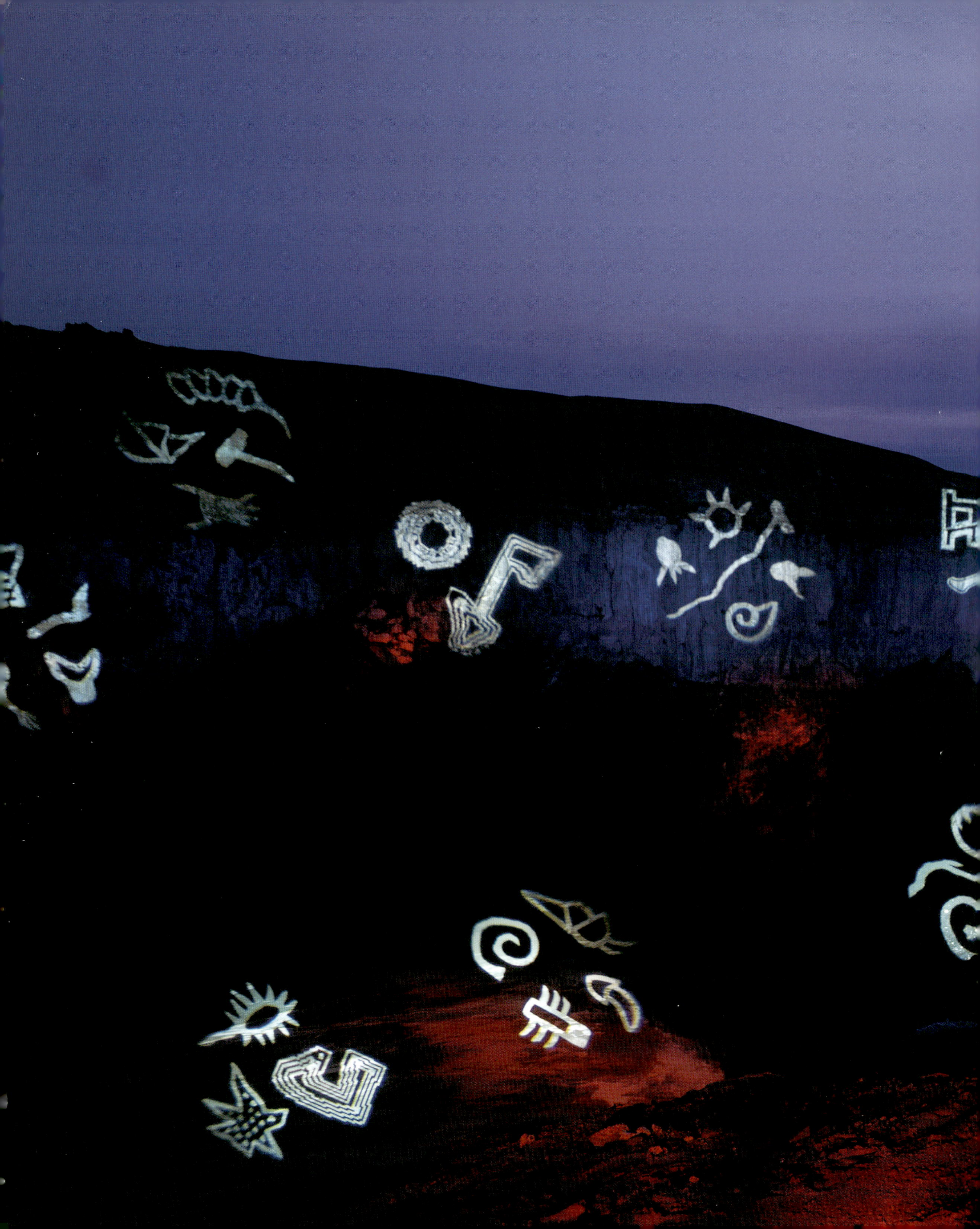

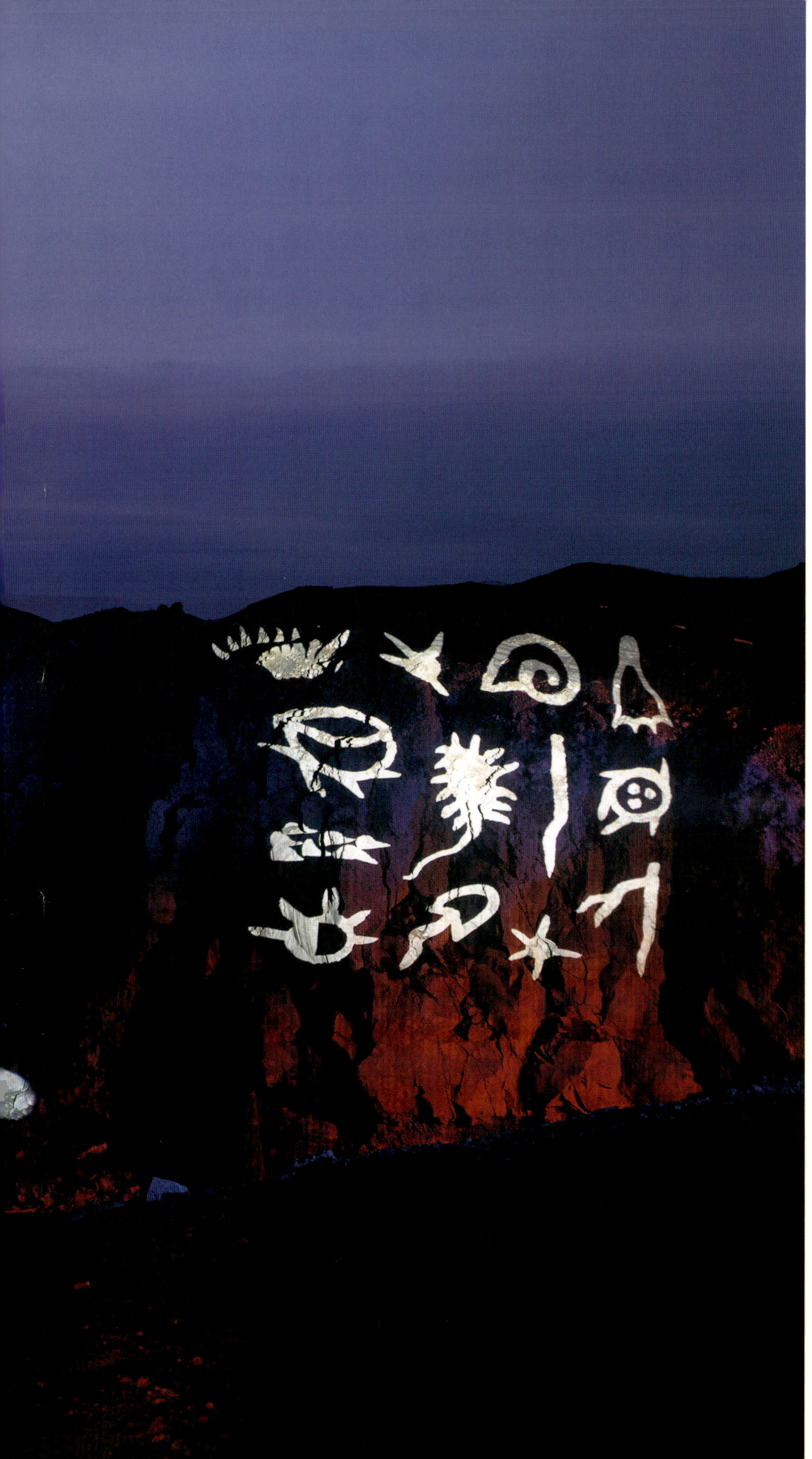

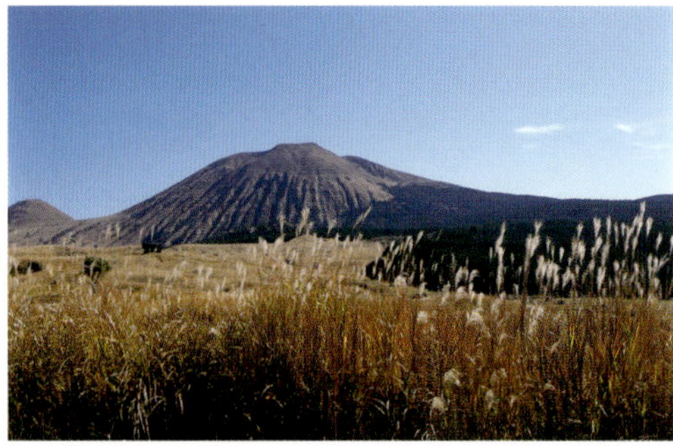

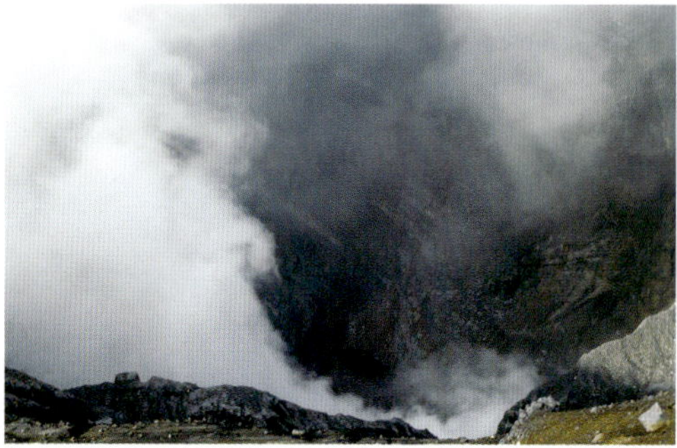

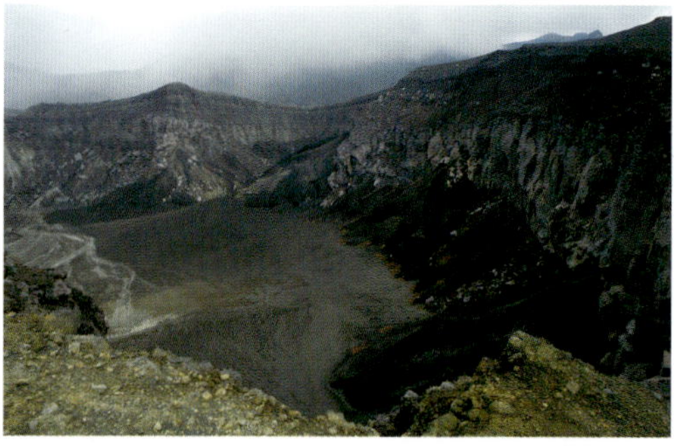

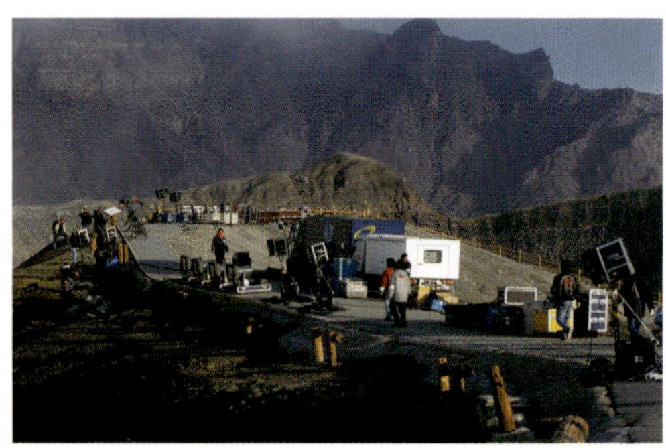

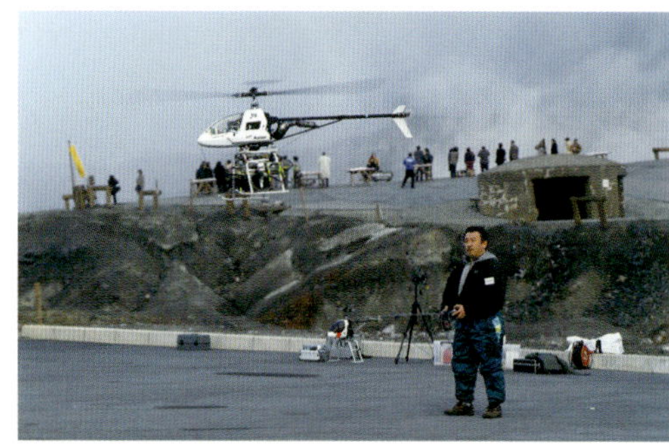

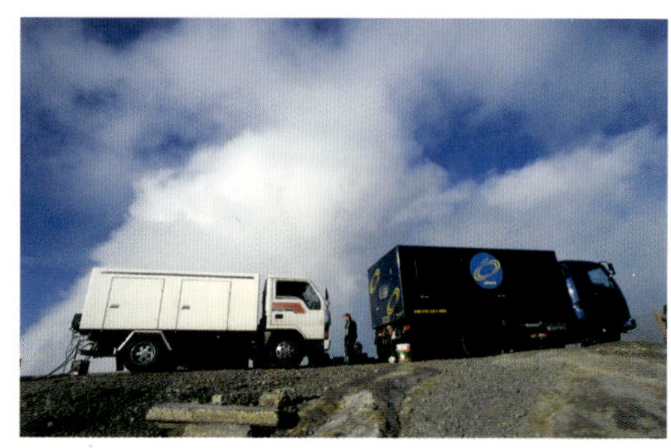

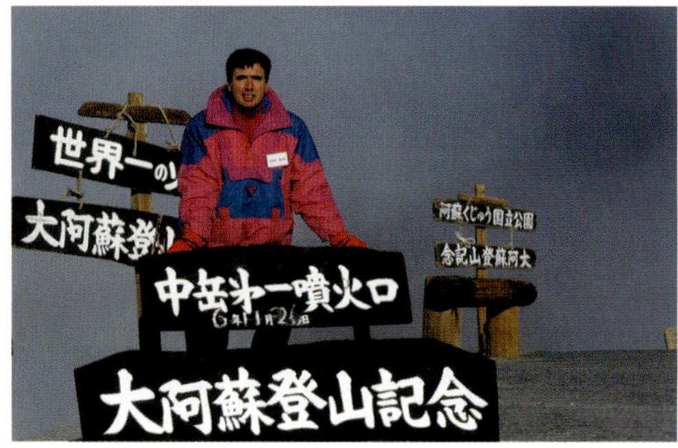

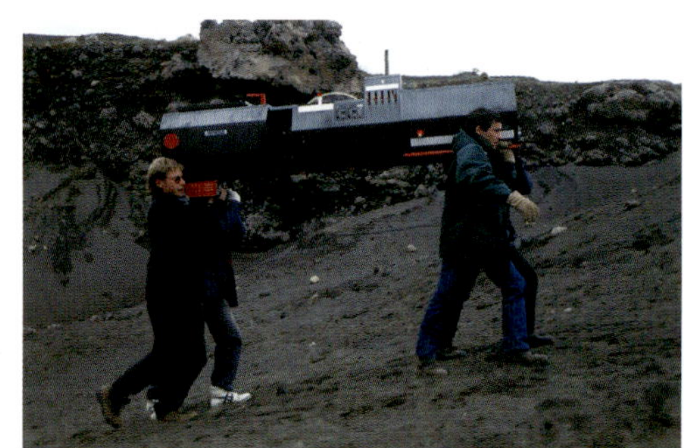

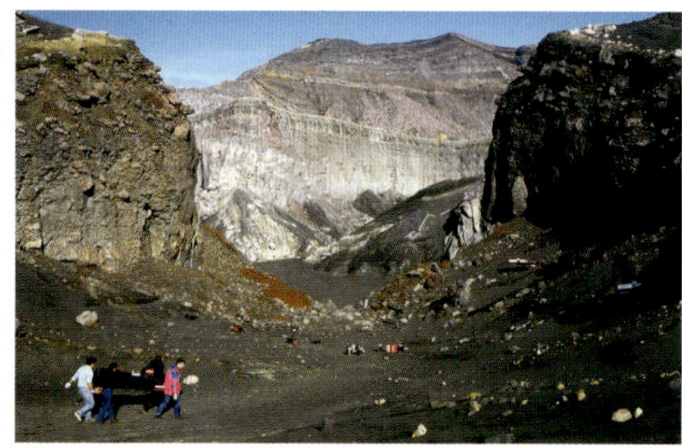

By invitation of Asahi Television Corporation Lucy+Jorge Orta were able to realise the most ambitious of the ephemeral Light Works for the Japanese audience, which was broadcasted during the special New Year's Eve arts programme in front of thirty million spectators. It took over two years for the artists to settle on the location after touring many mythical sites across Japan, including: the Buddhist temples, Shinto Shrines and 'Zen gardens' of Kyoto, the Hiroshima memorial, the island of Okinawa, the UNESCO World Heritage site of Himeji Castle, and Mount Fuji.

During the expedition, Lucy+Jorge Orta collected the natural and cultural imprints of the locations they explored, sketching signs and pictograms in a series of folding calligraphy sketchbooks they purchased from the monks in the temples of Kyoto. Each location was rigorously analysed, technical feasibility studies conducted and authorisations requested, ruling out sites that would compromise a monumental work. The artists finally narrowed down their choice to Mount Aso on Kyushu Island.

It was no coincidence that the artists selected the world's largest active volcano range, spewing ash and sulphur from the caldera. On the eve of the 50th anniversary of the bombing of Hiroshima and close to the city of Nagasaki, *The Cry from the Earth* on Mount Aso was a highly symbolic ephemeral action, marking an ethical dimension to the concept of Light Works. Delayed several months due to the eruptions, the 60-strong crew and several tons of

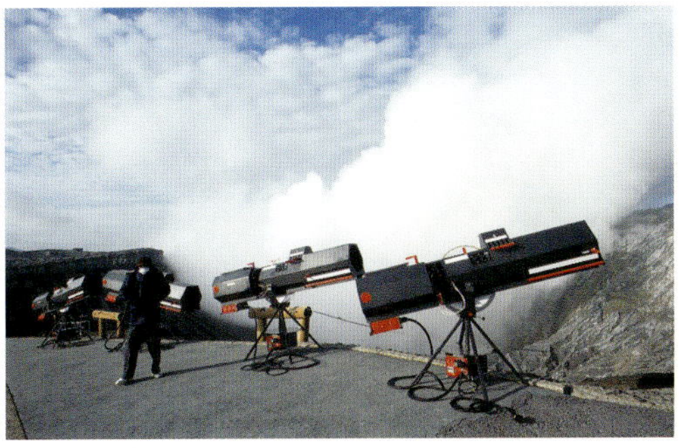
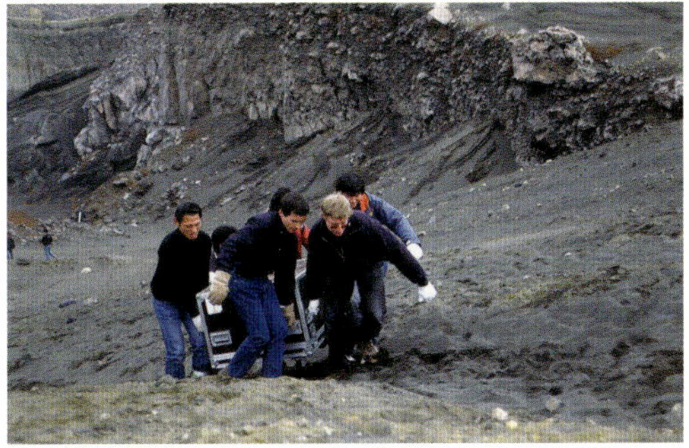
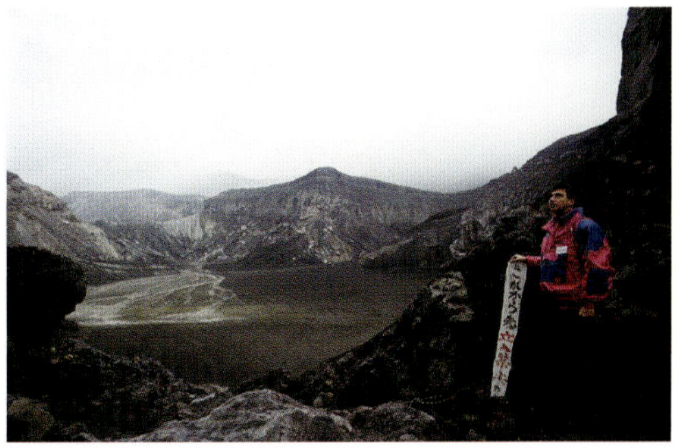
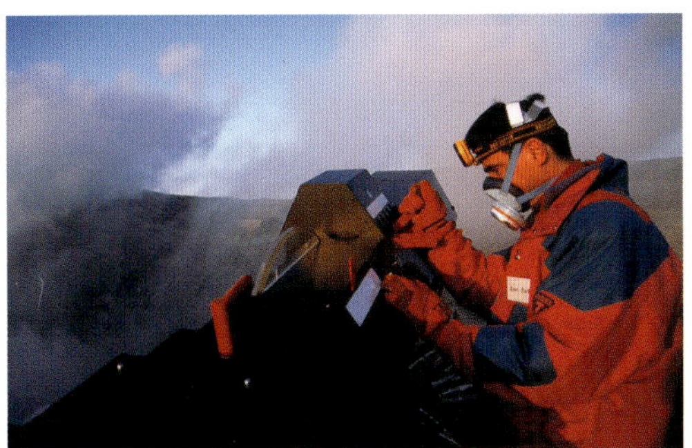
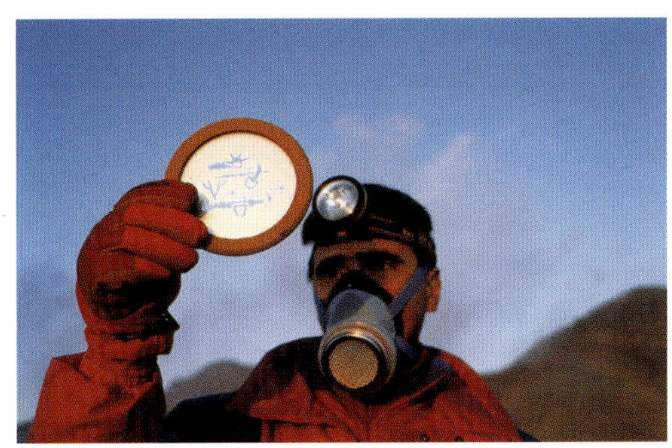
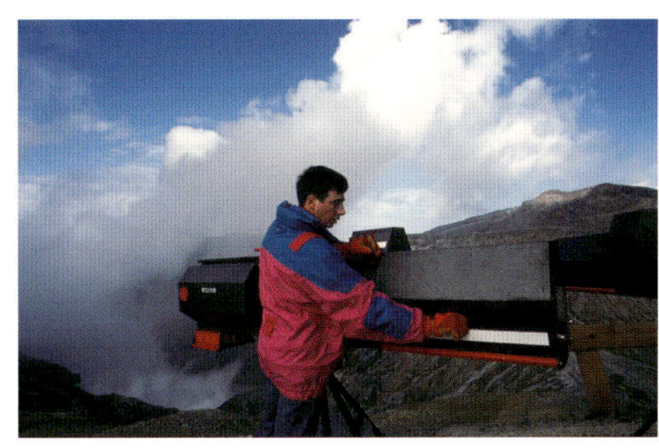
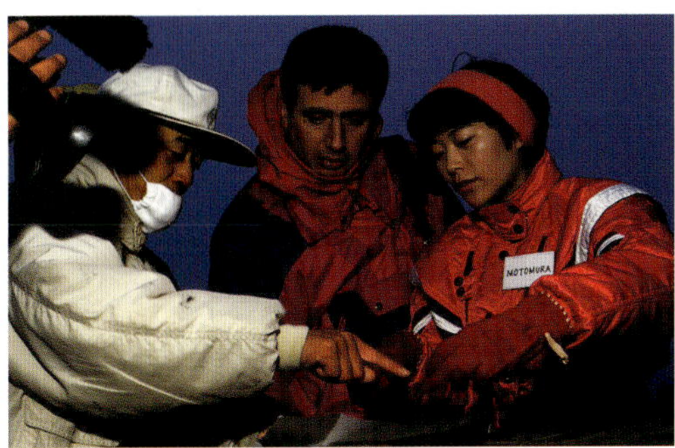
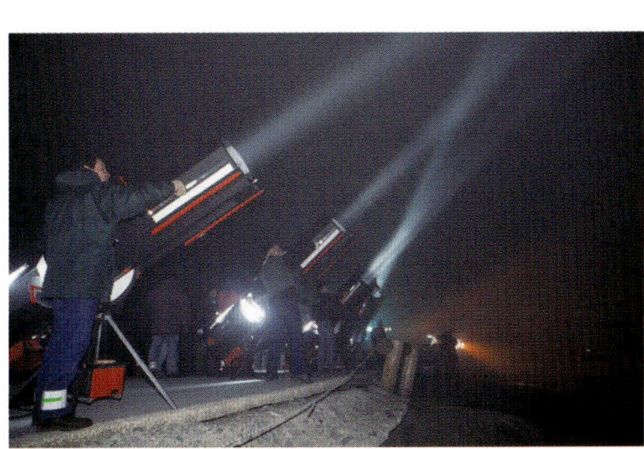
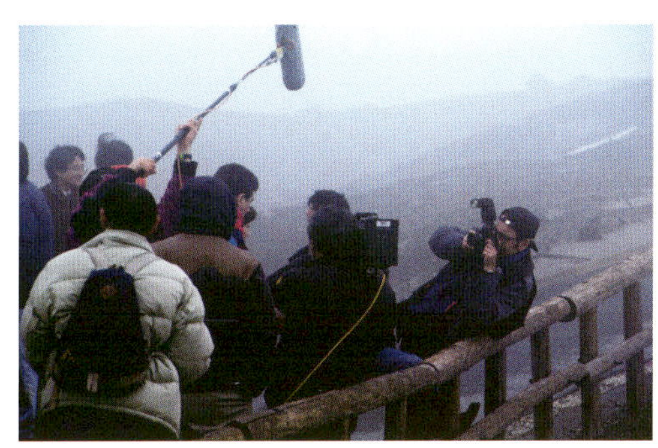

projection and camera equipment were transported to the edge of the crater. The images were projected onto the poisonous vapour clouds, resonating with the tragic memory of man's destructive trait and that of nature's own hostile forces.

The graphic score for the Light Works is composed of the artists' hand-drawn and digital pictograms, images of the volcanic eruptions and coded transcriptions of the electronic audio signals recorded on location. To create the concert, the artists experimented with the Xenakis UPIC sound research technologies, which converted their drawings into sound signals and the audio recordings of the volcanic eruption into images. The graphic analysis of the Mount Aso's volcanic activity is diffracted on the surface of the volcanic rock.

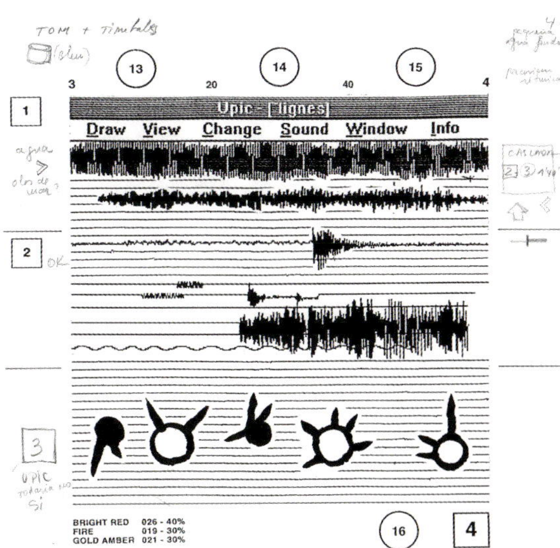

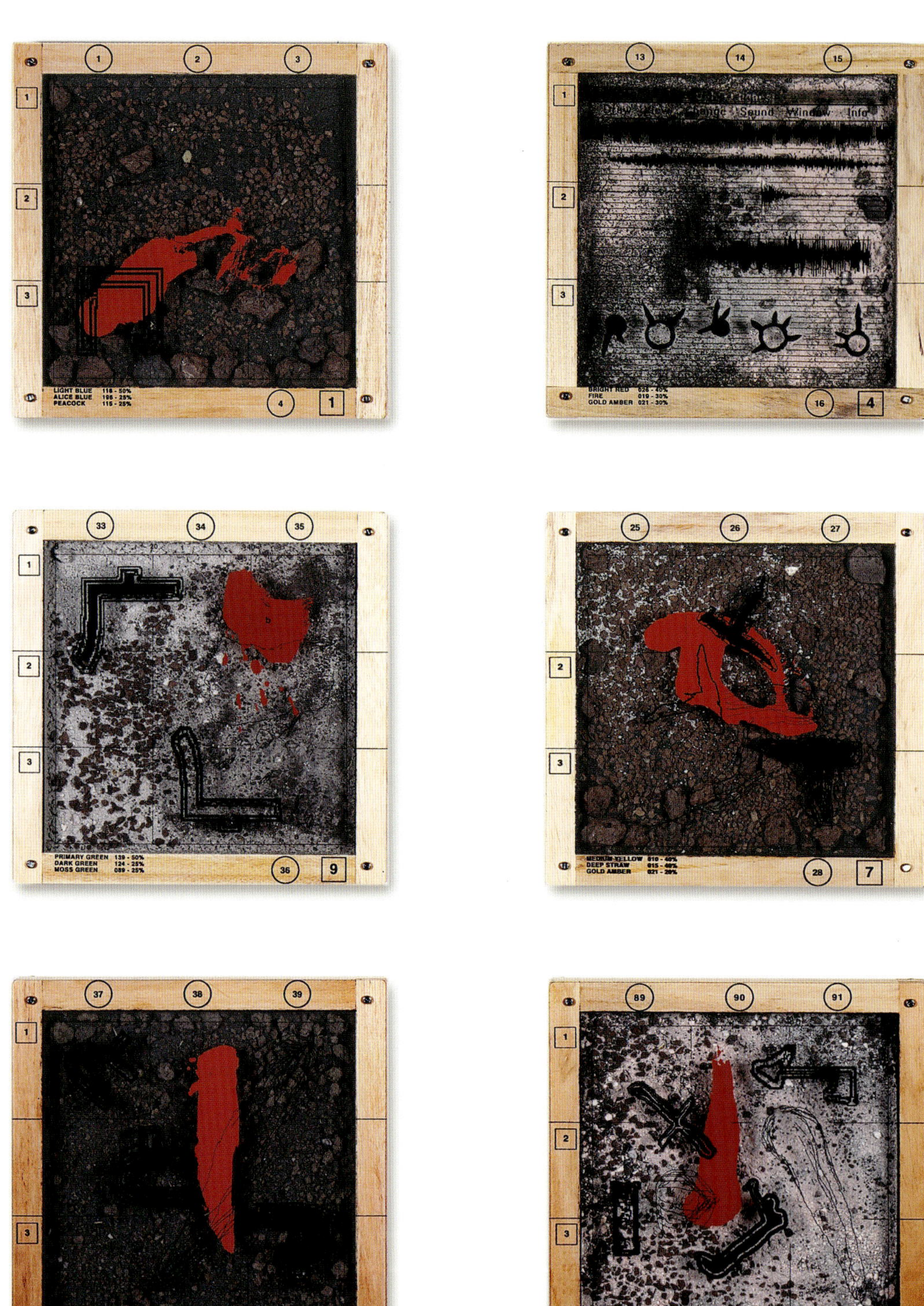

The Cry from the Earth, graphic score vitrine, 1995
Silkscreen print, Perspex, sand, volcanic ash, sulphur deposits
50 x 50 cm each module

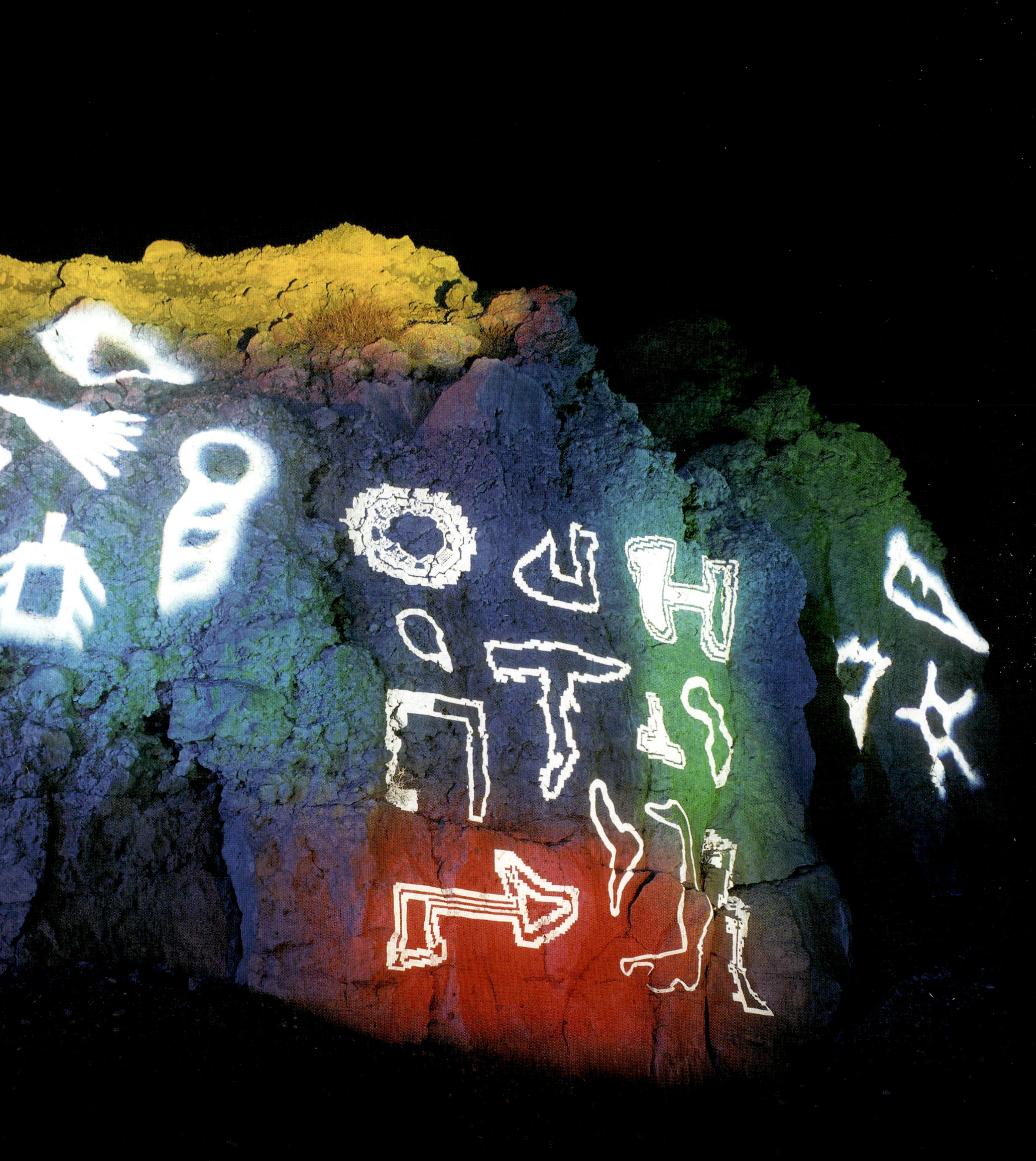

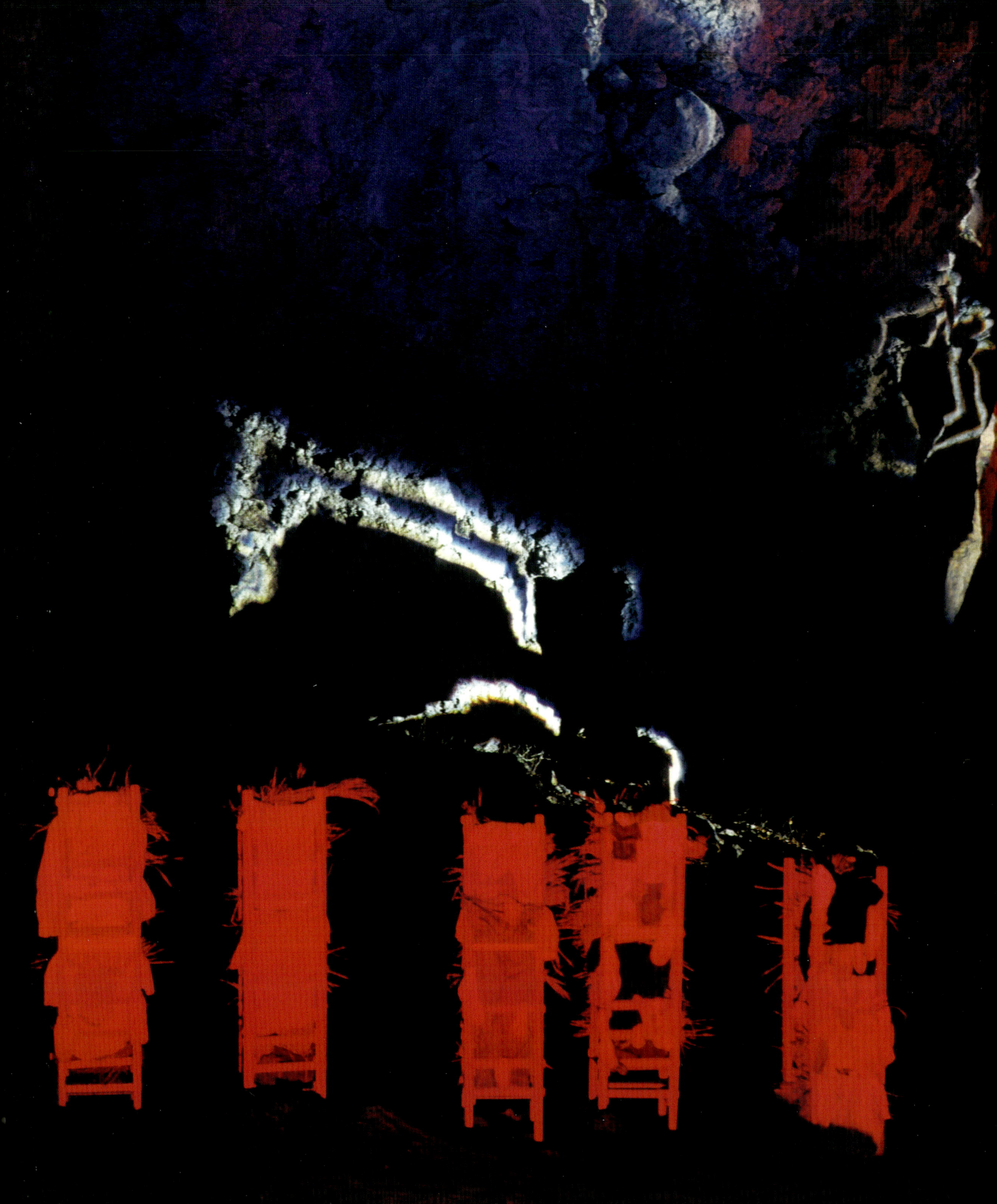

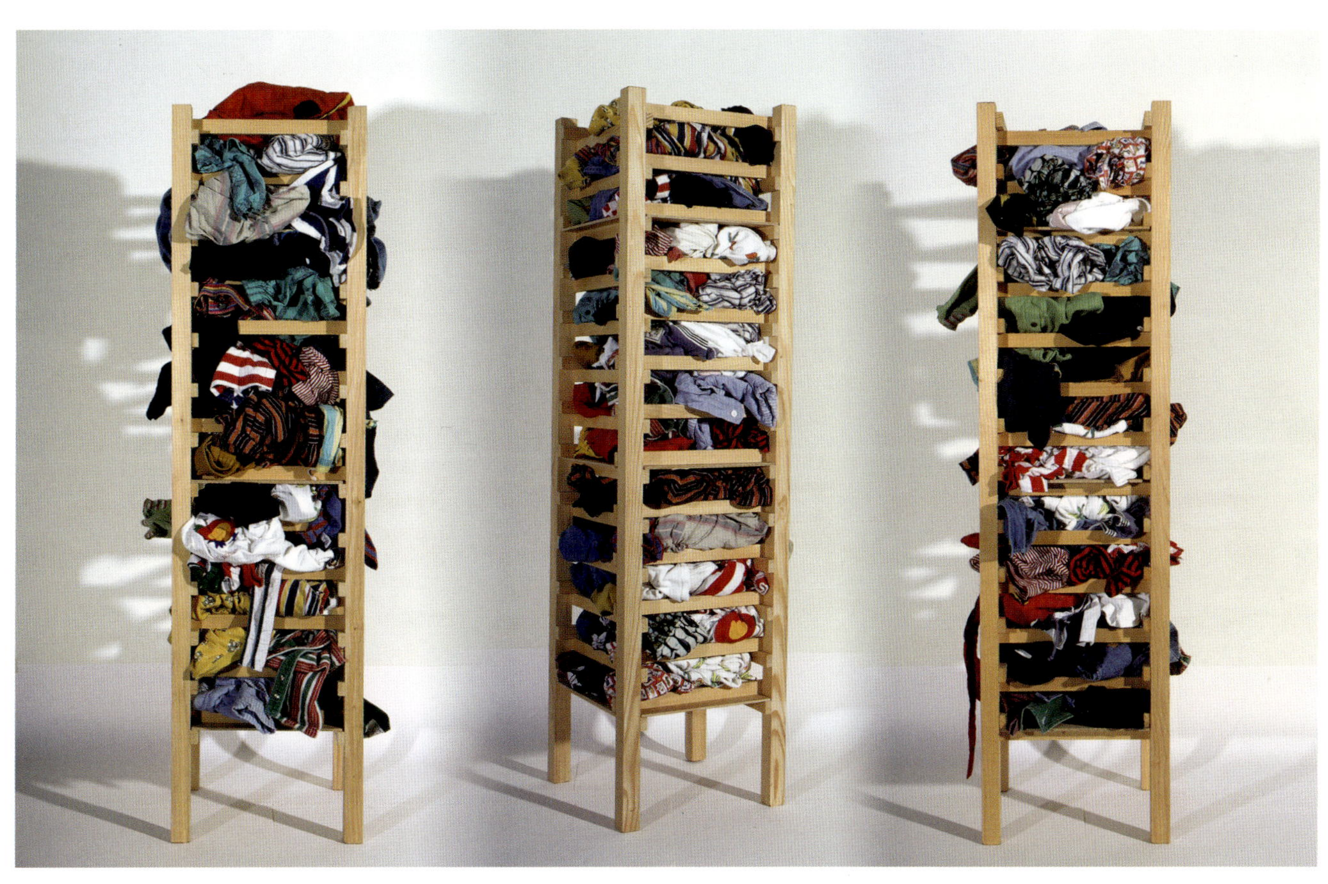

Mount Aso Totem, 1994
Wood, used clothes
170 x 50 x 50 cm each

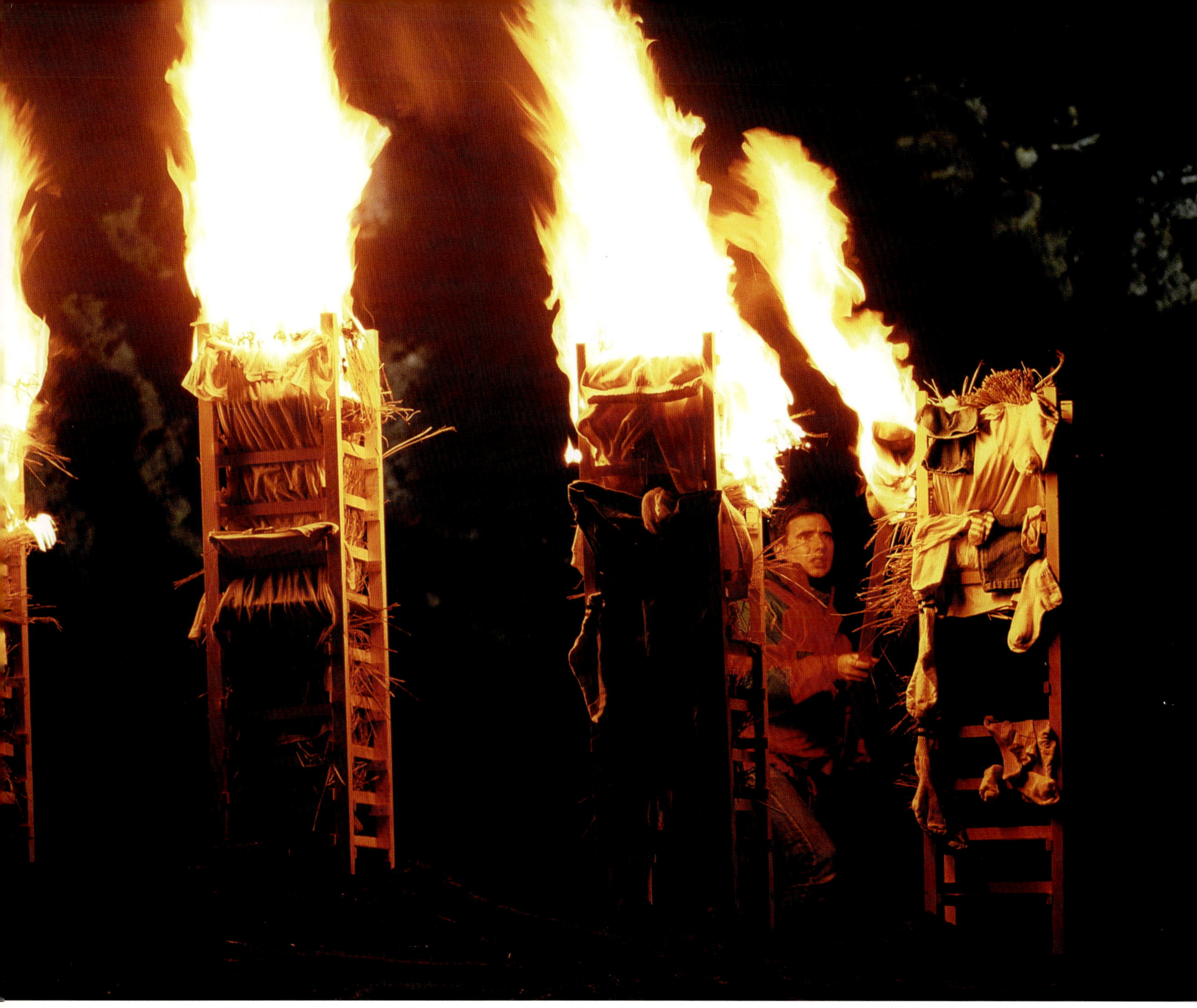

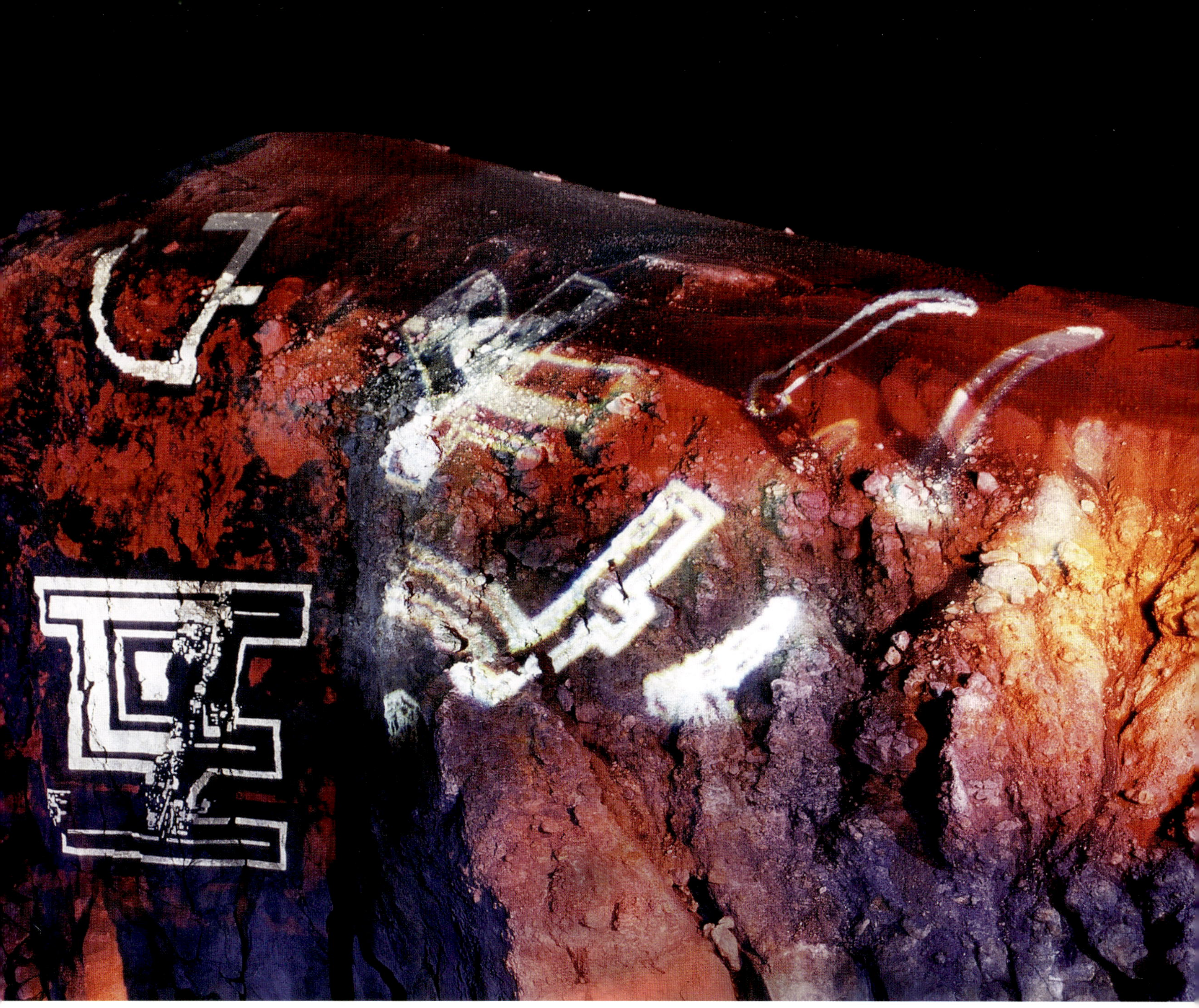

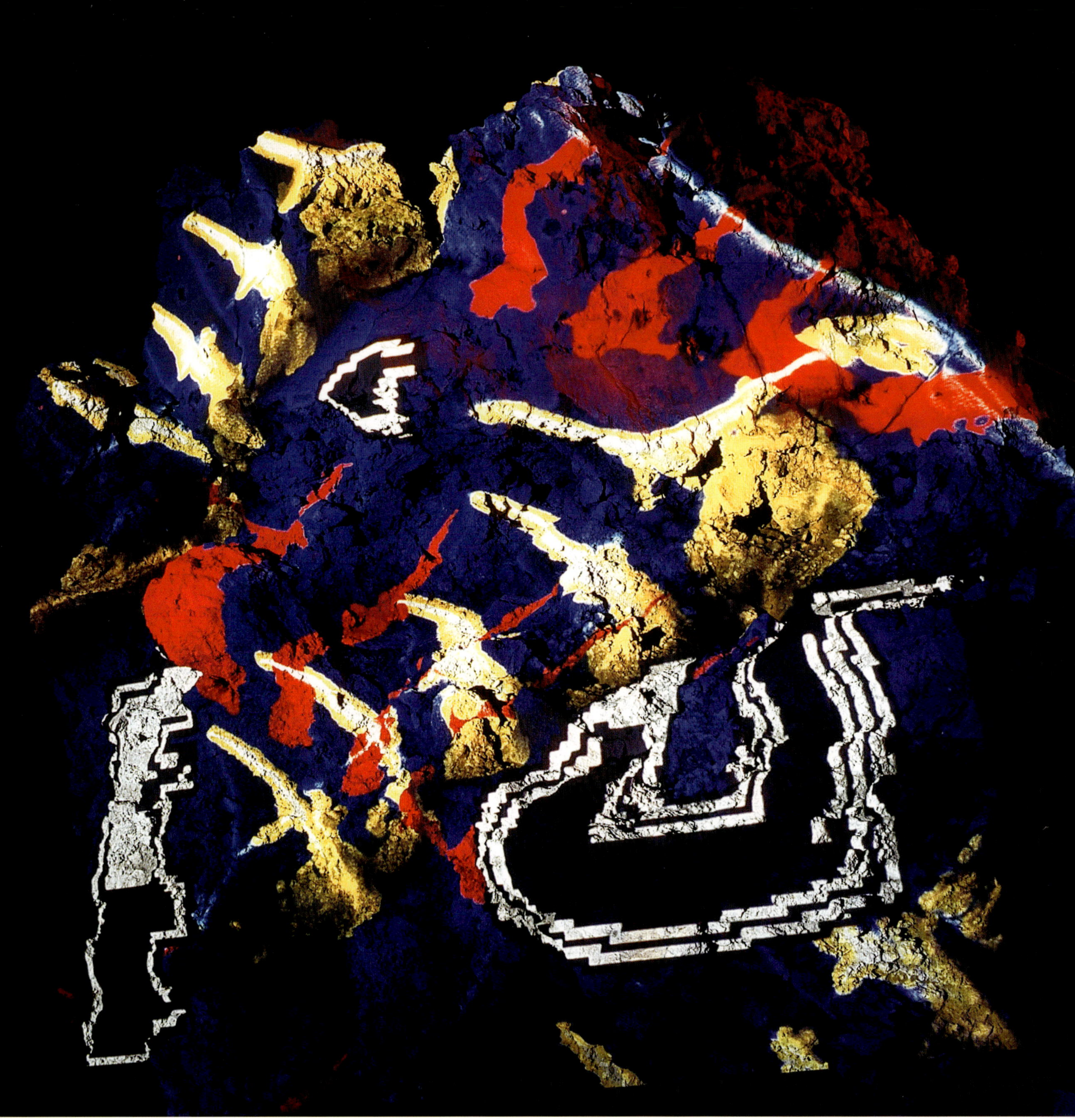

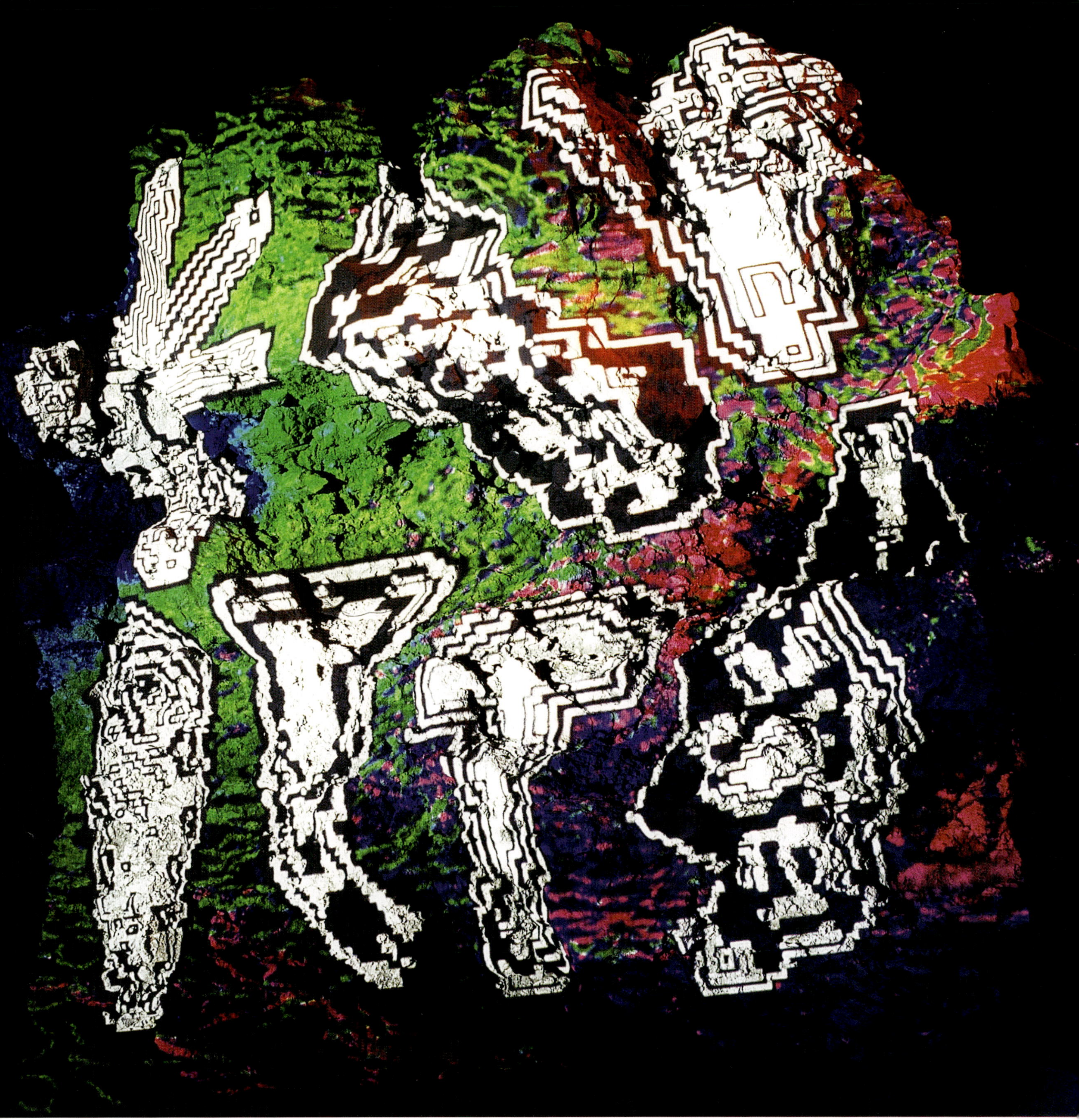

Menhir... Menhir onto which the strange birds have placed their signs. Signs that dislocate storms, divert the storm-cloud makers, quenching the fire of angles. And who show you the road to a friendly sky.

1995

WOVEN LIGHT

Cappadocia, Turkey

The unique geological, historic and cultural features of the eroded pillars and minaret-like forms in Göreme were the source of inspiration for the Light Works expedition to Cappadocia commissioned by the UCPA (French Union of Outdoor Sports Centres) to mark the 60th anniversary of the non-profit organisation. The soft volcanic deposits, dating back nine million years have been carved out to form houses, churches and monasteries by a succession of inhabitants across the Cappadocia region. The reminders of the layers of civilisations in the carvings and frescoes inside the churches and chapels date back to the ninth century.

The artists reflect on the symbiosis between nature and man, in the strange landscape chiselled by both their complementary energies. The geometric symbols the artists chose to project onto the edifices and inside the caves are taken from the Turkish kilim carpet motifs and tapestry woven over centuries to reflect ancient cults and ancestral beliefs. Themes of life, birth, marriage and fertility; spiritual life and happiness; love and unison; and death, passed on across generations forming the history and layers of the Anatolian civilisations that have inhabited the troglodyte villages find themselves re-inscribed temporarily onto the surface and crevices of the dwellings.

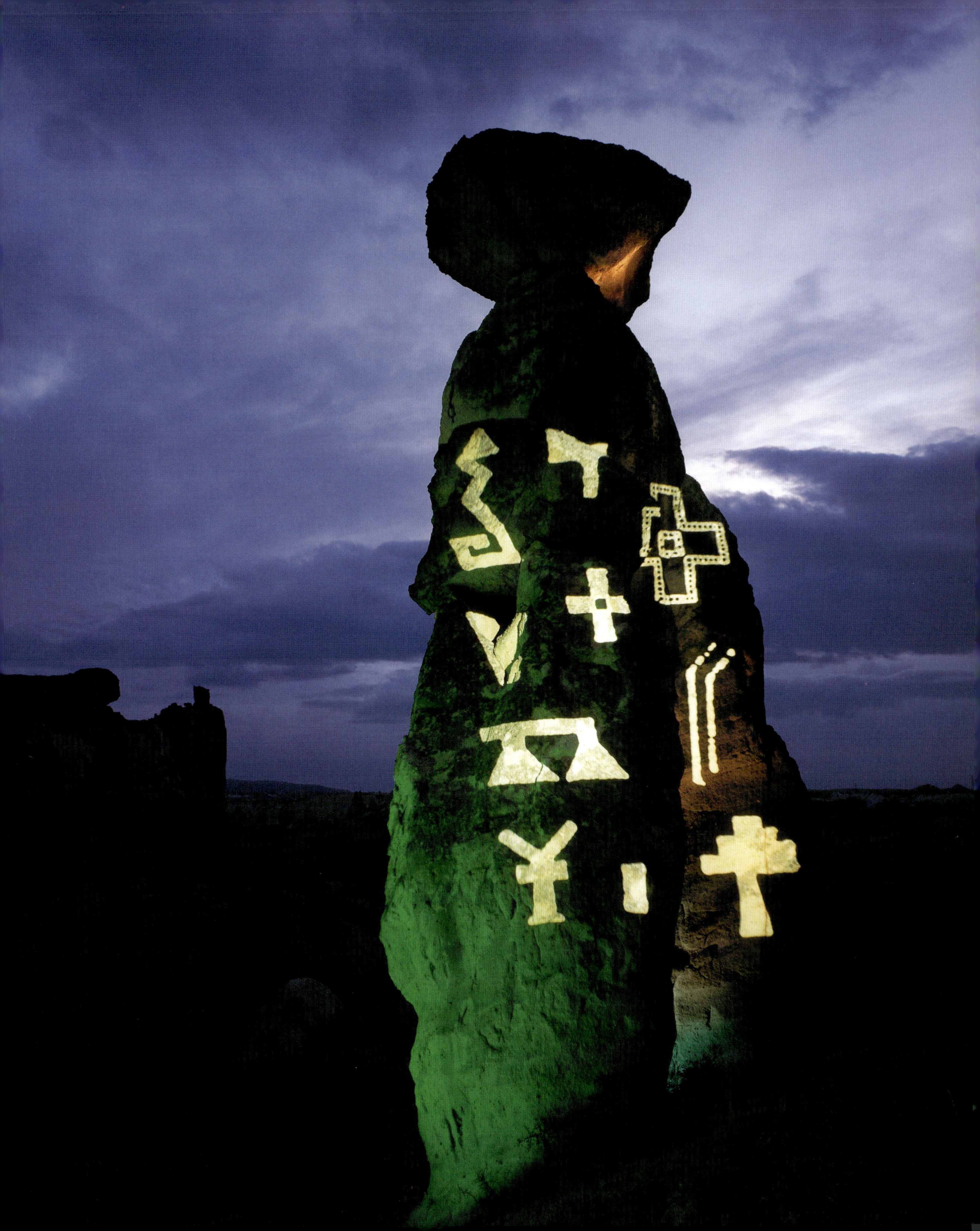

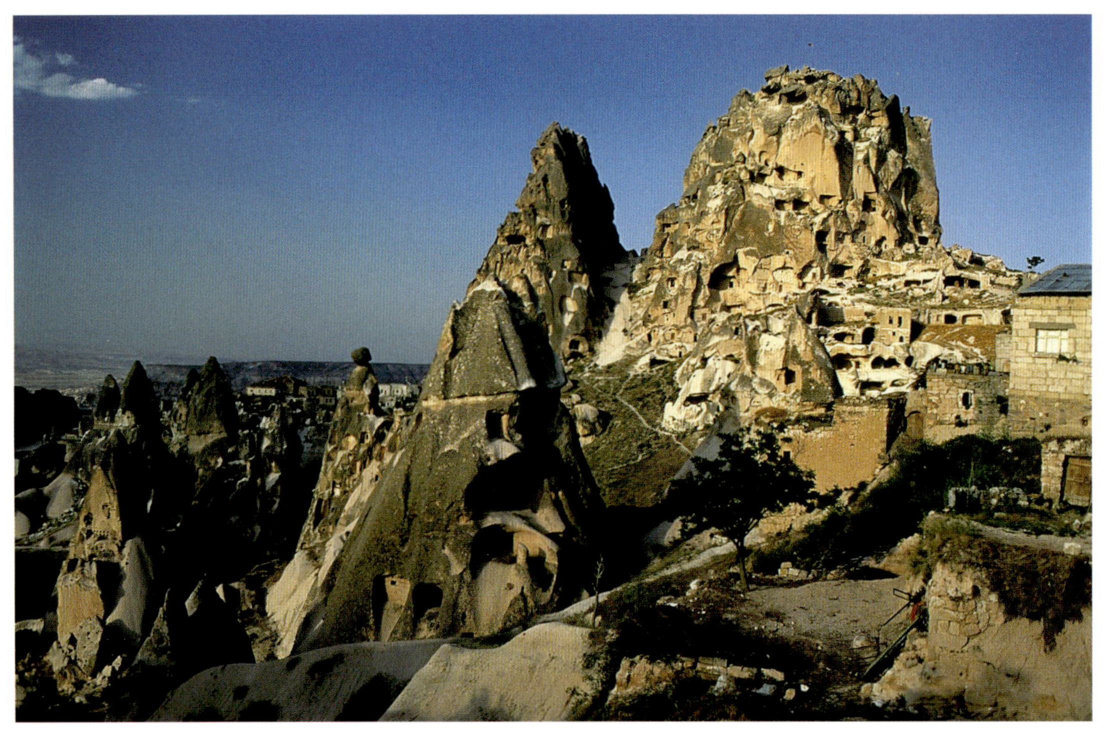

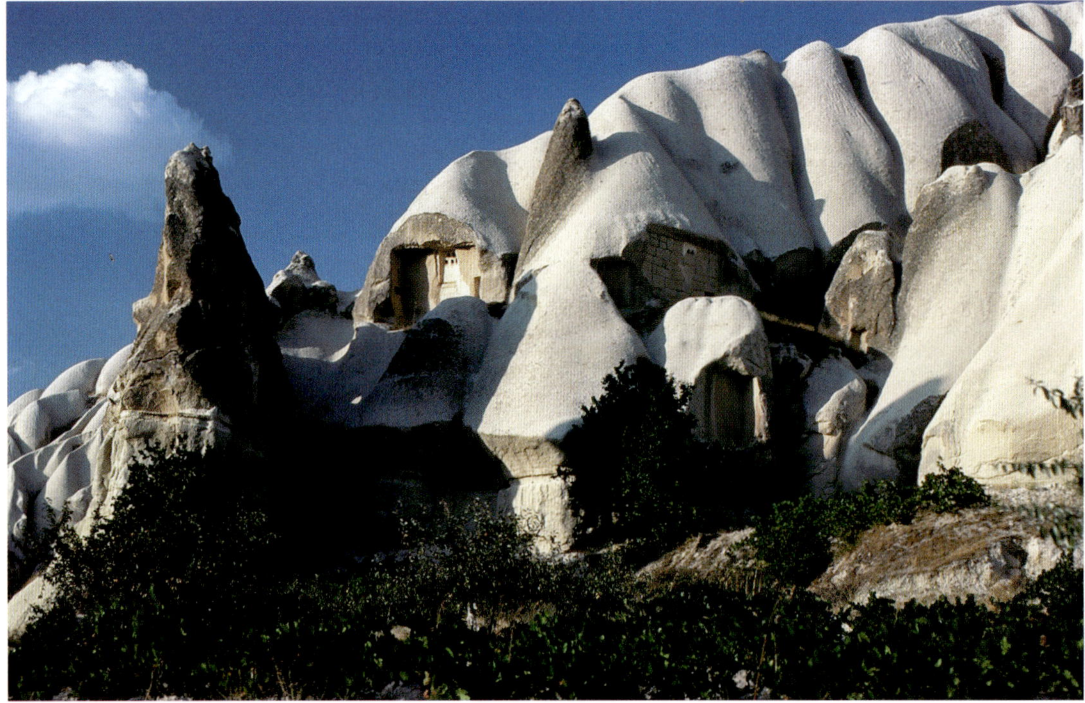

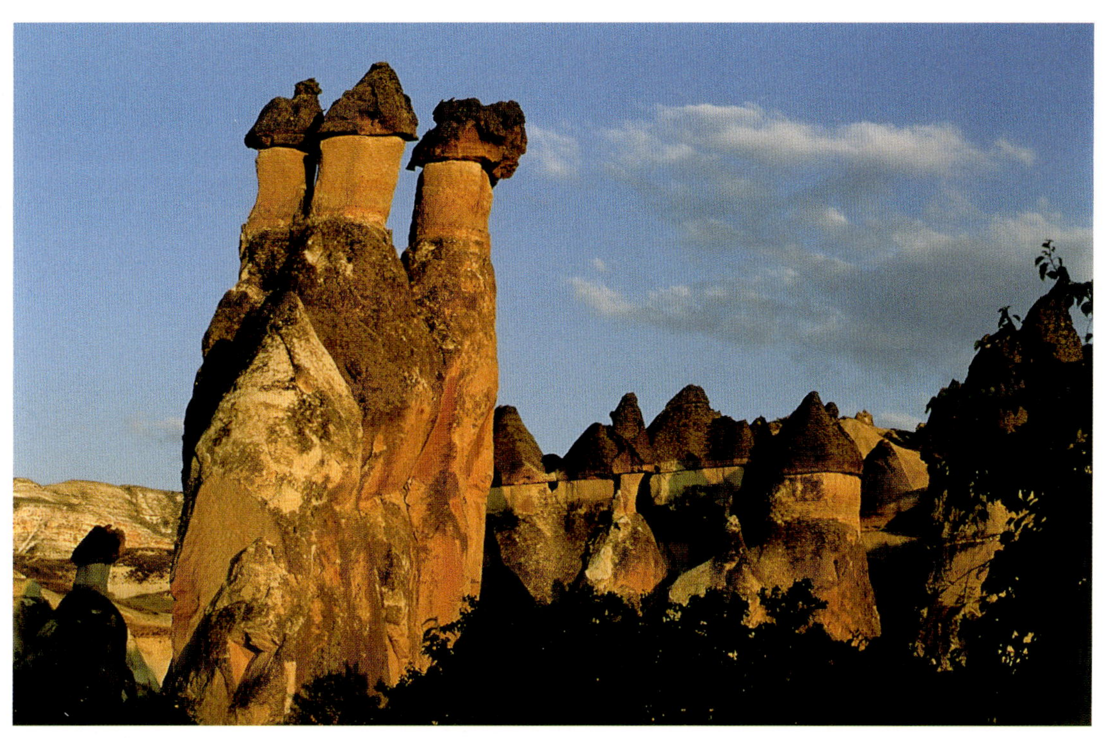

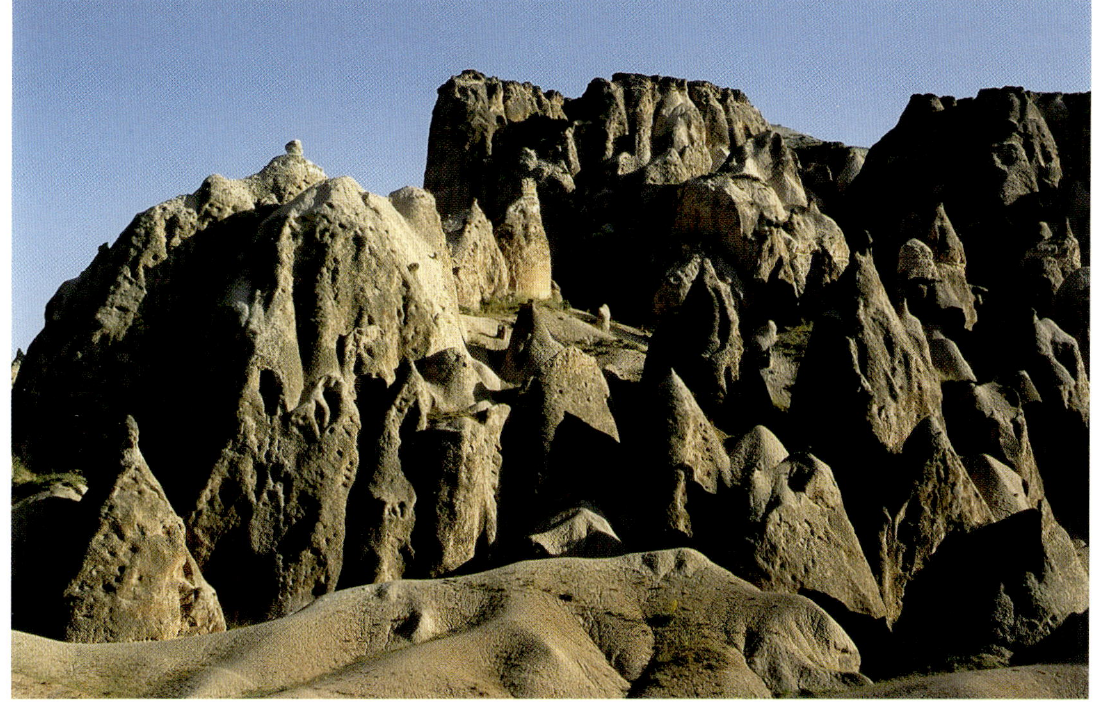

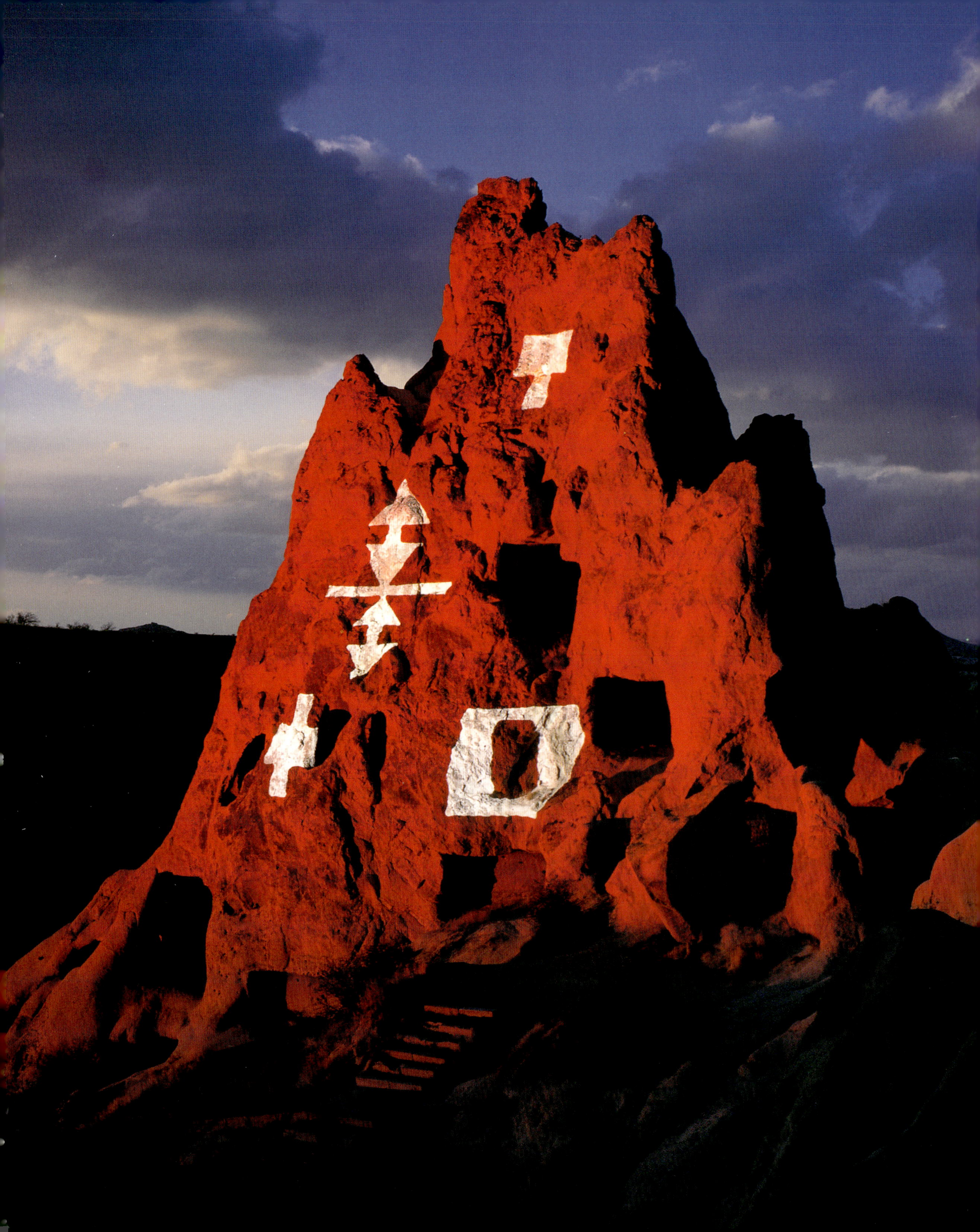

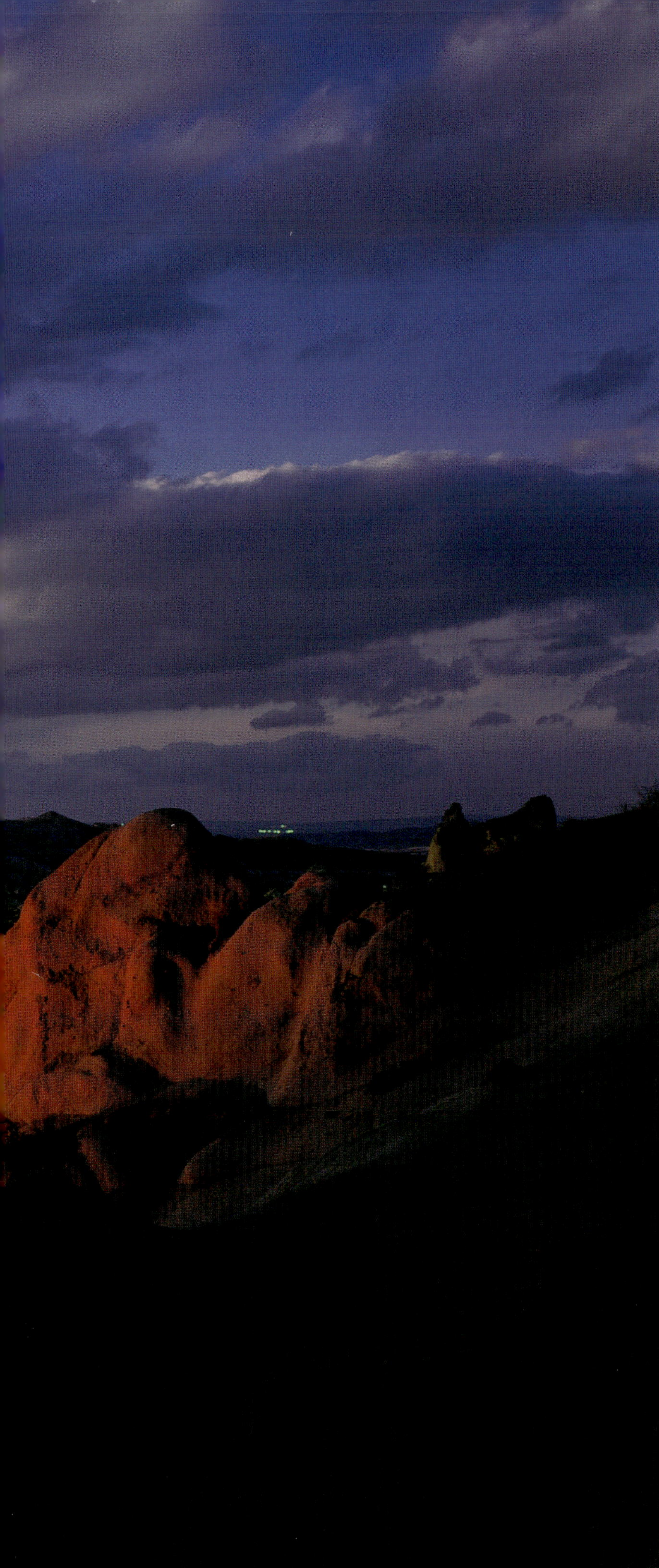

Red elevation to conjure Black from the sky. Don't be frightened of the dark caves: they are there to light the way, to help you cross the evening's rooms and discover the secret threshold of Cappadocia.

The Nunnery, Goreme

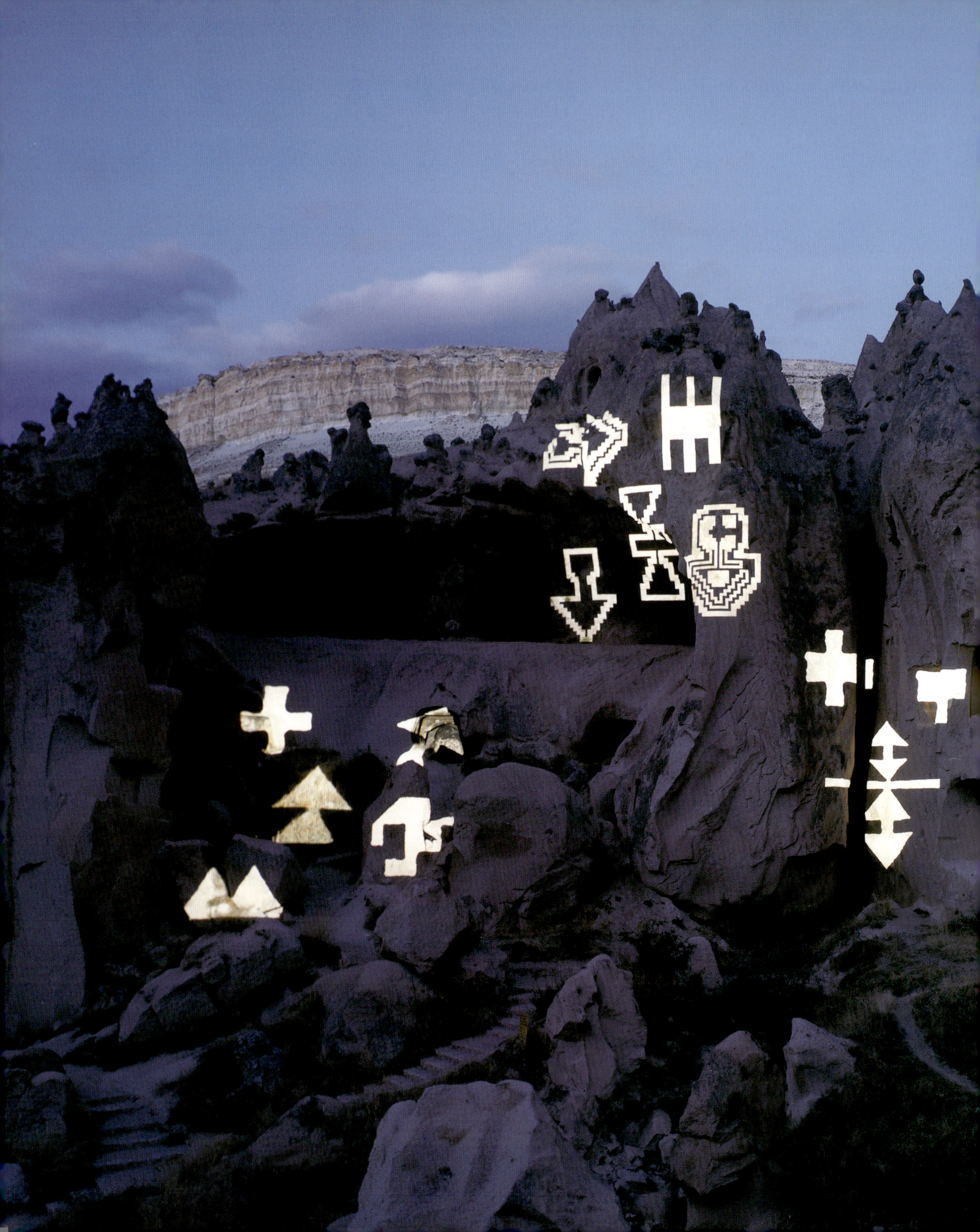

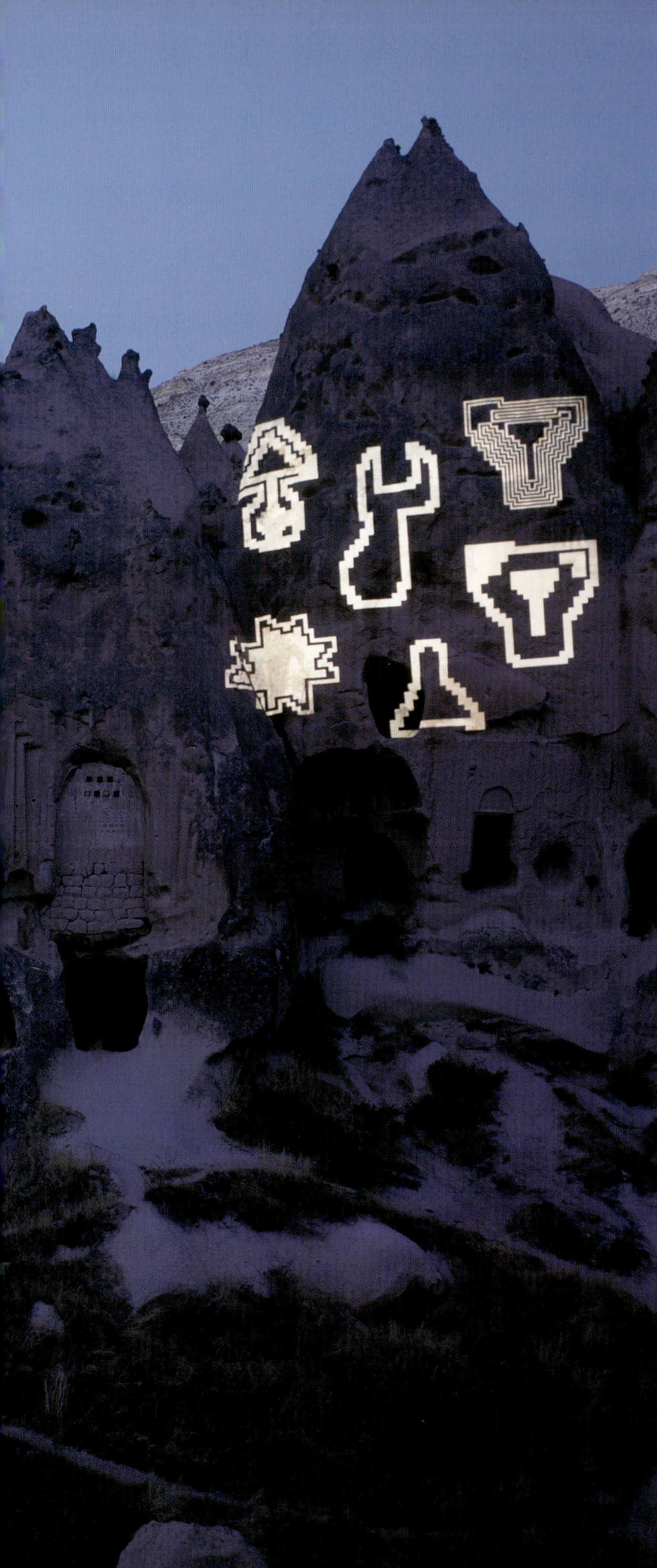

On the walls of the palaces crenellated with watchmen, dreams have arranged their familiar figures: mirrors of the future, thoughtful dragons, meanders, shadows' shell. With lips blue with dreams, just above, stammering dawn.

Zelve Valley, Avanos

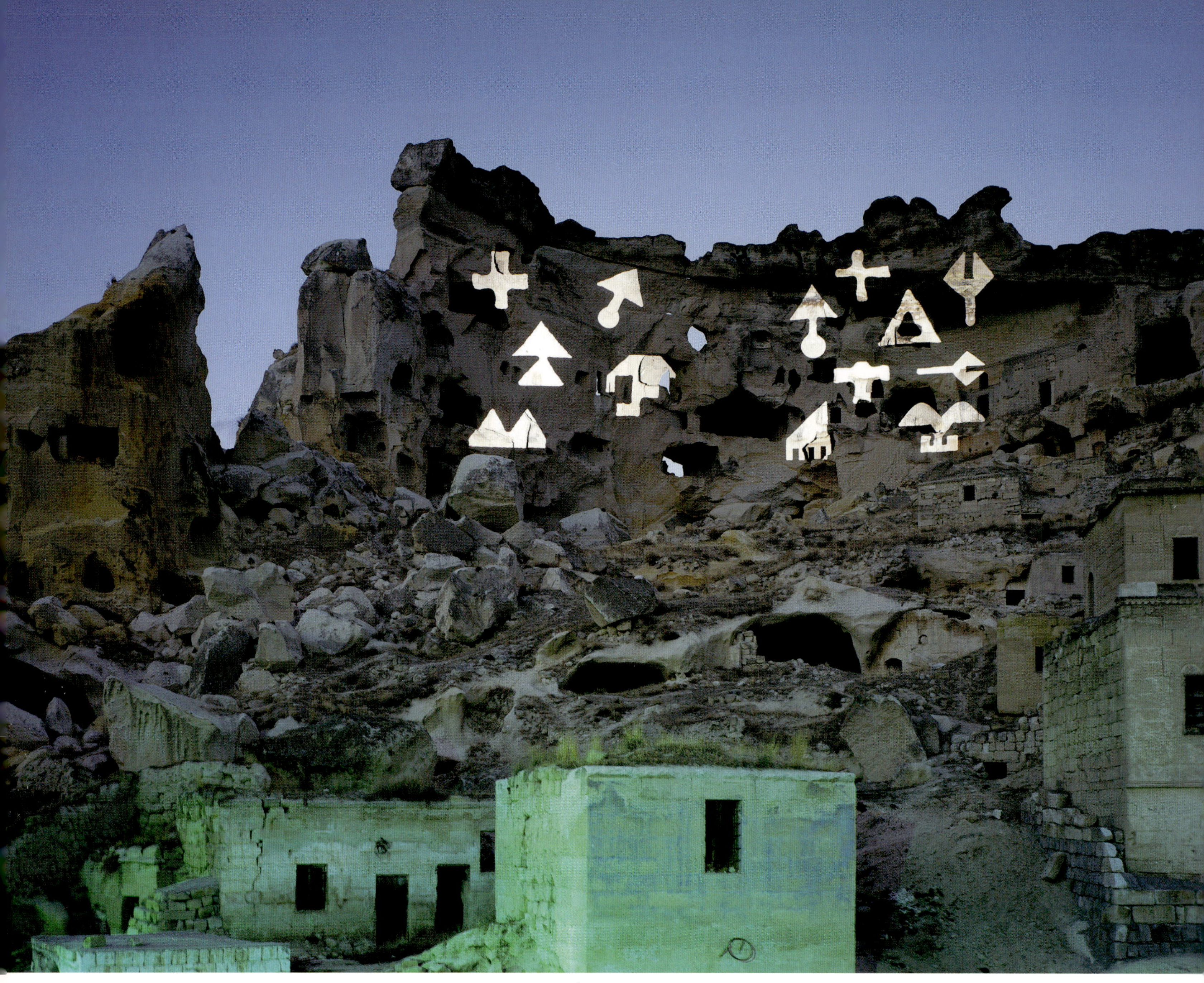

Signs on the cliffs, reefs emerged from Time. But what's happened to the shore? Where's the sea of yesteryear? And who, fairy, or mermaid, has sown, drawn these corals of light?

THE CLIFFS OF OLD CAVUSIN, AVANOS

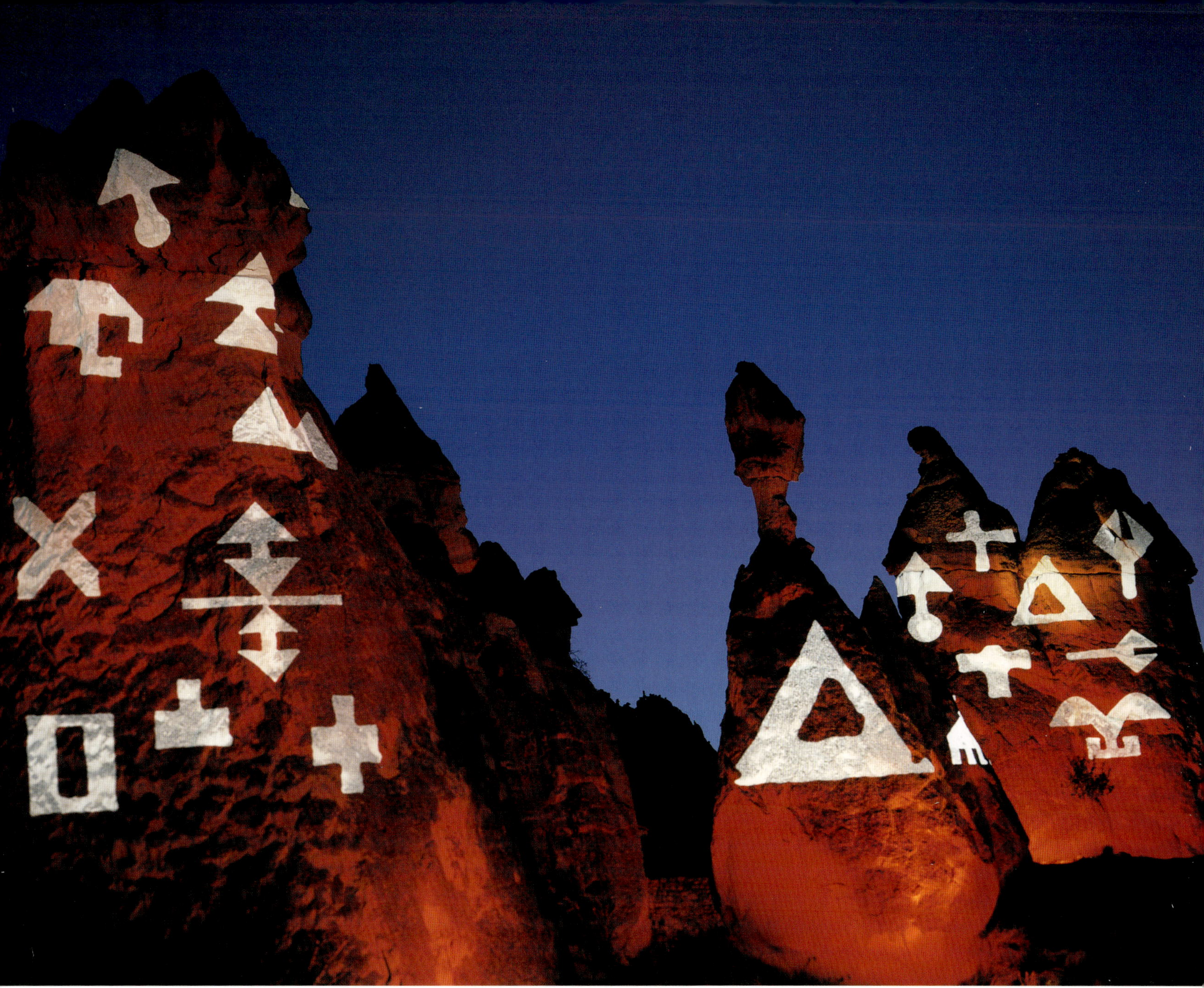

Here doors from elsewhere that probably lead to the centre of Earth. A doorkeeper will meet you and lead you. But you have to whisper into his ear: White triangle shall be the light of the shadow.

Jacques Lacarrière

Avanos Valley

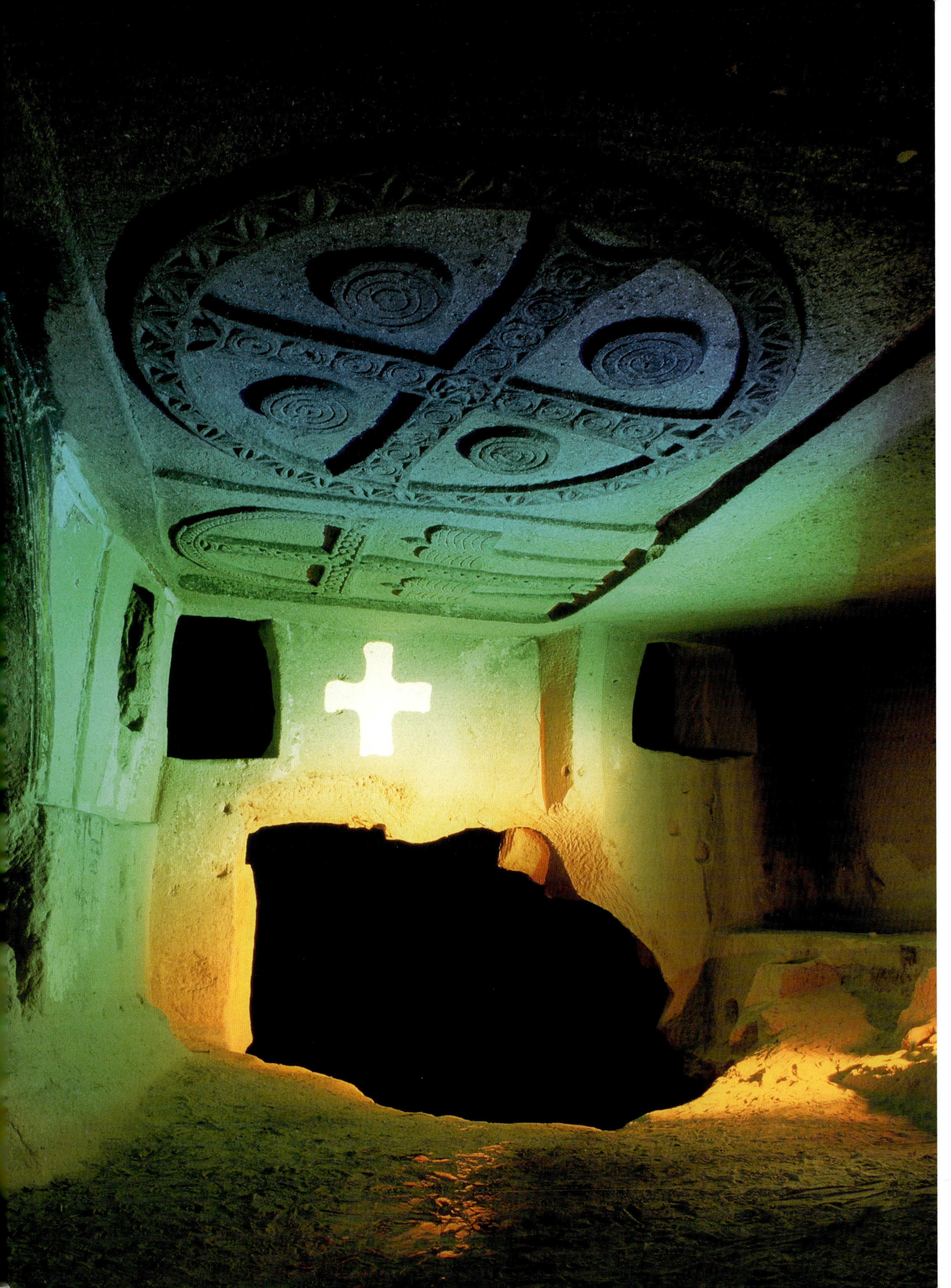

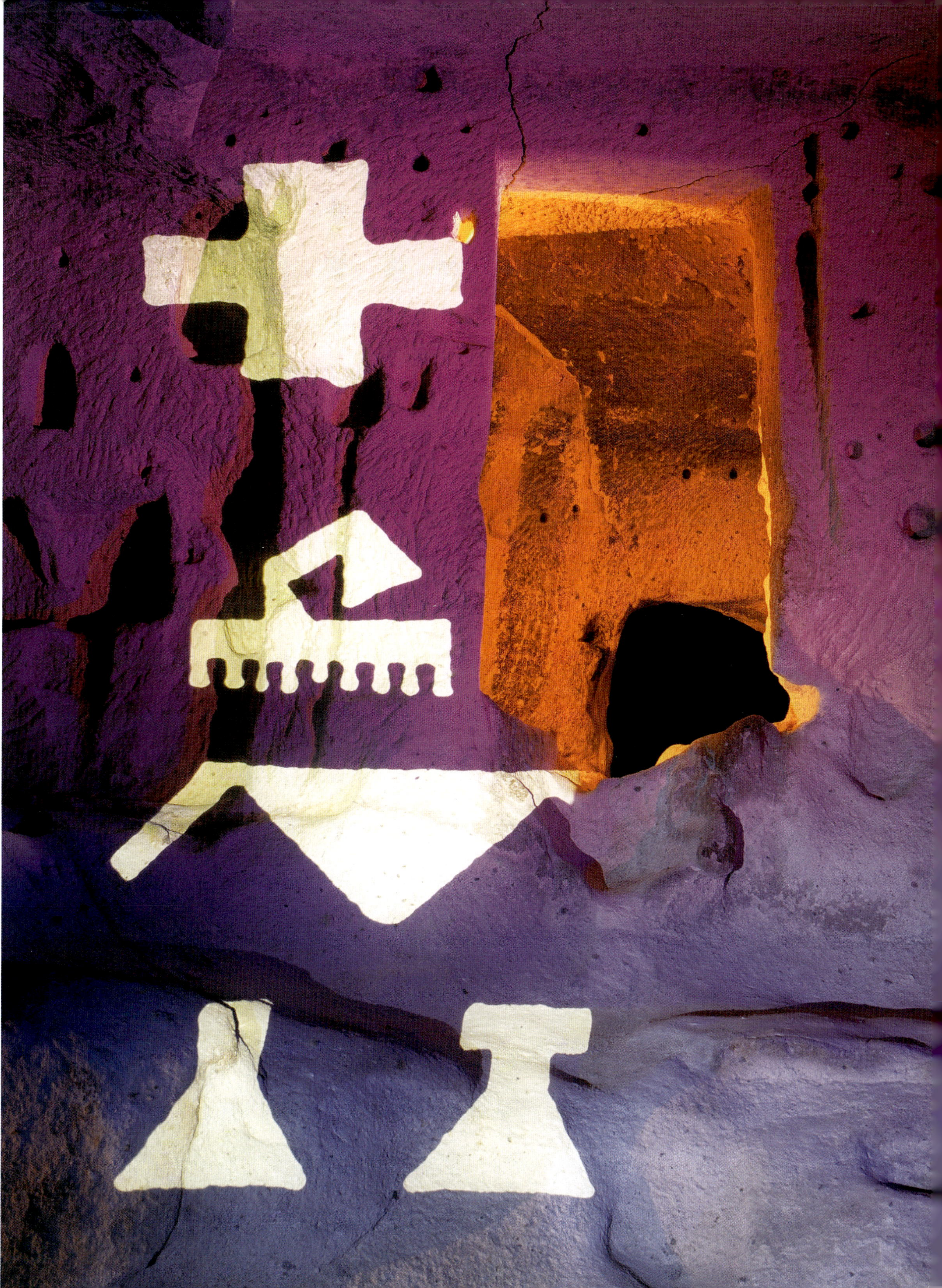

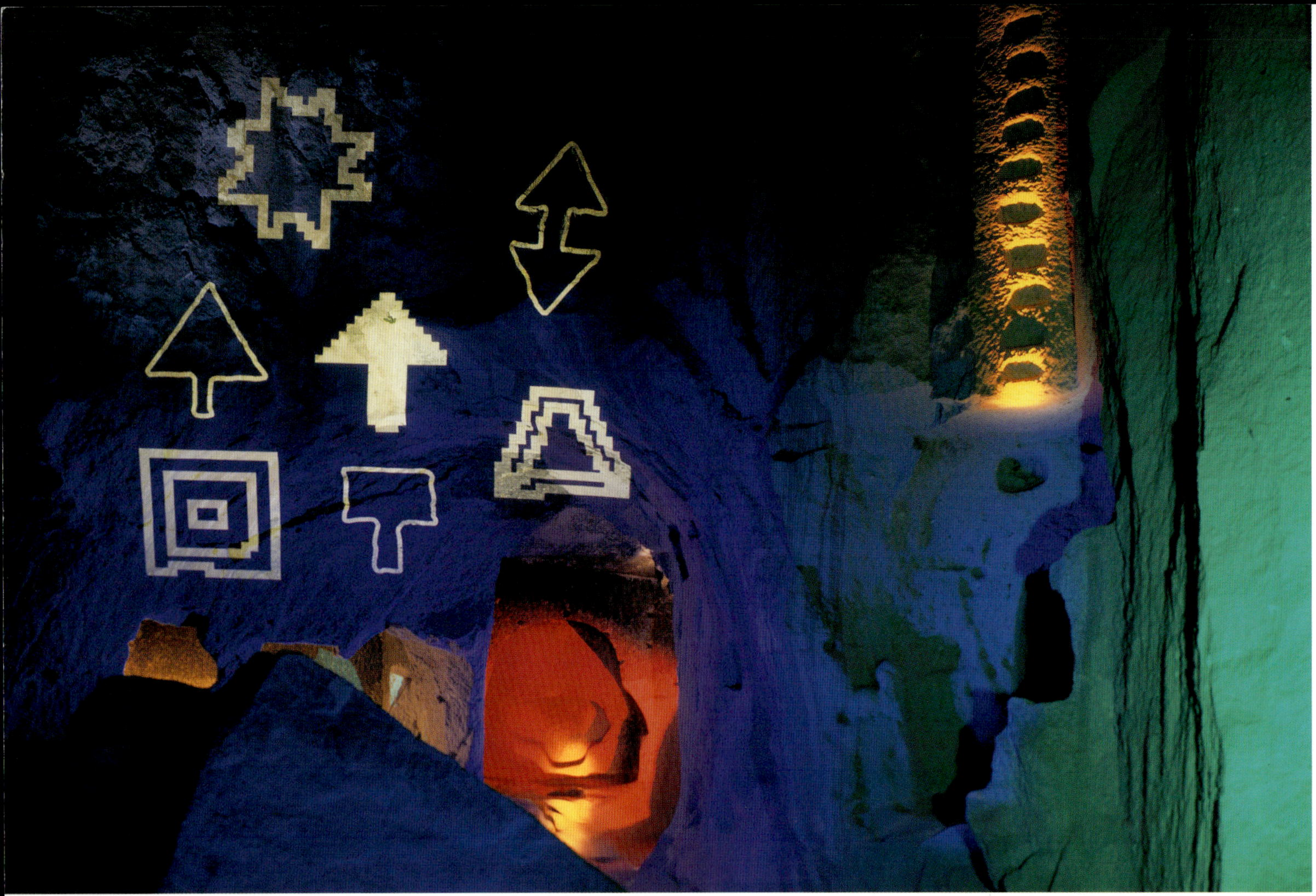

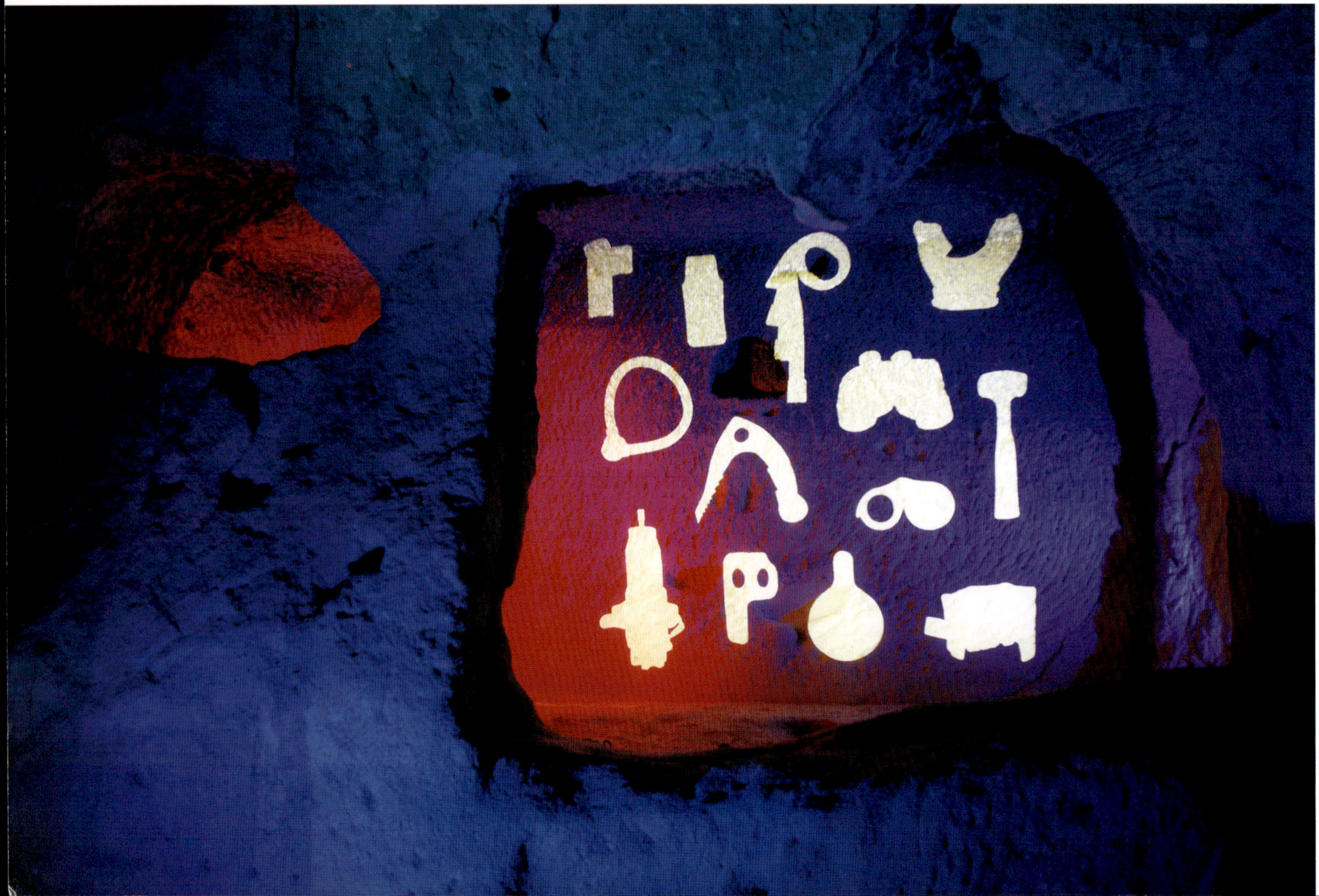

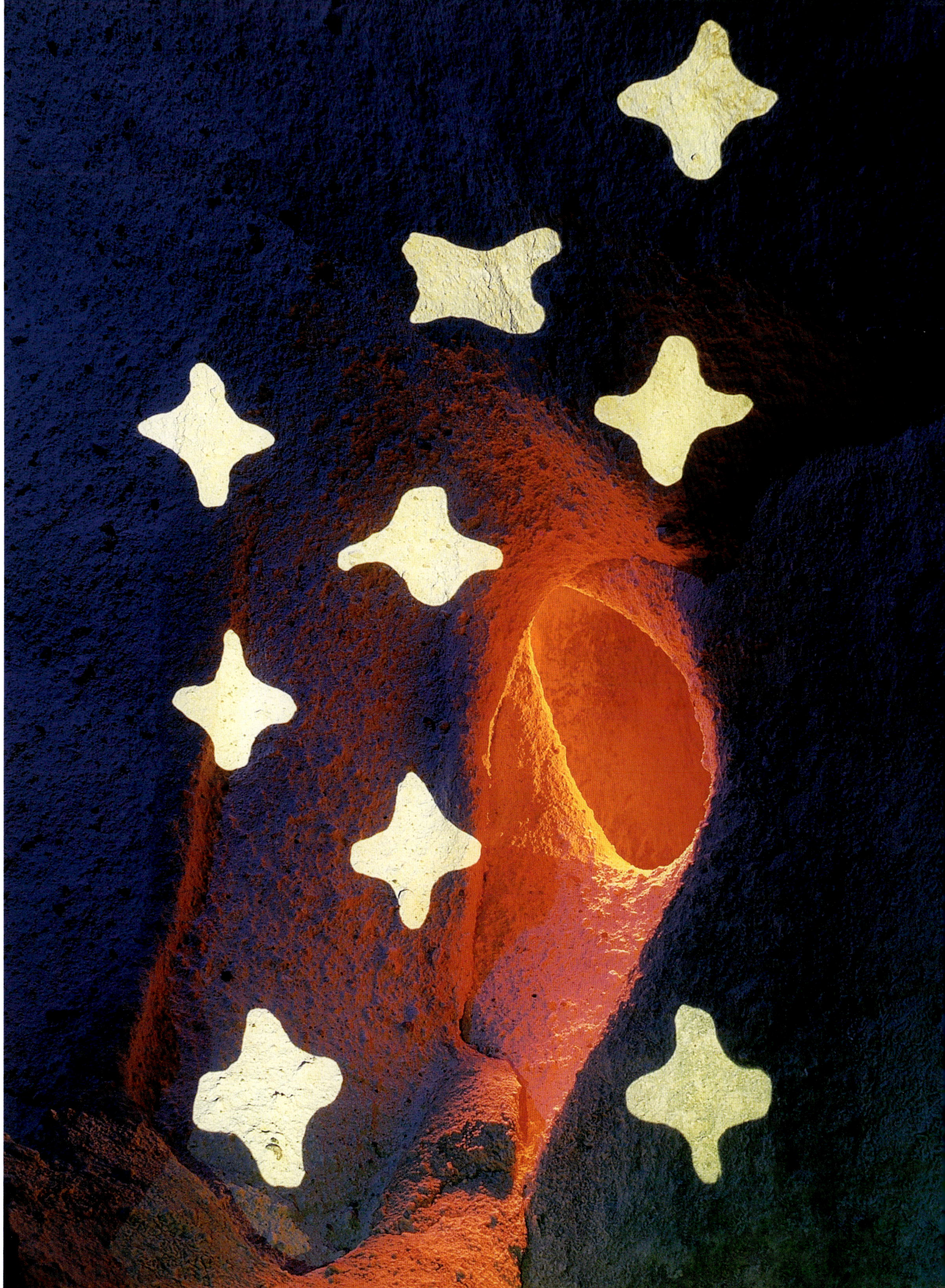

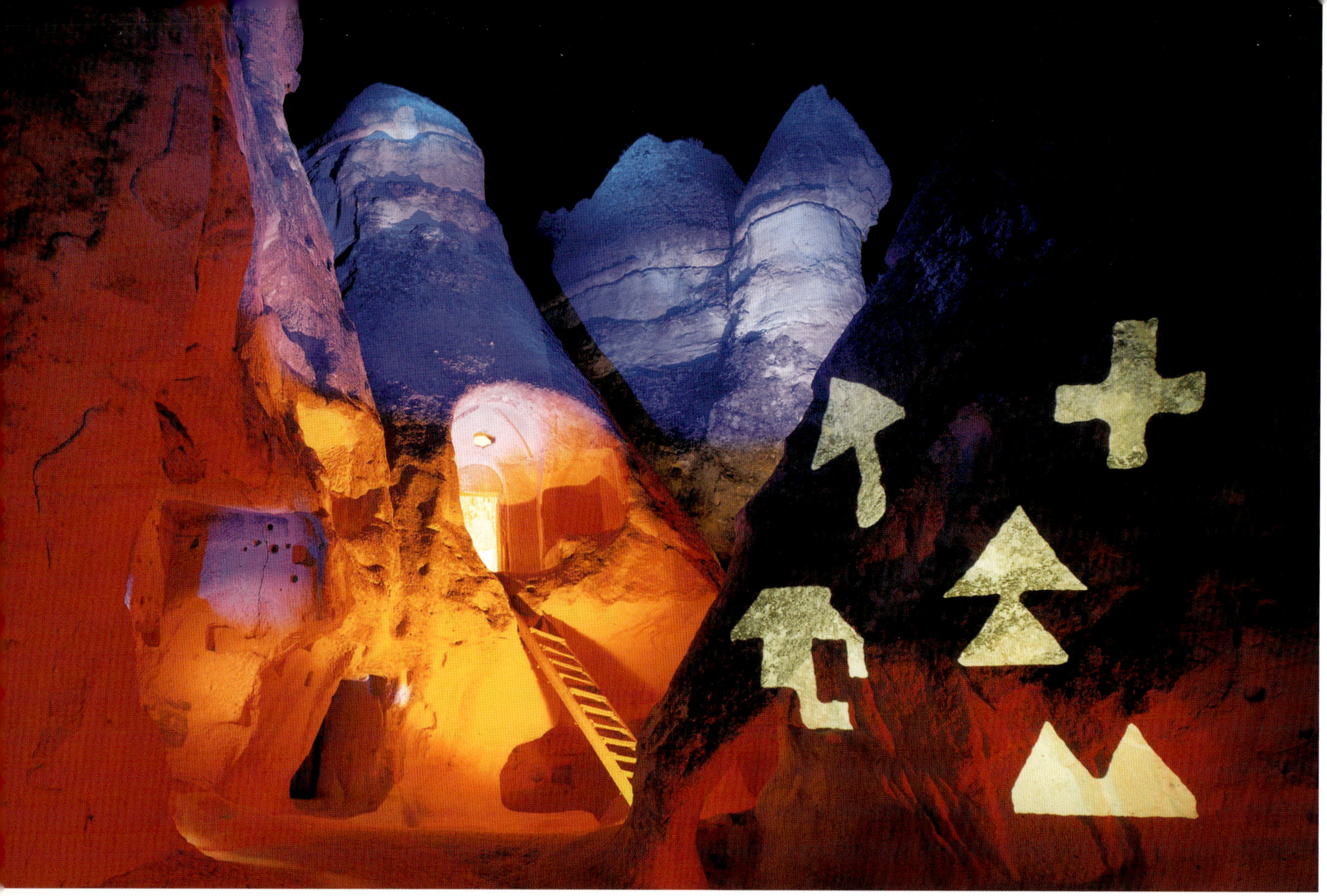

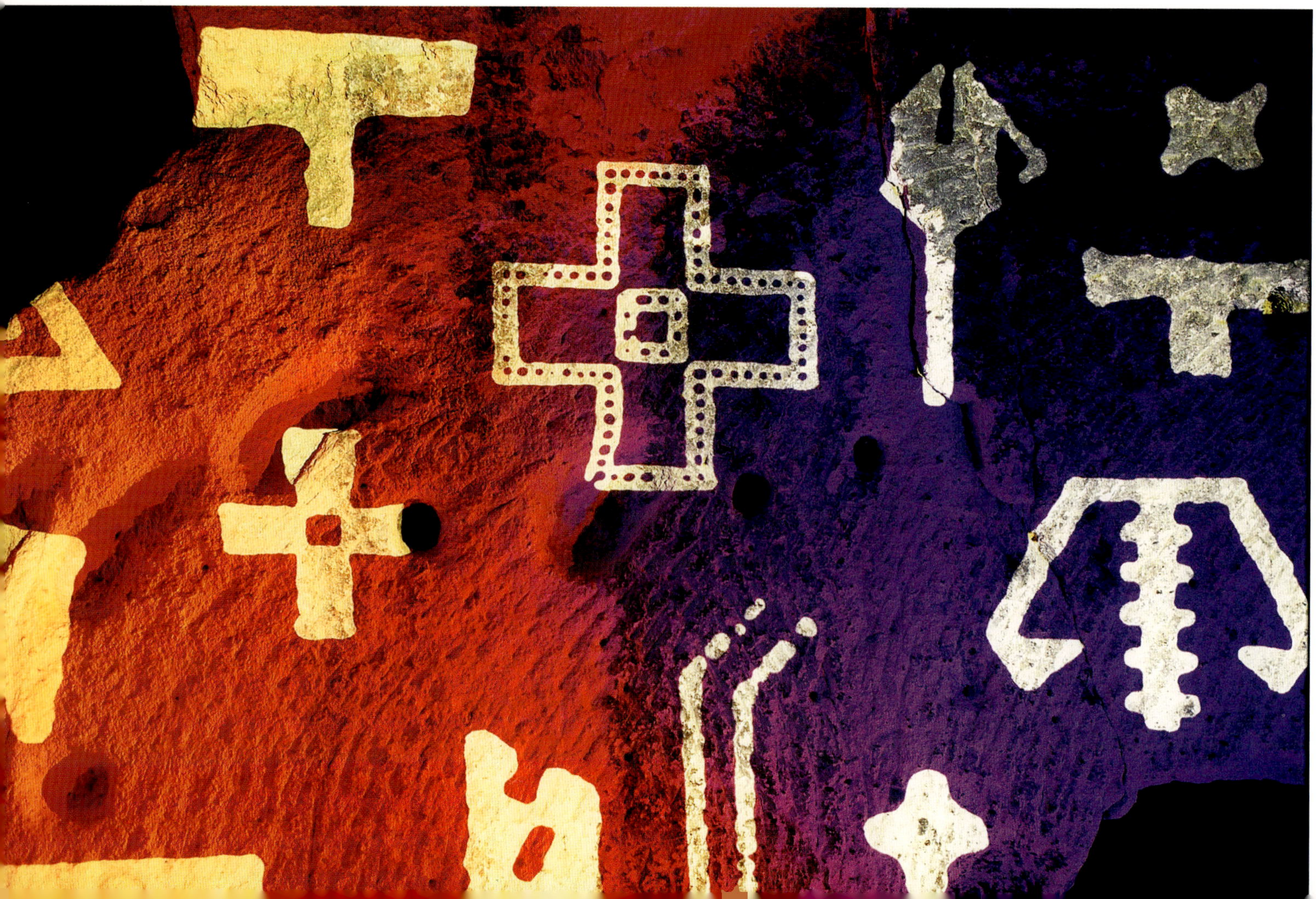

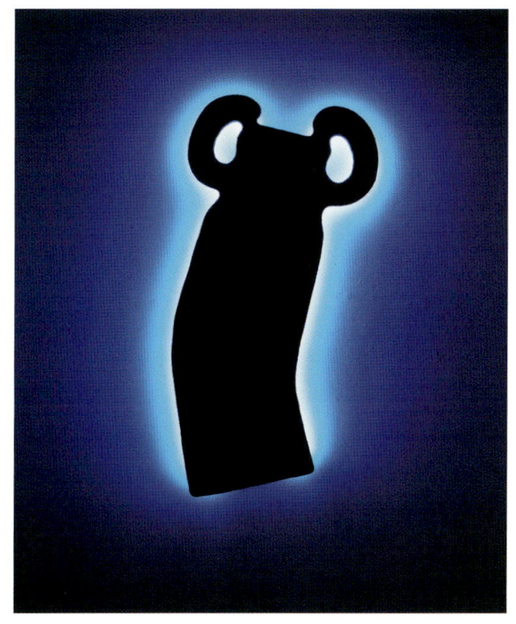

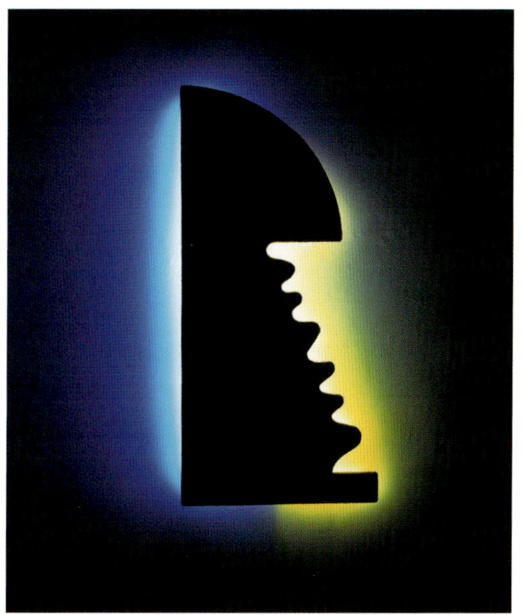

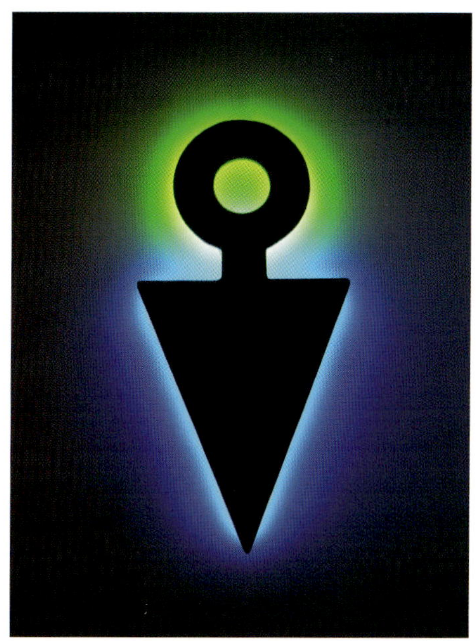

XIII Madrépora del tiempo sumergido, P.N., 1994
Wood, earth, volcanic ash, minerals, neon, speakers
122 x 50 x 9 cm

XXVI Torre sombrera, discussion de nieve, P.N., 1993
Wood, earth, volcanic ash, minerals, neon
122 x 56 x 7 cm

Túnica triangular, polen de piedra, P.N., 1993
Wood, earth, volcanic ash, minerals, neon
122 x 60 x 7 cm

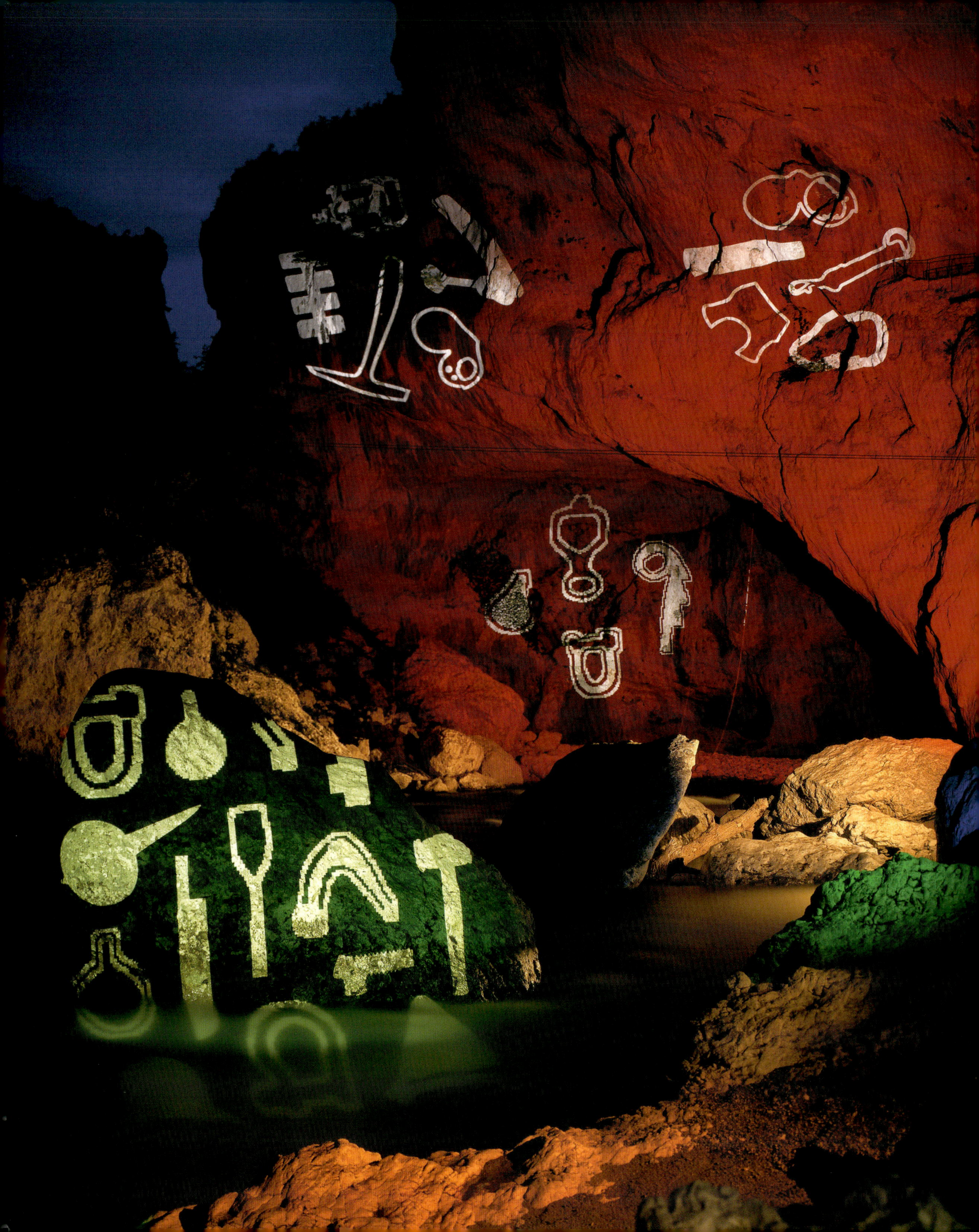

PATHS OF LIGHT

1995

Gorges du Verdon, France

Considered to be one of Europe's most beautiful river valleys, the Gorges du Verdon in southeastern France stretches 25 kilometres with steep cliffs of up to 700 metres high. The *Paths of Light* created by Jorge Orta was commissioned by the UCPA (French Union of Outdoor Sports Centres) to mark the sixtieth anniversary of the non-profit organisation. The images and symbols derived from extensive research into the UCPA archives were projected onto the crevices and pools of startling 'verdon' turquoise-green waters, after which the limestone canyon has been named.

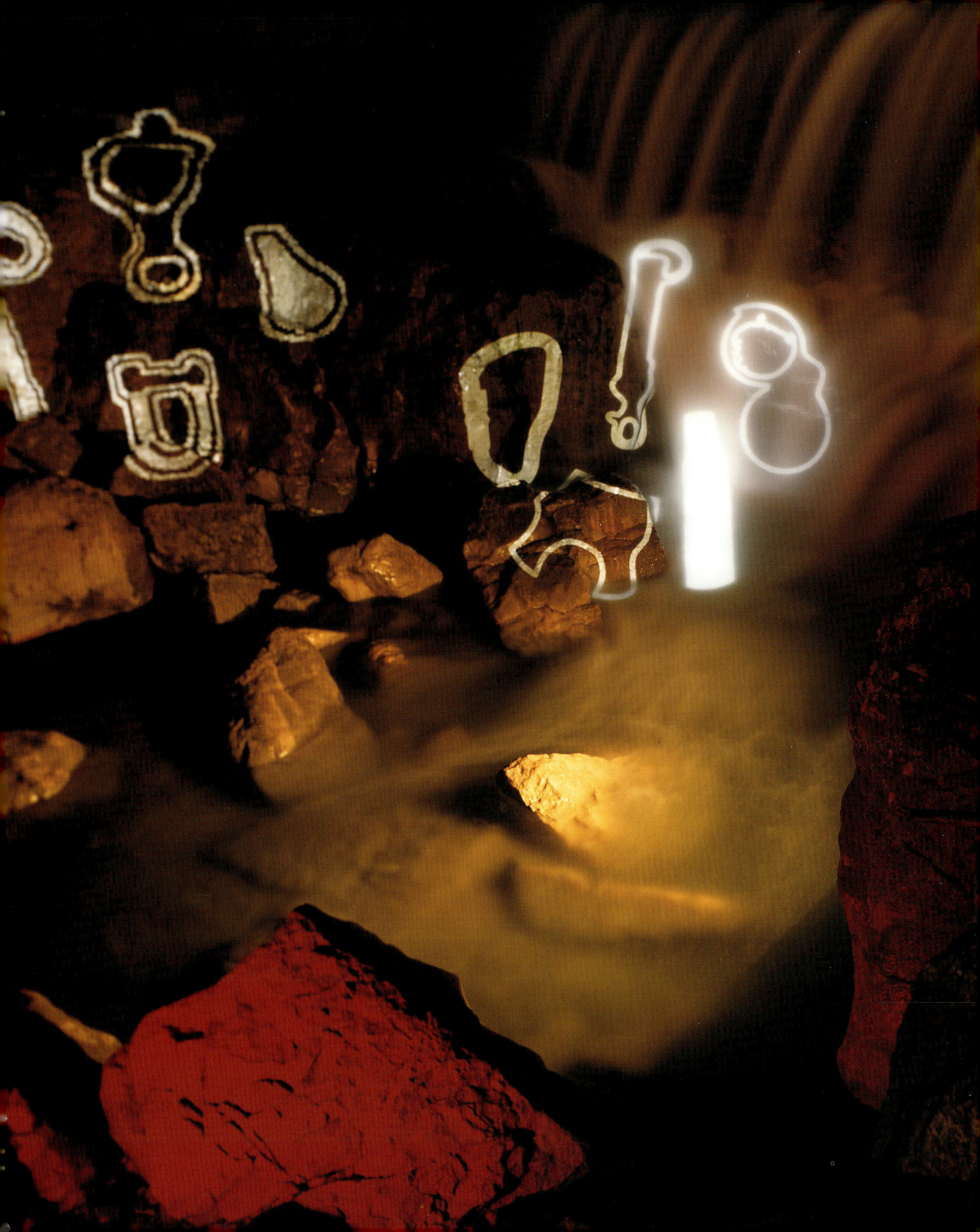

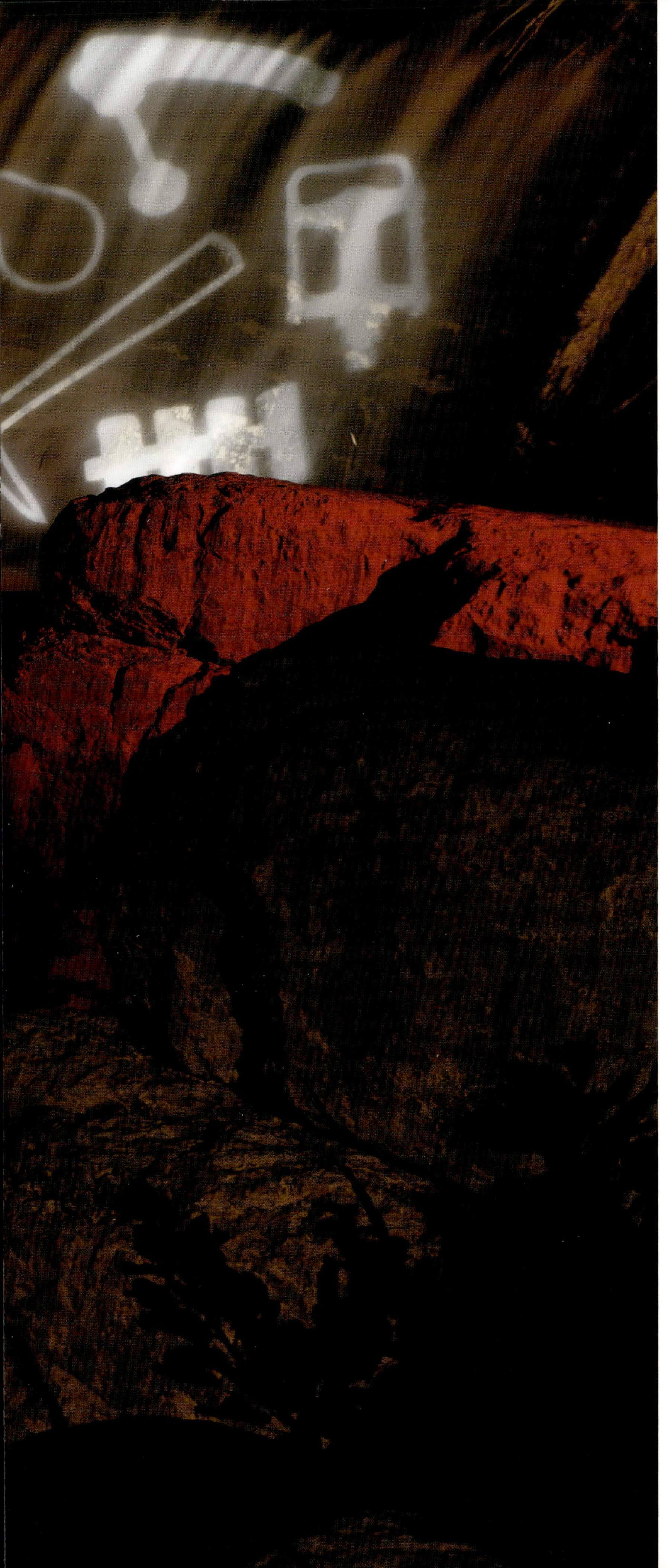

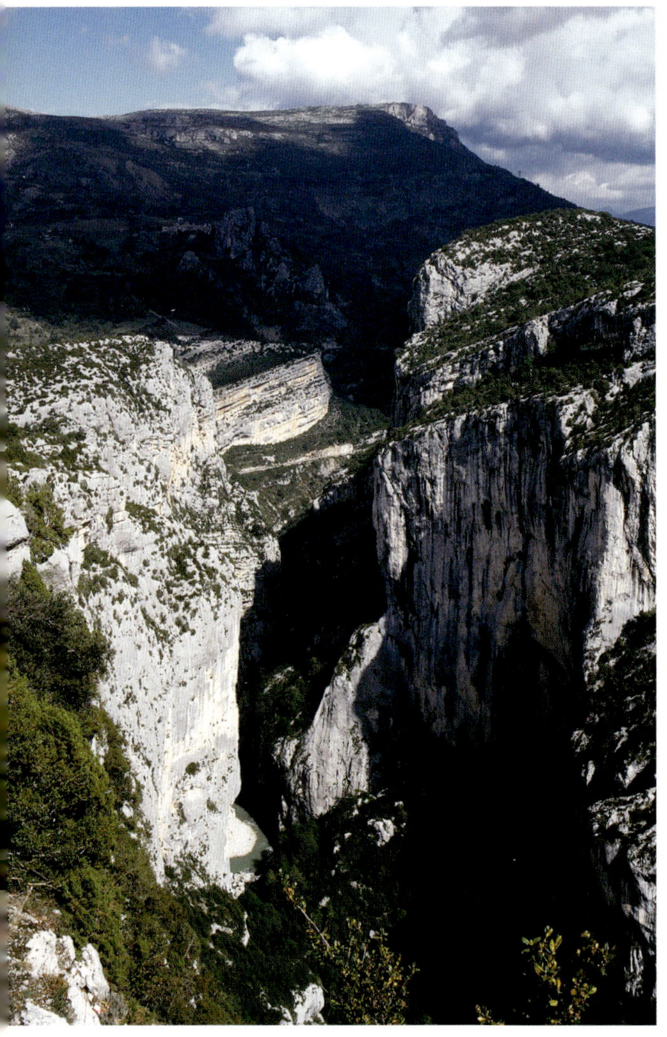

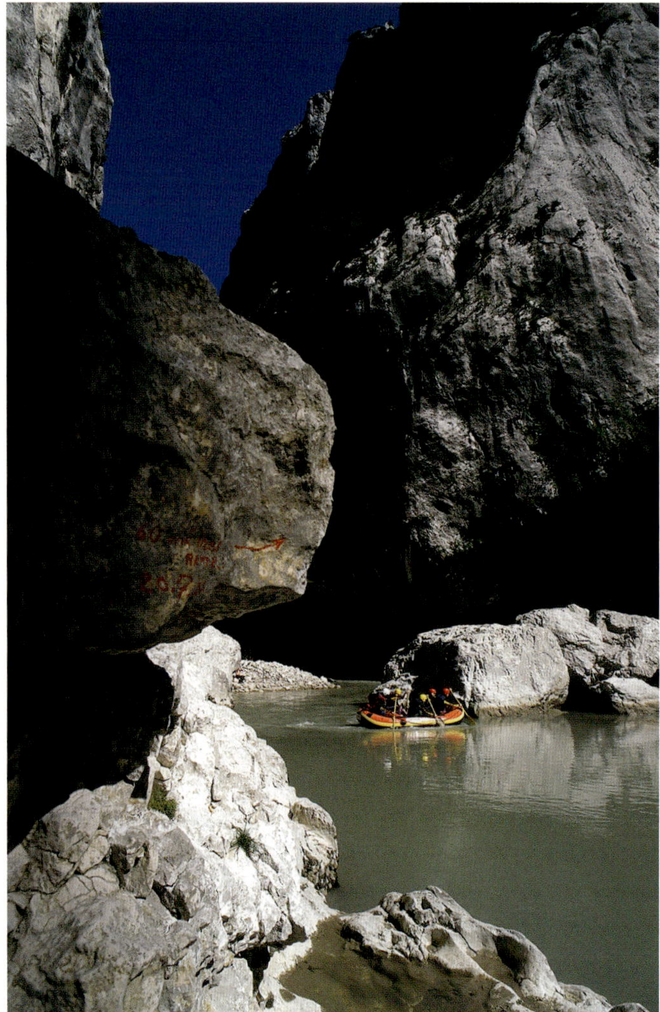

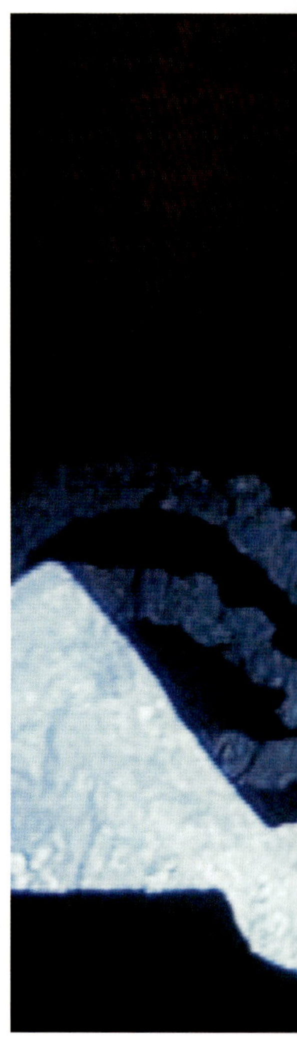

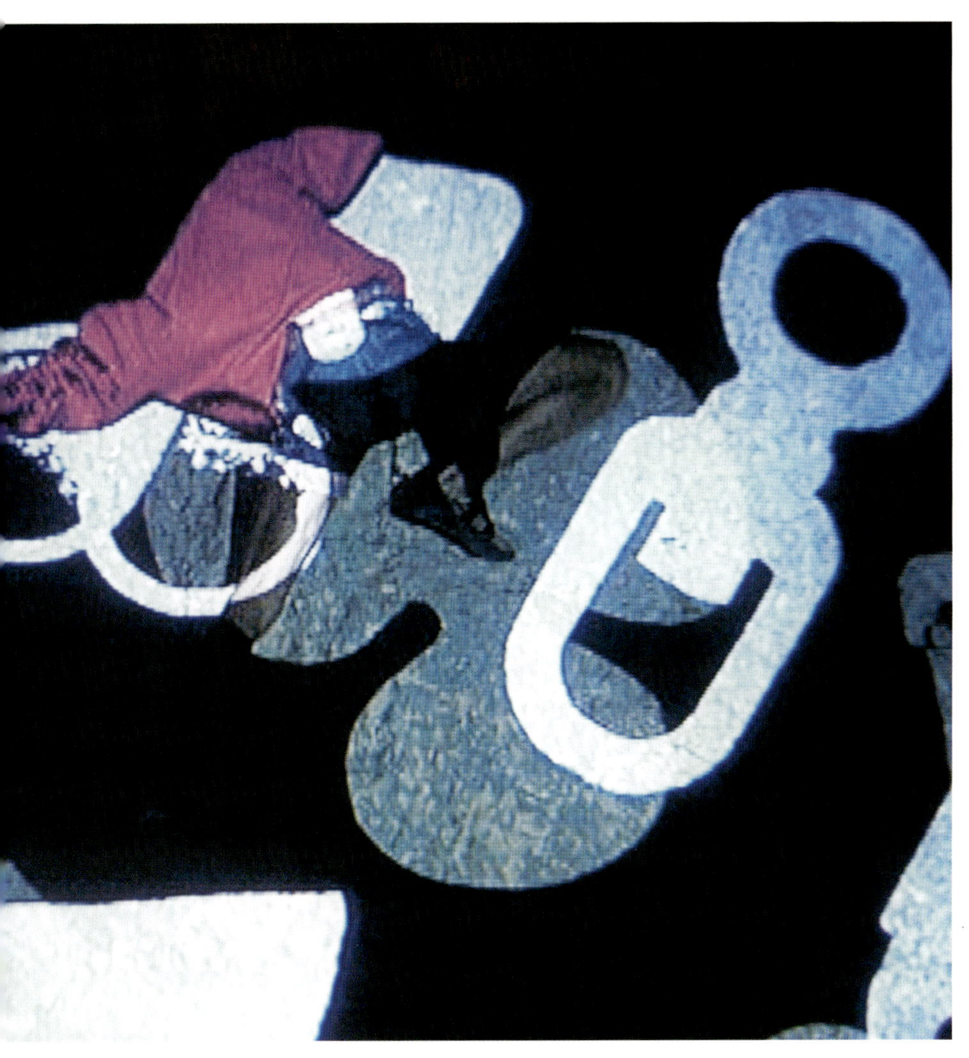

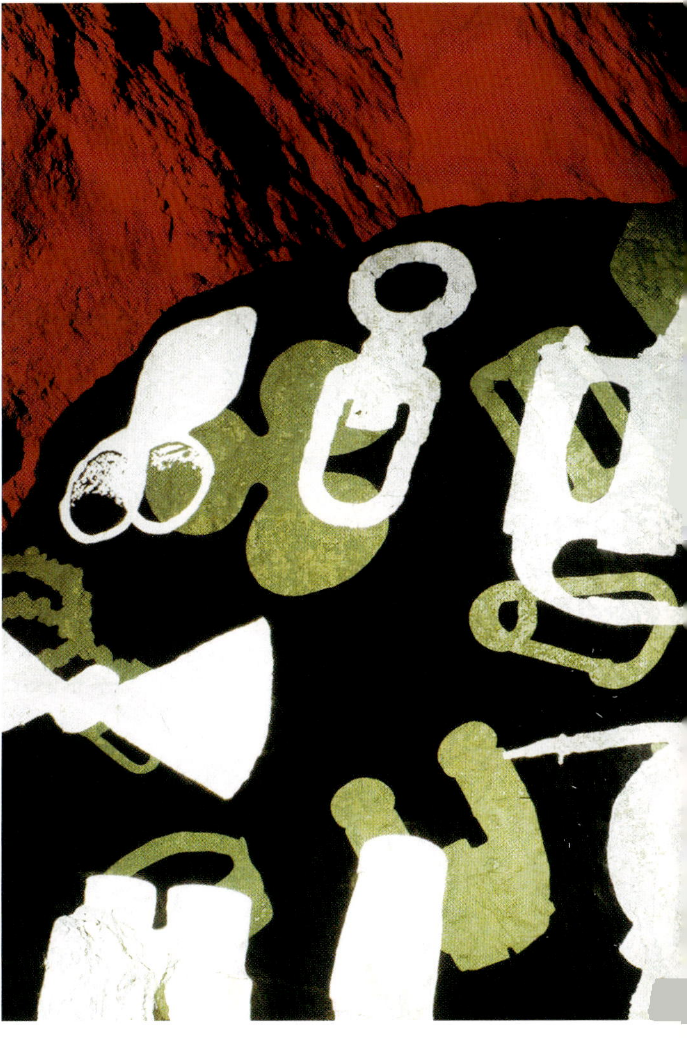

1995

LIGHT MESSENGER

Canal Grande, XLVI Biennale di Venezia, Italy

I am, me, the Salute, the result of an act of grace. Don't forget! Longhena, baroque and triumphant, conceived me so that the terrible plague of 1630 could cease, unforgiving and unforgettable. So what's this reappearing, from time to time, on my stone skin, strange mixtures, coloured incandescence, I'm not offended by them! On the contrary!

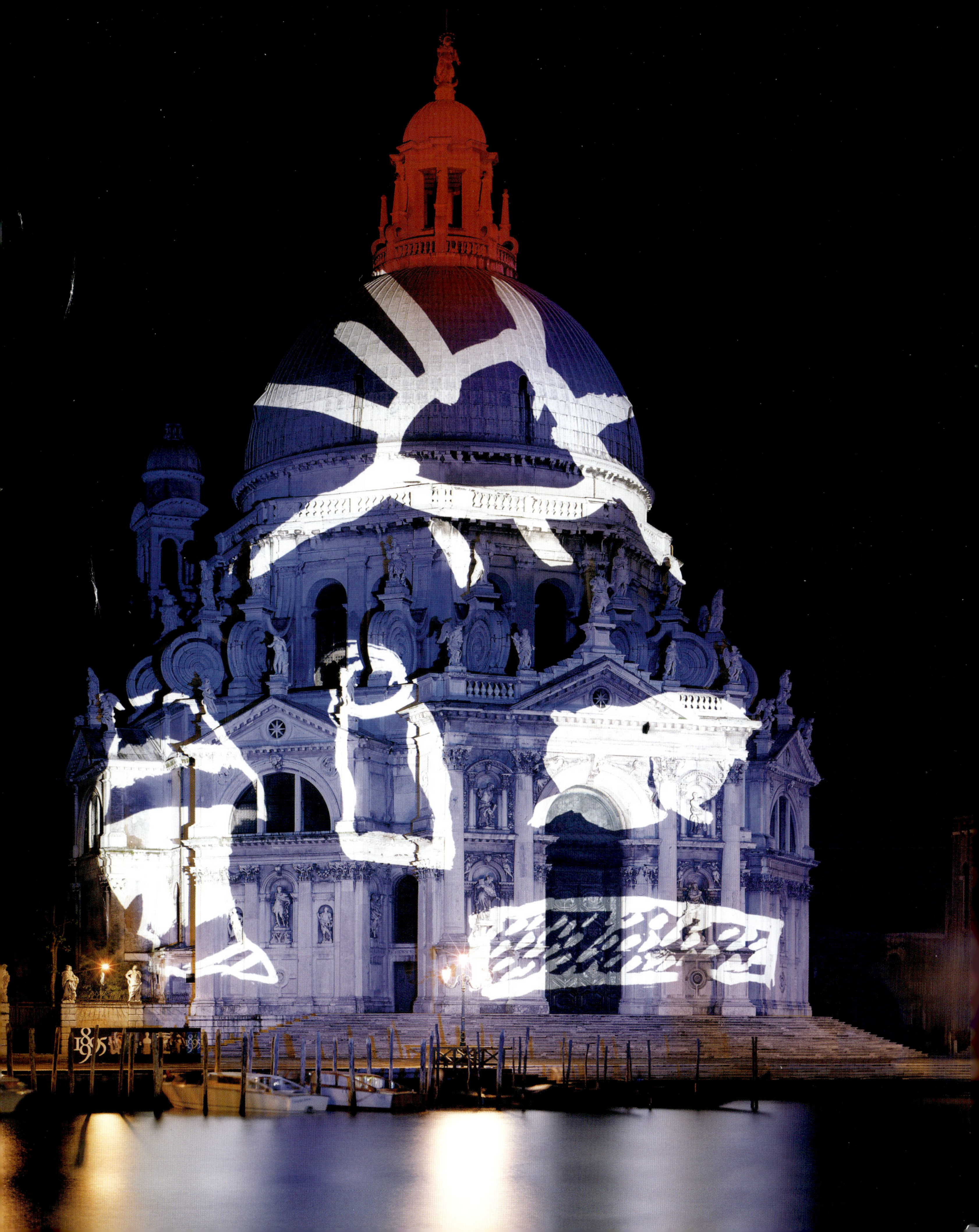
1895
1895

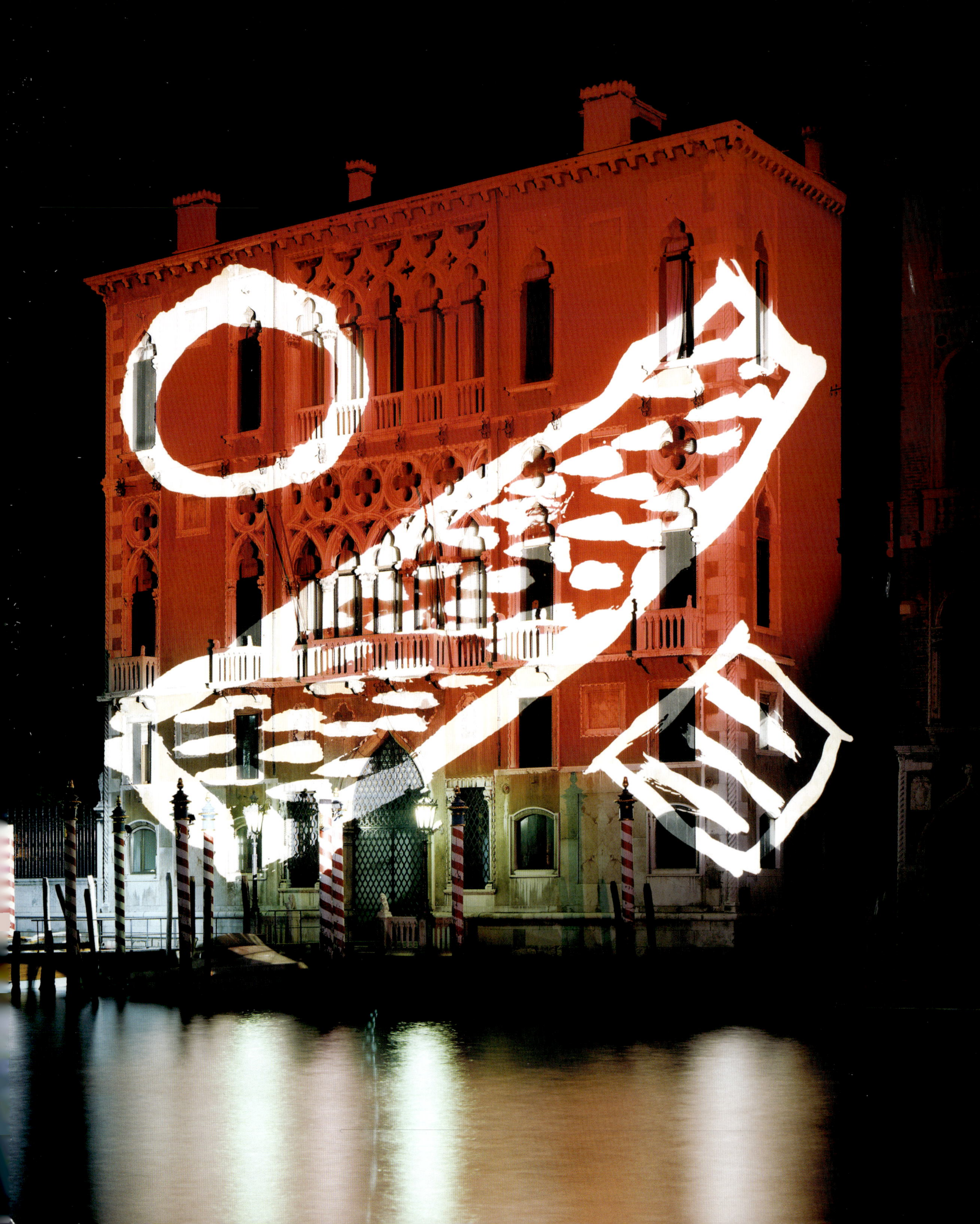

One is a stiff and dignified palace, erect on the Grand Canal! One does not mind dressing up from time to time. To partake in the festivities and to pay for fantasised dreams. Some evenings, yes, when, shame is drunk, all is permitted!

Palazzo Cavalli

Oh! All right! Do what you want with me! All of my facade is yours. Your dreams and fantasies, your whims don't displease me! I accept everything! Yes! To play diva as much as the diva themselves. However, don't forget I'm watching you, from the skylight, up there, on the right.

Palazzo Grimani

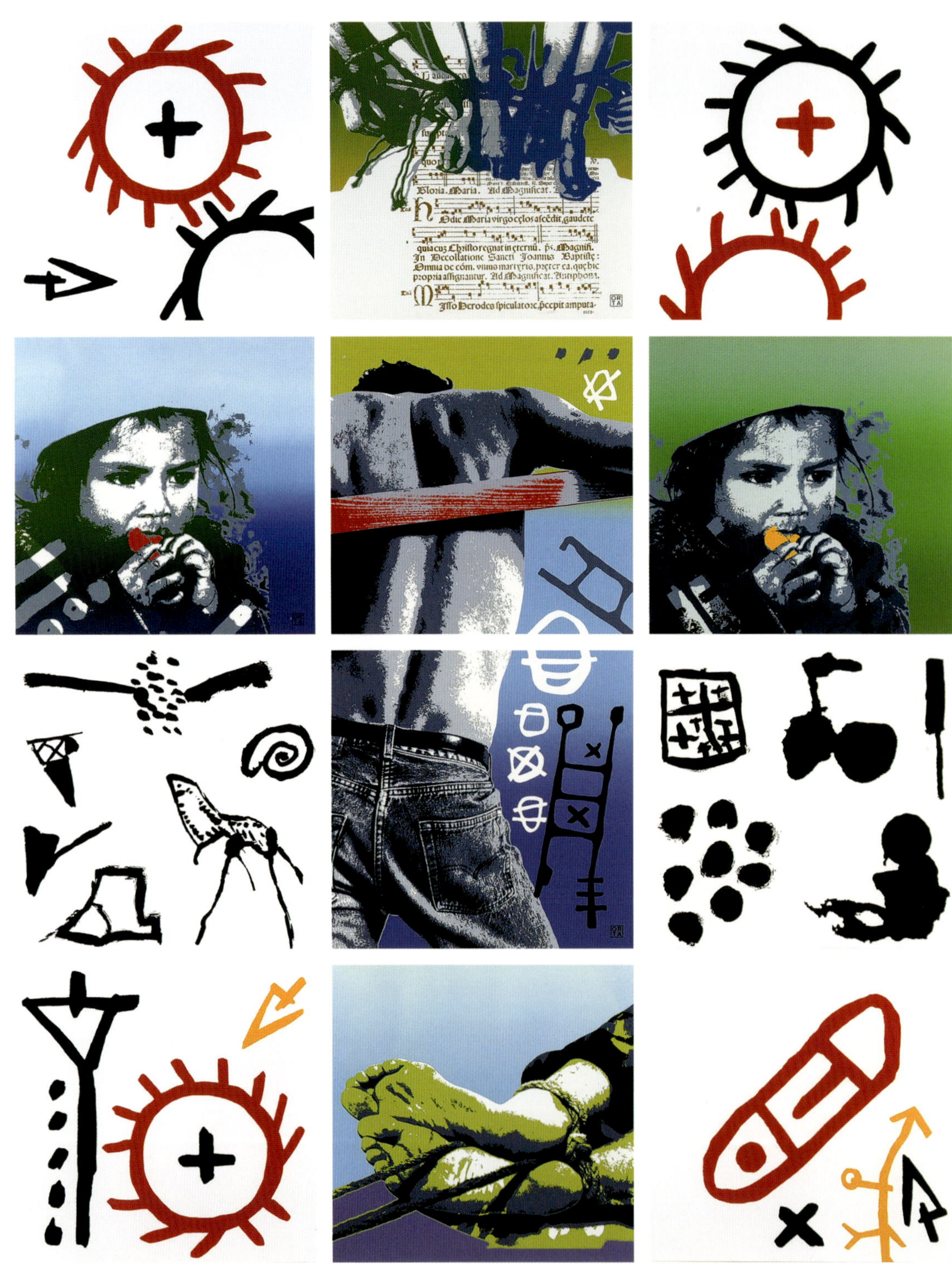

Módulos, 1995
Silkscreen print on paper
160 x 215 cm

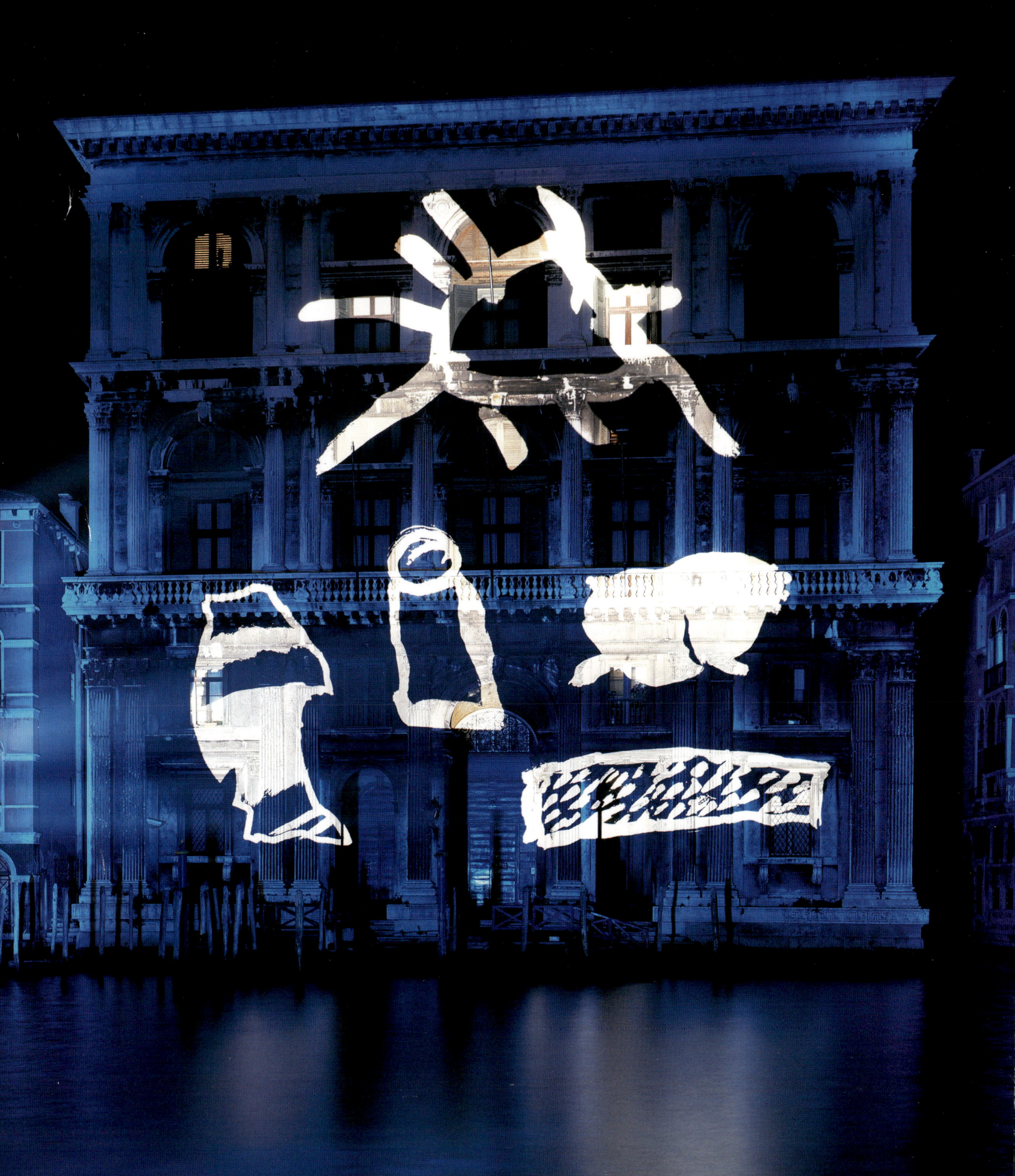

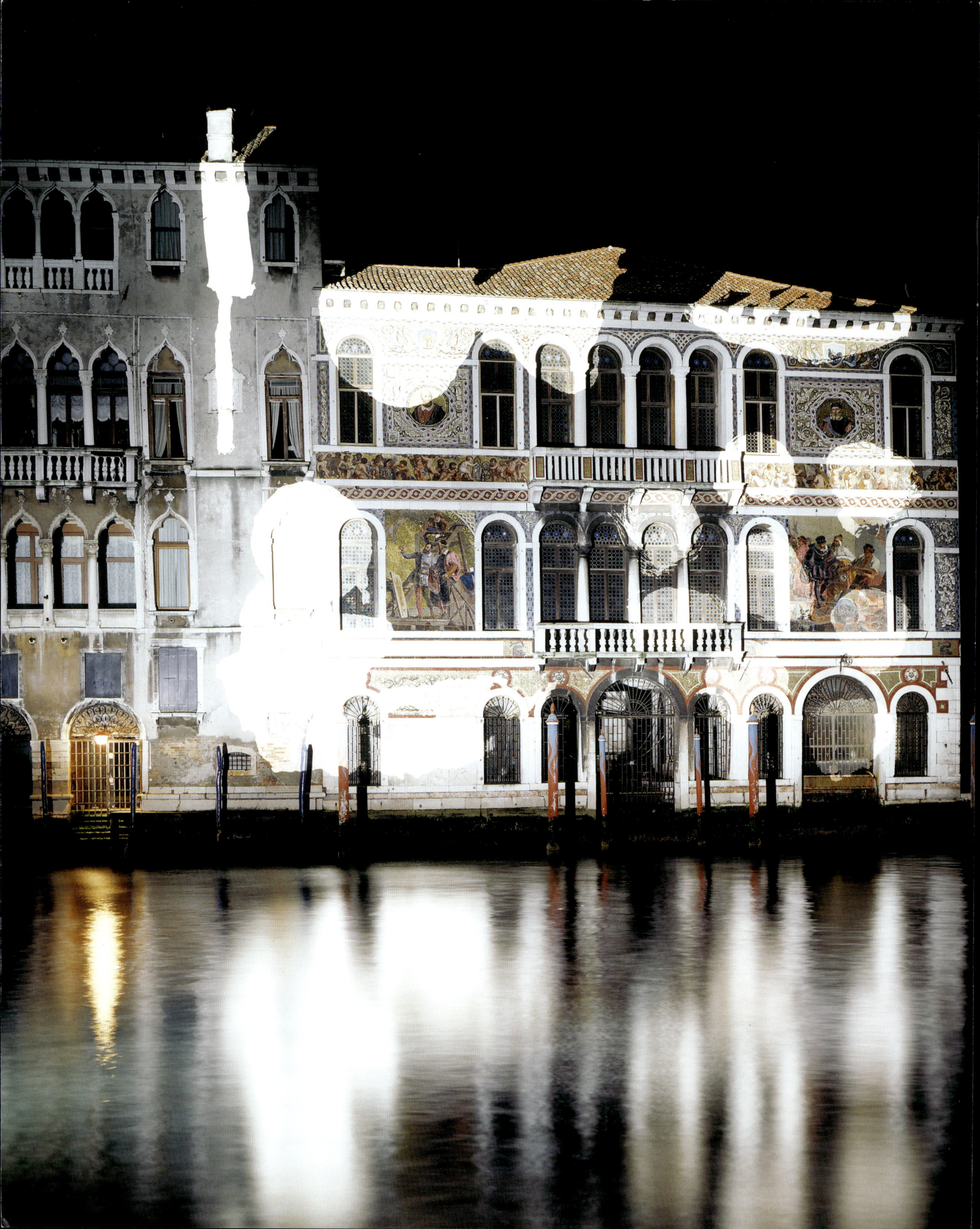

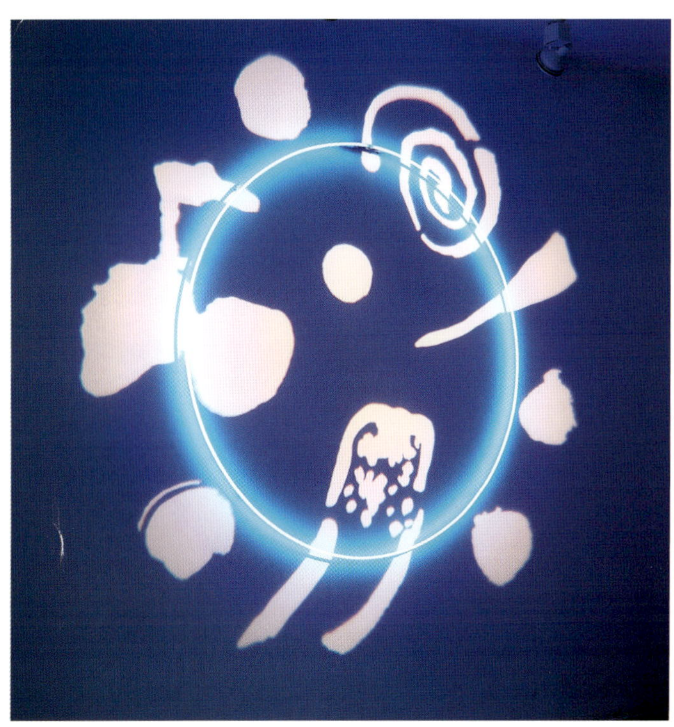

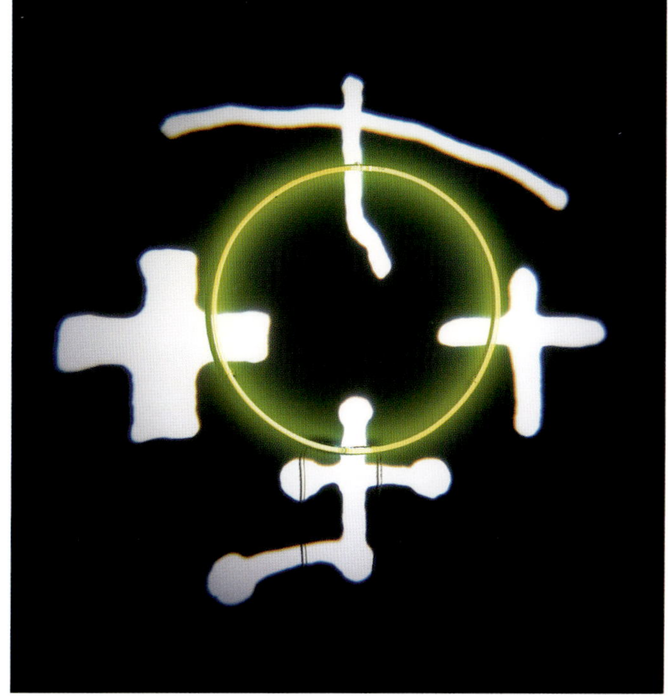

Venice: our second Mona Lisa!
Made-up, even decked with moustaches...
her mystery remains intact!

PALAZZO BARBARIGO

Réseau Poussière (Networks of Dust), 1995
Neon, light projector, gobo
300 x 300 cm
Collection of La Cité Numérique Lille, France

Croix Cardinale, 1996
Neon, light projector, gobo
120 x 120 cm

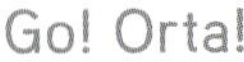

Go! Orta!
Don't you mind! Go on! This tattoo séance doesn't displease me. I approve of it, and in addition your fantasy, all, in the clam and the euphoria. Age has rendered me serene!

BERNARD HEIDSIECK

FONDACO DEI TURCHI

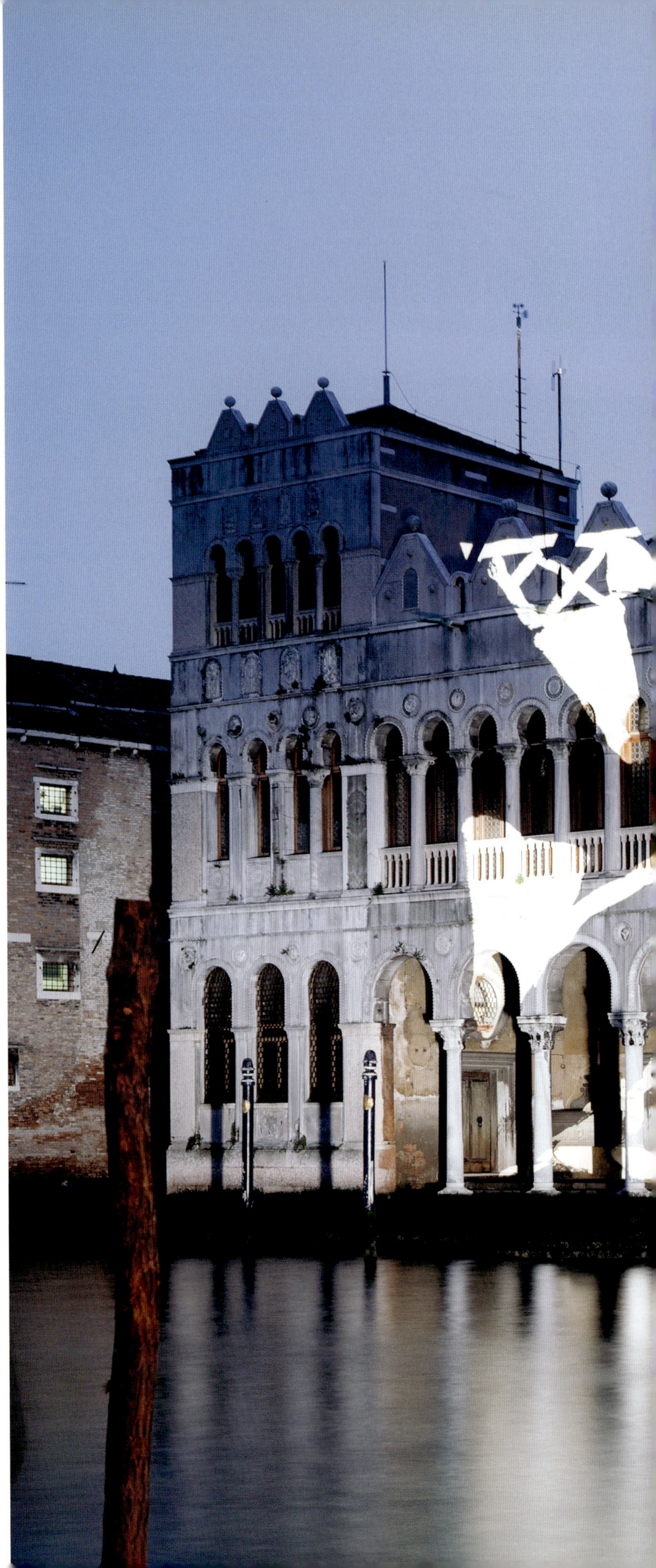

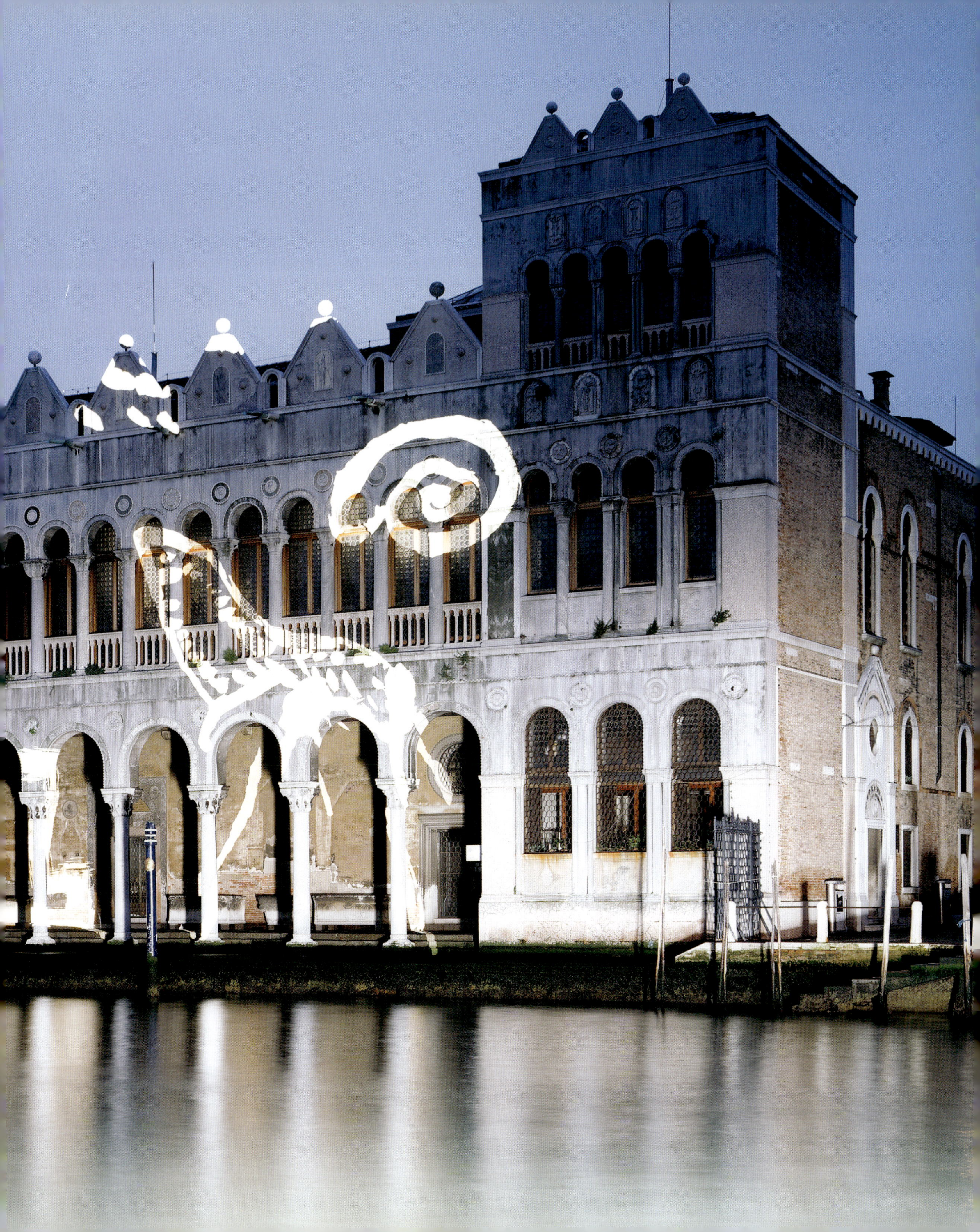

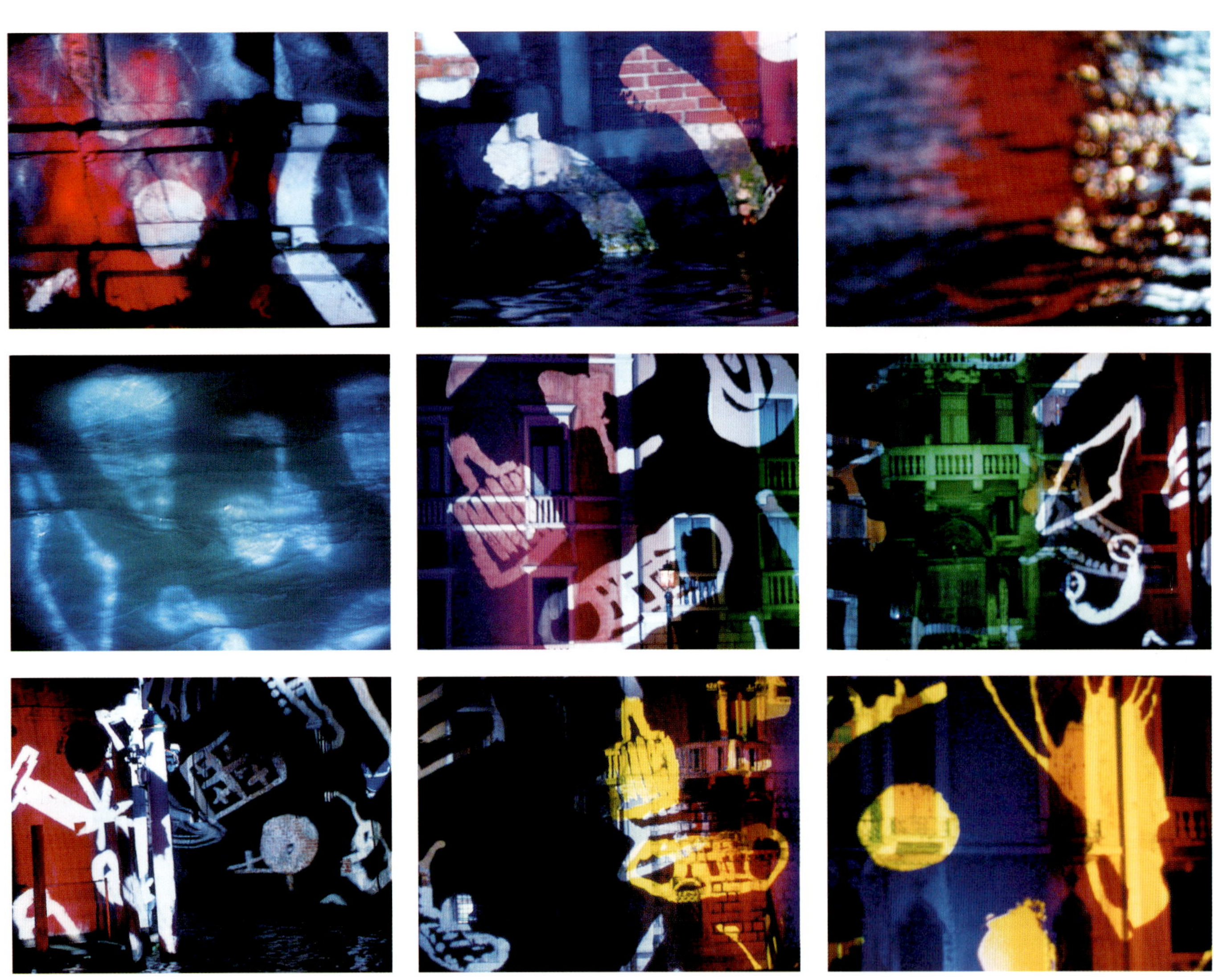

Light Messenger, 1995
Video stills

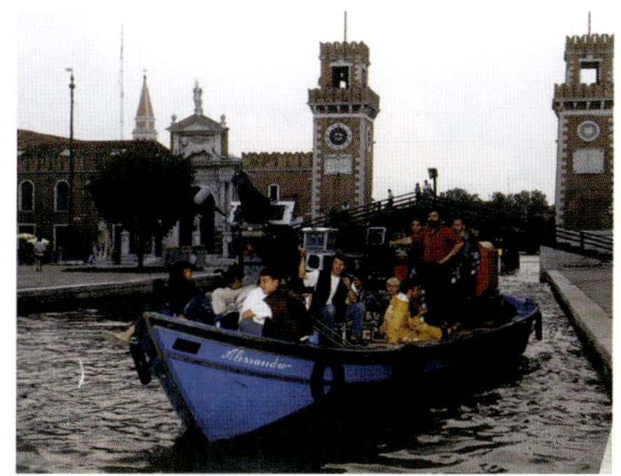

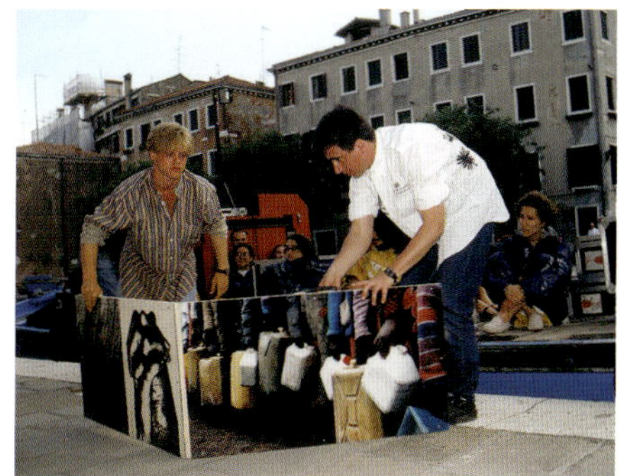

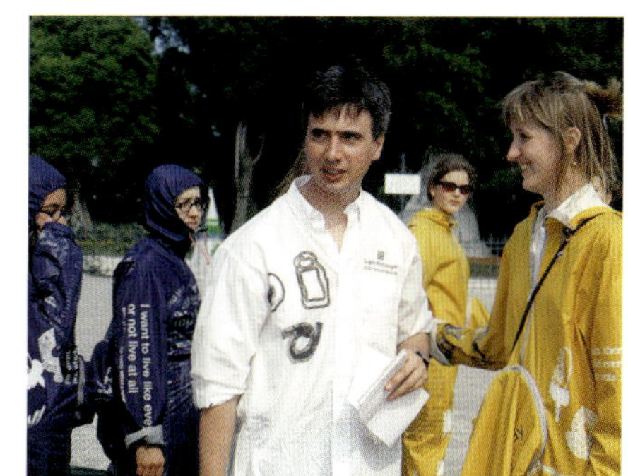

Representing Argentina for the 46th Venice Biennale by invitation of the curator Jorge Glusberg, Jorge Orta created a mobile ephemeral work to celebrate the majestic floating city by using the water's surface as a mirror, creating unusual shimmering light reflections on the surface of the buildings.

During three inaugural nights of the Venice Biennale, a silent Venetian cargo boat, carrying a giant image projector, navigated the Grand Canal, passing the extraordinary eleventh century Basilica di Santa Maria della Salute, and the sumptuous palaces: Palazzo Cavalli-Franchetti, Palazzo Bernardo, Palazzo Barbarigo, Fondaco dei Turchi, Cà d'Oro. Using the gondola moorings at various points along the canal, these temporary platforms provided a stage from which to 'graffiti' the facades of the buildings, playing host to the night festivities.

The pictograms projected onto the Venetian palaces and churches were created during community workshops run by the artists with children from a village in Jorge's hometown of Rosario and homeless youths in Paris, depicting personal belongings such as combs or seashells; with others computerised using the latest computer graphic programs. Together they represent the silent visual language of marginalised communities.

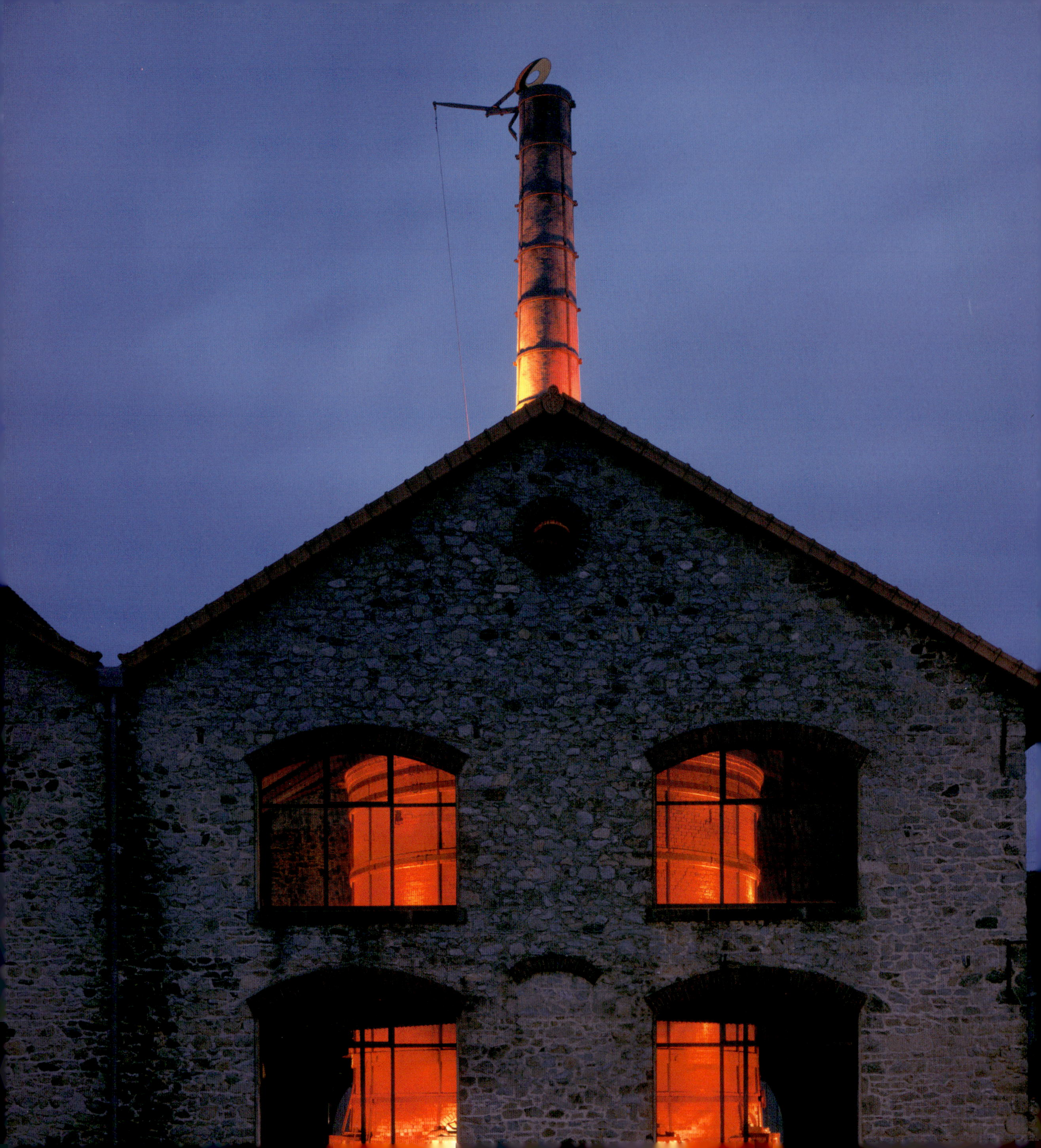

HEART OF THE MOON

Four du Casseaux, Limoges, France

1996

The Casseaux firing kiln is closely linked to the Limoges porcelain story and remains stoic monument to the memory of the craftsmanship of Occidental porcelain manufacture. Listed as a historical monument in 1987, it is one of the most eminent traces of the nineteenth century Limousin industrial heritage and one of the last kilns that can still be viewed in the city. The Light Works commissioned by the DRAC French Ministry of Culture, together with the manufacture of one hundred porcelain heart sculptures, *The Gift*, constituted the first chapter in a series of ephemeral public works around the theme of the heart—under the heading *OPERA.tion Life Nexus*.

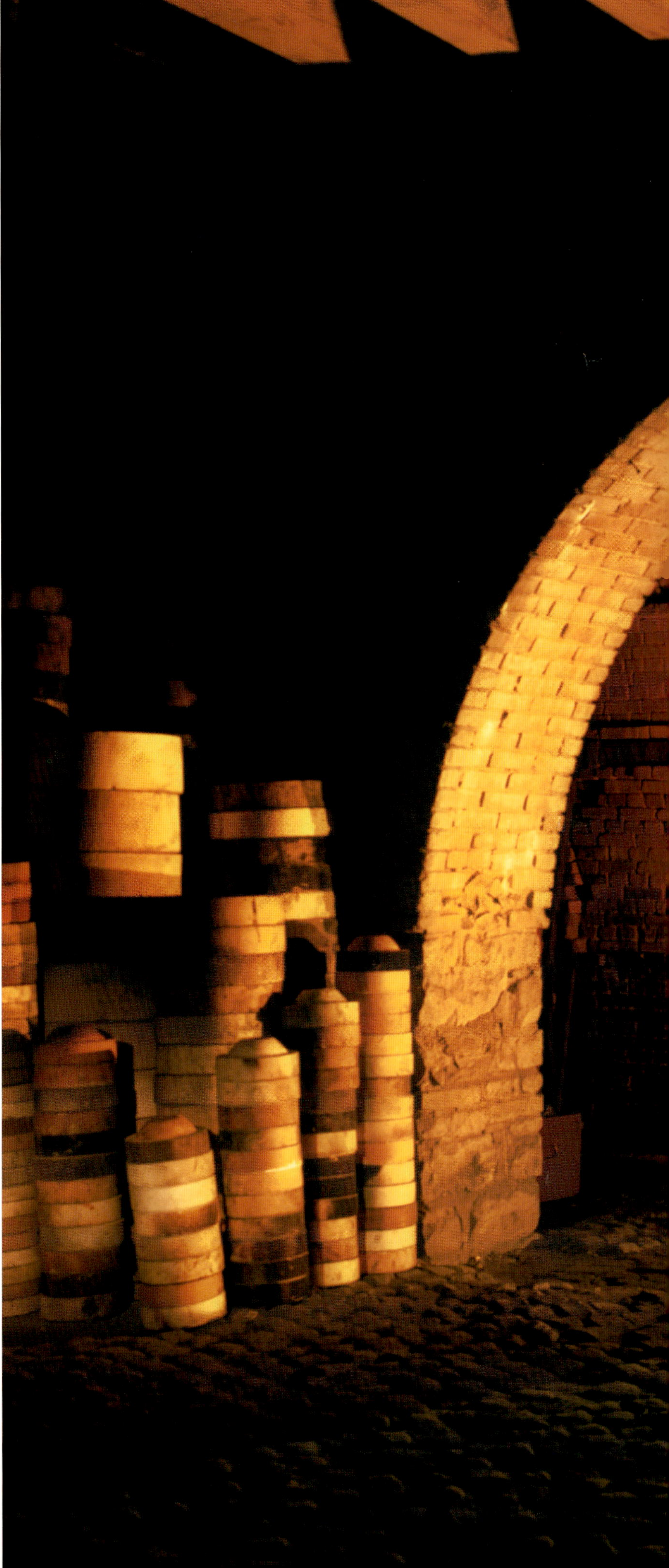

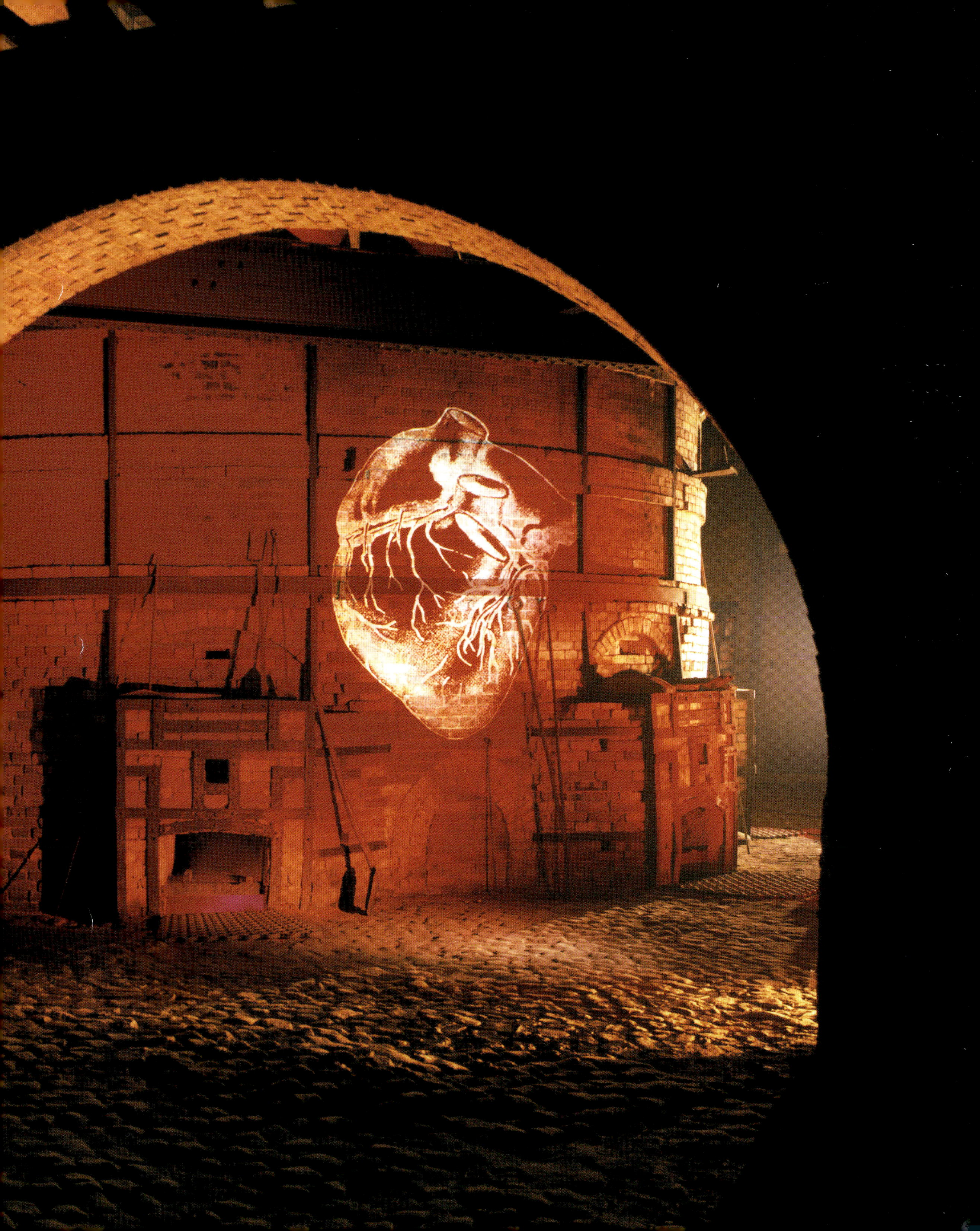

VIA CRUCIS

1996

Cloître de la Cathédrale de Saint-Étienne de Cahors, France

The configuration of the artwork *Via Crucis (Way of the Cross)* commissioned for the annual contemporary art festival Le Printemps de Cahors, refers to the depiction of the final hours of Jesus. 14 points throughout the cloisters of the Cahors Cathedral were illuminated replicating a symbolic journey of sorrows. Commencing with the courtyard, we find a small audio-wall work, and dividing a fu rther series of light boxes are four large image projections emphasising the cardinal points and implying different schools of thought. In total 40 light projectors illuminate the sculptured recesses of the Gothic arches.

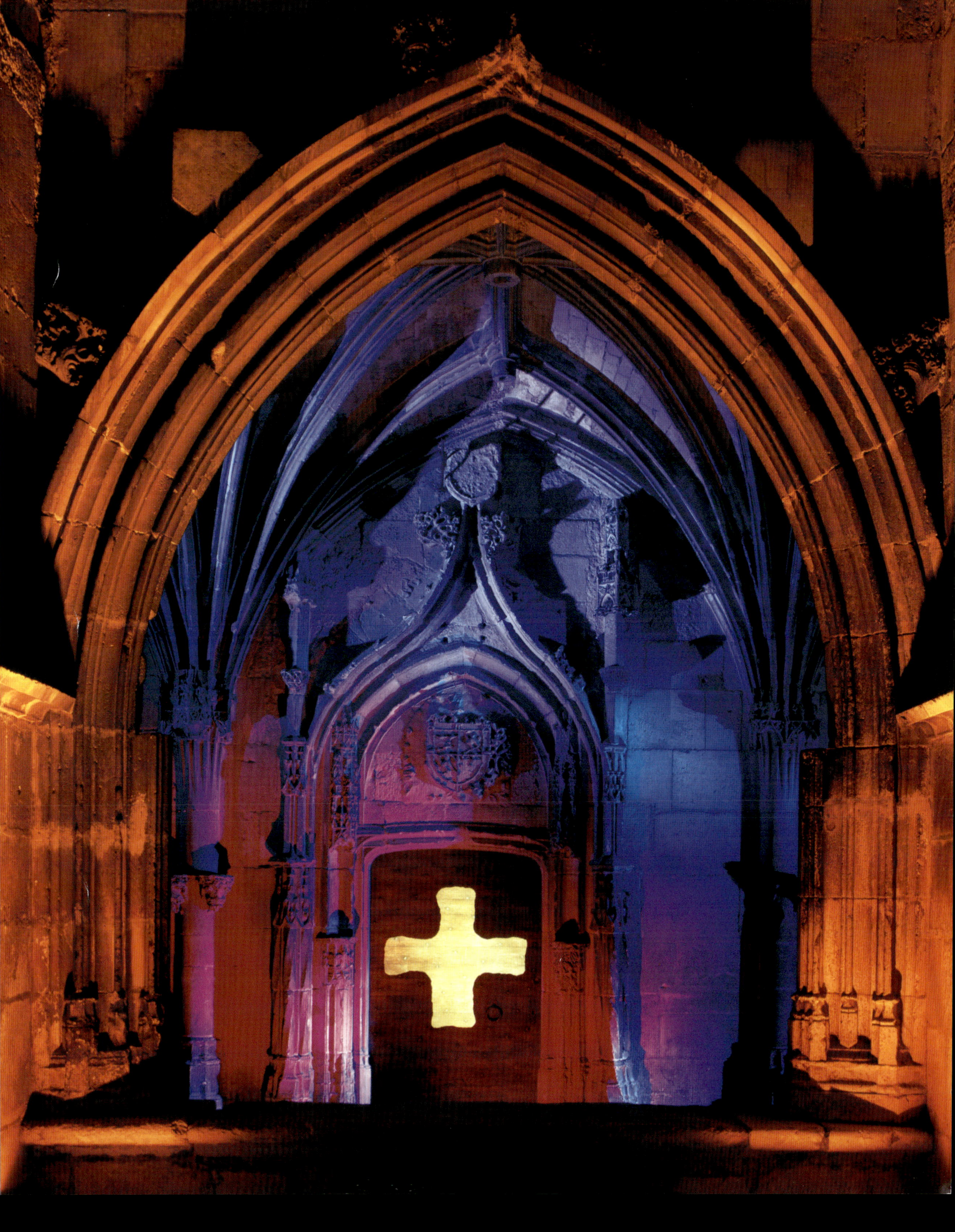

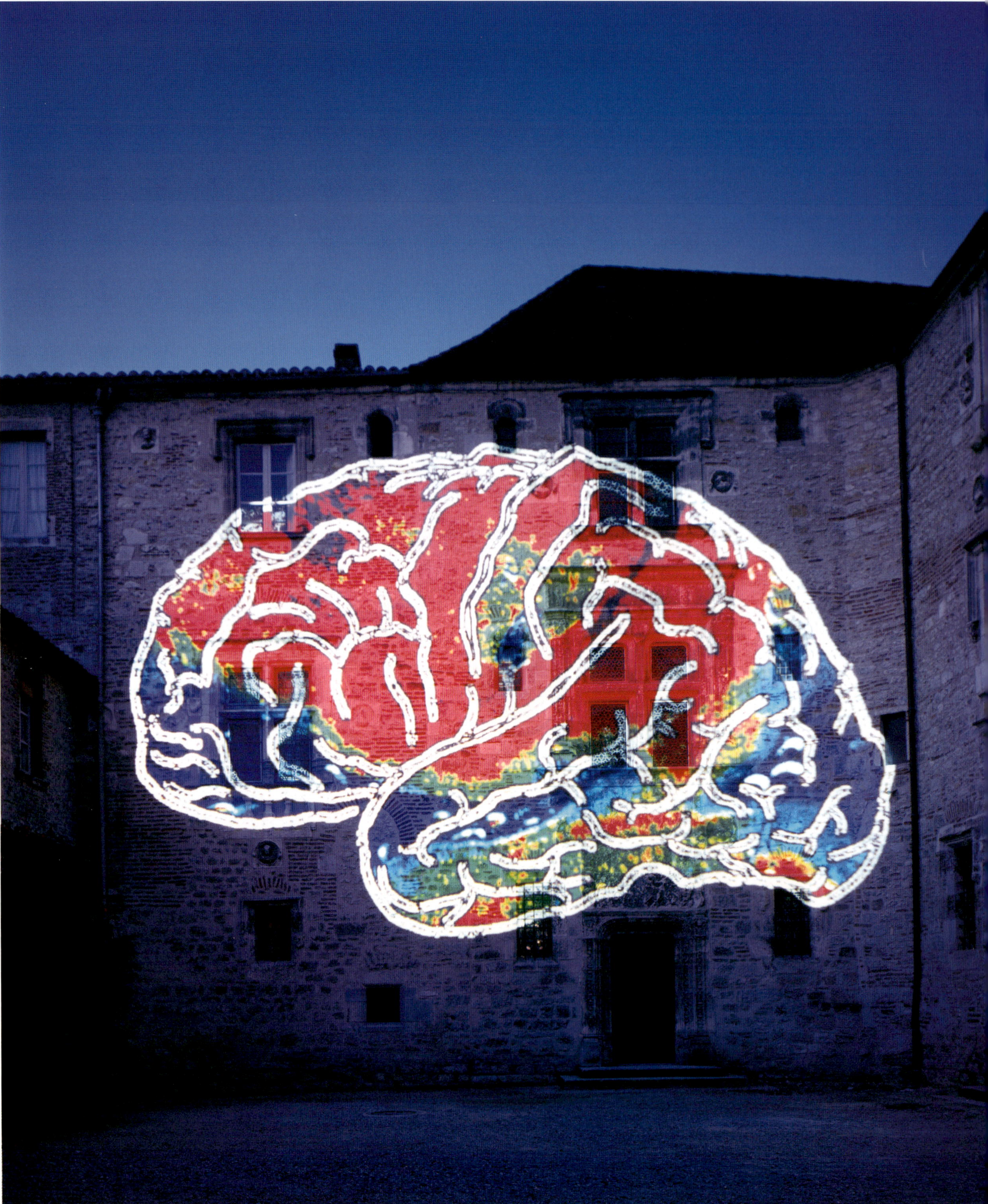

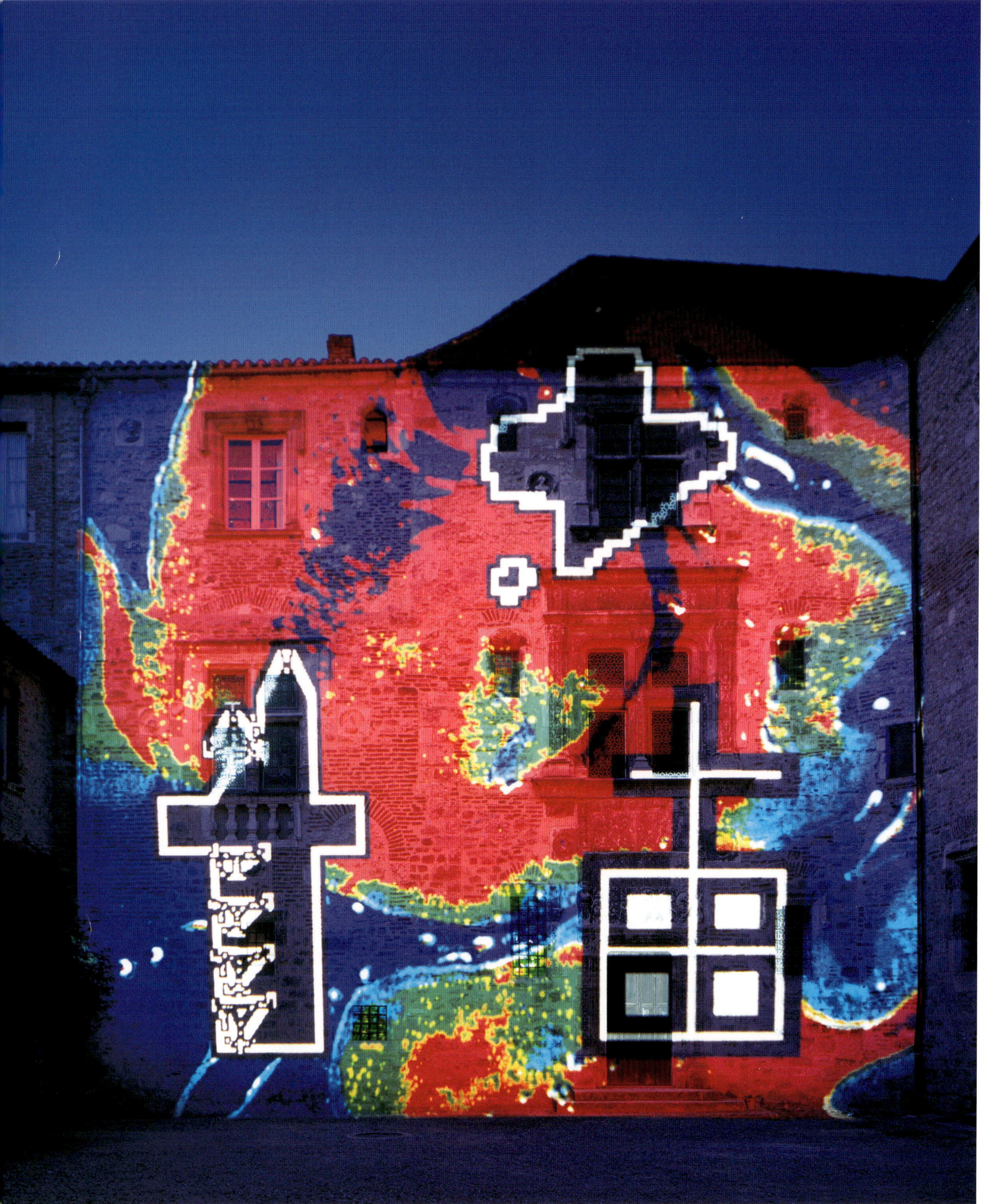

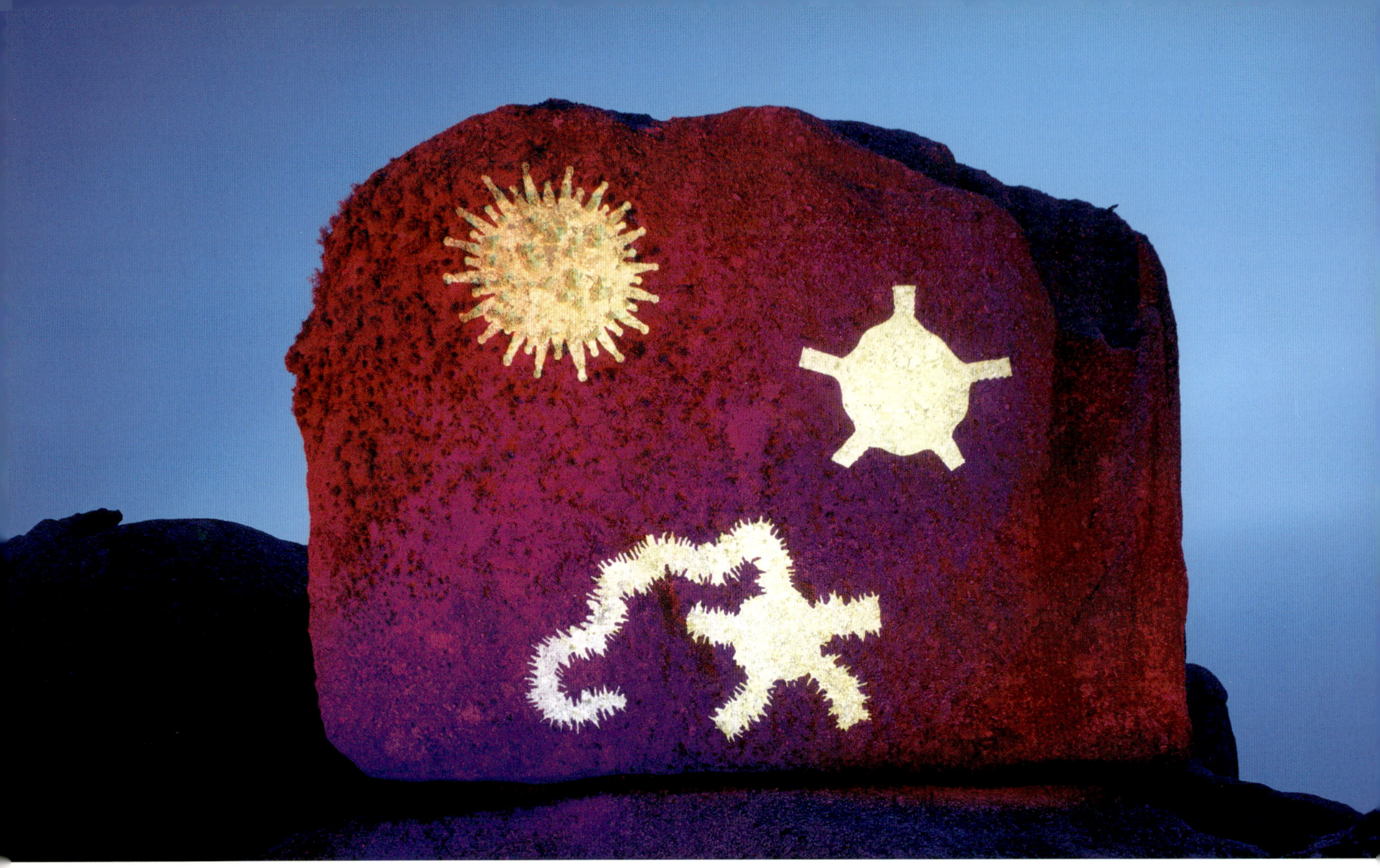

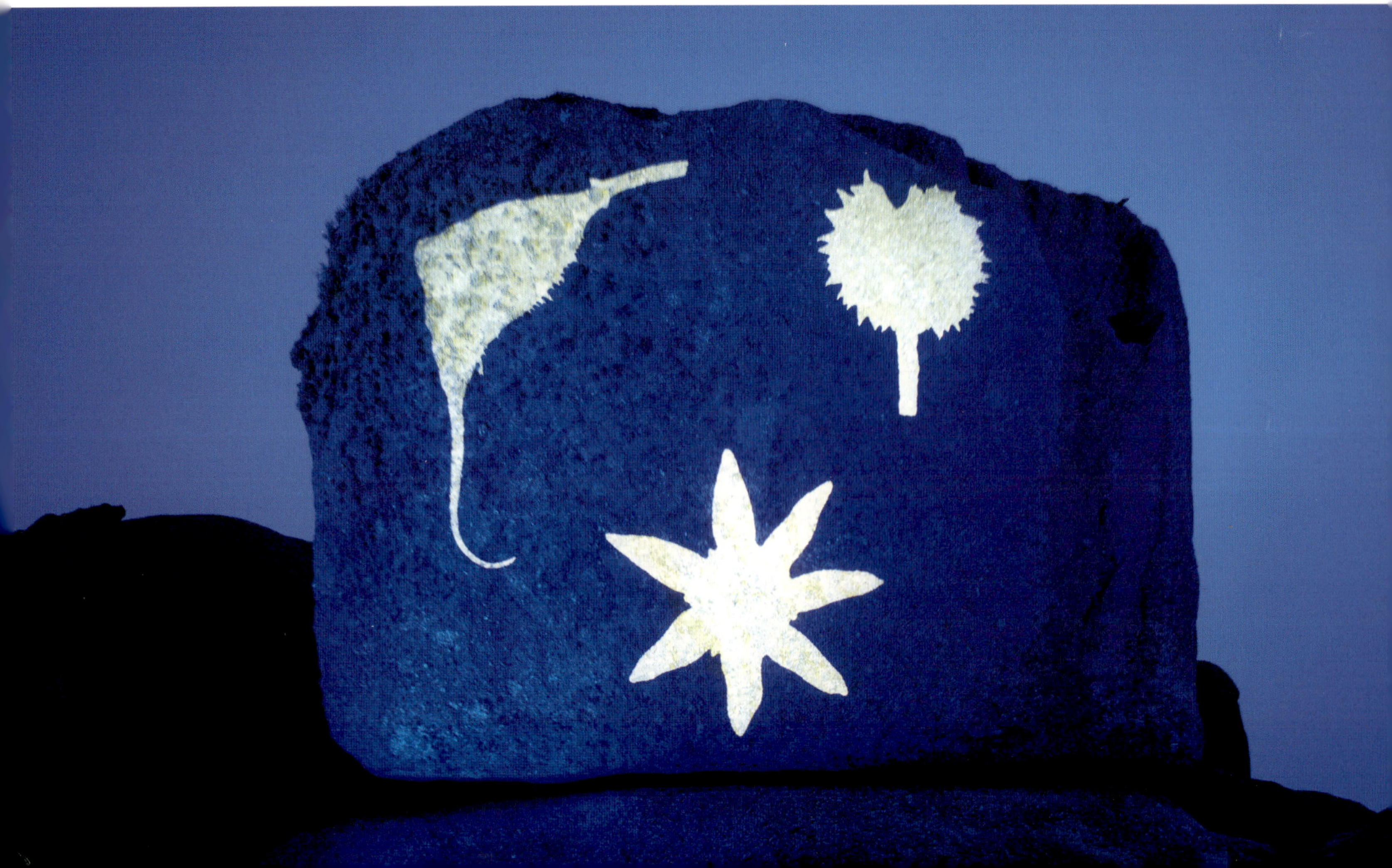

LIGHT MESSENGER

1996

Parc du Dourven, Brittany, France

The intermittent flickering of light along the coastline of the Dourven peninsula represents the transitory nature of our environment, the ebb and flow of the tide, constantly evolving in a cycle of birth and death. The graphic symbols projected onto the perdurable granite cliffs and monoliths are versions of the microscopic unicellular species that cohabit the park, here larger than life, reminding us of their fragile existence.

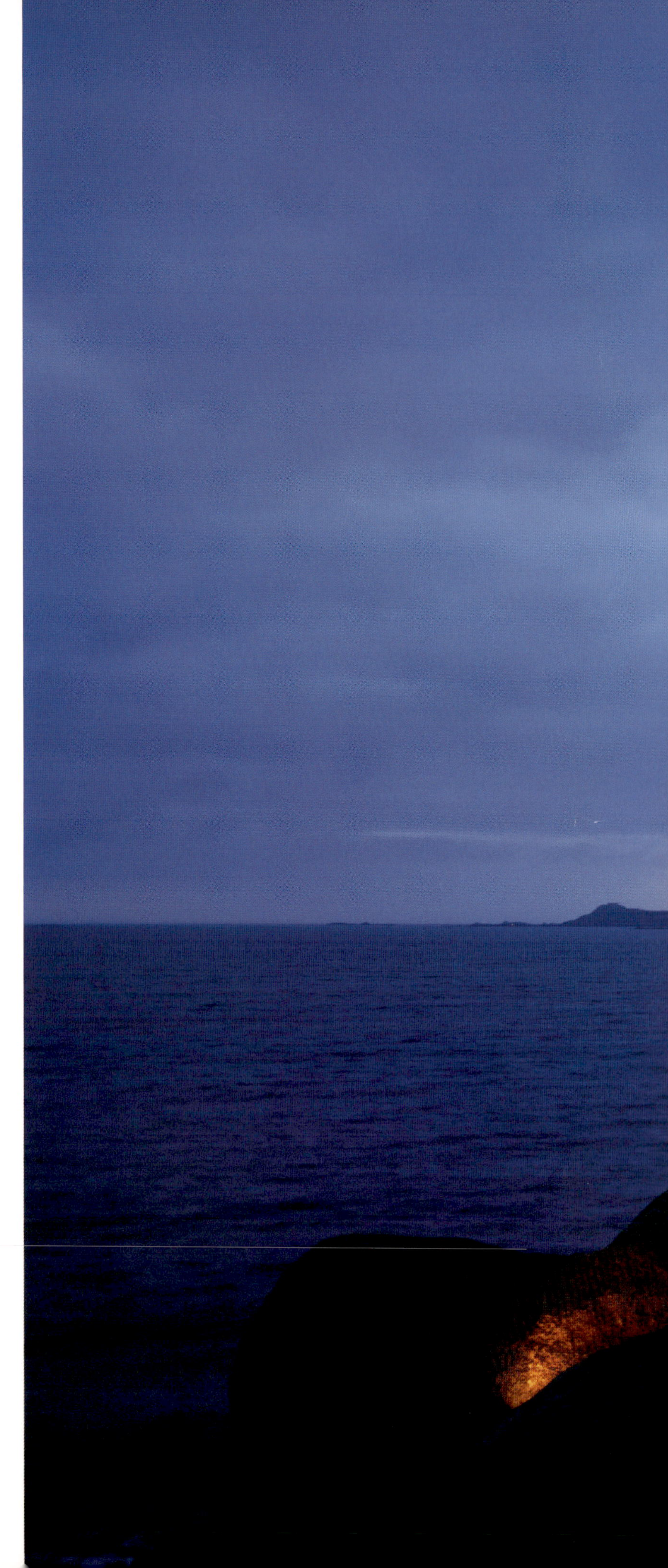

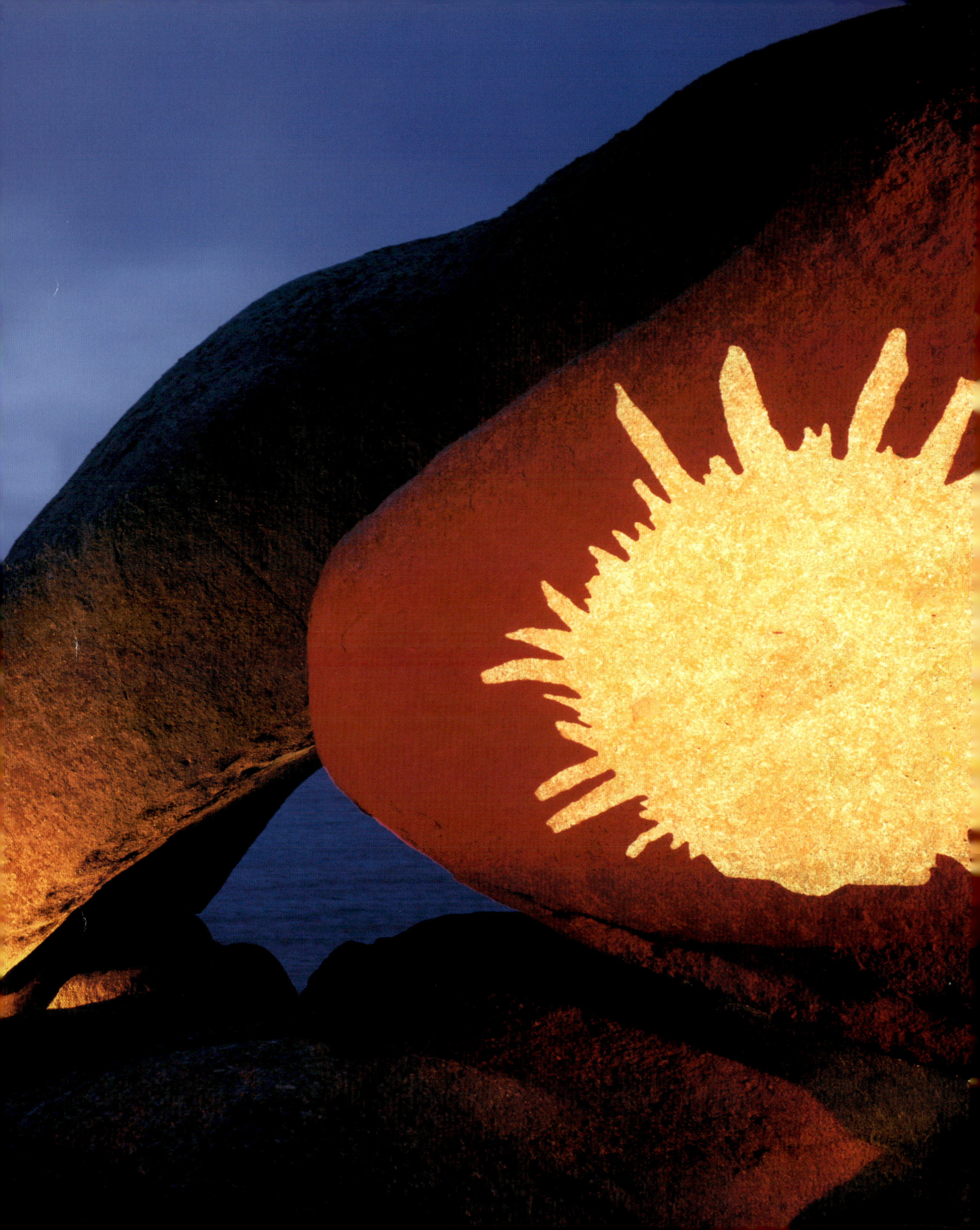

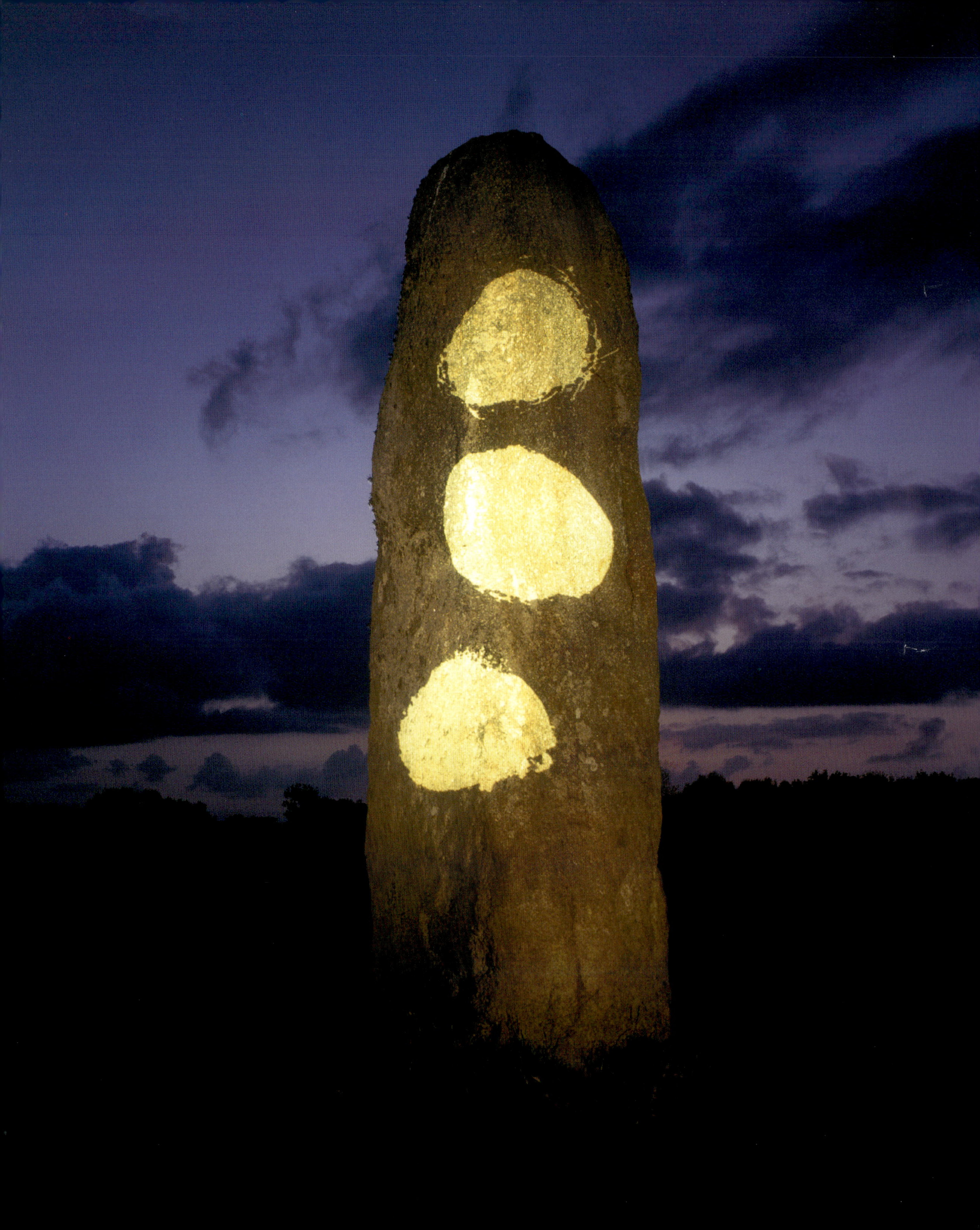

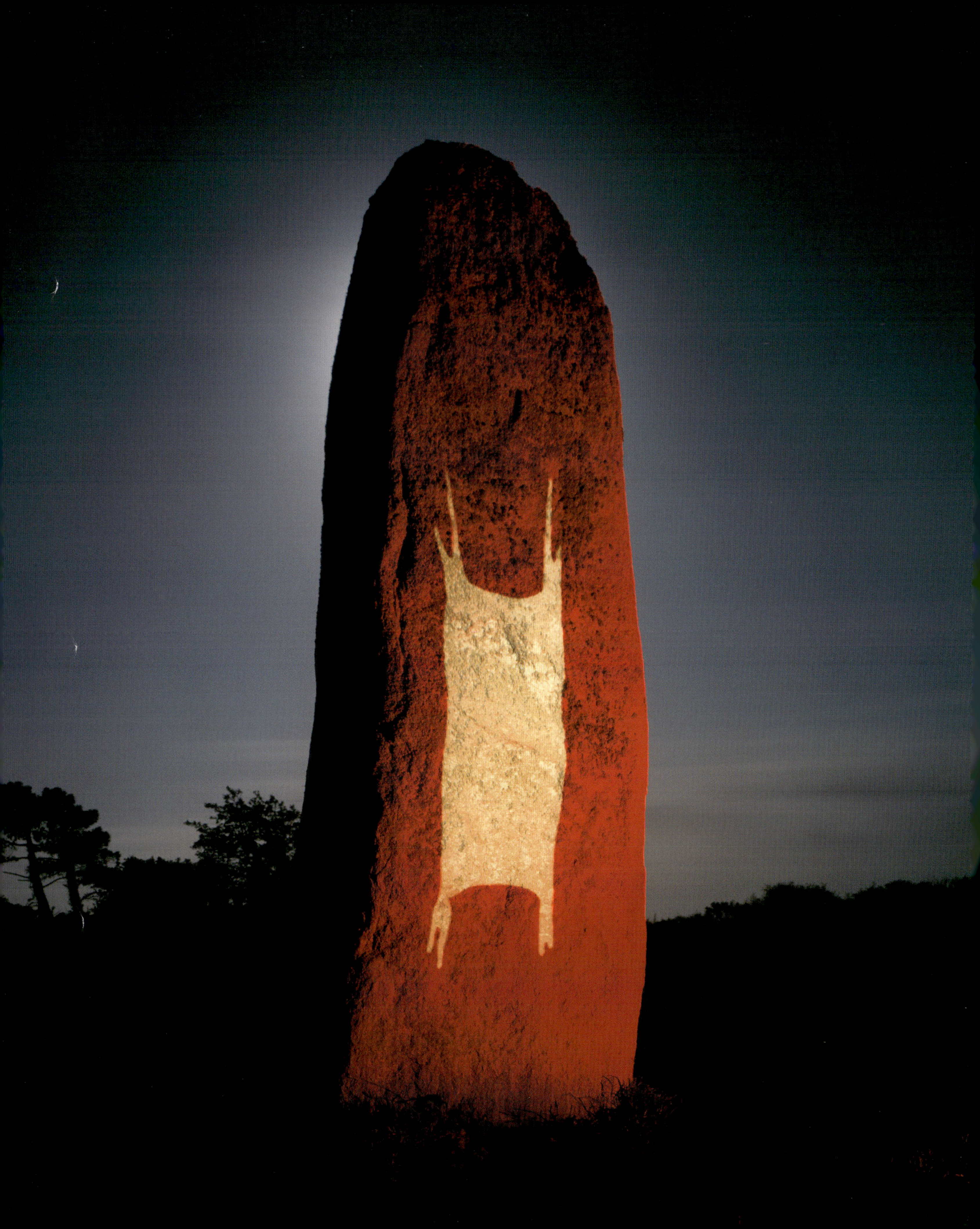

In a time of spiritual drought, illuminating our natural surroundings allows us to contemplate on our existence, origin and destiny more carefully. “Originality is returning to one’s origins” were the words of Gaudi, so let’s rediscover the great Temple of Nature. A temple with mountains for walls, the celestial vault for a dome, the sun’s glow for windows, and melodies of the streams, the leaves rustling and animal voices; a temple built by cosmic forces that brings us closer to Harmony. As the sun fades to half-light the sky is adorned with the most unpredictable colours. In this vast temple, light reveals the ephemeral within the infinite and Light Works attempt to crystallise this union—a spec of mankind in the immensity of the universe.

JORGE ORTA (*NETWORKS OF DUST*, 1996)

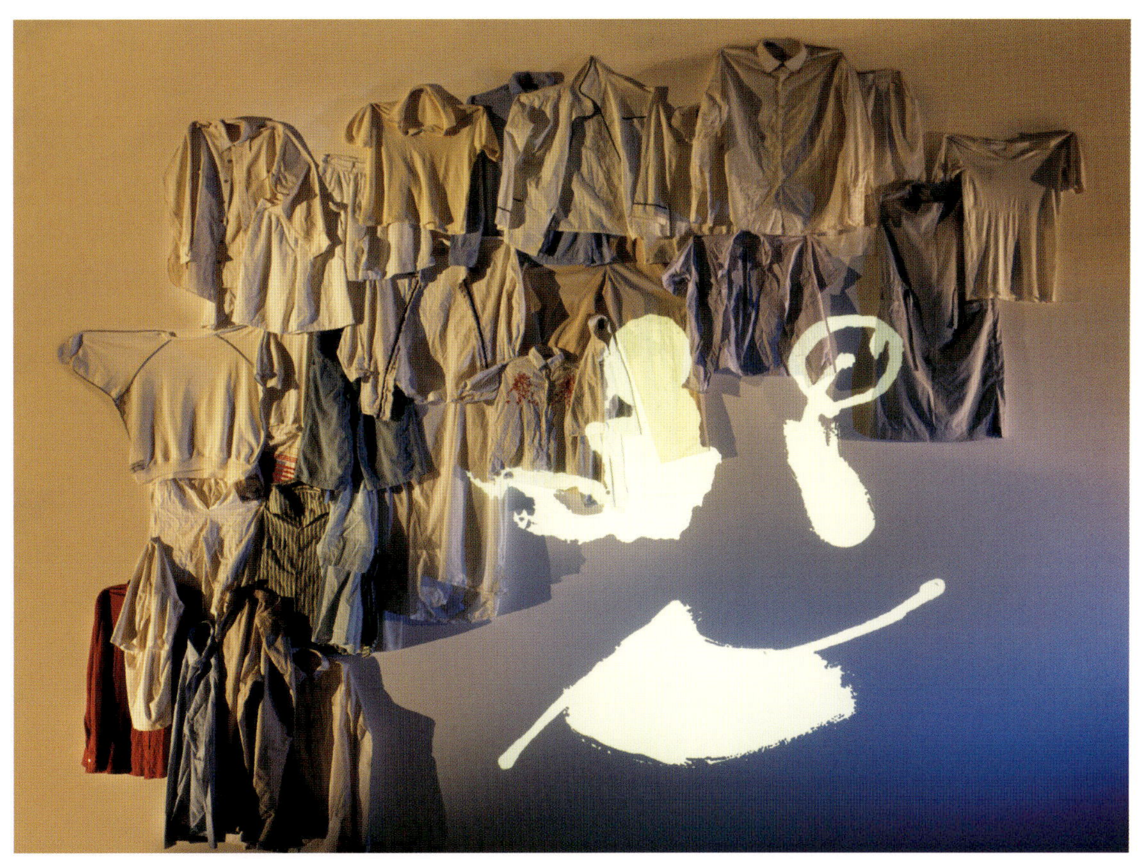

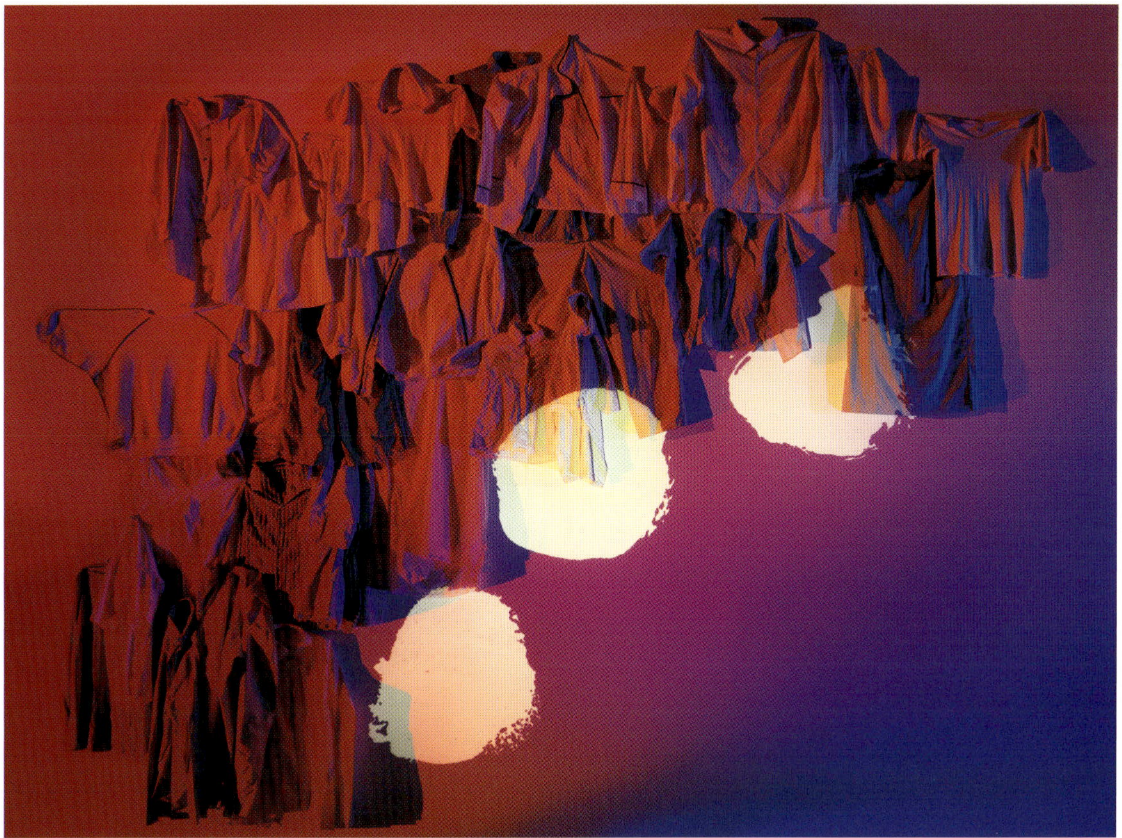

Light Messenger, 1996
Light installation with used clothes, light projector, gobo
Variable dimensions
Courtesy of La Galerie du Dourven Brittany, France

CROSSROADS

Cathédrale d'Évry, France

1996

Commissioned by the Diocese of Évry-Corbeil-Essonnes *Crossroads* was created to inaugurate Evry Cathedral, which was designed by Swiss architect Mario Botta. Jorge Orta conducted extensive research on the symbol of the cross throughout cultures, religions and history, to create a universal and spiritual ephemeral work. Using the cathedral as a beacon and the public space as a stage, he bathed them in 22 light compositions with an accompanying audio installation, creating a moving public event drawing a crowd from all walks of life.

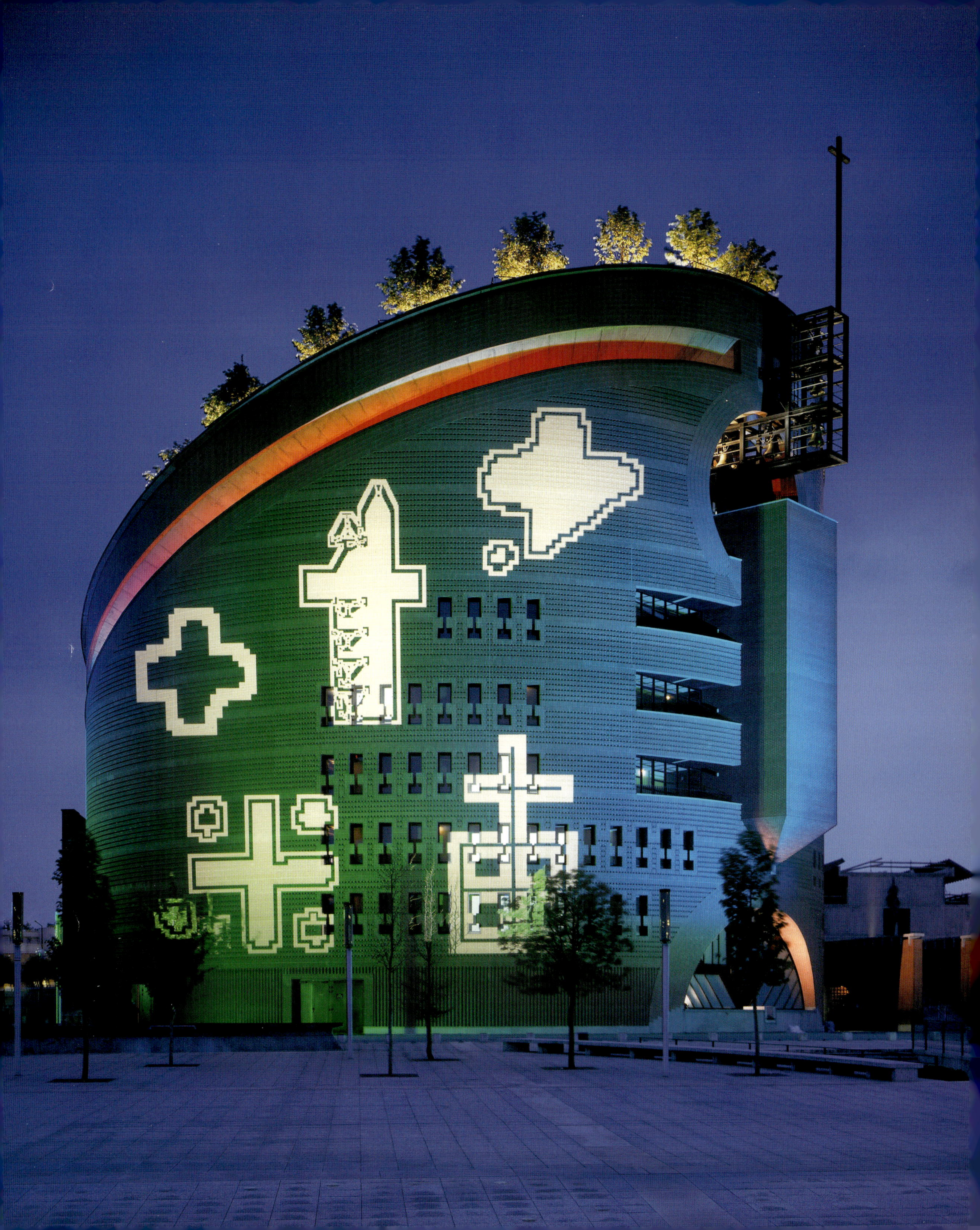

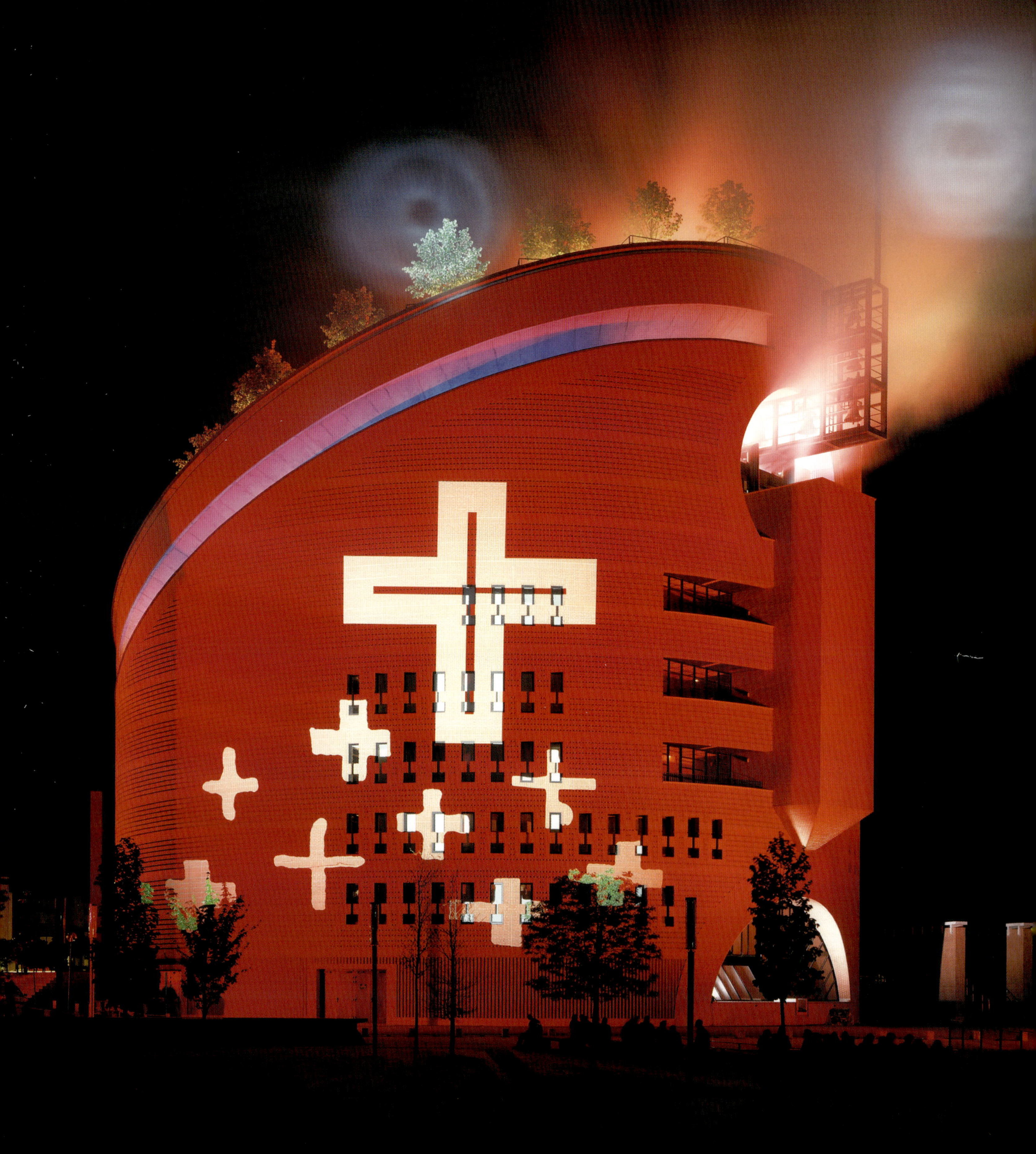

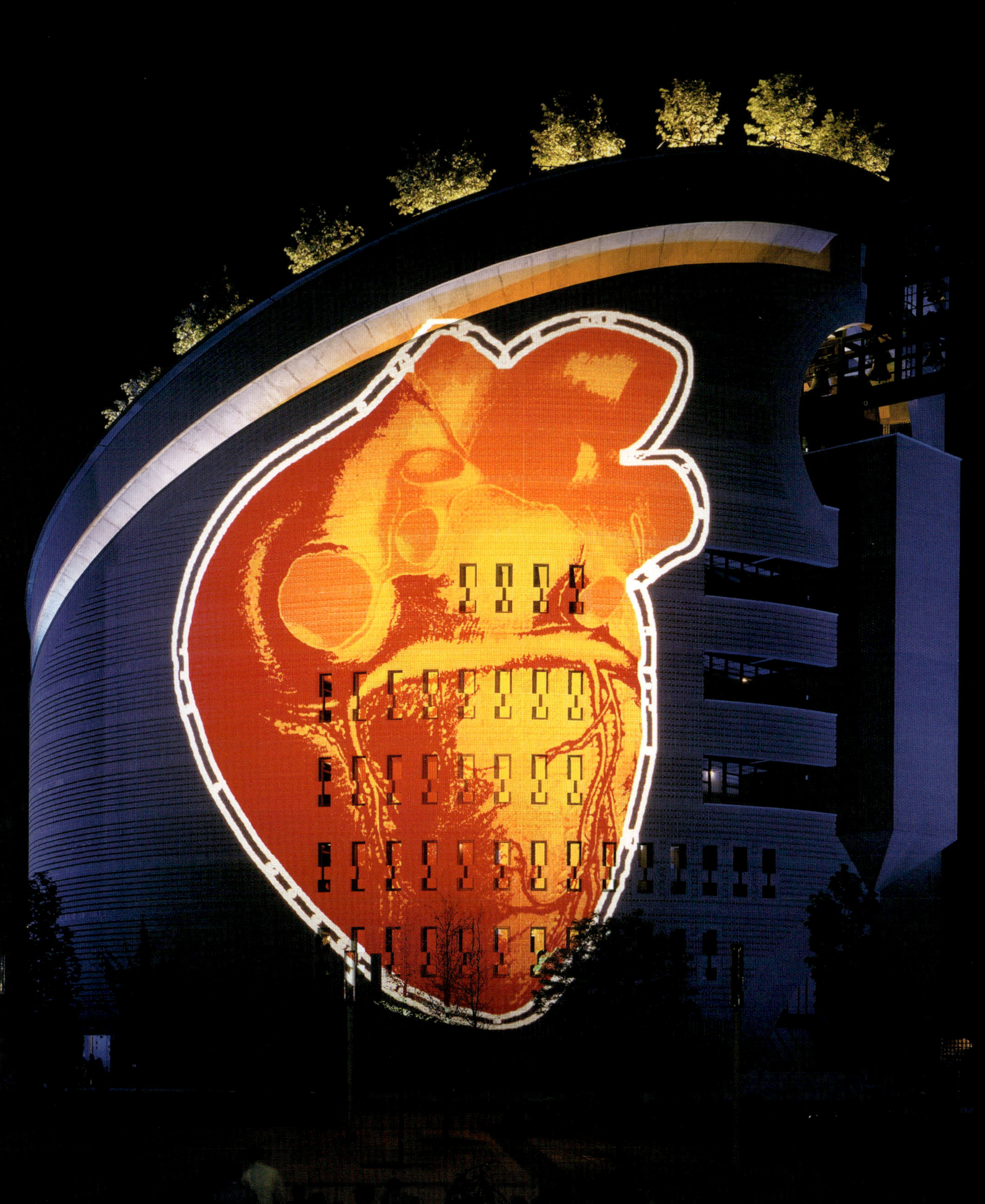

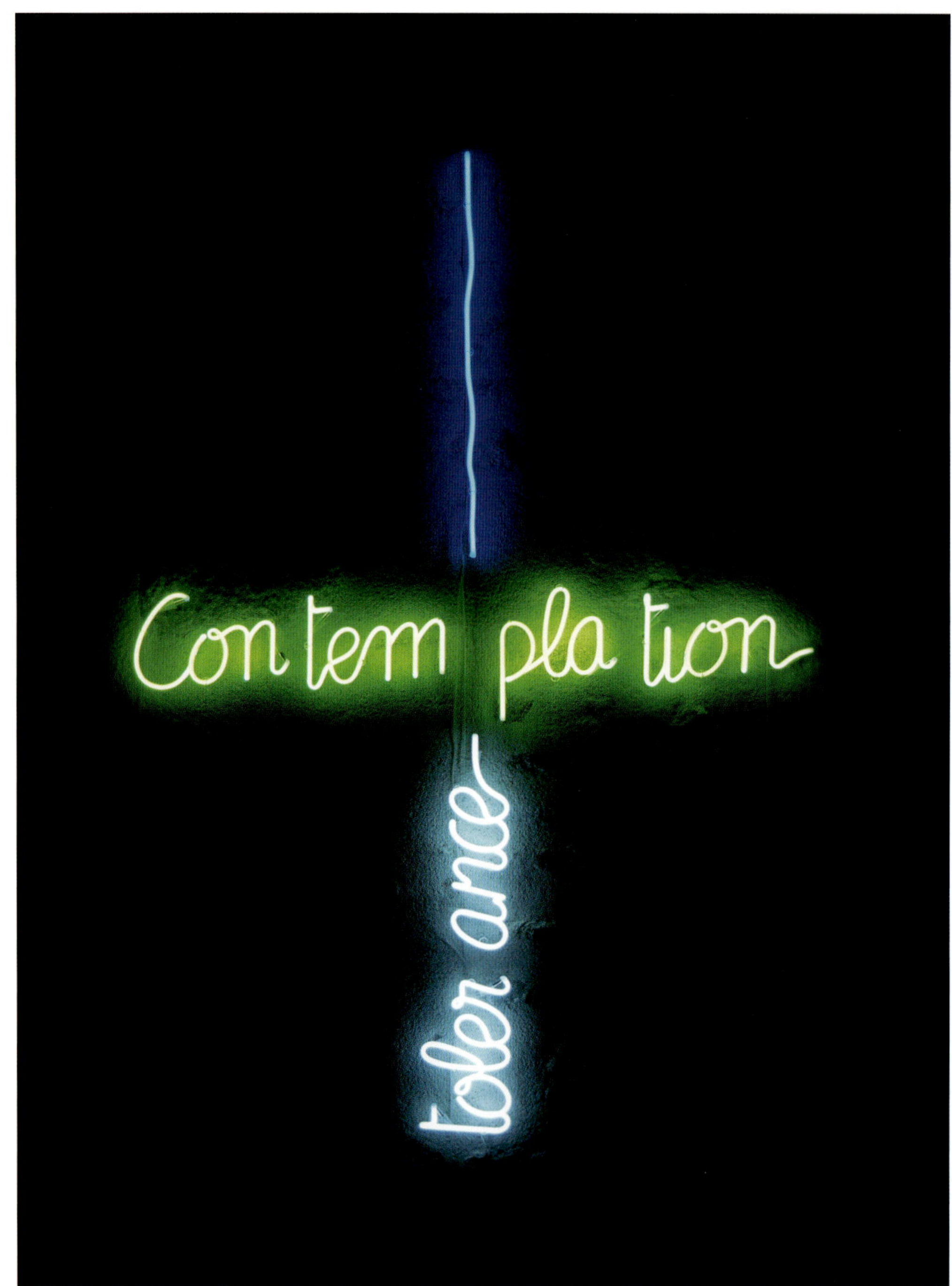

Contemplation, 1996
Neon
150 x 100 cm
Courtesy of Le Musée d'Art et d'Archéologie de Guéret, France

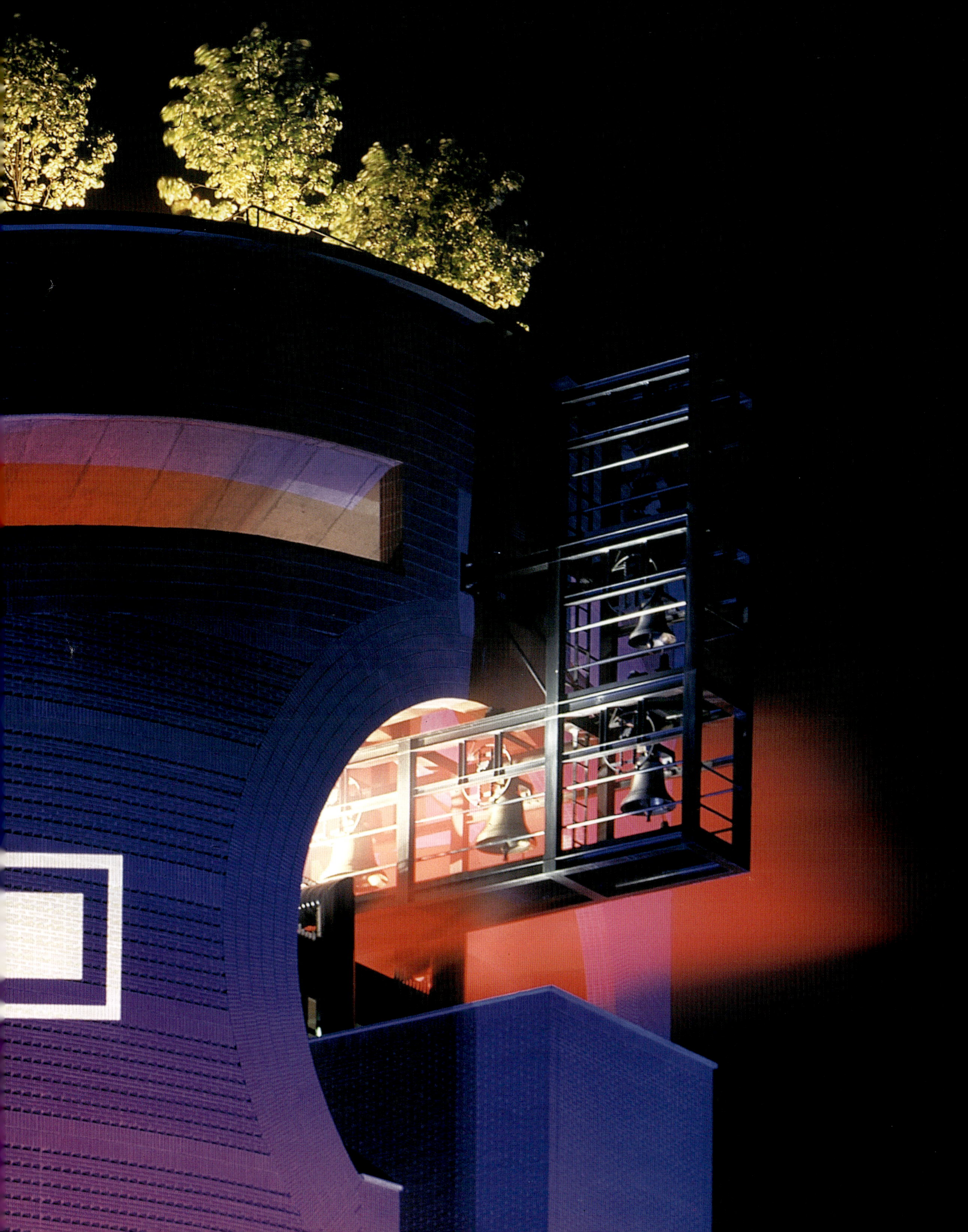

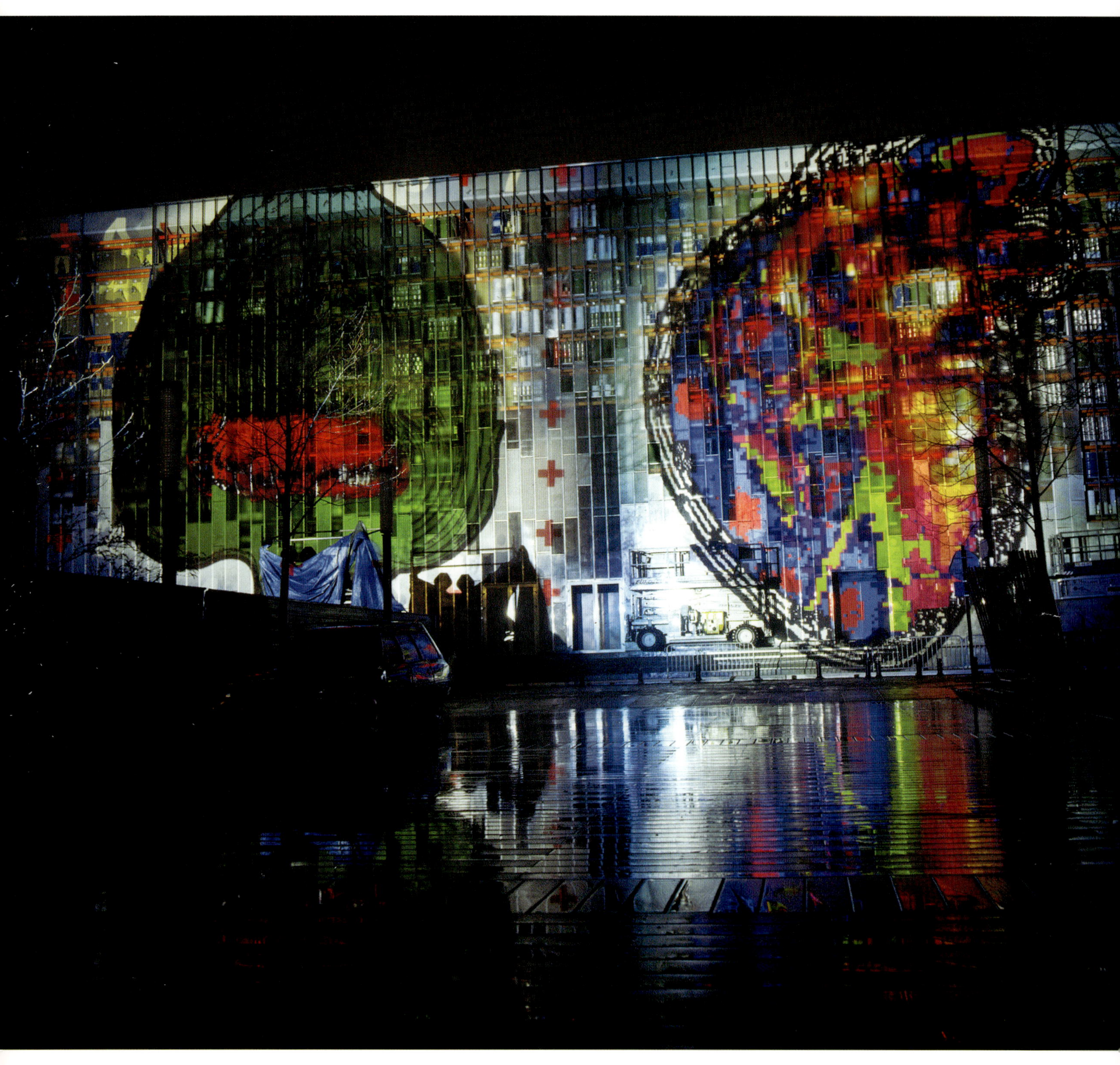

OPERA.tion LIFE NEXUS Act IV—Millennium

Lieu Unique LU, Nantes, France

2000

Behind the glass facade of the former LU biscuit factory, now a dynamic multidisciplinary cultural centre are 16,000 steel safe boxes—mini time capsules—each containing a personal object donated by the local inhabitants of Nantes. At midnight on 31 December 1999 Lucy+Jorge Orta created a Light Works to commemorate the sealing of the last of these vaults, which is has been named *Le Grenier du Siècle* (*Store of the Century*). Contemporary artist Patrick Raynaud imagined this enormous city attic, which will be opened 100 years later on 1 January 2100 at 5pm precisely. The double-layered translucent glass proved to be one of the most interesting projection experiments, as the light refracted off the white steel vaults just behind the glass wall.

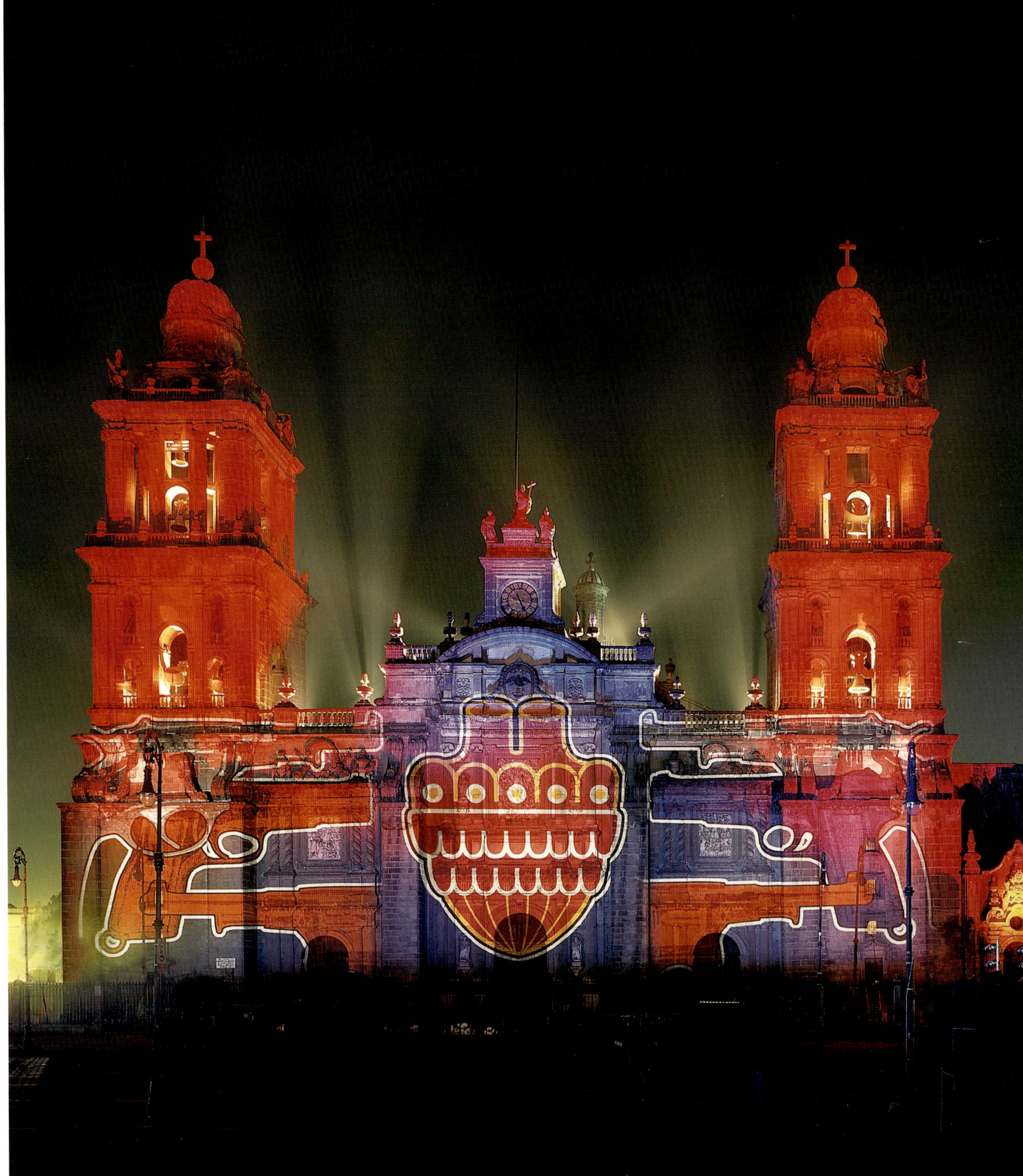

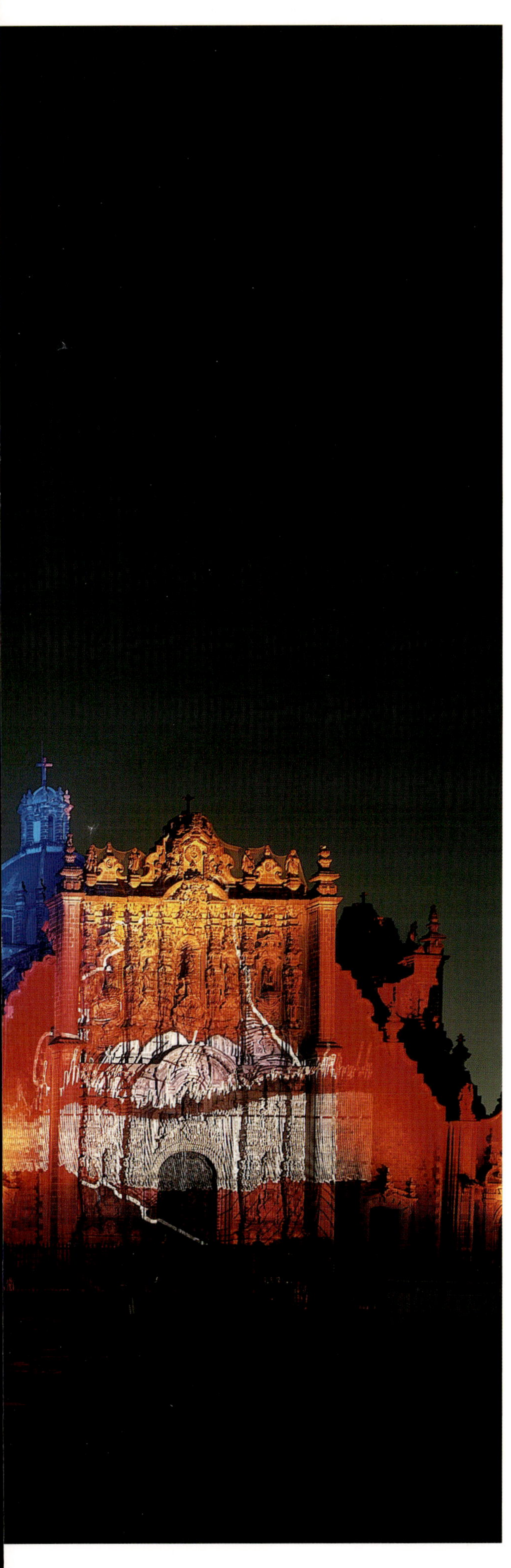

NEXO CORAZÒN Act V

El Zócalo, Mexico City, Mexico

Prior to the V act of *OPERA.tion Life Nexus*, Jorge Orta conducted a series of community workshops with inhabitants living around the historical district of the Zócalo. Local artists, street vendors, homeless children, and prostitutes dropped into the Ex-Santa Teresa Alternative Art Center, to assist with the creation of the graphic score, depicting the scenes they witness daily on the streets of Mexico city, which would form the backdrop to the visual iconography. Cultures France (AFAA), the French Embassy and the XVII Festival del Centro Histórico commissioned Orta and French composer Pierre Henry to create an integrated visual-sound installation for an audience of 200,000.

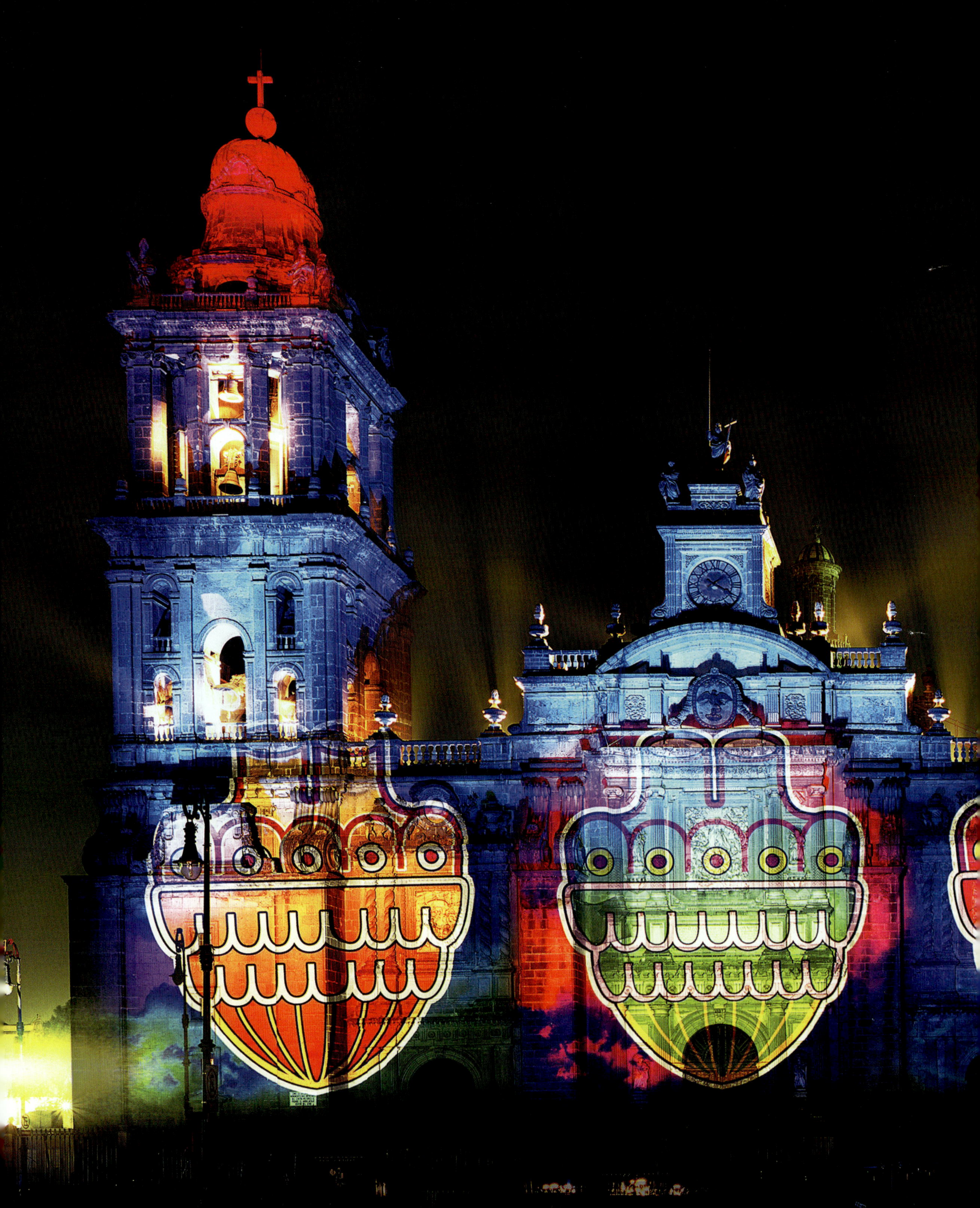

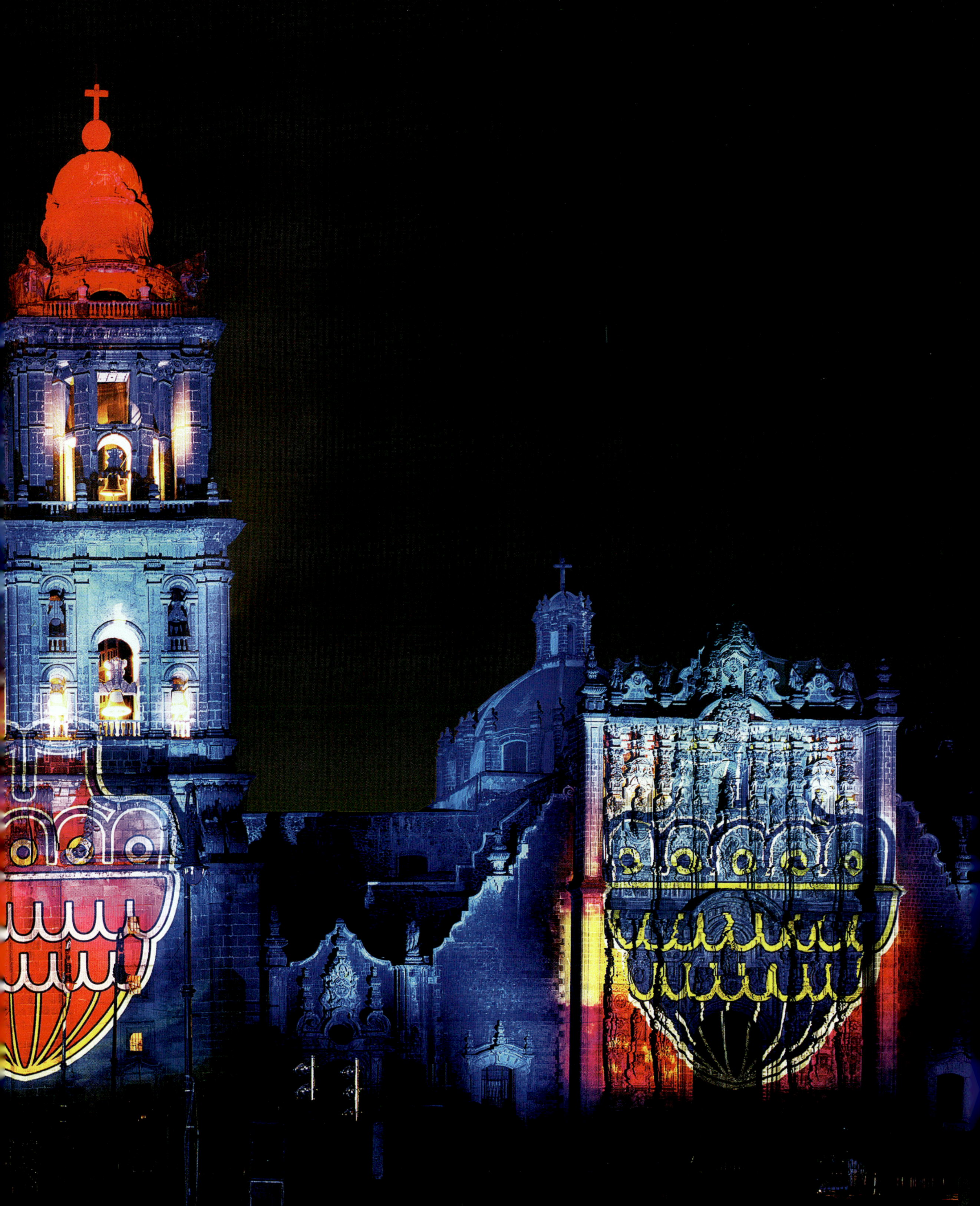

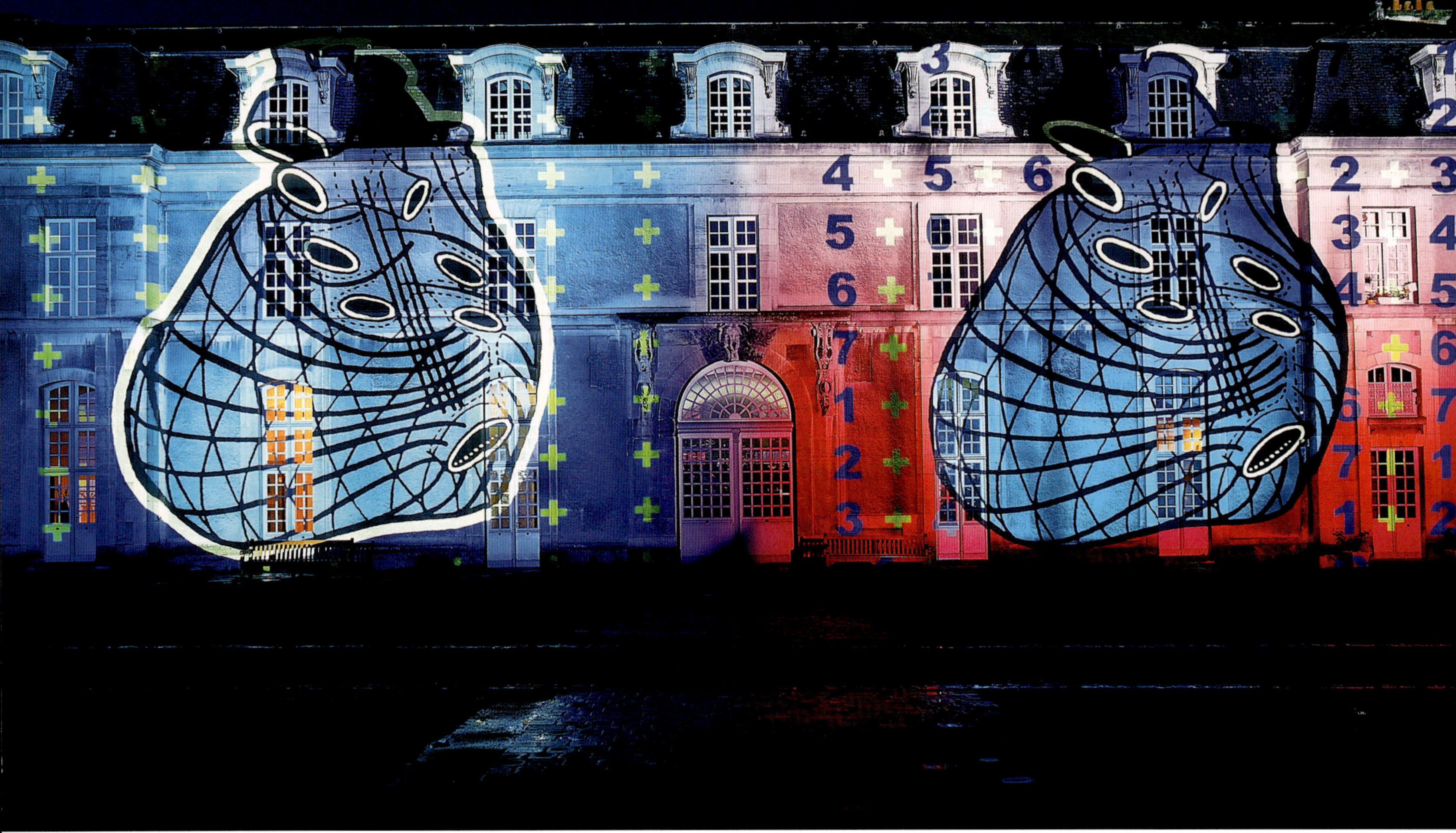

OPERA.tion LIFE NEXUS Act VI—Battement des Grands Jours

2001

Palais de Tau, Cathédrale de Reims, France

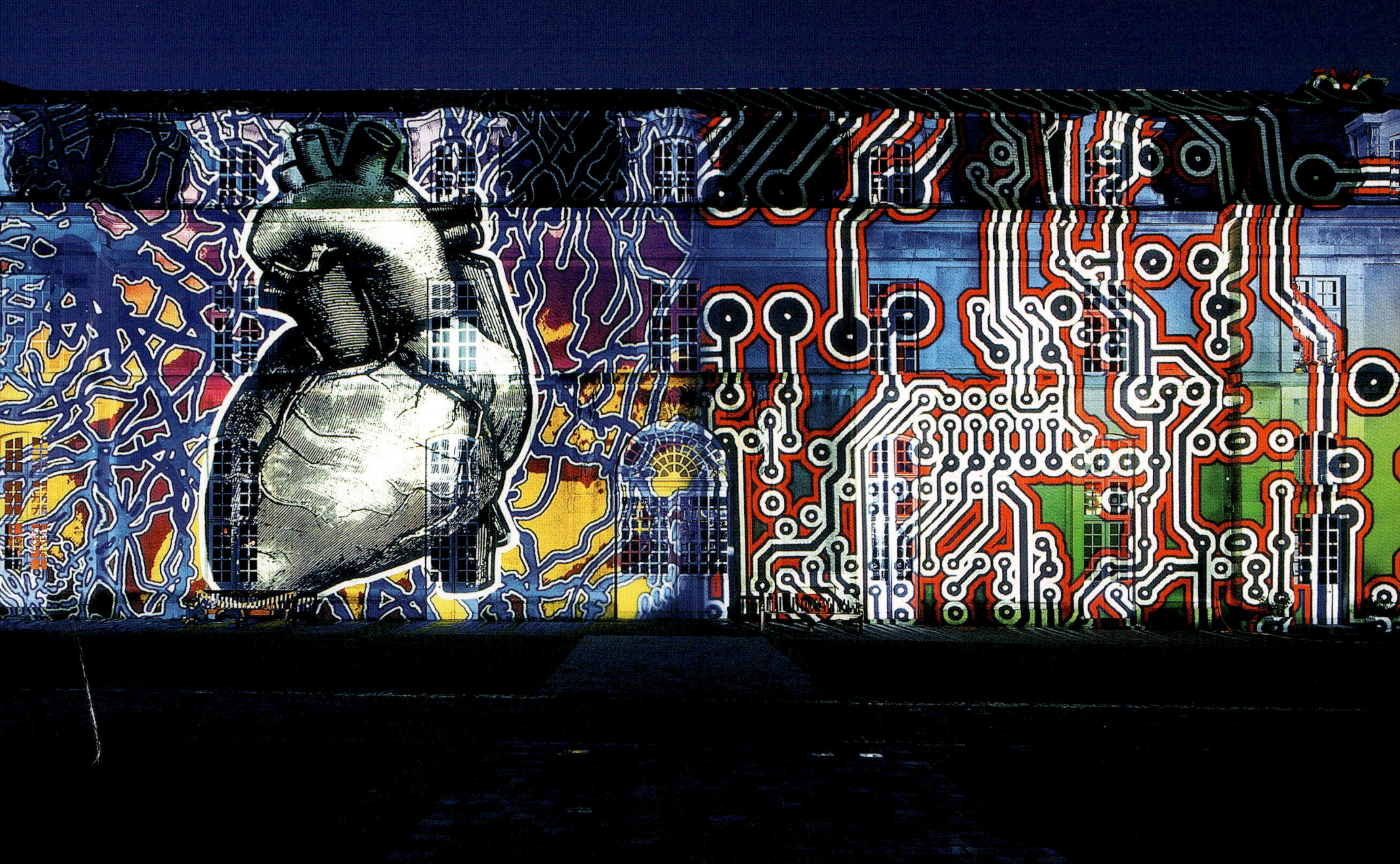

The Palais de Tau was the Episcopal residence associated with the coronation of 32 French kings, from the eleventh century to the reign of Charles X in 1825. Both the palace and the neighbouring cathedral are on the UNESCO World Heritage List. This splendid setting became the site of intervention for the VI act in the series *OPERA.tion Life Nexus*. Lucy+Jorge Orta collaborated with Spanish composer Llorenç Barber, who improvised a concert using the cathedral bells as the images embellished the palace facade.

The Palais de Tau is now an important museum conserving the city of Reim's Medieval artefacts and tapestries. The Light Works on the facade coincided with the opening of the exhibition Twenty Centuries of Cathedrals, showing public treasures and hidden masterpieces from the cathedrals all over France, enlightening the public to the role of the founding saints and donors who have contributed to the construction and enrichments of the cathedrals as an important societal phenomena and unique architectural works of art. As Victor Hugo has so justly written, "a total work of art" associating spiritual life, with artistic creation, recreational and administrative and activities.

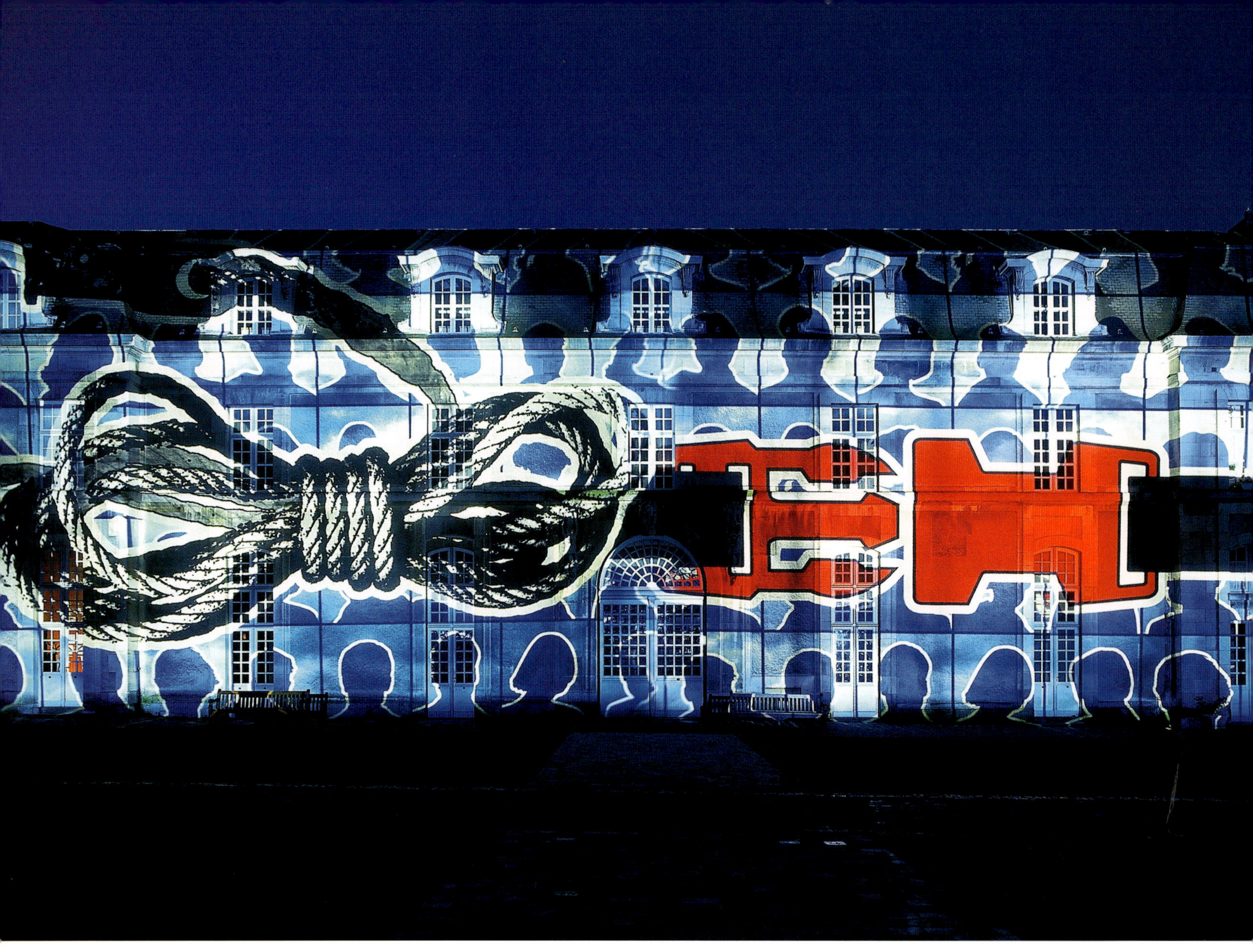

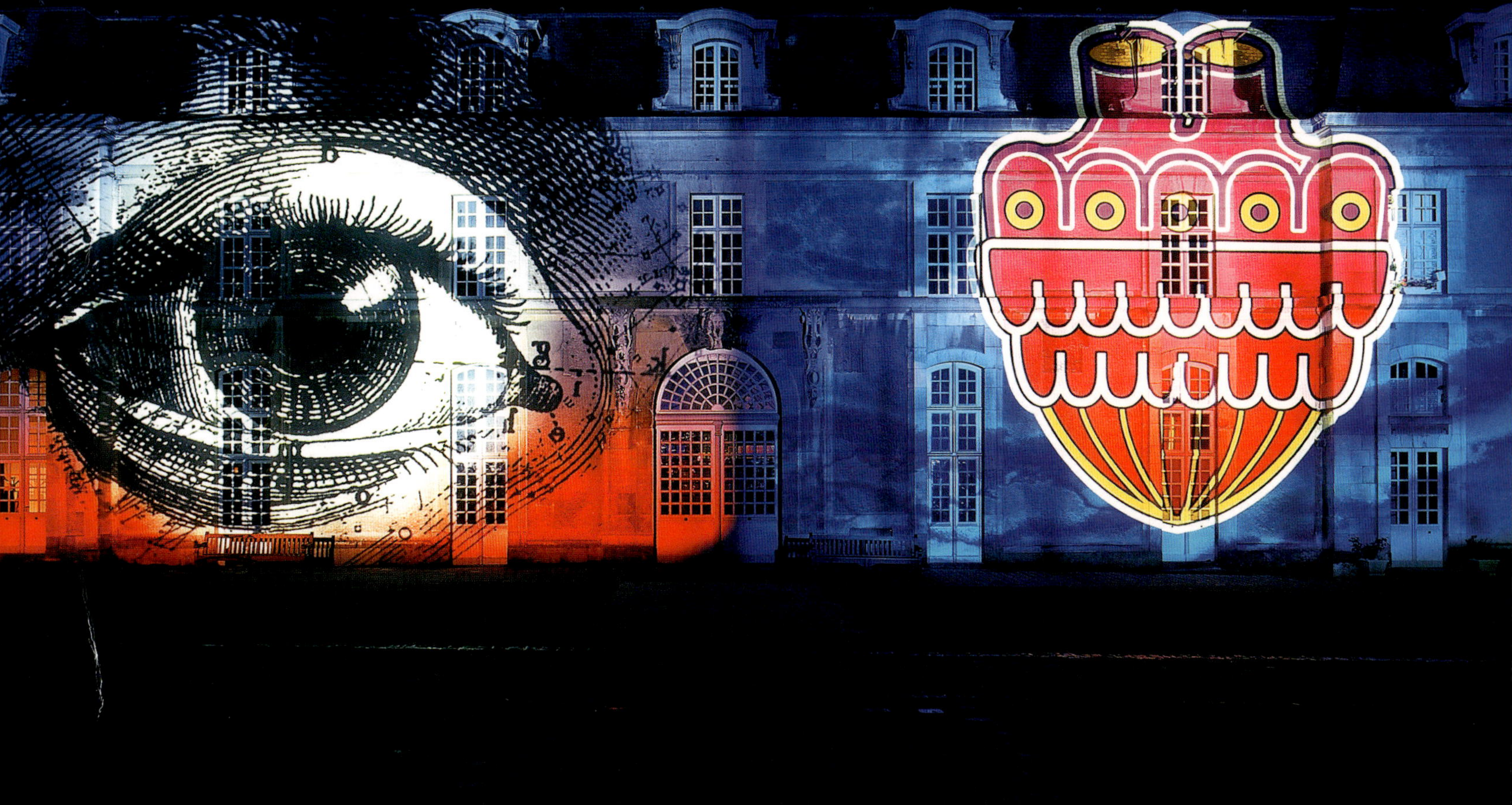

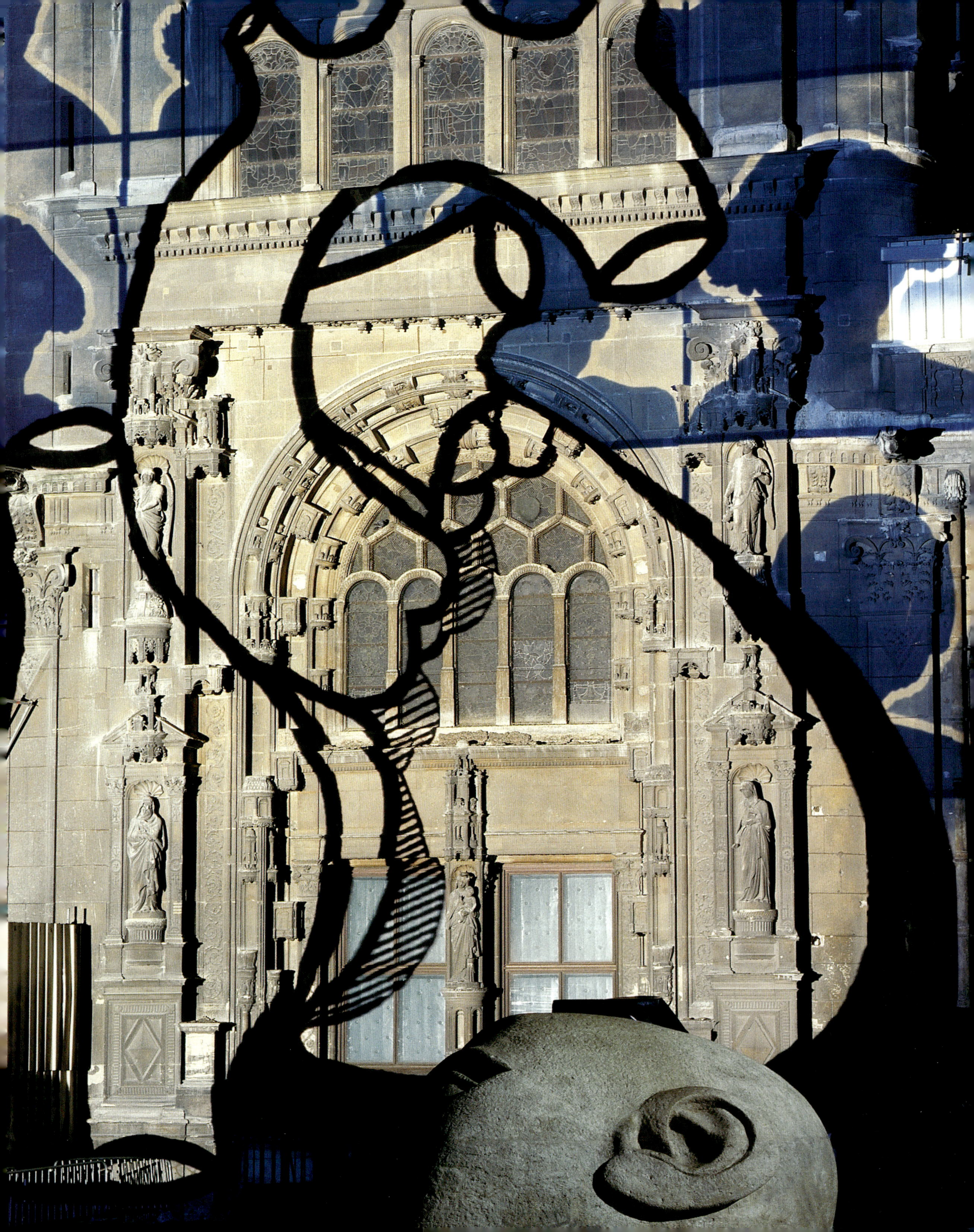

OPERA.tion LIFE NEXUS Act VIII

2002

Église Saint-Eustache, Paris, France

Commissioned by a department of the Health Ministry EFG (Etablissement français des greffes), the XIII Light Works in the series *OPERA.tion Life Nexus*, was created for the open-air music festival La Fête de la Musique. The artists invited German composer Simon Stockhausen to create an original score based on their ongoing artistic research on the symbol of the heart. The facade of the church, undergoing renovation proved an interesting site for experimenting with light and live performance, as Stockhausen suspended his orchestra in the scaffolding above the Les Halles gardens.

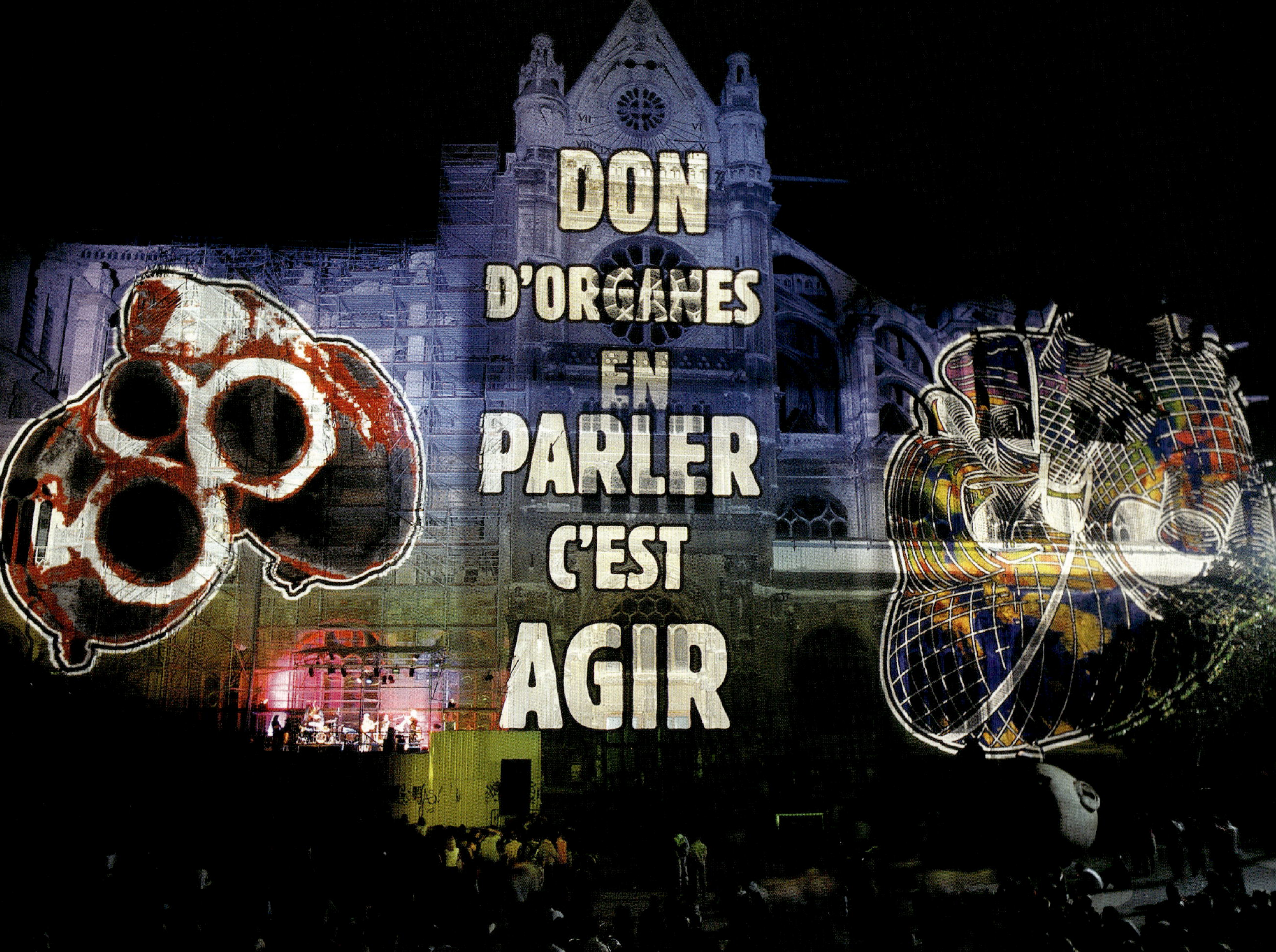
DON
D'ORGANES
EN
PARLER
C'EST
AGIR

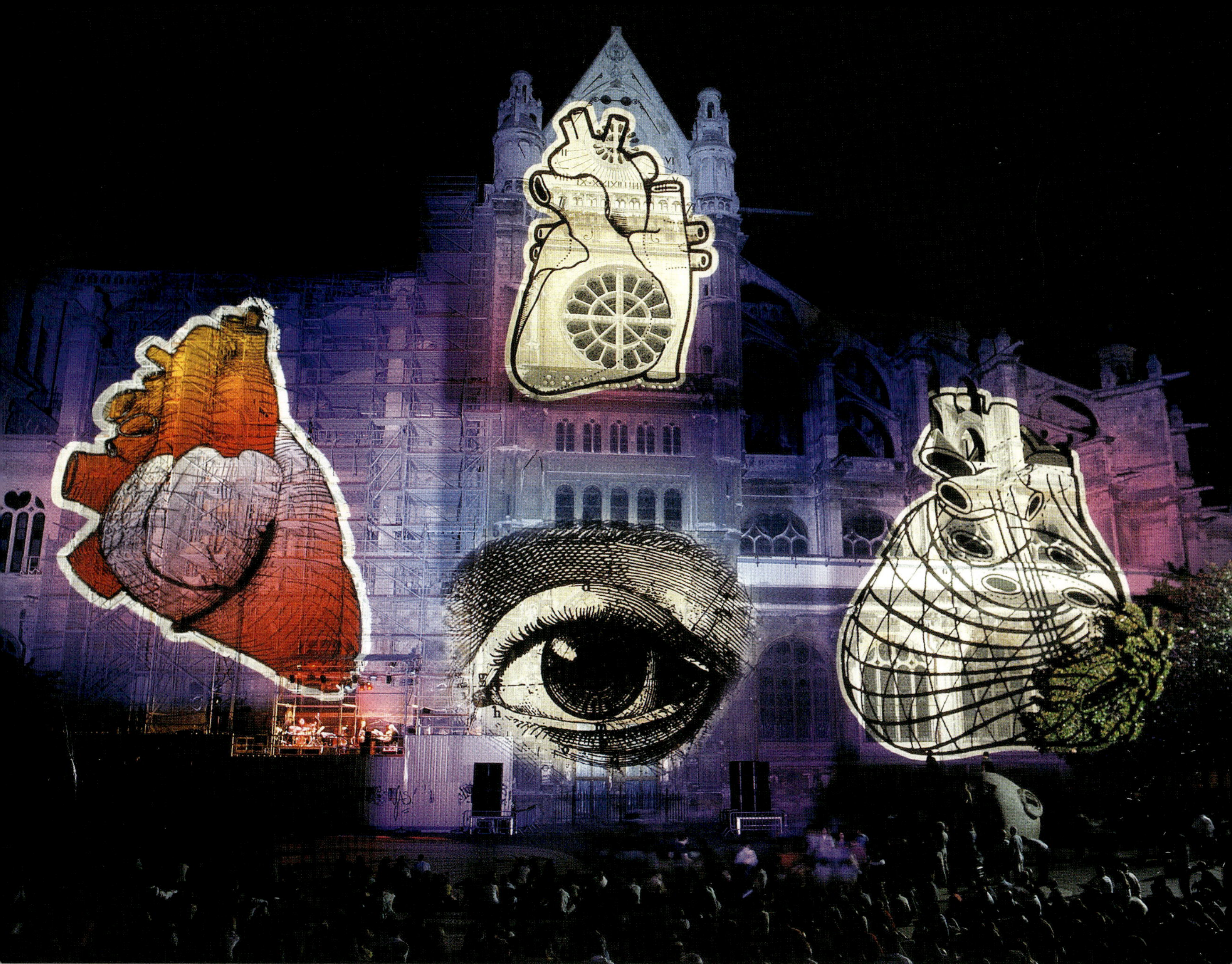

The unifying theme of the series of works OPERA.tion Life Nexus is that of Heart = Life, expressed creatively through both symbolic and human perspectives. The universal nature of the Heart is able to ally cultural, social and religious differences, opening up a new vision of the medical problem of donation, to a message of hope.

Jorge Orta

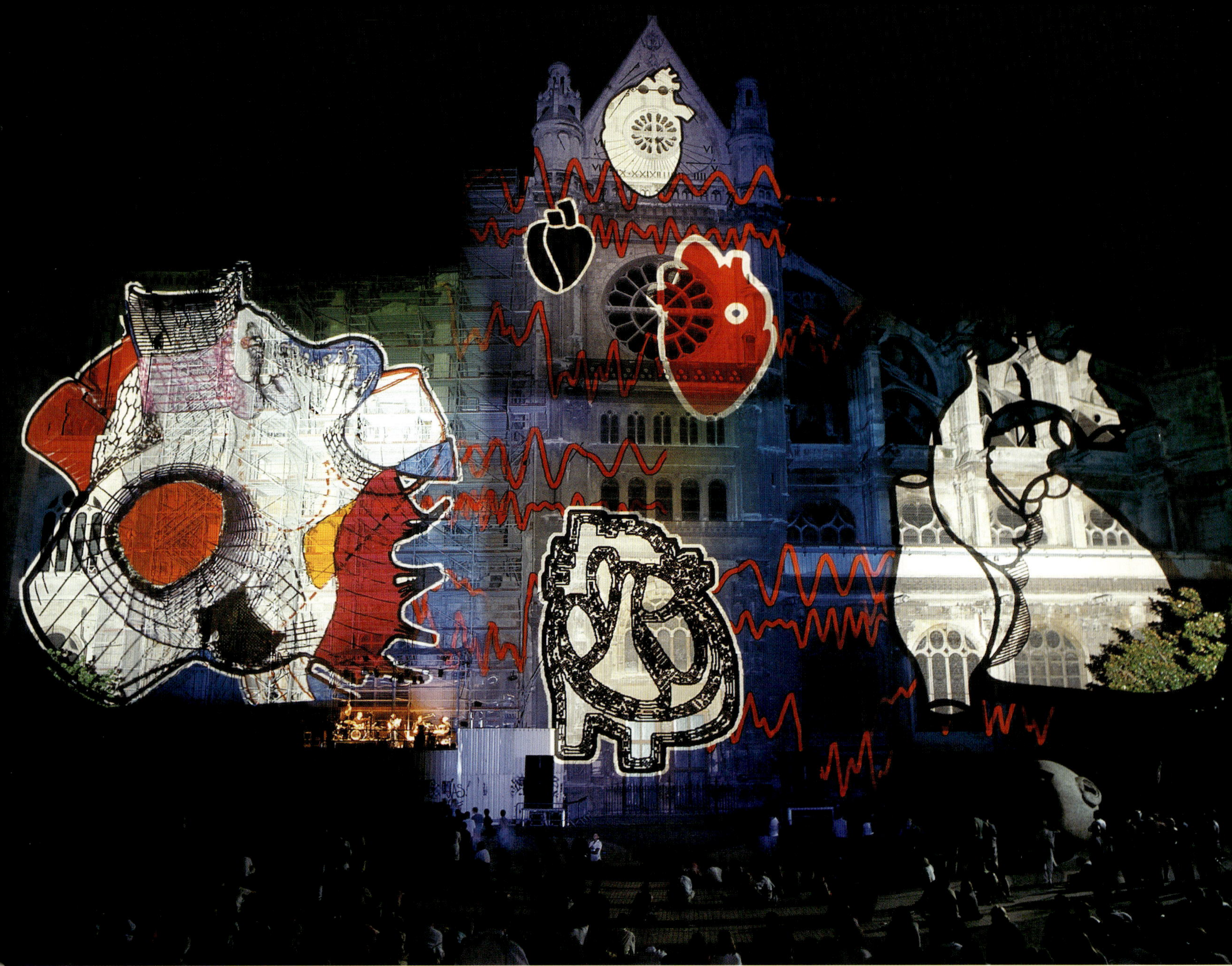

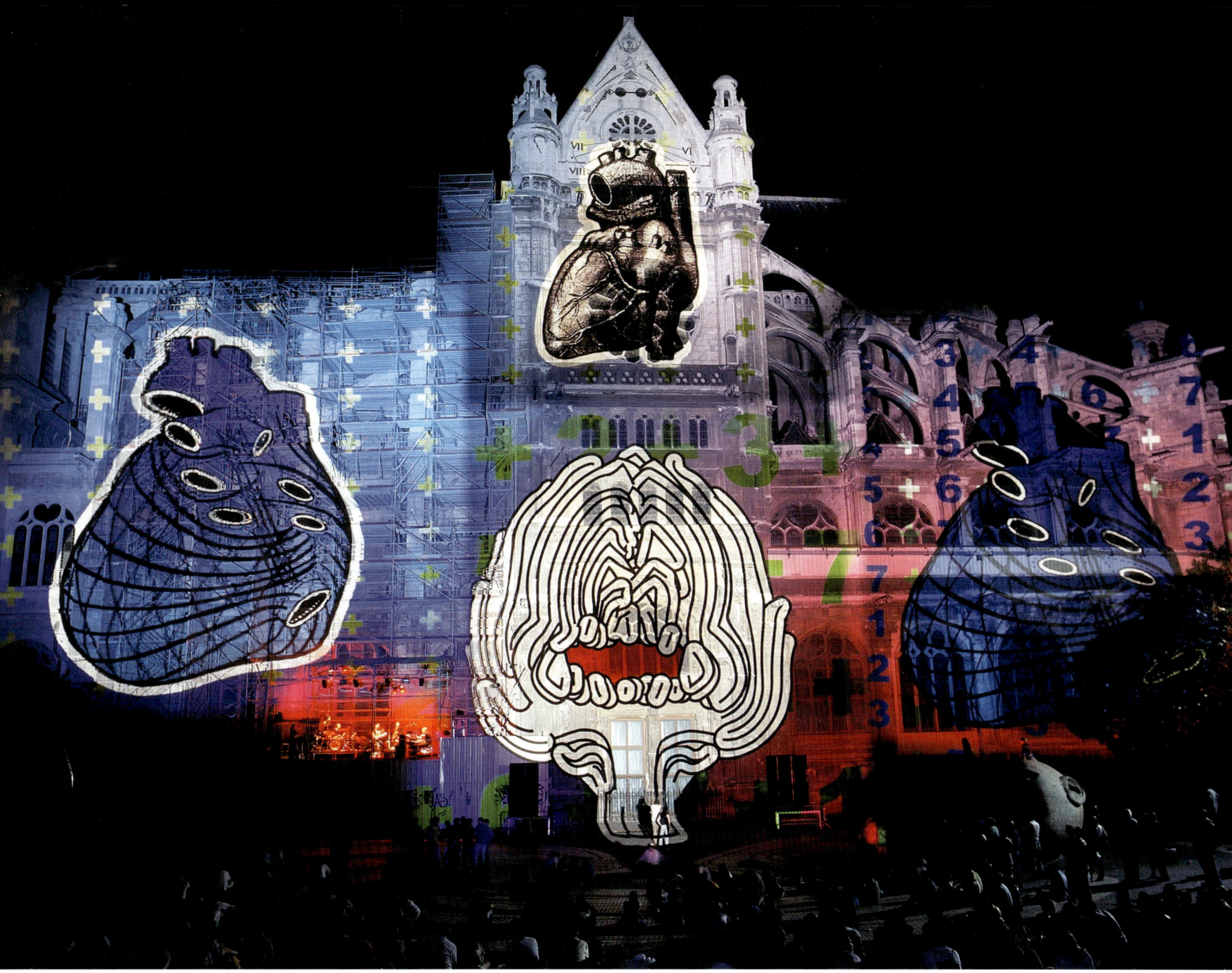

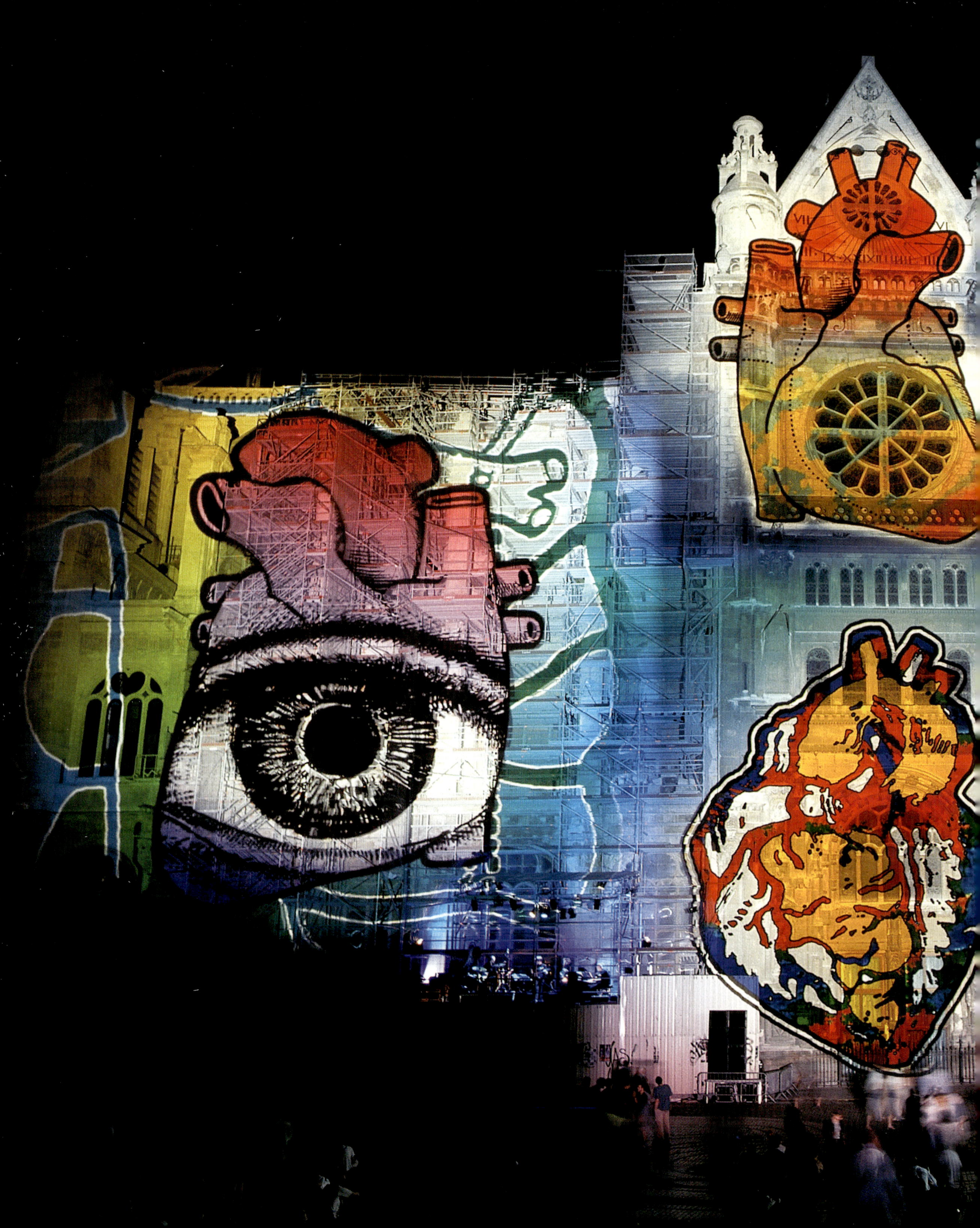

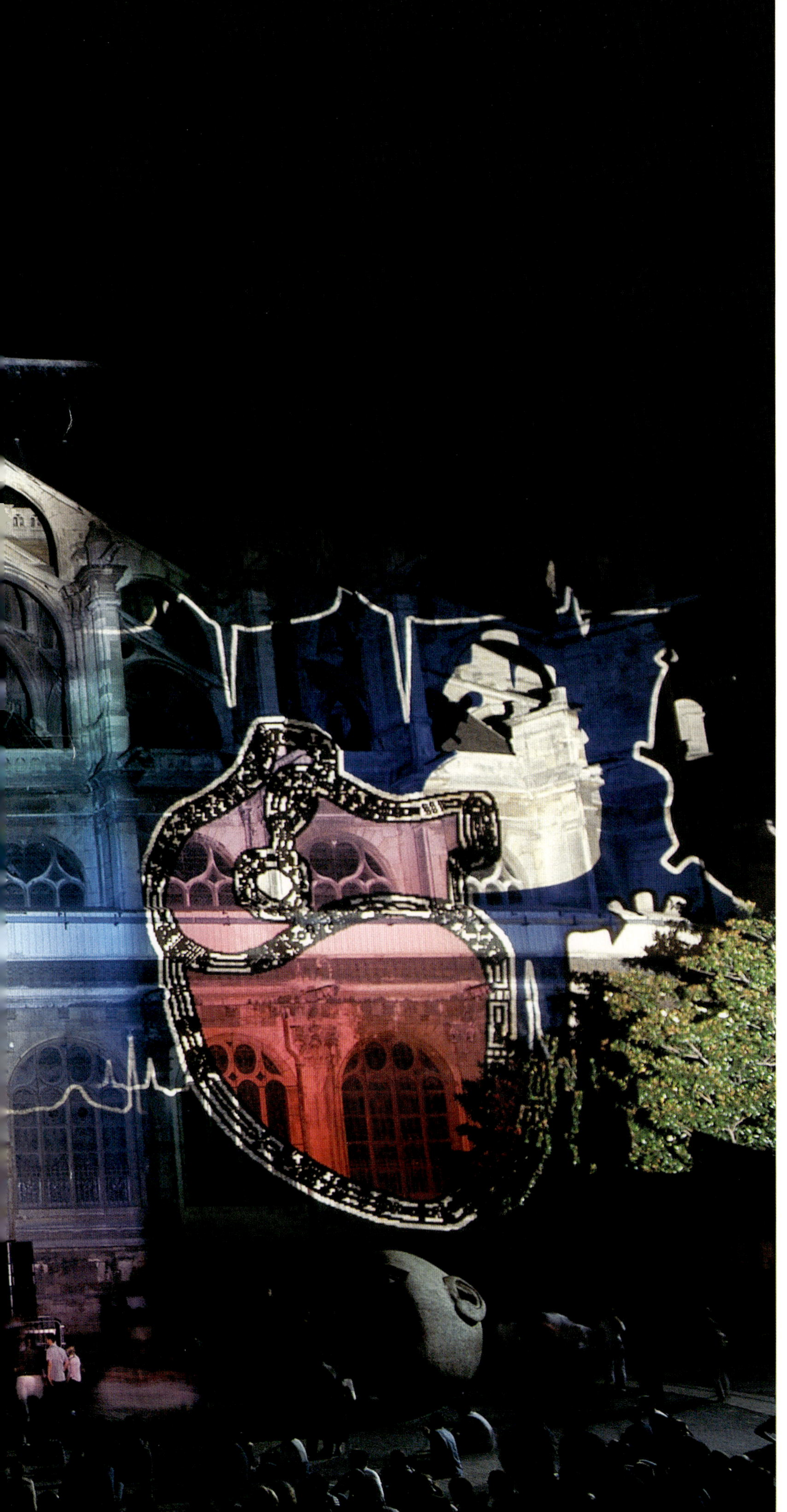

OPERA.tion LIFE NEXUS Act IX

Place Stanislas, Nancy, France

To inaugurate the 14th World Transplant Games hosted by the city of Nancy, the IX Light Works in the series *OPERA.tion Life Nexus* marks the closure of a decade of artistic research on the symbol of the heart. As well as creating one of the most memorable *Light Works* and a concert together with French composer Pierre Henry in the Place Stanislas, a UNESCO listed heritage site, the artists rallied the support of the regional council with and collaboration of over 35,000 college students across the region of Meurthe-et-Moselle. Together they drew up the first universal code of ethics for organ donation: *The Gift*. This charter can now be found enclosed in one of the 70 gold hearts at the tip of a five metre public sculpture created by Jorge Orta for the Place de la République of Nancy.

As the sun set, tens of thousands of people, 1,500 transplant athletes and their coaches from around the world converged on the Place Stanislas to partake in the IX act of the series *OPERA.tion Life Nexus*. The grandiose ephemeral Light Works combining the striking heart iconography and a musical creation, composed and arranged by Henry, created a choreography of giant images projected onto the facades of the Hotel de Ville, Grand Hotel de la Reine and the two cafes, Faith and Commerce. It was a unique moment of artistic creation dedicated to organ donation and its values.

2003

Over a year leading up to the Light Works, 35,000 college students with their families or in schools with their teachers, were given information on and time to exchange views on organ donation before giving free rein to their imagination and inventiveness to express their opinions or their sensitivity to organ donation. Lucy+Jorge Orta provided each of them with a blank heart-shaped sketchbook in which to inscribe a short sentence expressing their feelings on the subject, or to represent it by a drawing, collage, painting or poetry that inspires organ donation. Collected and synthesised, the sketchbook responses led directly to the writing of the code of ethics for organ donation. The Charter, instigated by the artists, with the support of the EFG (Etablissement Français des greffes) and medical scientists has the ambition to emanate a universal founding document for all the aspects of care that engender organ donation and transplantation: human, sociological, philosophical, medical, religious, humanistic and legal.

In the Place de la République stands, *Le Cœur du Grand Nancy*, a striking public sculpture and the lasting trace of the collective efforts of the community of Meurthe-et-Moselle, around the issue of organ donation. Standing four meters high, over sixty bronze hearts are positioned on a pedestal inscribed with fragments of the texts collected during the workshops by Lucy+Jorge Orta. At the tip of the flame-like assemblage is a single gold heart. Inside this heart, the universal code of ethics for organ donation—*The Gift*—representing the desires to share thoughts and hearts with others.

Le Coeur du Grand Nancy (The Gift), 2003
Bronze, gold
5 metres
Public sculpture, Place de la République, Nancy, France

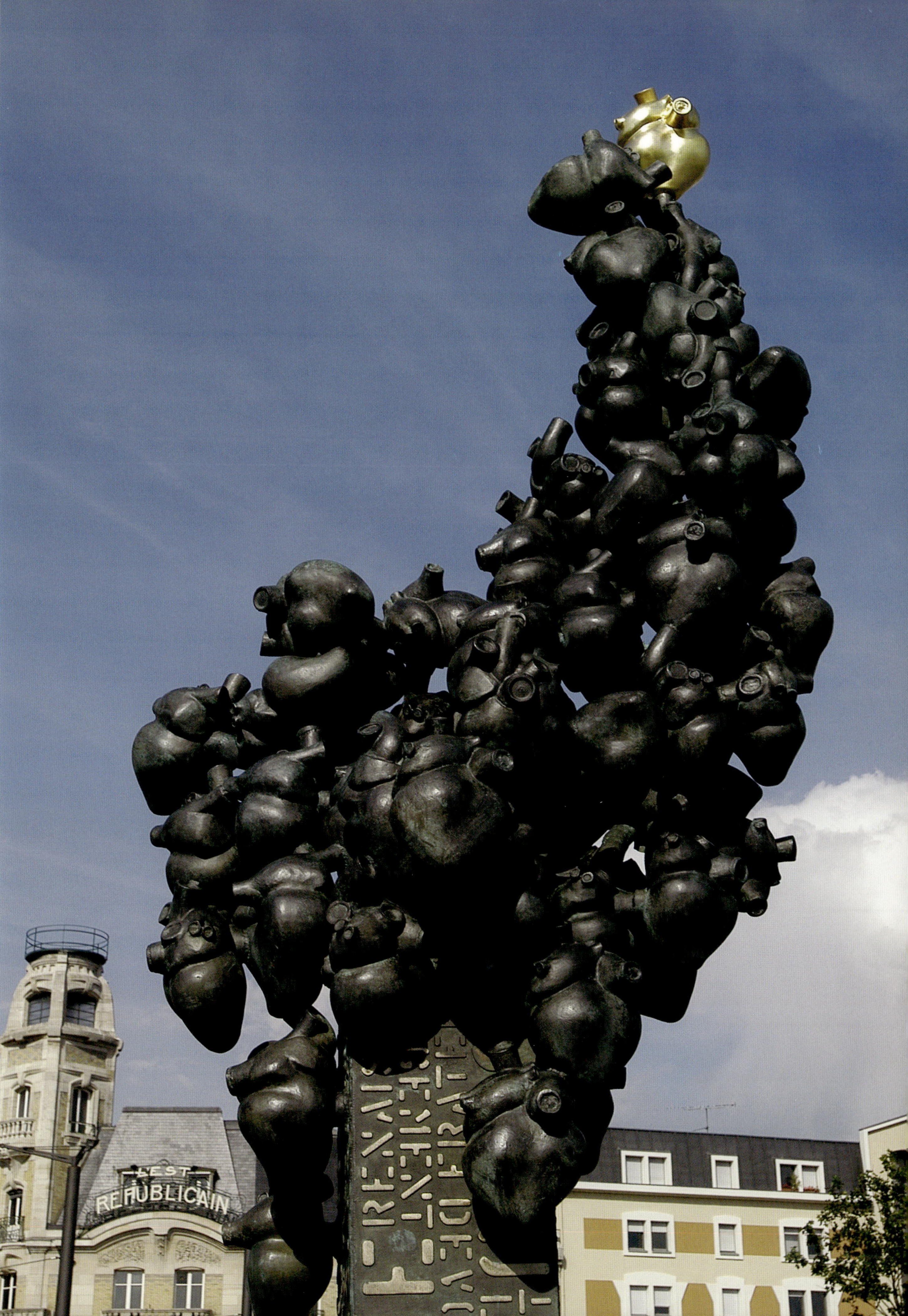
L'EST
REPUBLICAIN

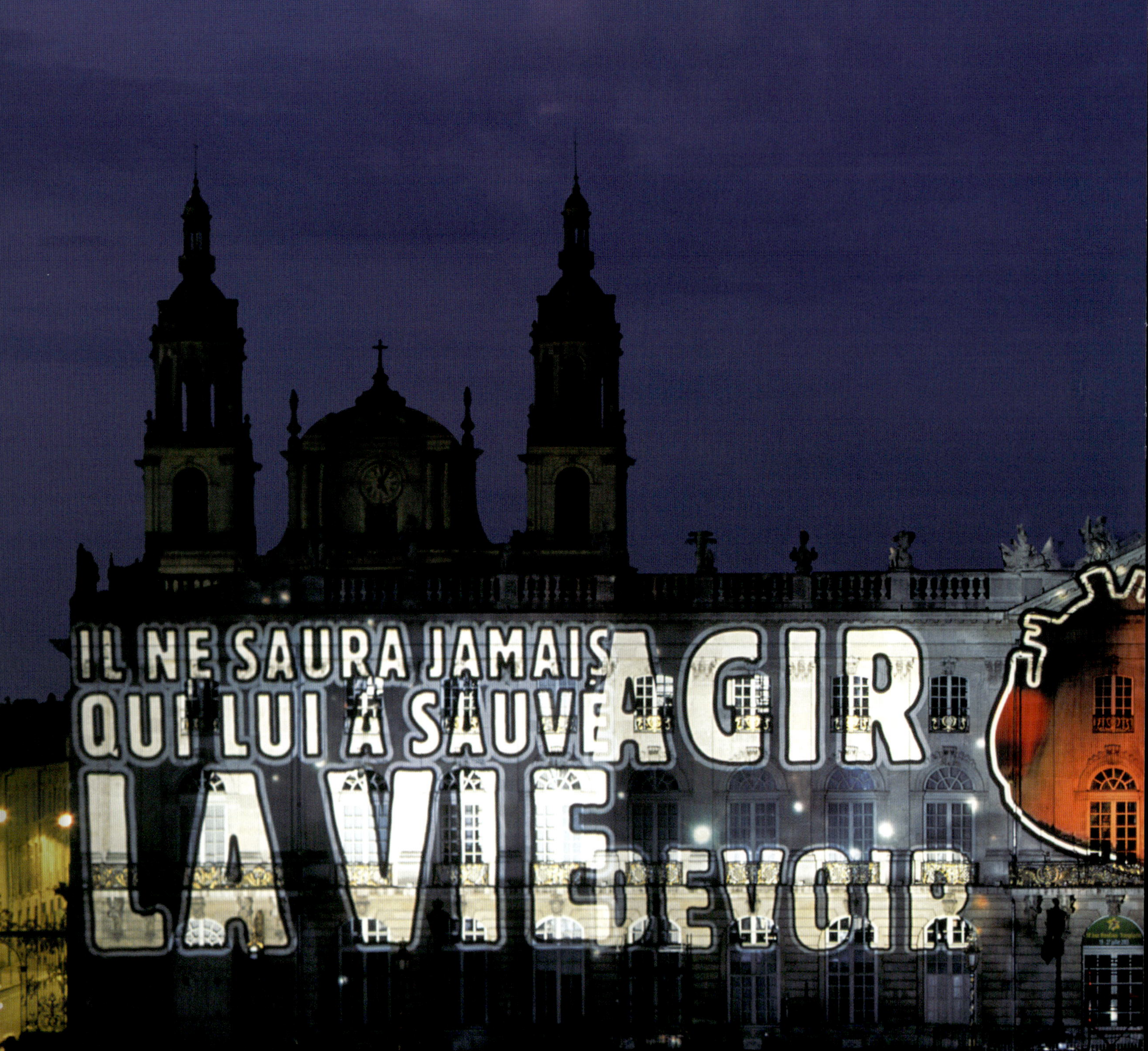
IL NE SAURA JAMAIS
QUI LUI A SAUVÉ
LA VIE
AGIR
DEVOIR

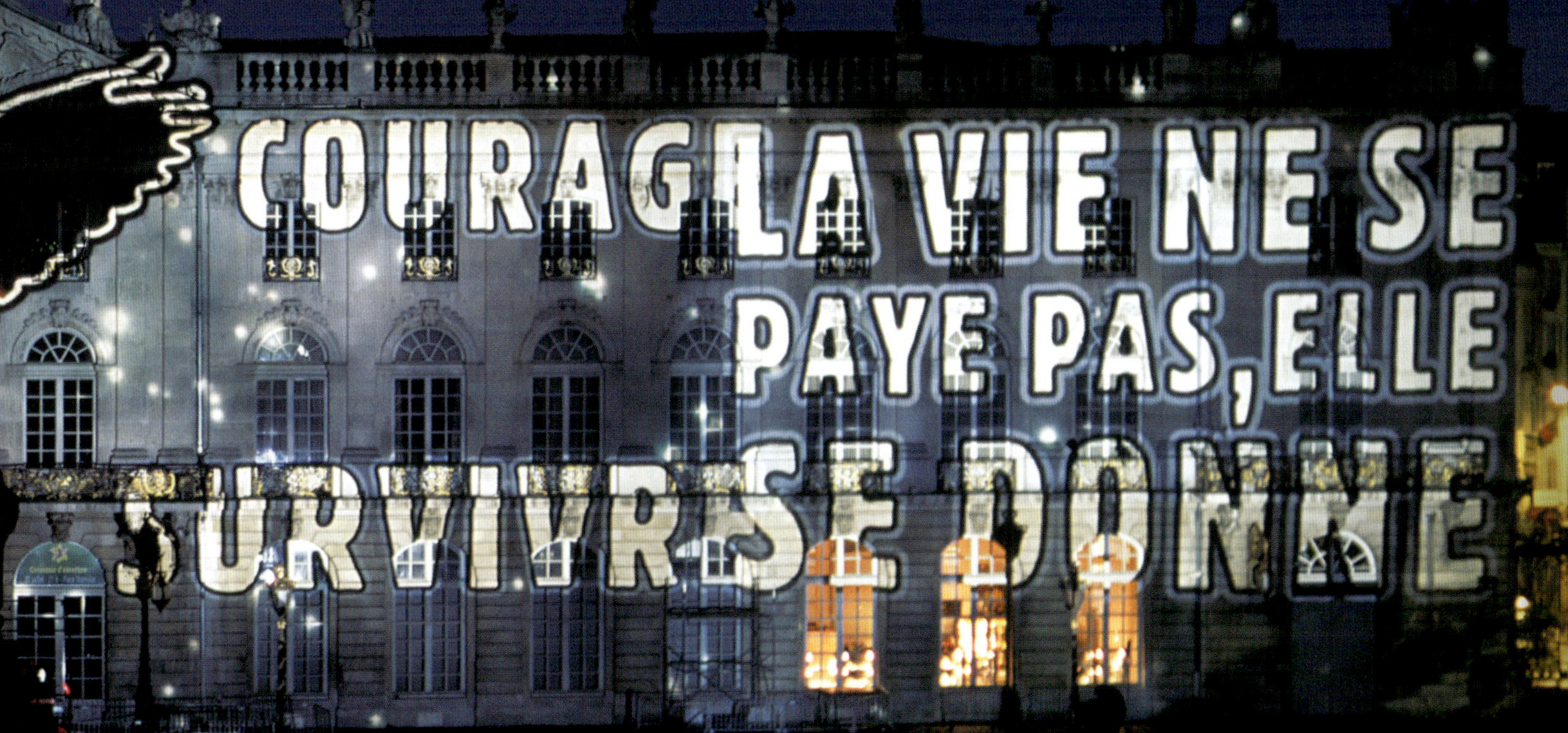
COURAGLA VIE NE SE
PAYE PAS, ELLE
SURVIVRSE DONNE

The mobilisation of young people and their families encourages the awareness of the concept of organ donation and how to act against the shortage of donations across France. The literal and figurative, texts written by the young people for The Gift, the universal code of ethics will be inscribed forever onto the city's public sculpture, taking on an even greater meaning.

JORGE ORTA

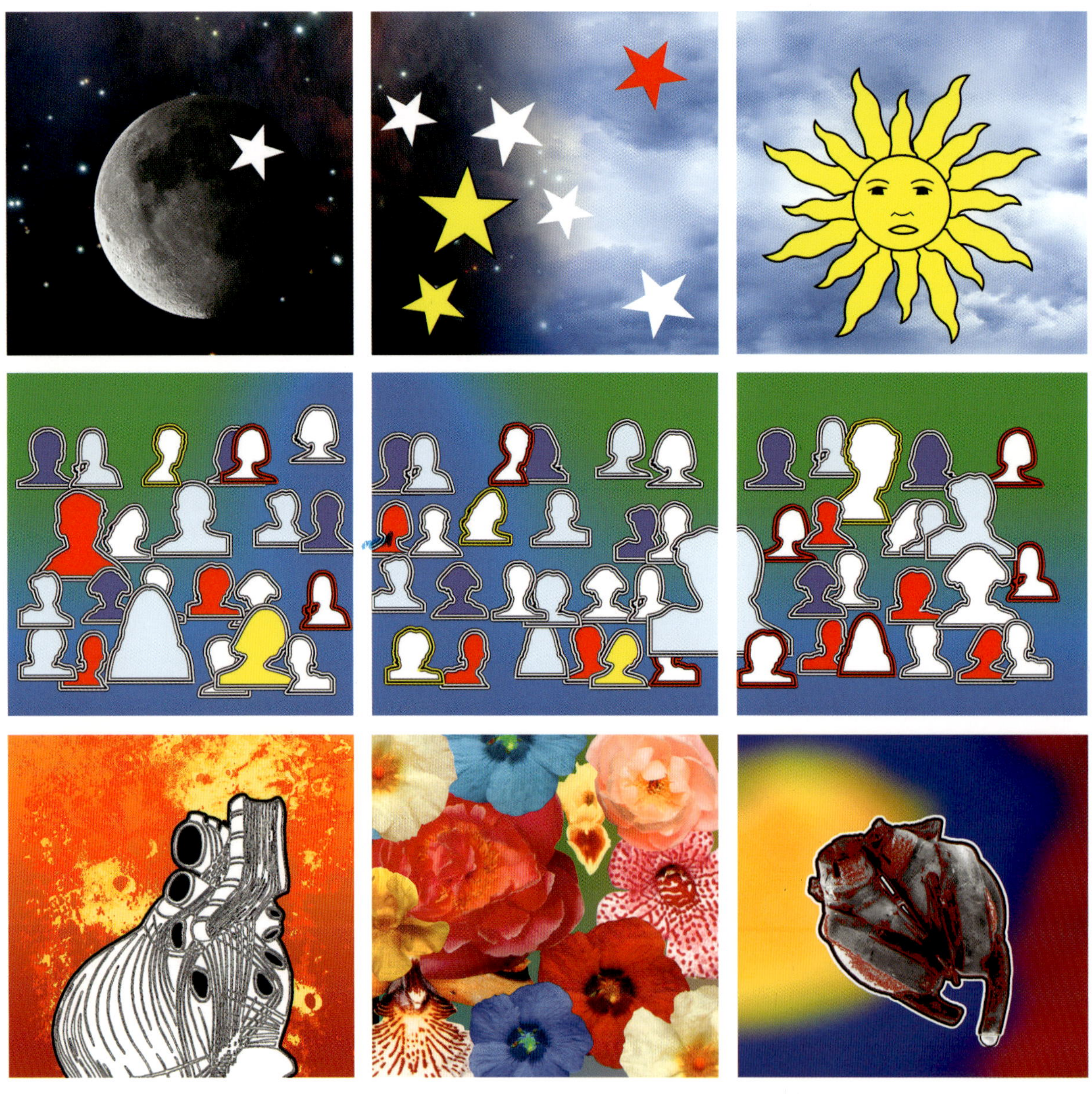

Falling Star, 2003
Laminated Lambda photograph
190 x 190 cm

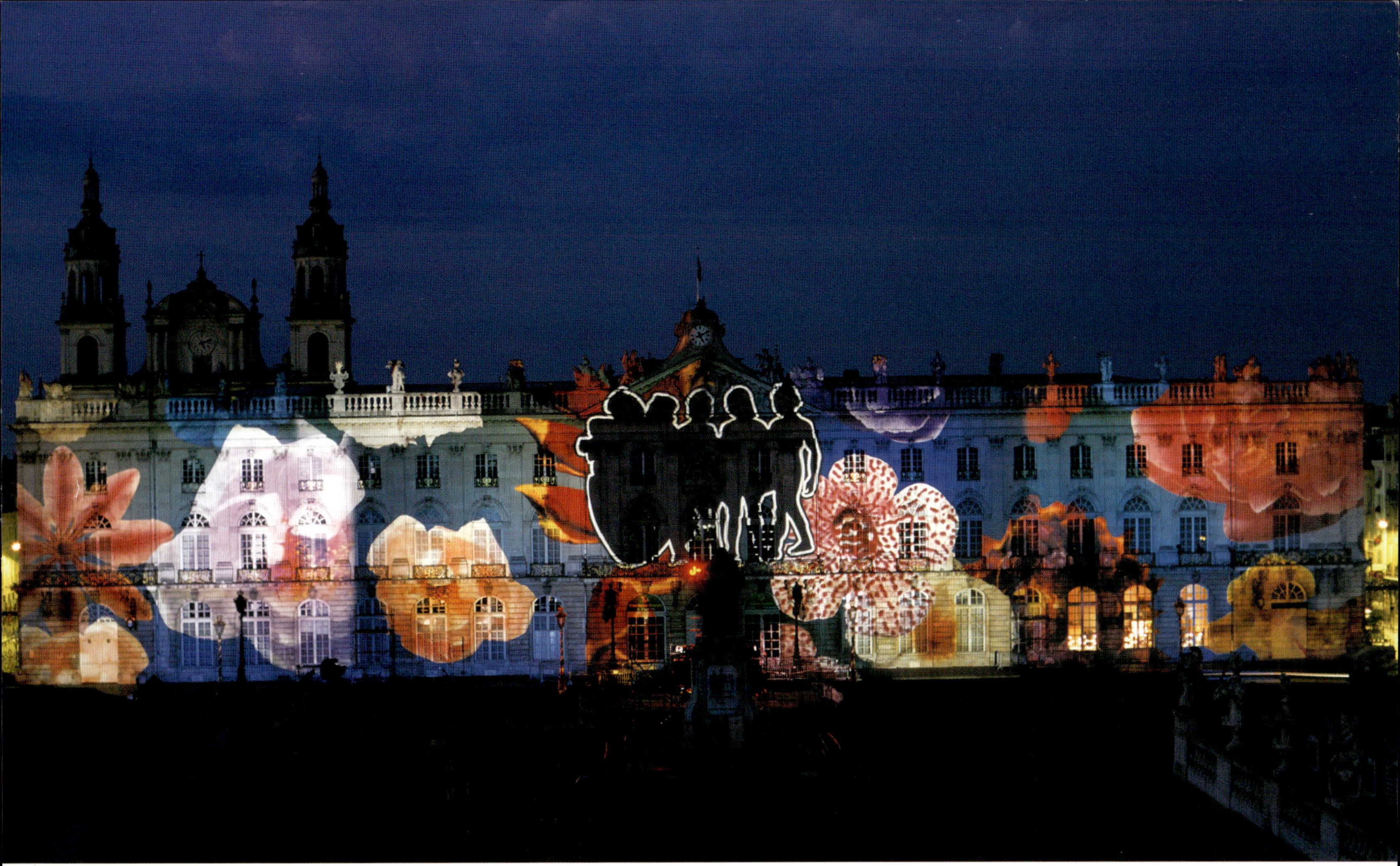

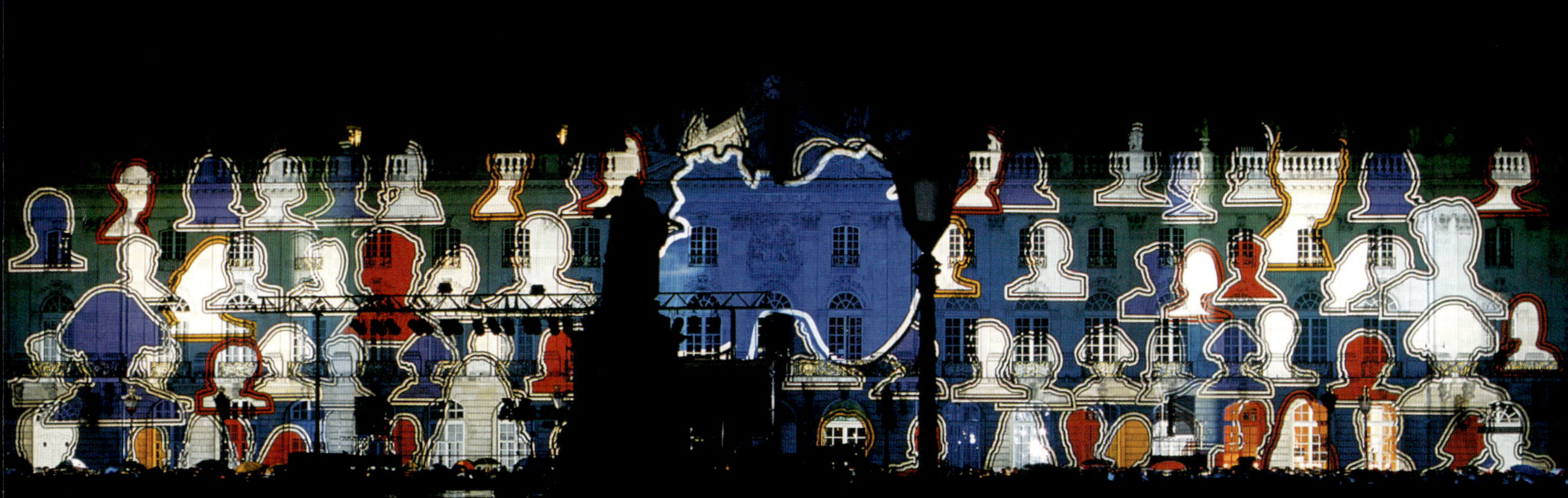

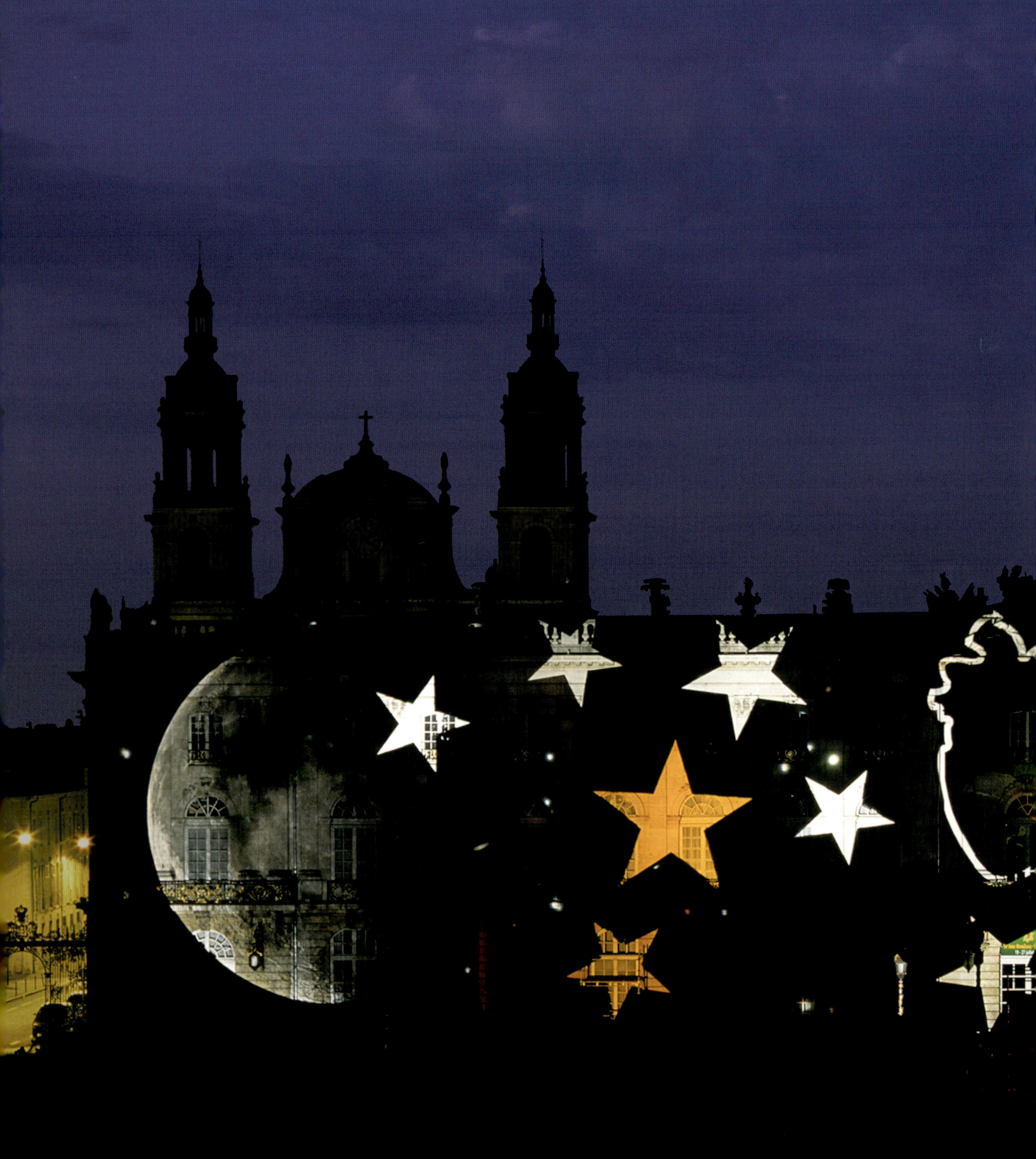

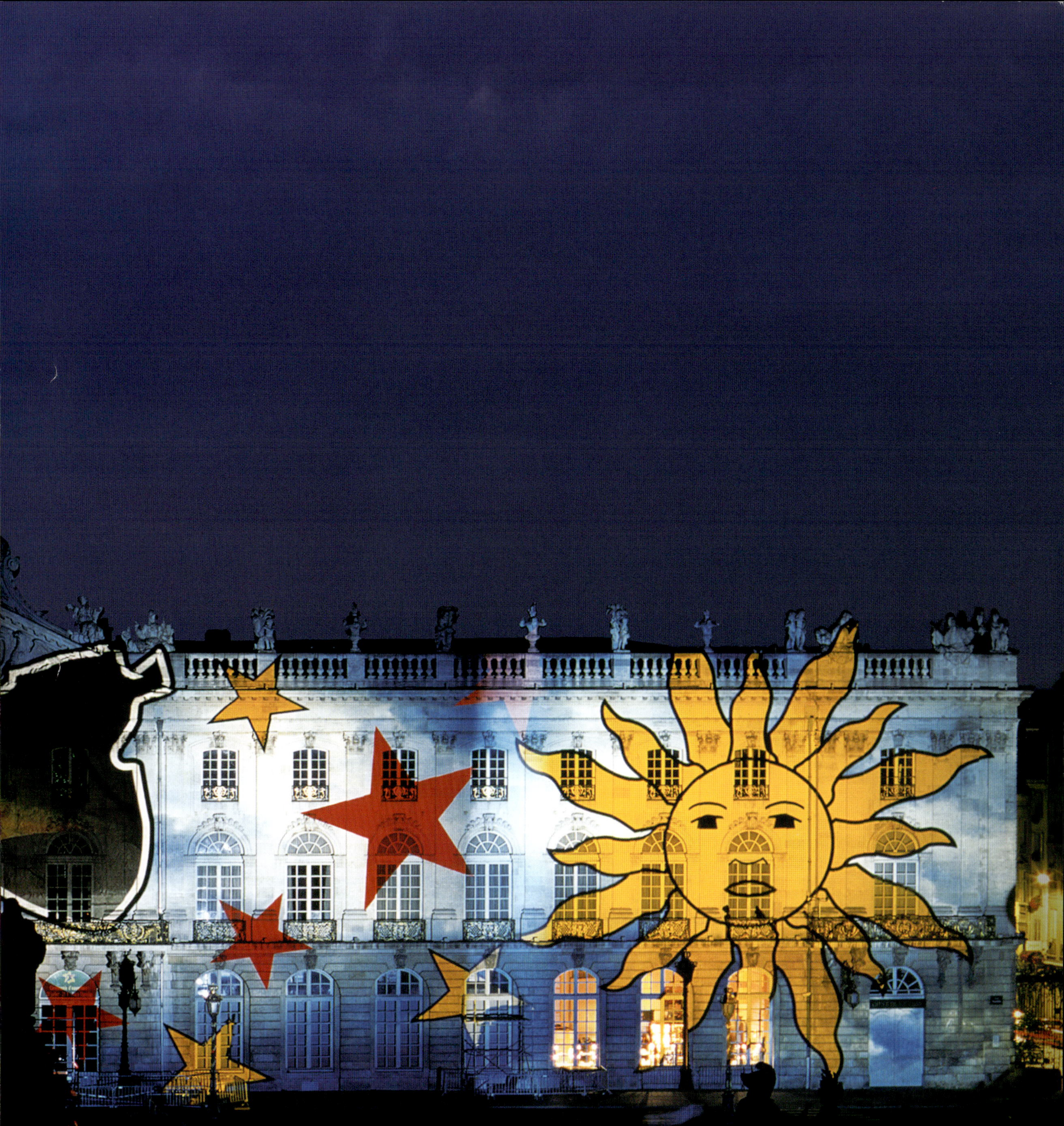

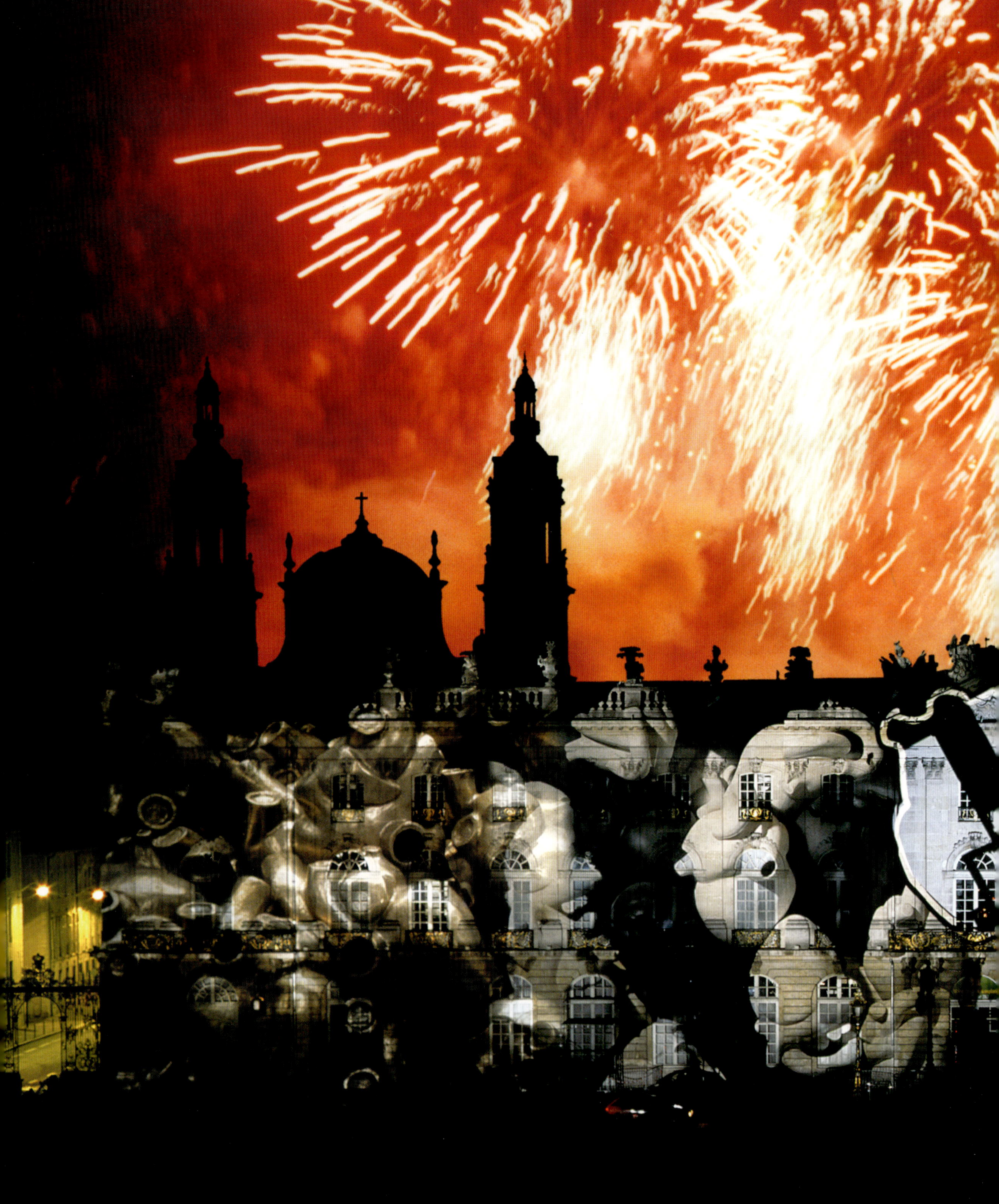

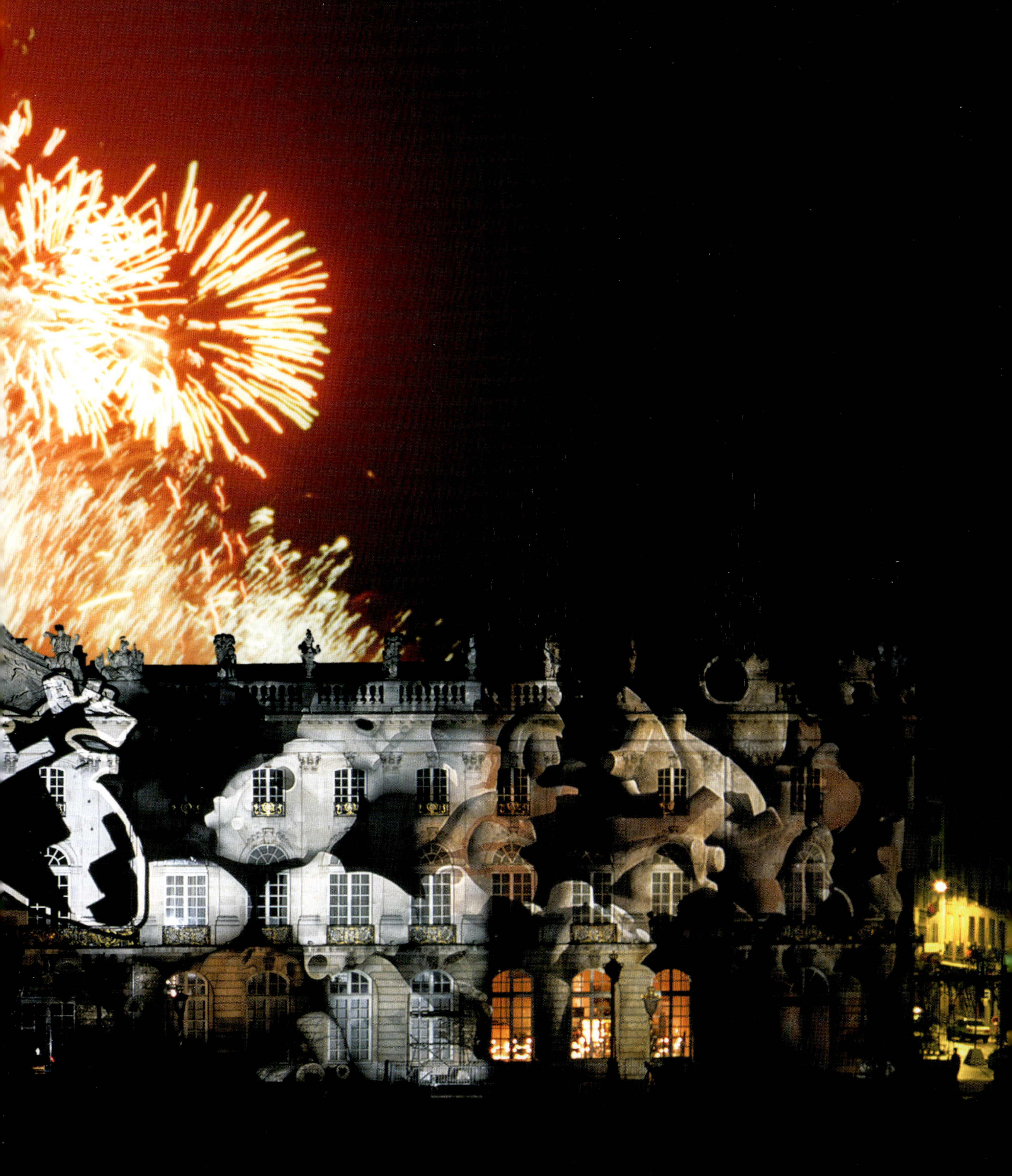

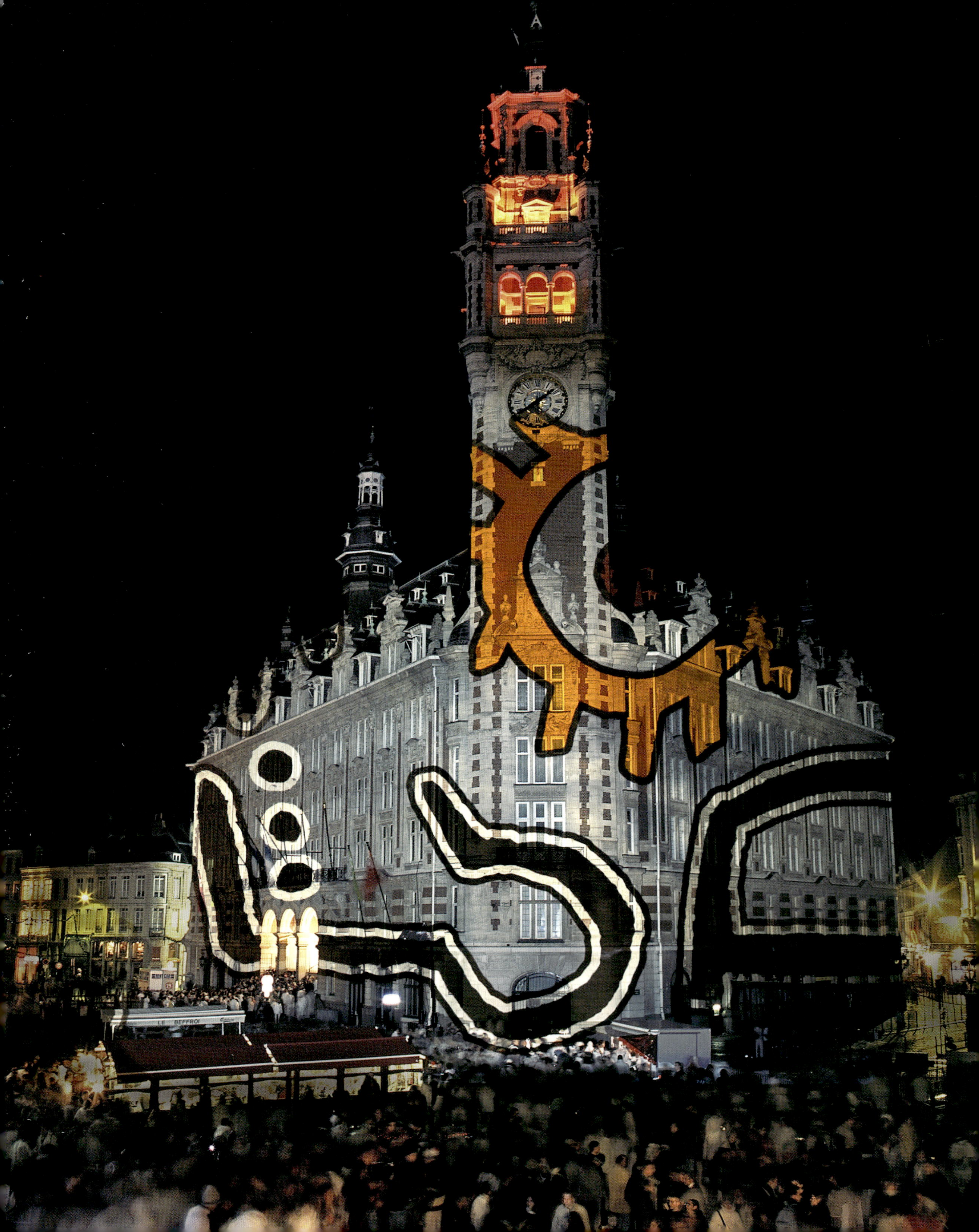
LE BEFFROI

LILLE LIGHTS

2003-2004

Opéra, Chambre de Commerce and Beffroi, Lille, France

On the 6 December 2003, and to inaugurate the European Cultural Capital, Lille 2004, the city commissioned Lucy+Jorge Orta and French composer Pierre Henry to create an open-air concert in front of the Lille Opera House, the Chamber of Commerce and Belfry tower. Around 750,000 visitors took part in the night's festivities.

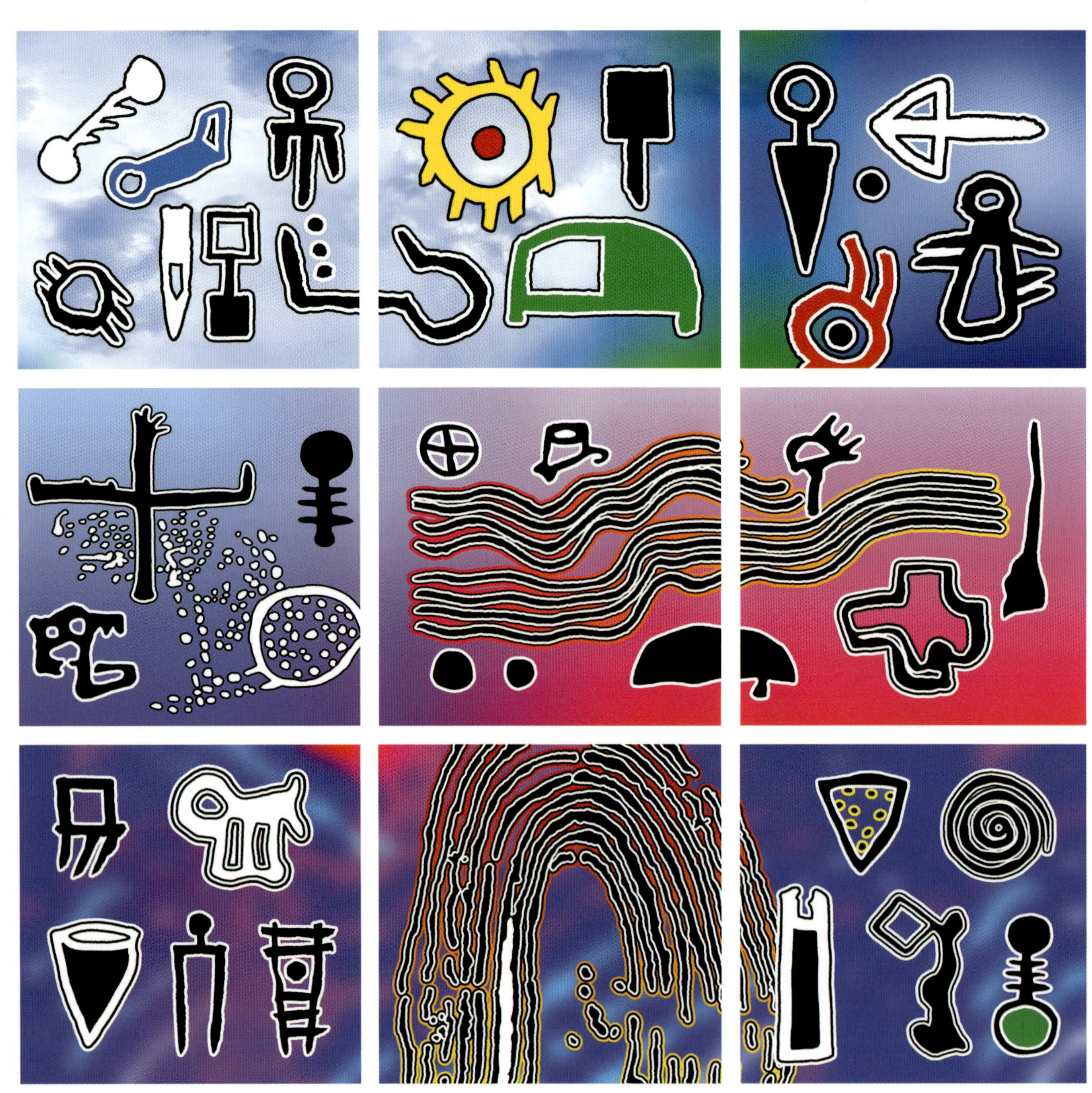

Planetary Alphabet, 2003
Laminated Lambda photograph
190 x 190 cm

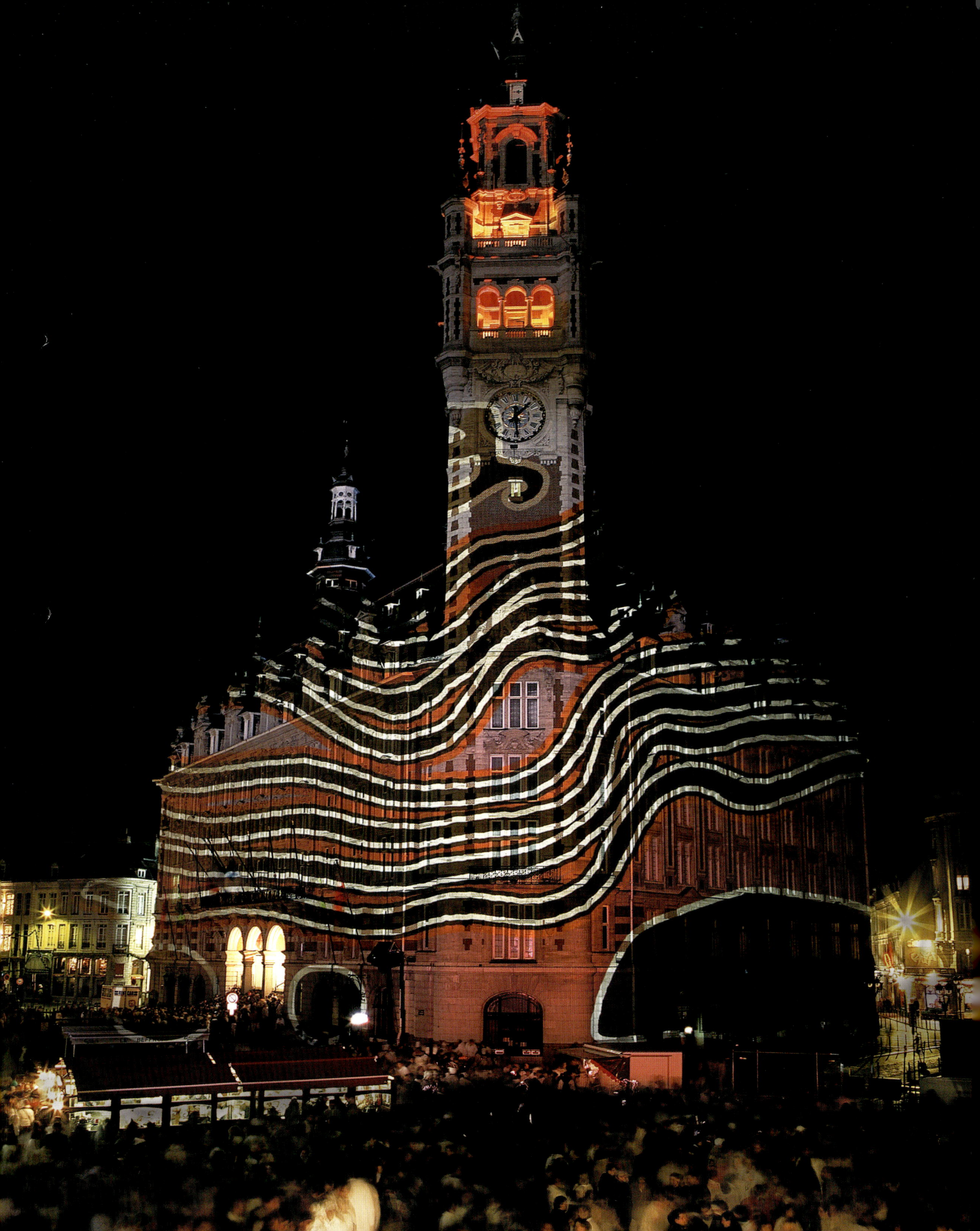

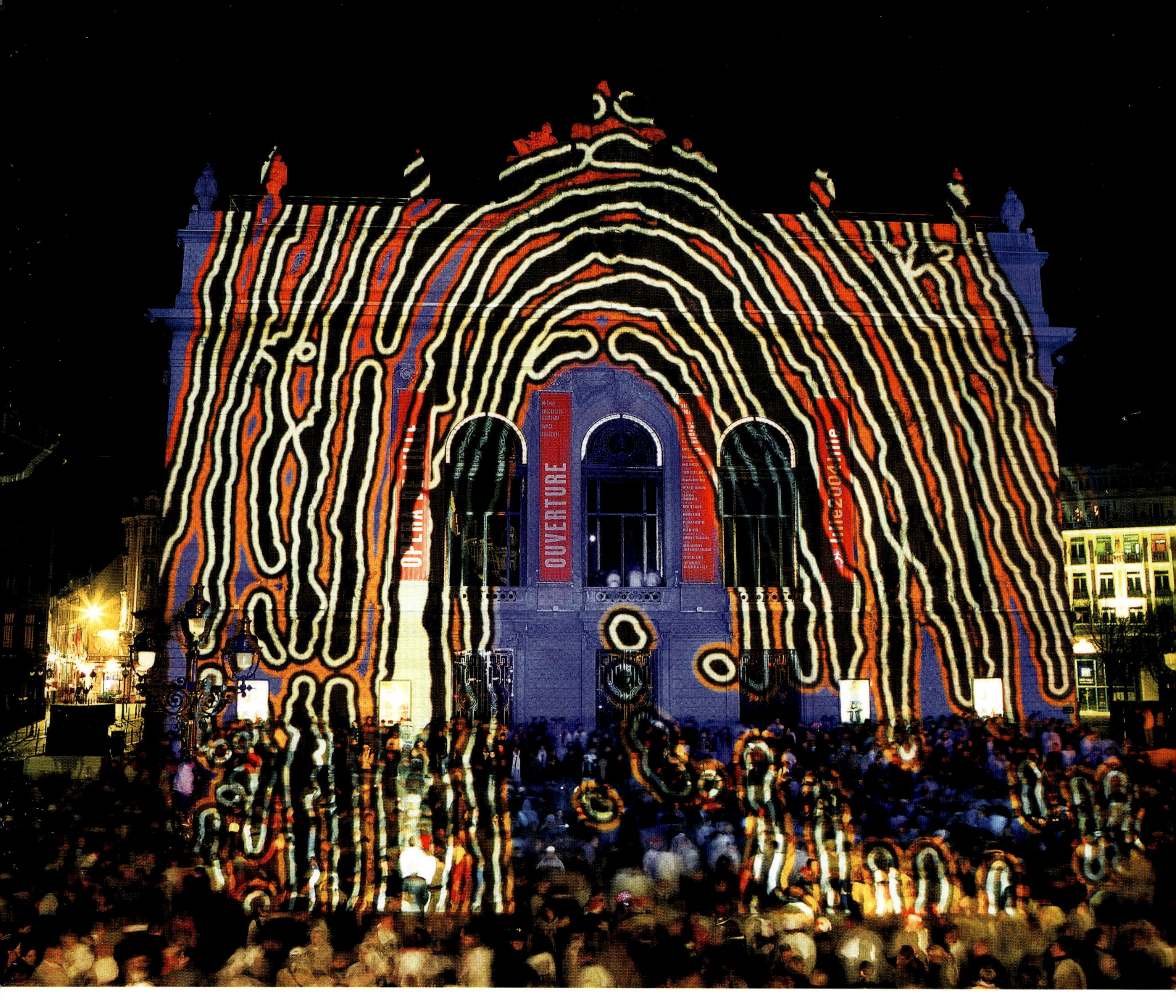
OUVERTURE

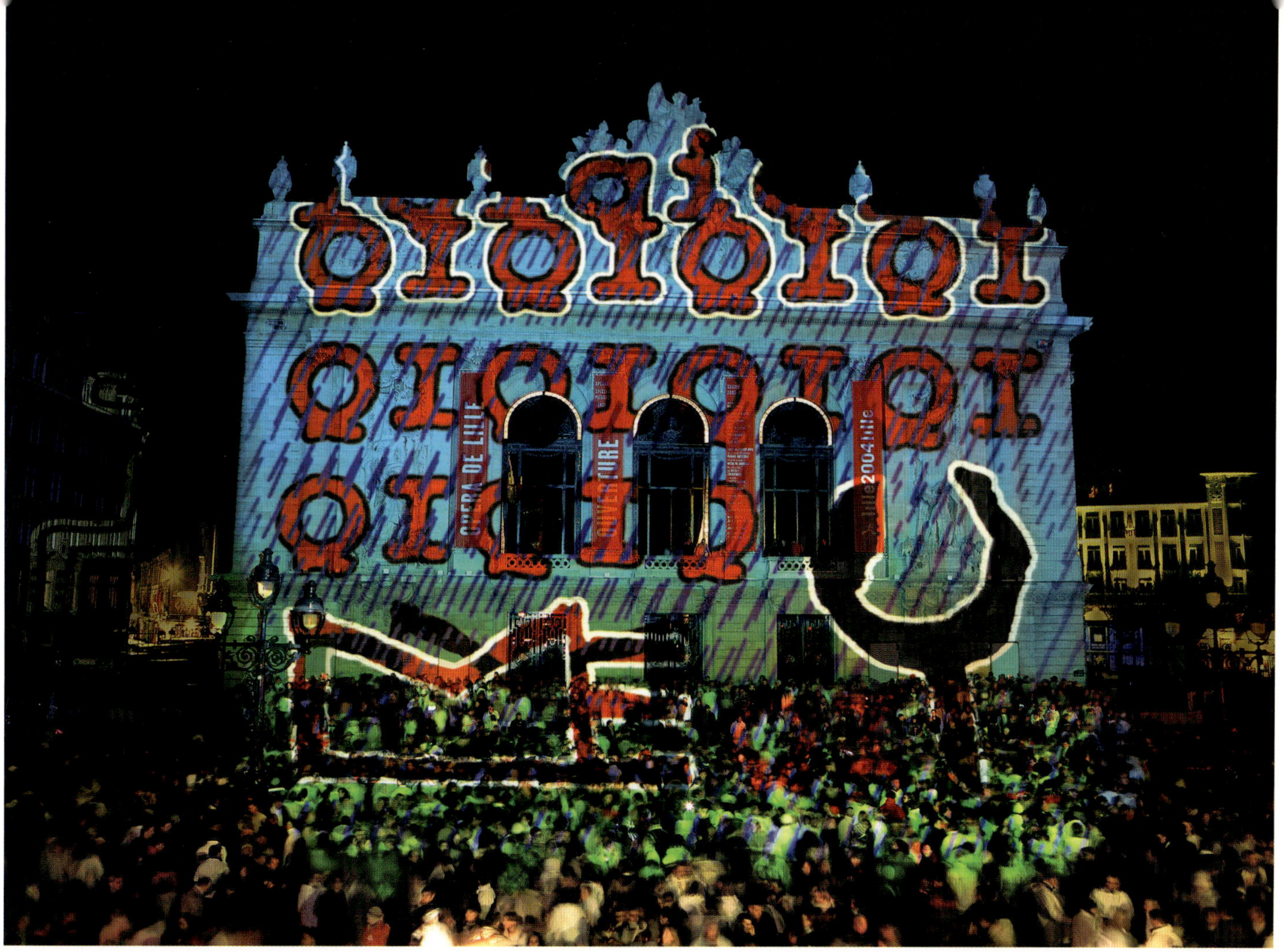

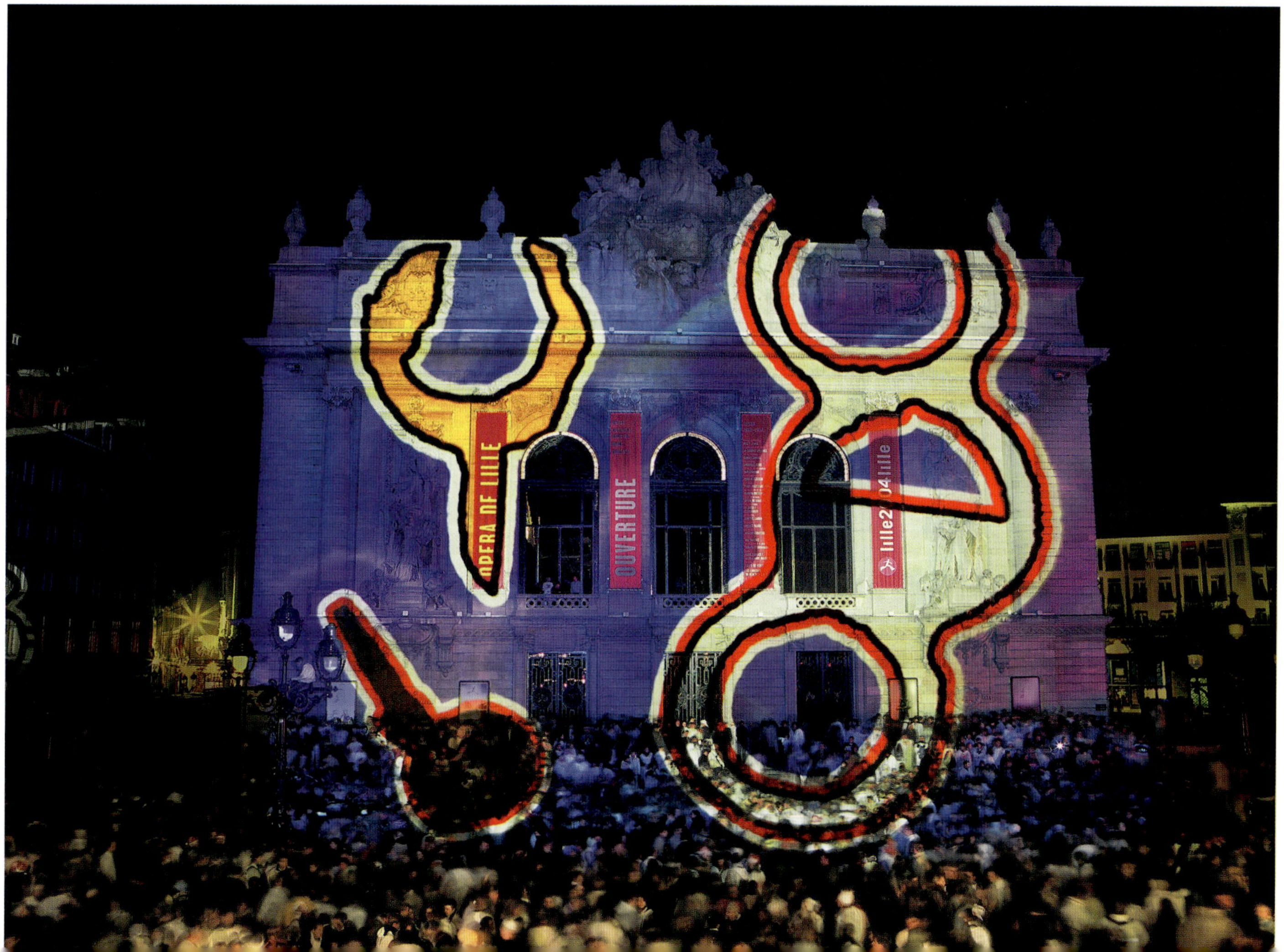

2006

CASA ABIERTA

Casa Argentina, London, UK

To celebrate the London Open House architectural event during the weekend of 16–17 September, the Argentine ambassador's residence in Belgrave Square, London was 'casa abierta' (open house), showcasing an exhibition of work by some of the most important Argentine and Argentine-related contemporary artists. During the nine days of Casa Abierta a series of artistic performances took place, including Lucy+Jorge Ortas' *70 x 7 The Meal*, taking the form of an Argentine banquet and the projections of luminographic paintings across the residence's facade.

Designed by Thomas Cubitt (1788–1855), the imposing Belgrave home of the Argentine ambassador has played a rich and varied role in fostering friendship and understanding between Argentine and British people. Always much more than a house with official functions, the residence is an authentic place of encounter and cultural exchange and the artists' works pays tribute to its tradition whilst looking to the future. The sequence of images Jorge Orta composed for Casa Abierta includes elements of the iconography from his work in Argentina during the late 1970s, such as the cross-shaped silhouettes and fragmented figures, completed with new digital interpretations.

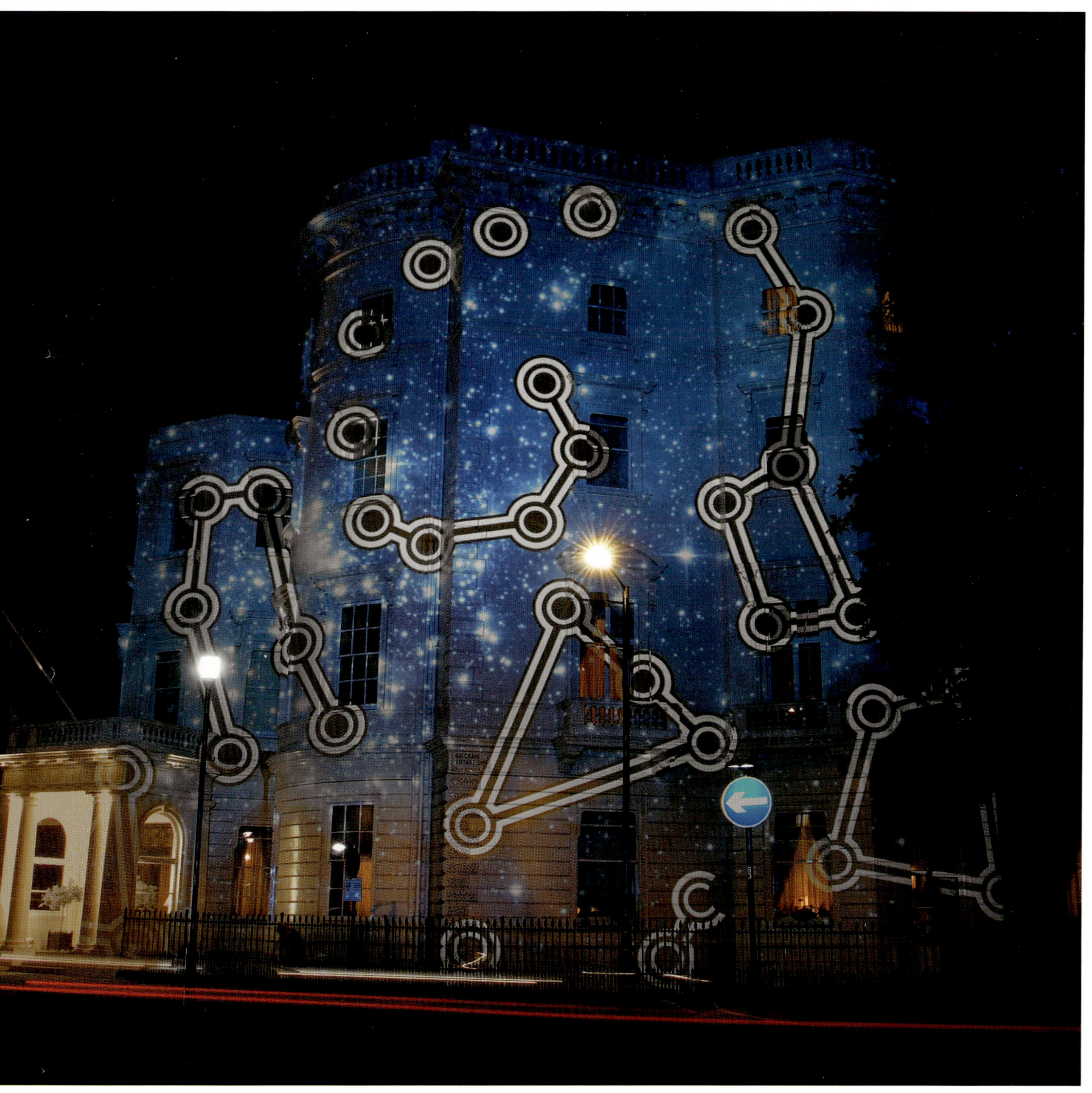

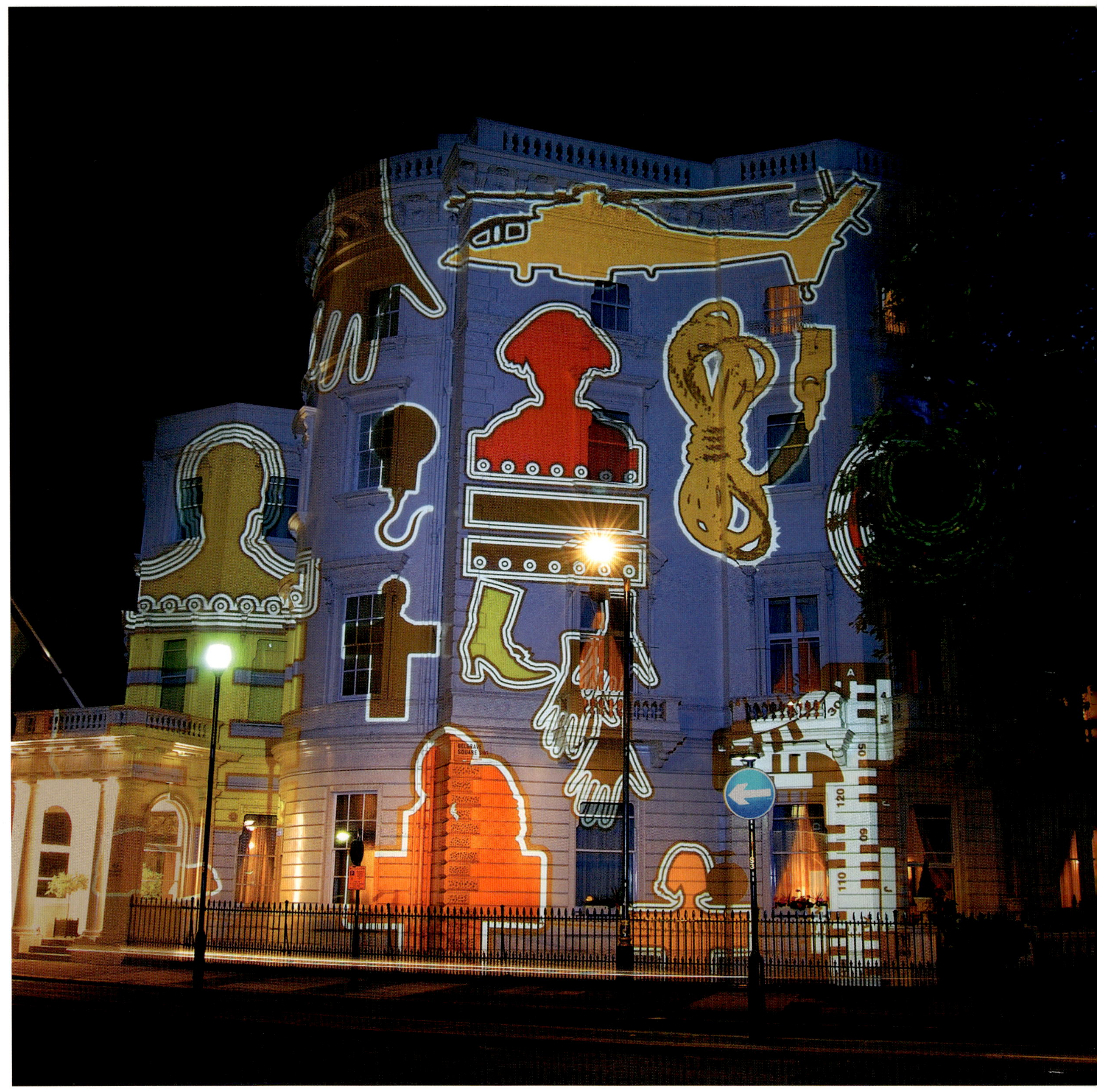

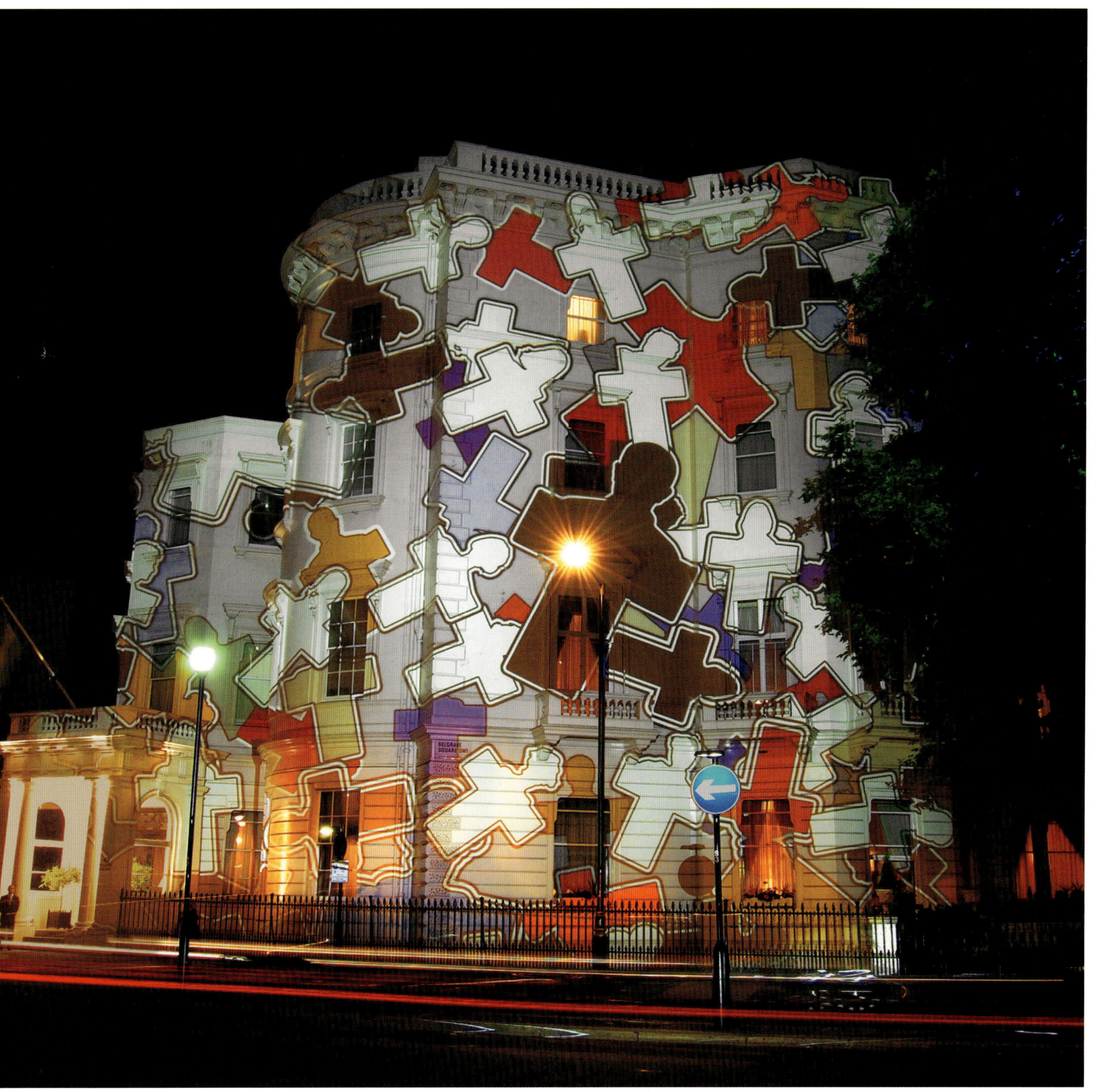

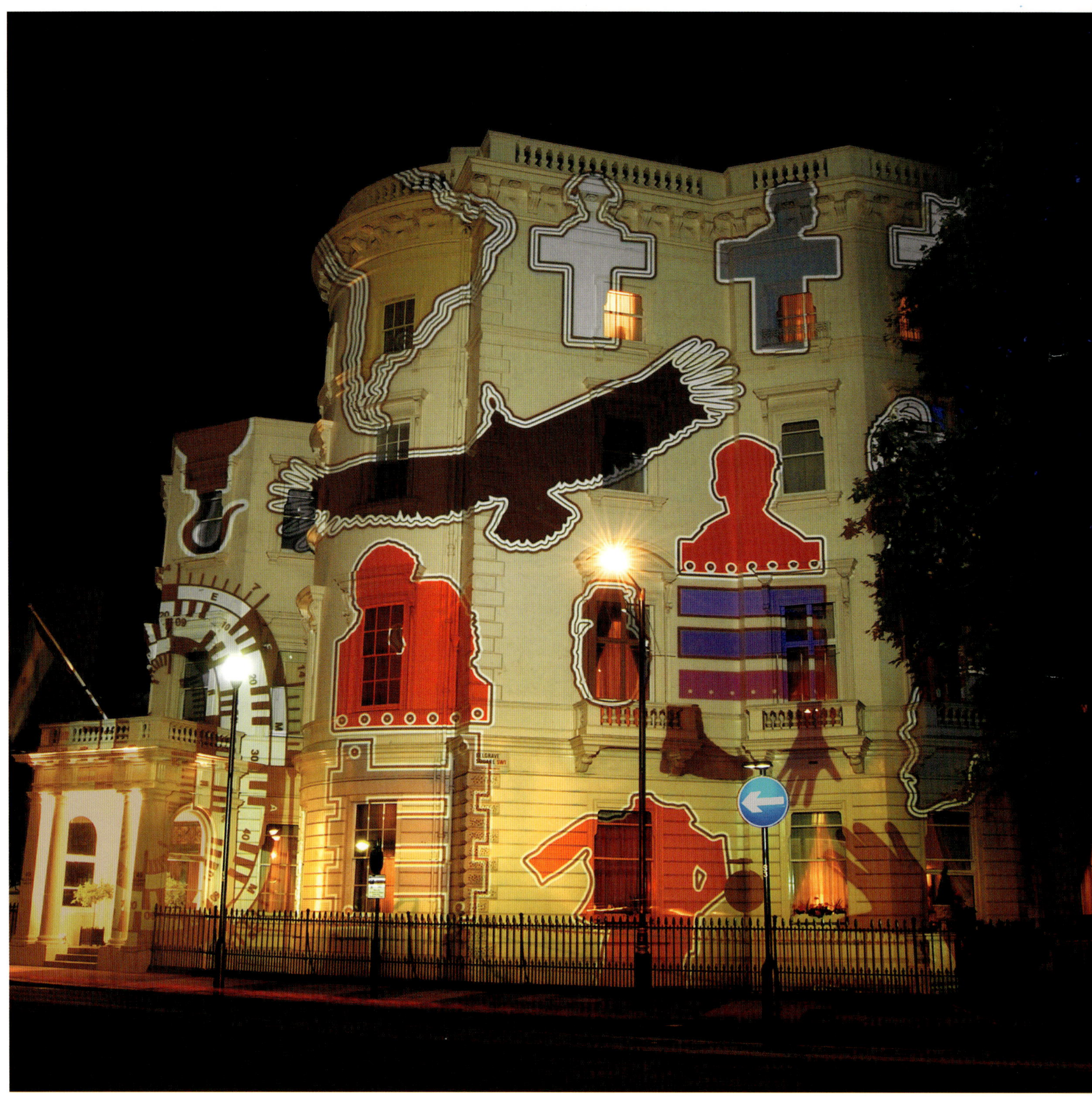

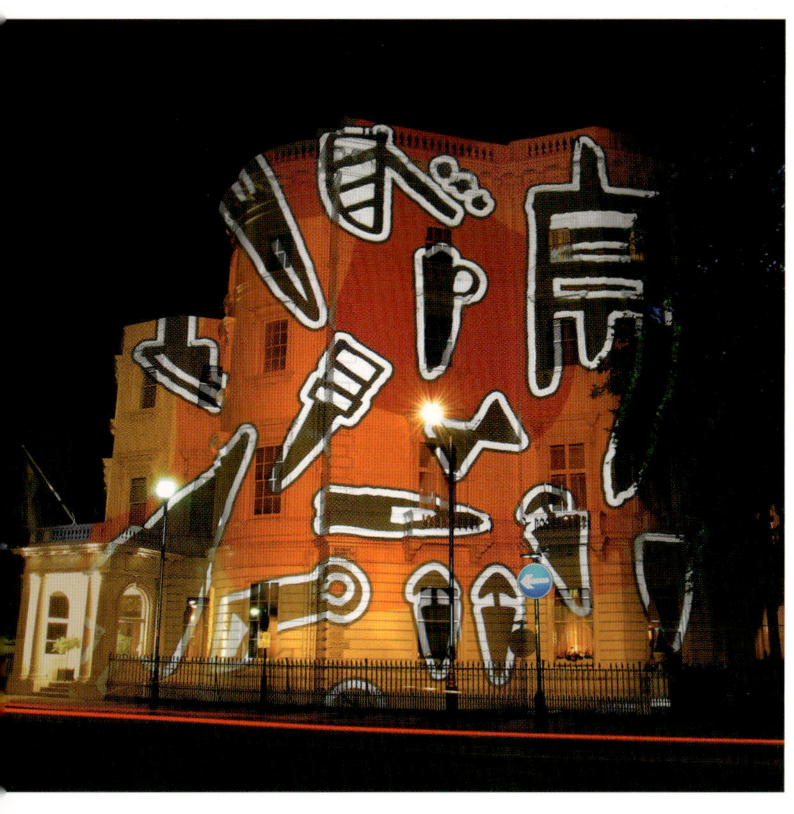

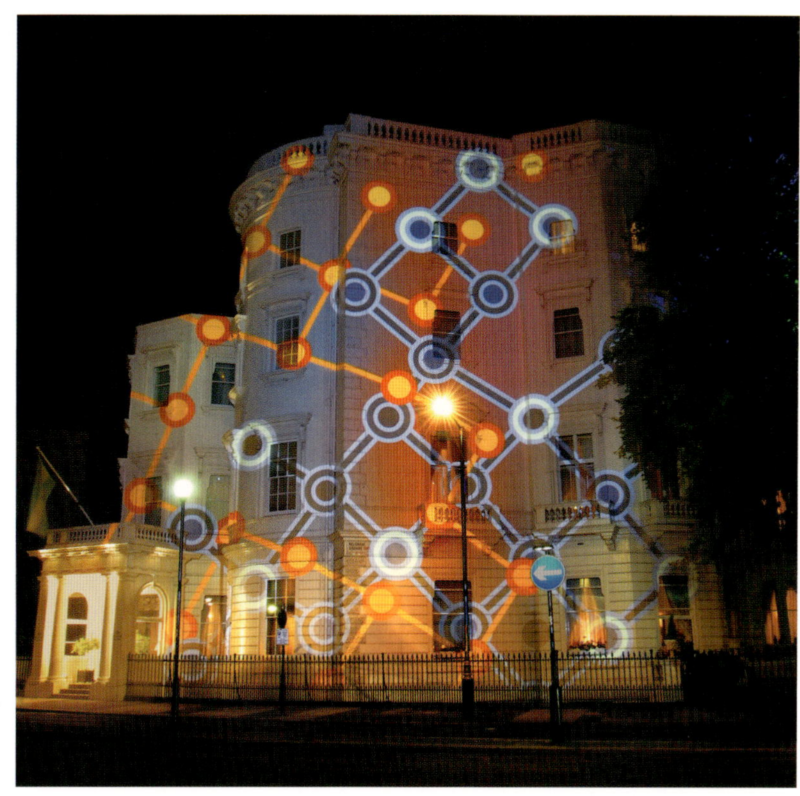

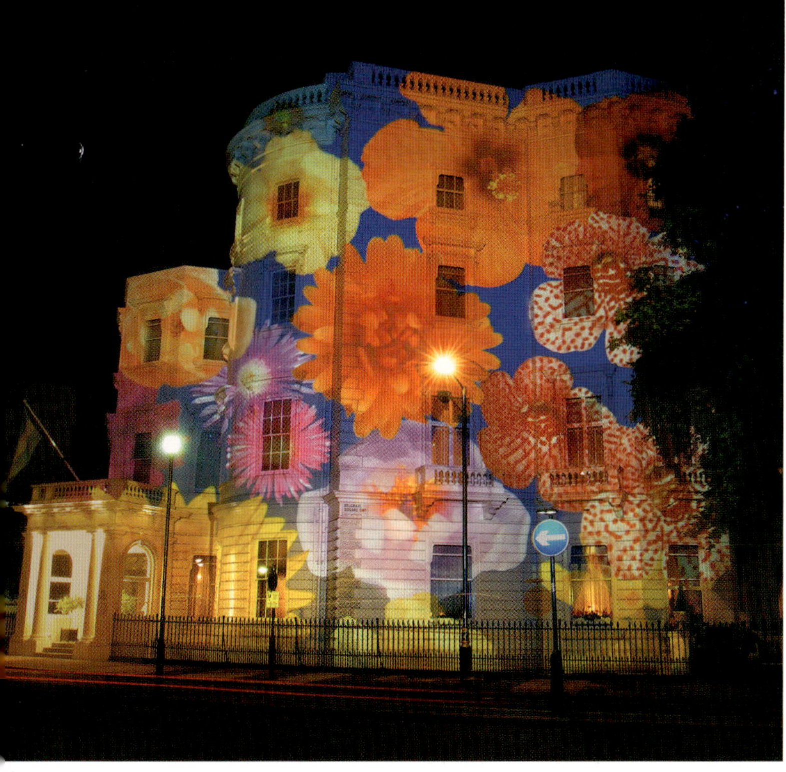

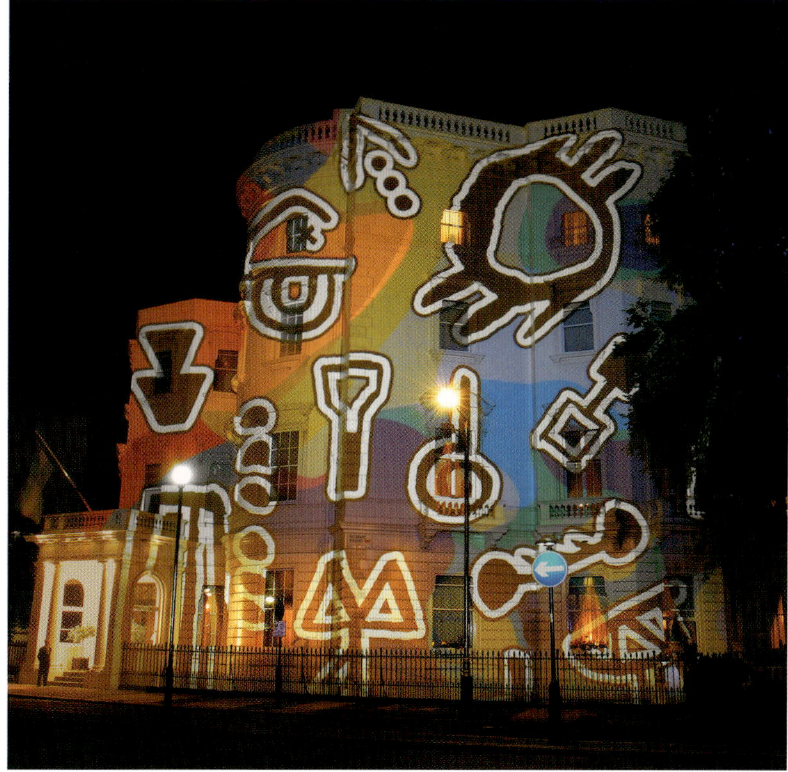

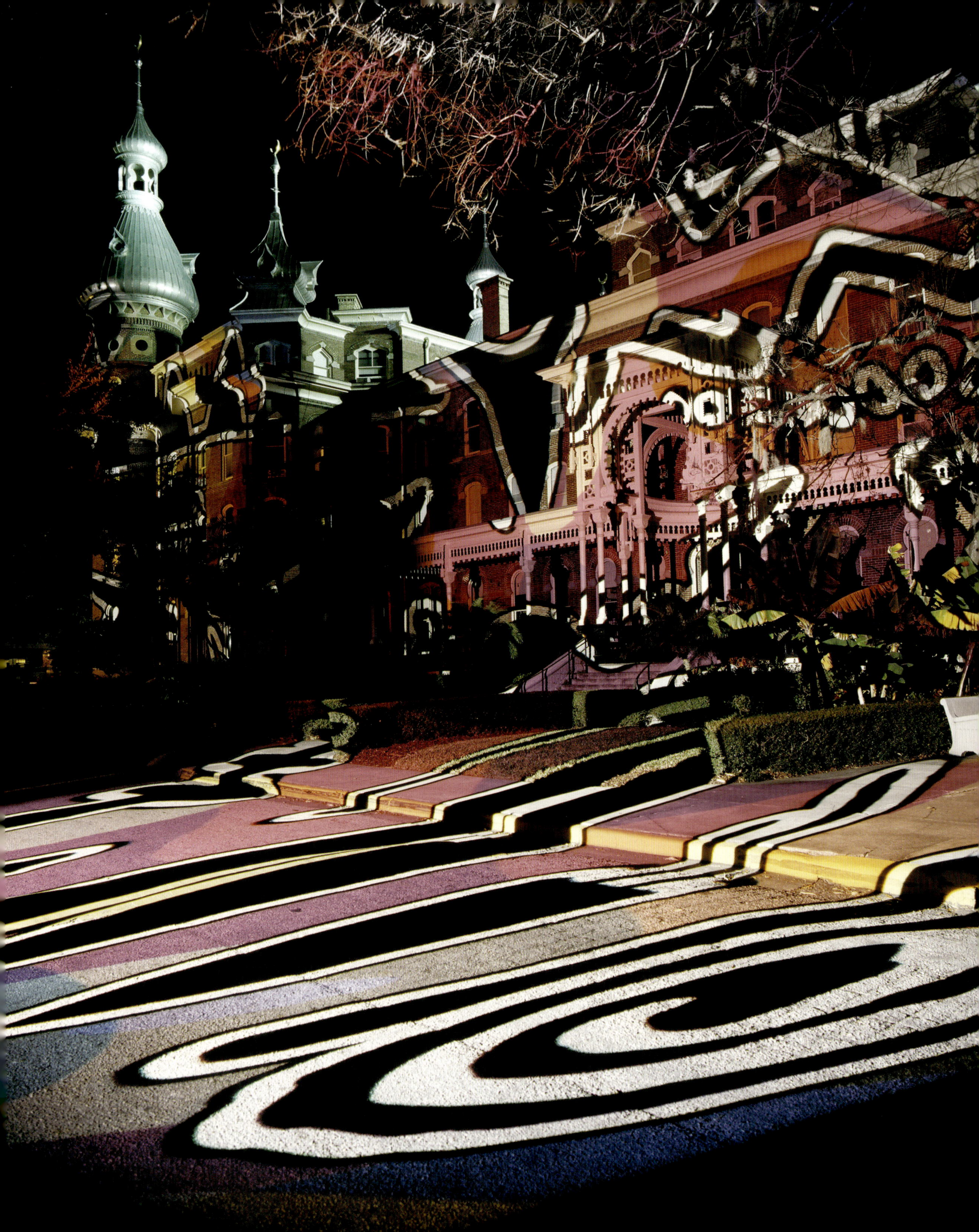

LIGHTS ON TAMPA

Tampa Bay Hotel, South Florida, United States

2006

Commissioned by Tampa City Public Art Program to inaugurate *Lights on Tampa*, the artists chose the Tampa Bay Hotel, home to the University of Florida to experiment for the first time the 'enveloping technique', imprinting the architecture and surrounding urban space with light images. The imagery is part of an ongoing visual language that the artists create, according to each context and often with the participation of local residents. From the early ideograms signs imagined in Argentina, enriched overtime with metasocial signs, silhouettes, objects, images, and sounds that connect peoples and cultures.

The participation of local residents, young and old, during workshop sessions enables a special moment of interactivity between people of all walks of life. Together they can discuss and imagine the visual imagery as well as addressing the underlying issues of the ephemeral artwork. Lucy+Jorge Orta become the mediator of a process, constructing the artwork with people, to ensure that it is an integrated part of the fabric of the city and a cohesive and interactive poetry. Even though the artists are using the latest in light projection technology, they believe that the challenge of each Light Work is not so much the technological, but the message's content and the involvement of the community—a 'catalyst art'.

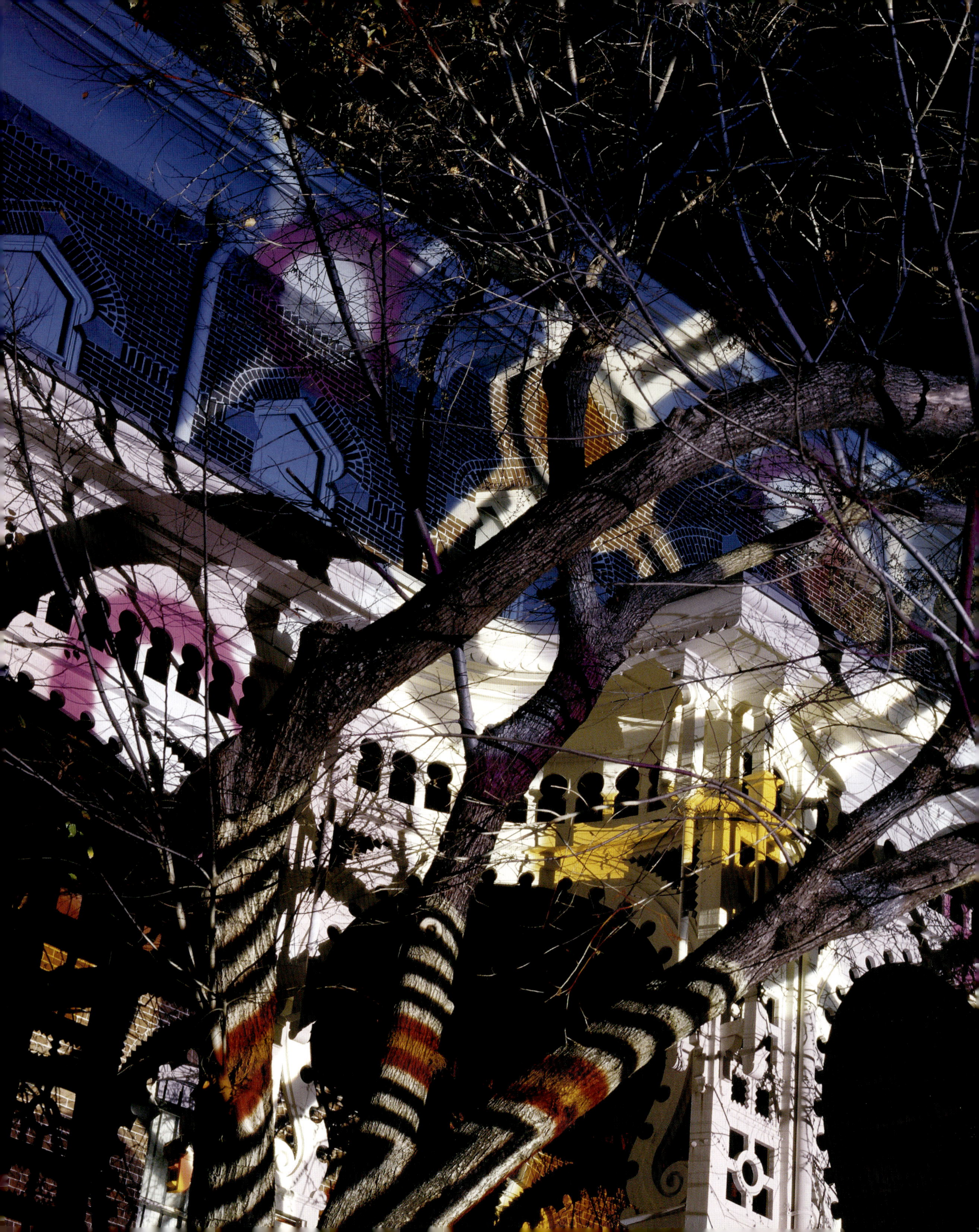

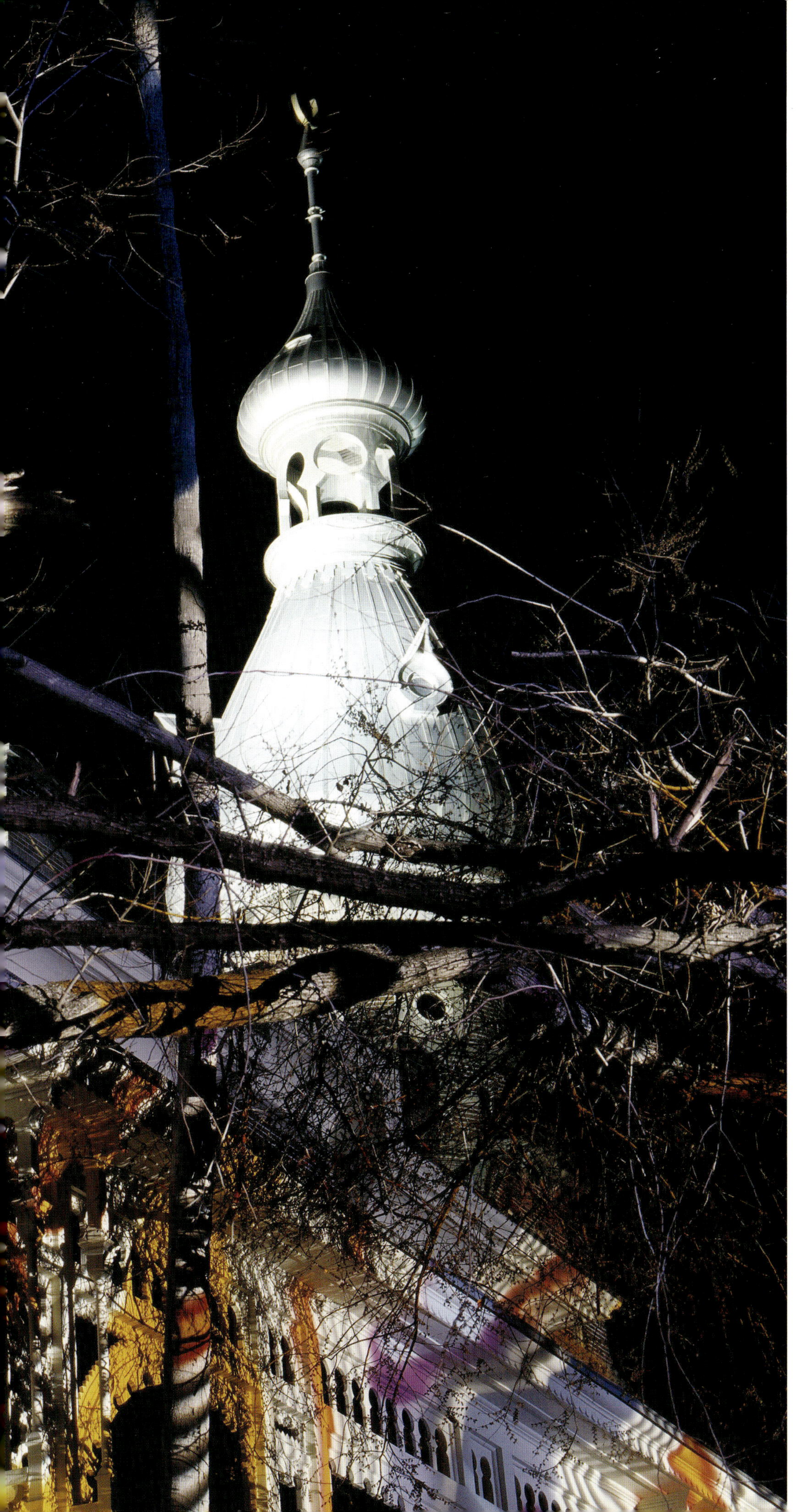

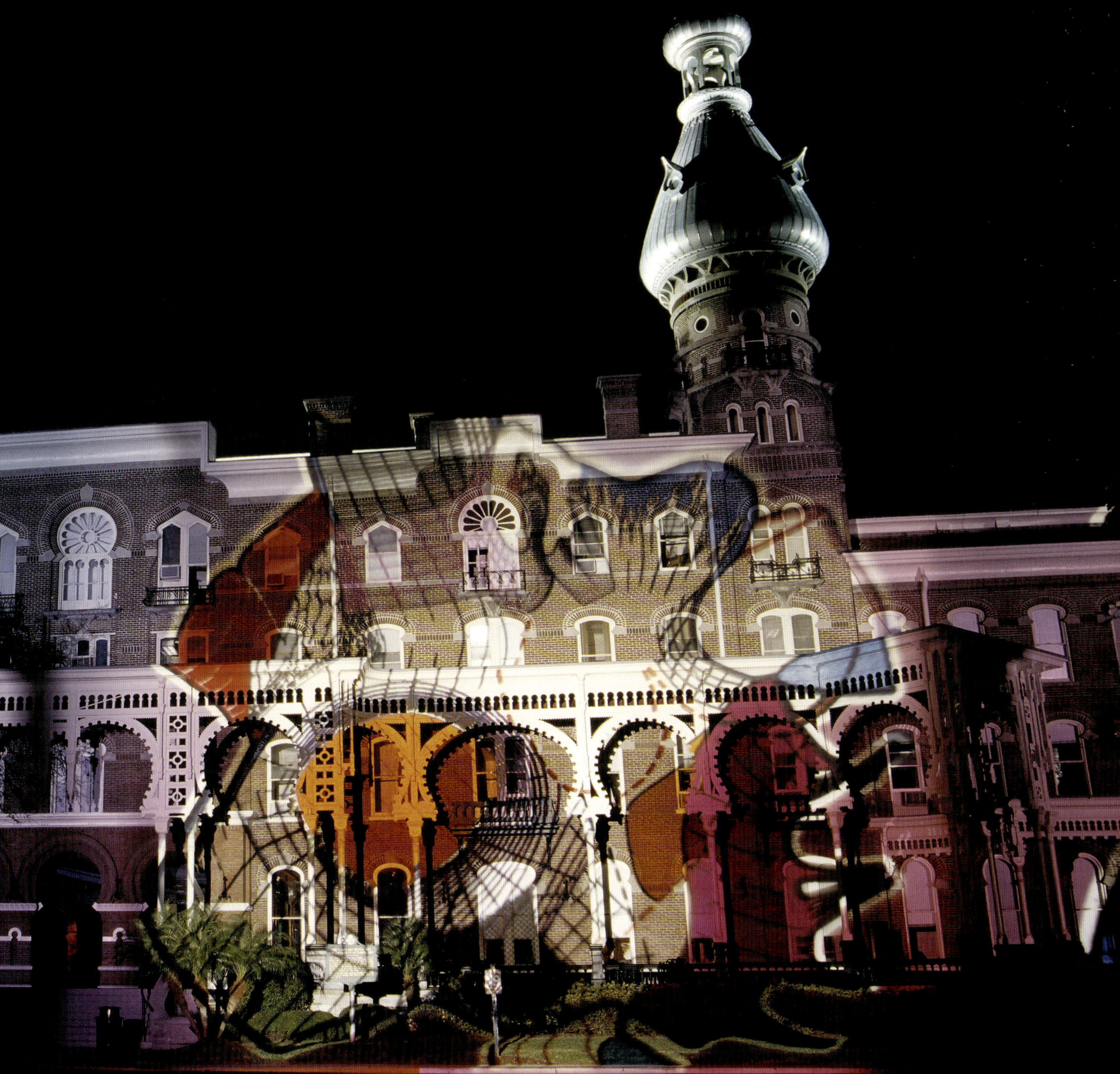

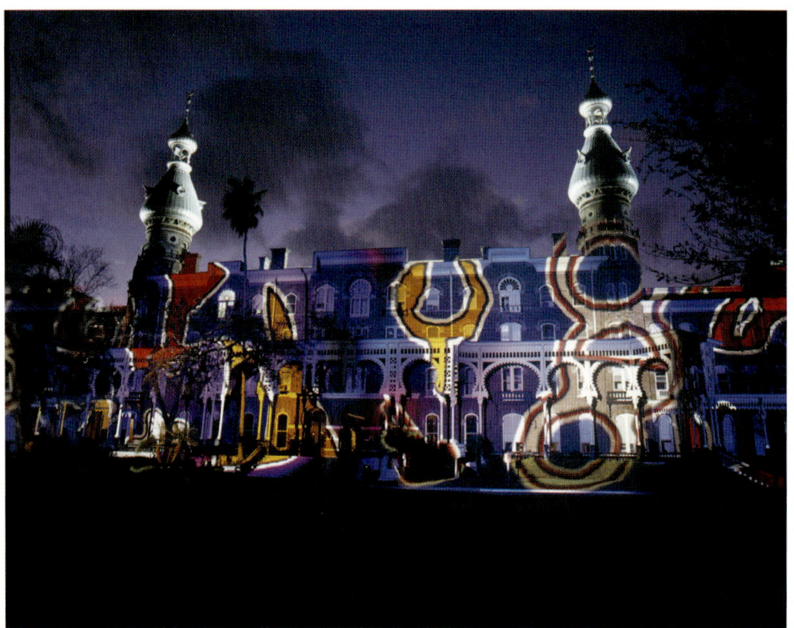
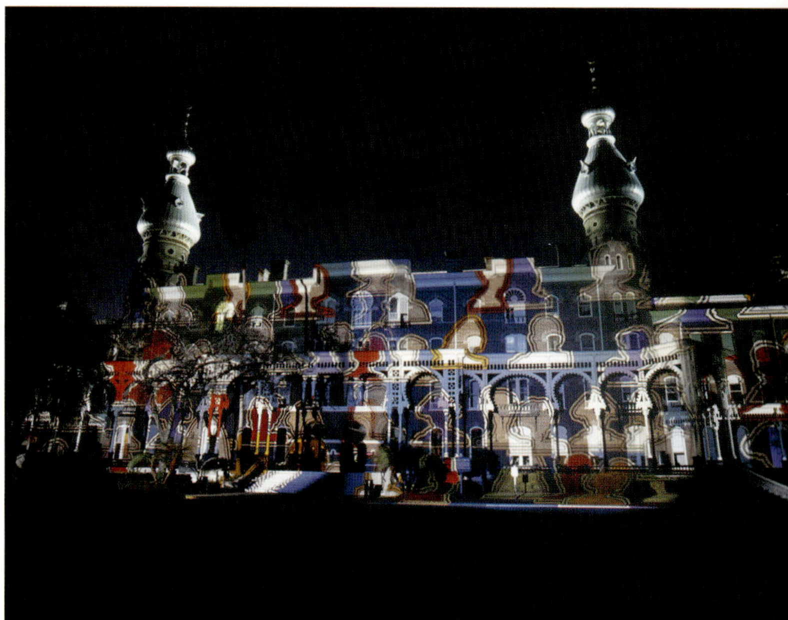
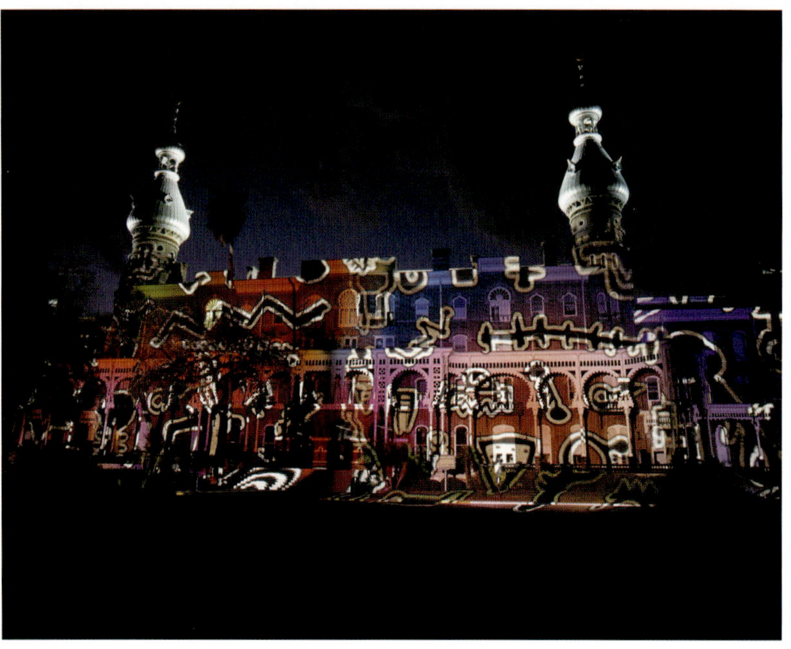
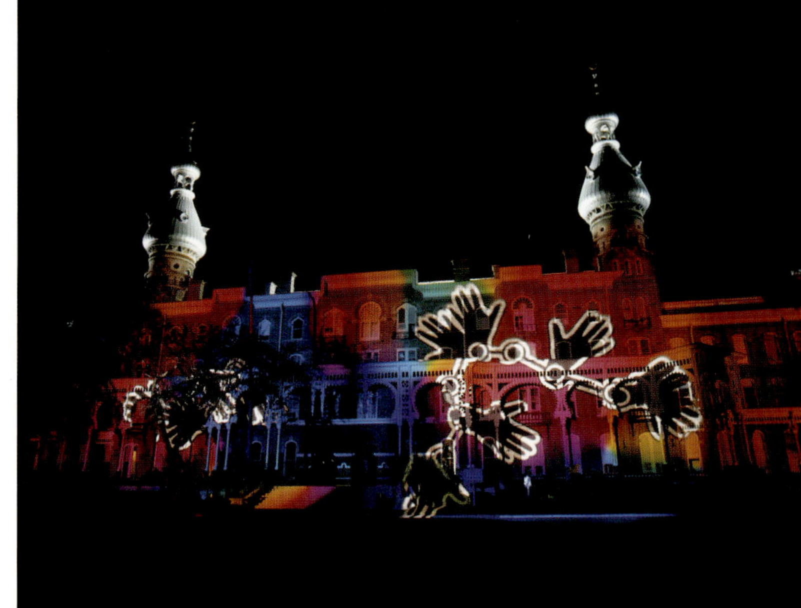

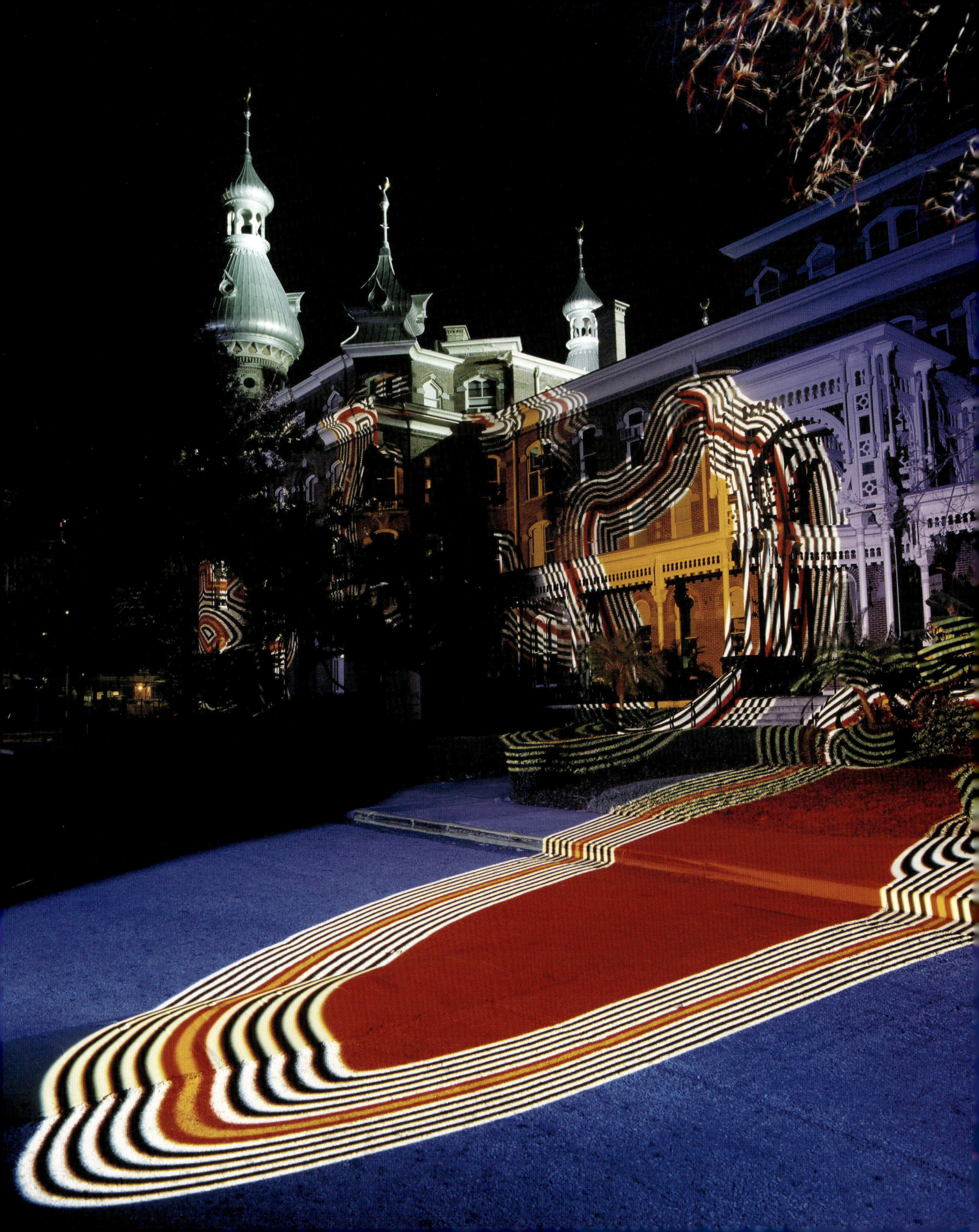

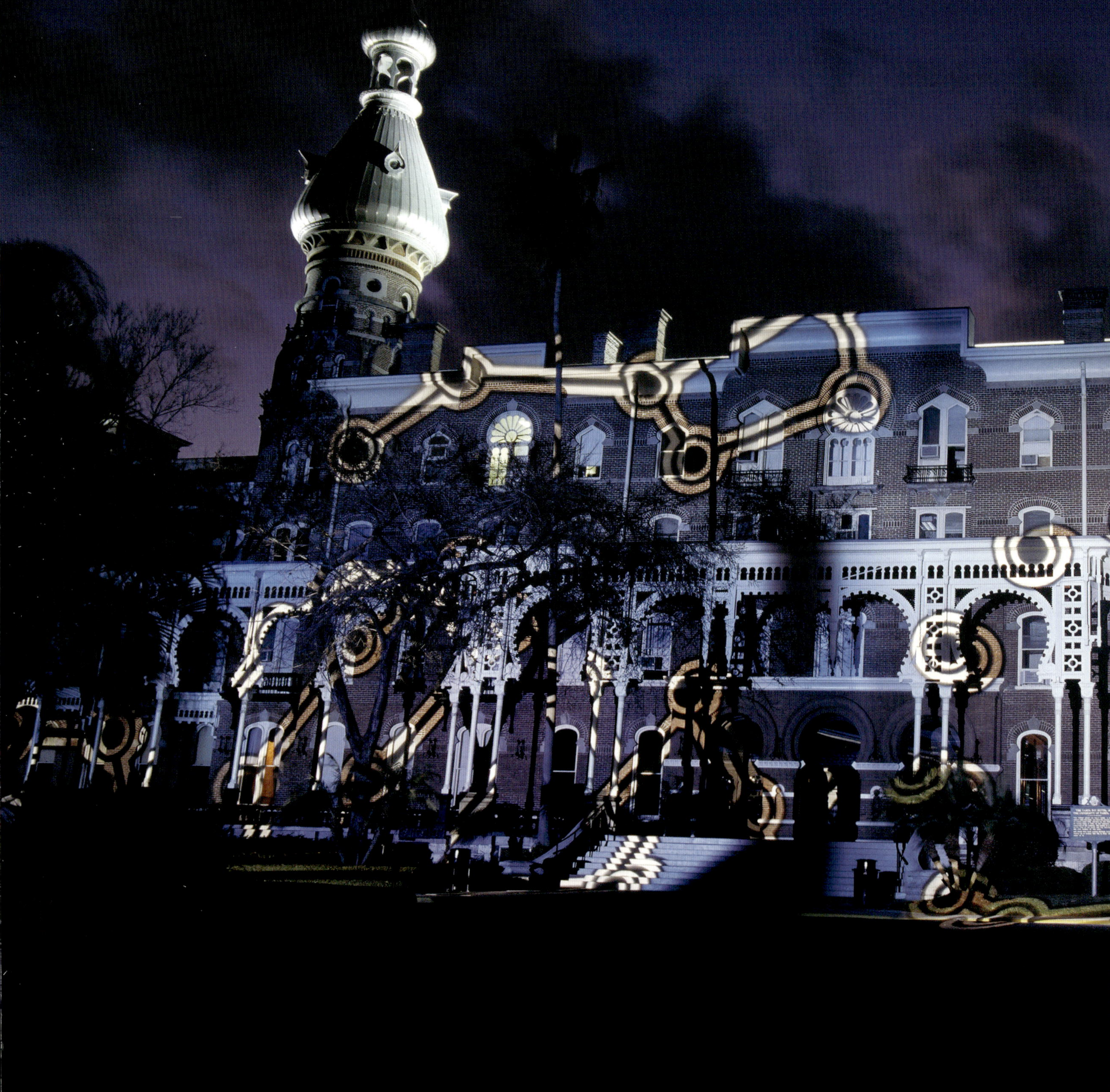

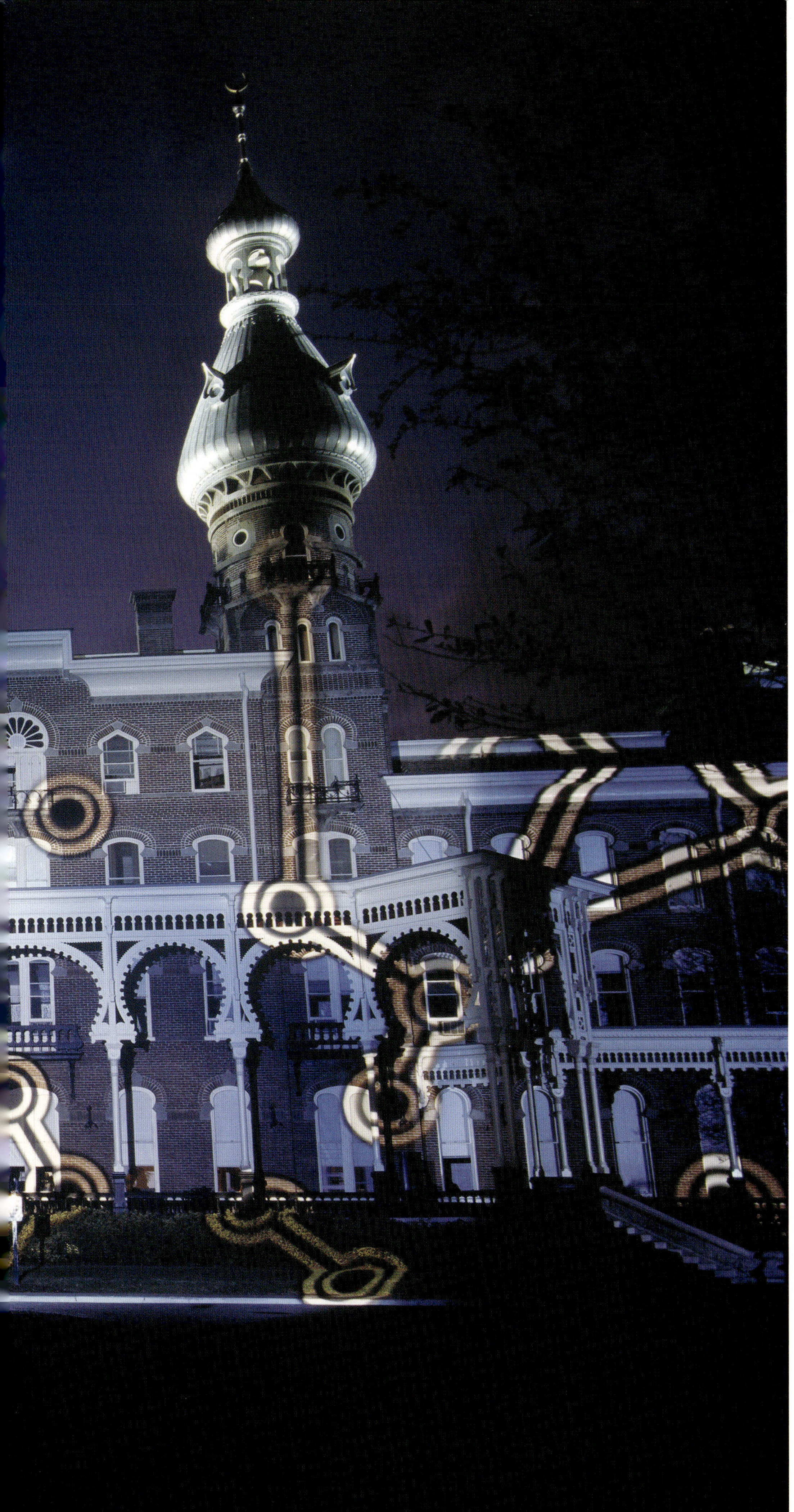

BRASILIA EM LUZ

Brasilia, Brazil

2009

On the National Day of Brasilia and to celebrate the Year of France in Brazil, Lucy+Jorge Orta proposed three simultaneous Light Works for the National Museum of Brasilia, the Brazilian parliament and the cathedral of Brazil. The artists chose to reflect on the natural world and man's impact on the equilibrium of the ecosystem. The city of Brasilia was created in a sparsely populated region of the neo-tropical savannah Amazon, once rich in biodiversity. The iconic architectures of Oscar Niemeyer stand out in contrast to this biome, now one of the most threatened in South America.

Their point of departure for the iconography of Brasilia em Luz was the legend of *Manto de Tupinambá*, a ceremonial mantel or cape created entirely from feathers. After meeting Oscar Niemeyer, the artists imagined the museum's iconic breast-womb clothed in successive layers of textures and rich with symbolic messages referencing the fragility of our natural environment. The domed architecture was ceremoniously 'dressed' and 'undressed' with a patterned mantel of abstract signs, ideograms, silhouettes, beetles, butterflies and flowers.

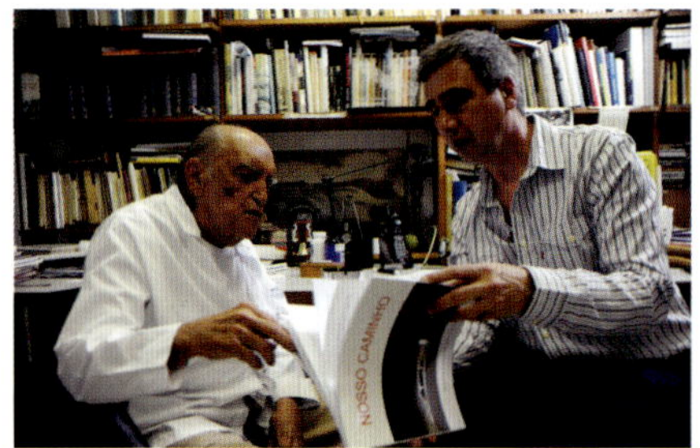

Oscar Niemeyer and Jorge Orta

The constellations and insects evoke the different scales, diversity and fragility of our global ecosphere. A minute entomologic world, invisible to eyes that are not accustomed to looking, versus the immensity of the millions of stars and galaxies—species and stars disappear without us even noticing, yet millions are still to be discovered. The mesh and connective structures represent our networked world and are a metaphor for the social ties and nexus that bind us together. The abstract human heart symbolise the act of giving and recognition of the other. The pictograms and graphic symbols, a common universal alphabet forming an imaginary dialogue between cultures.

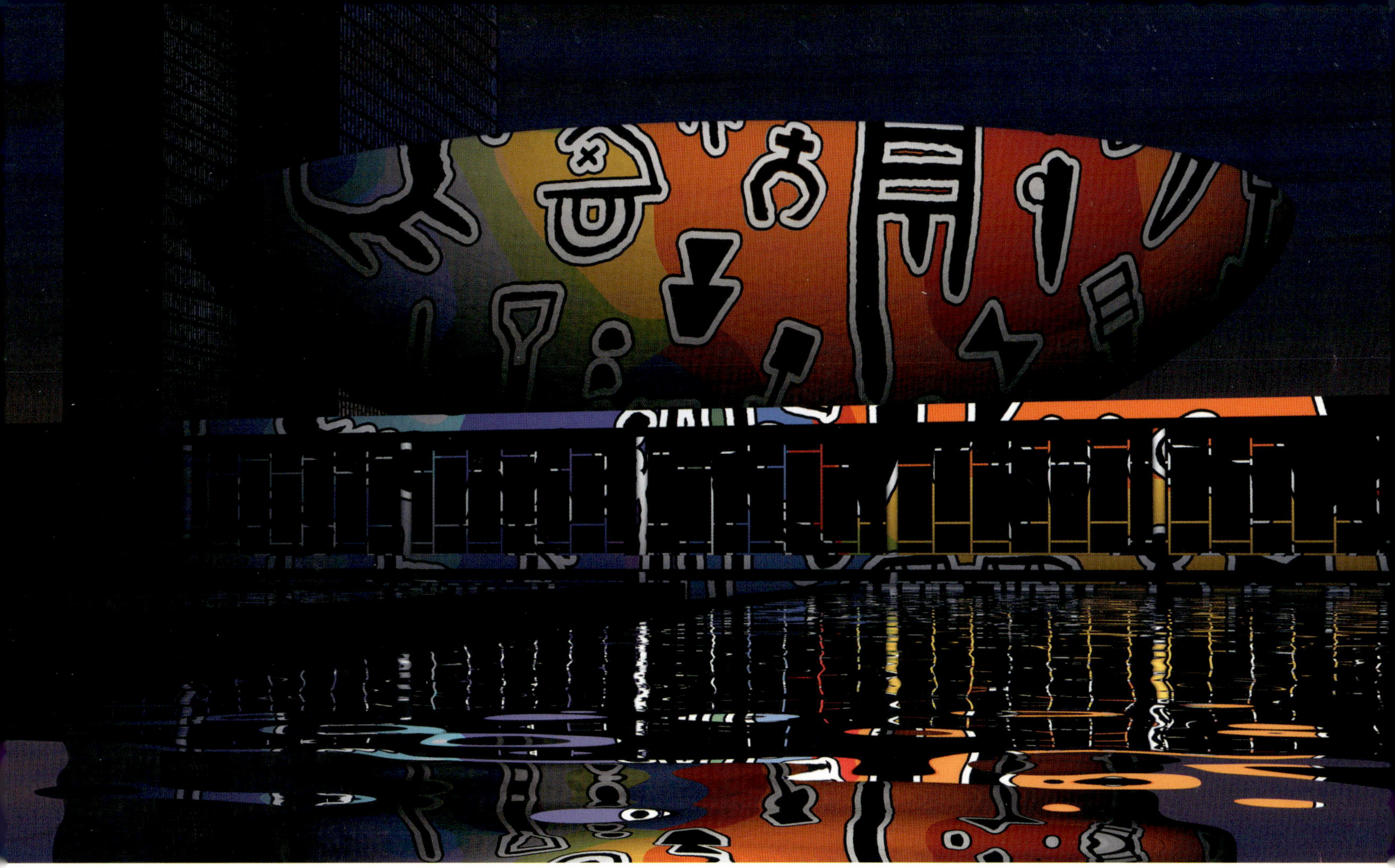

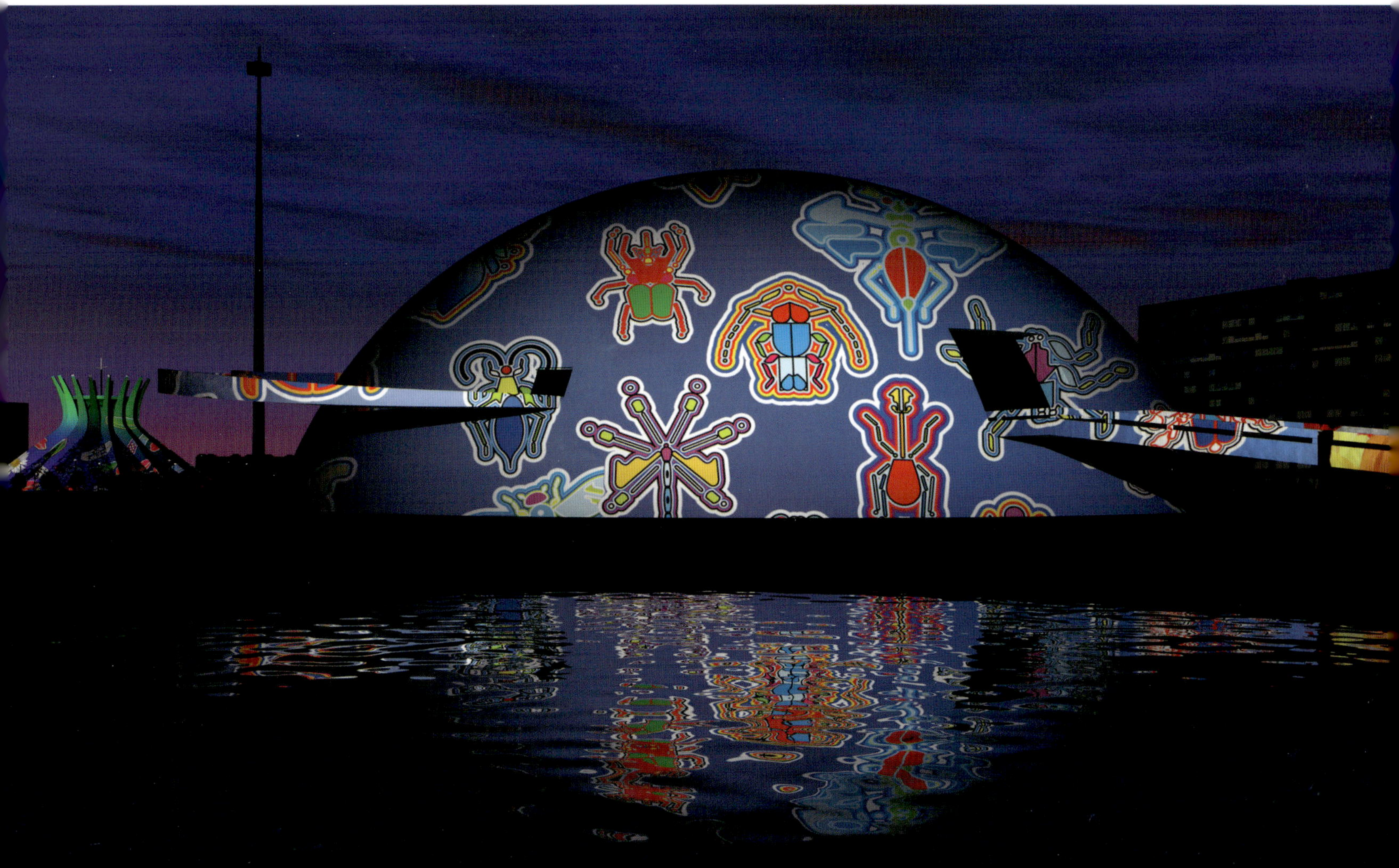

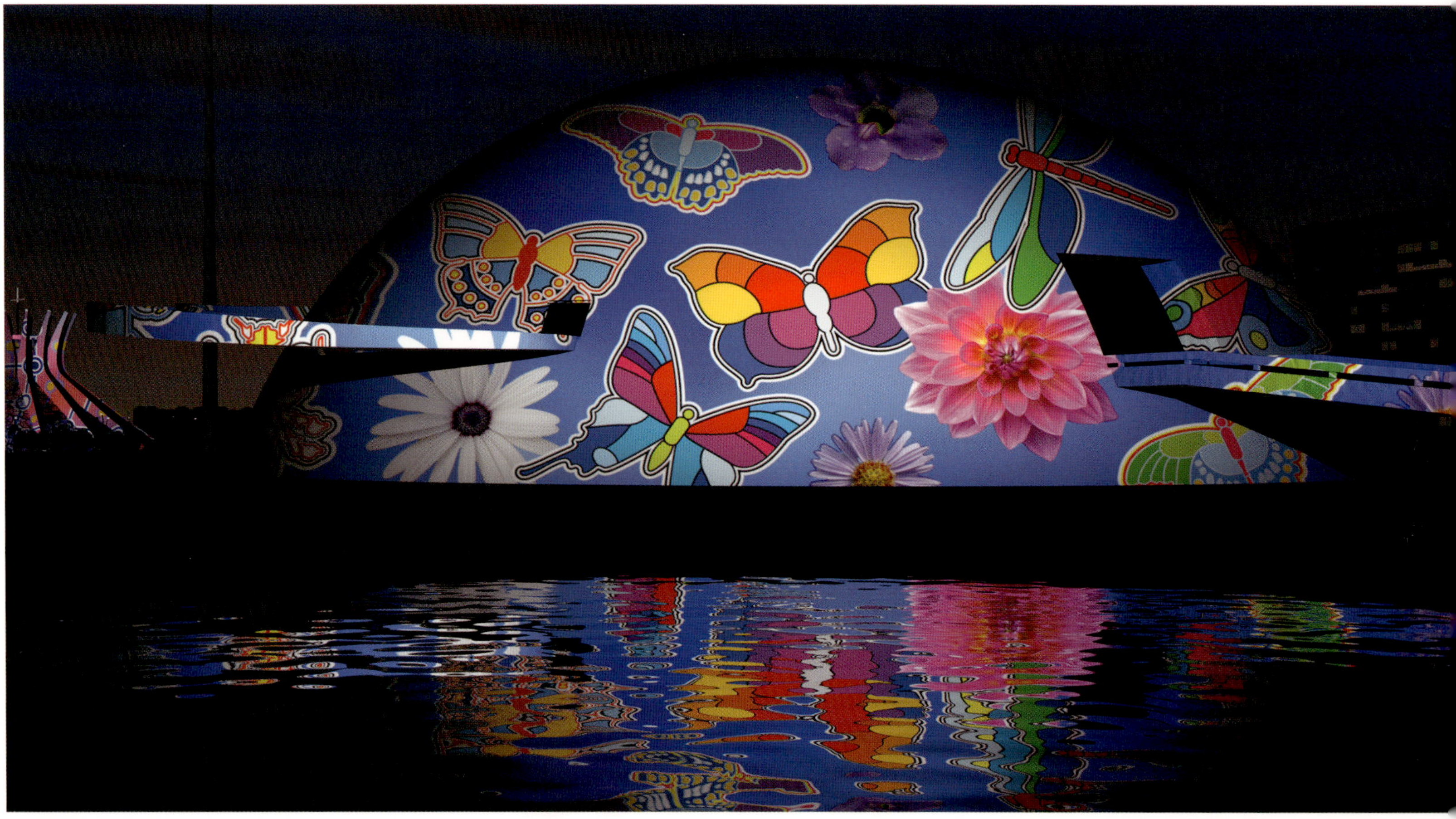

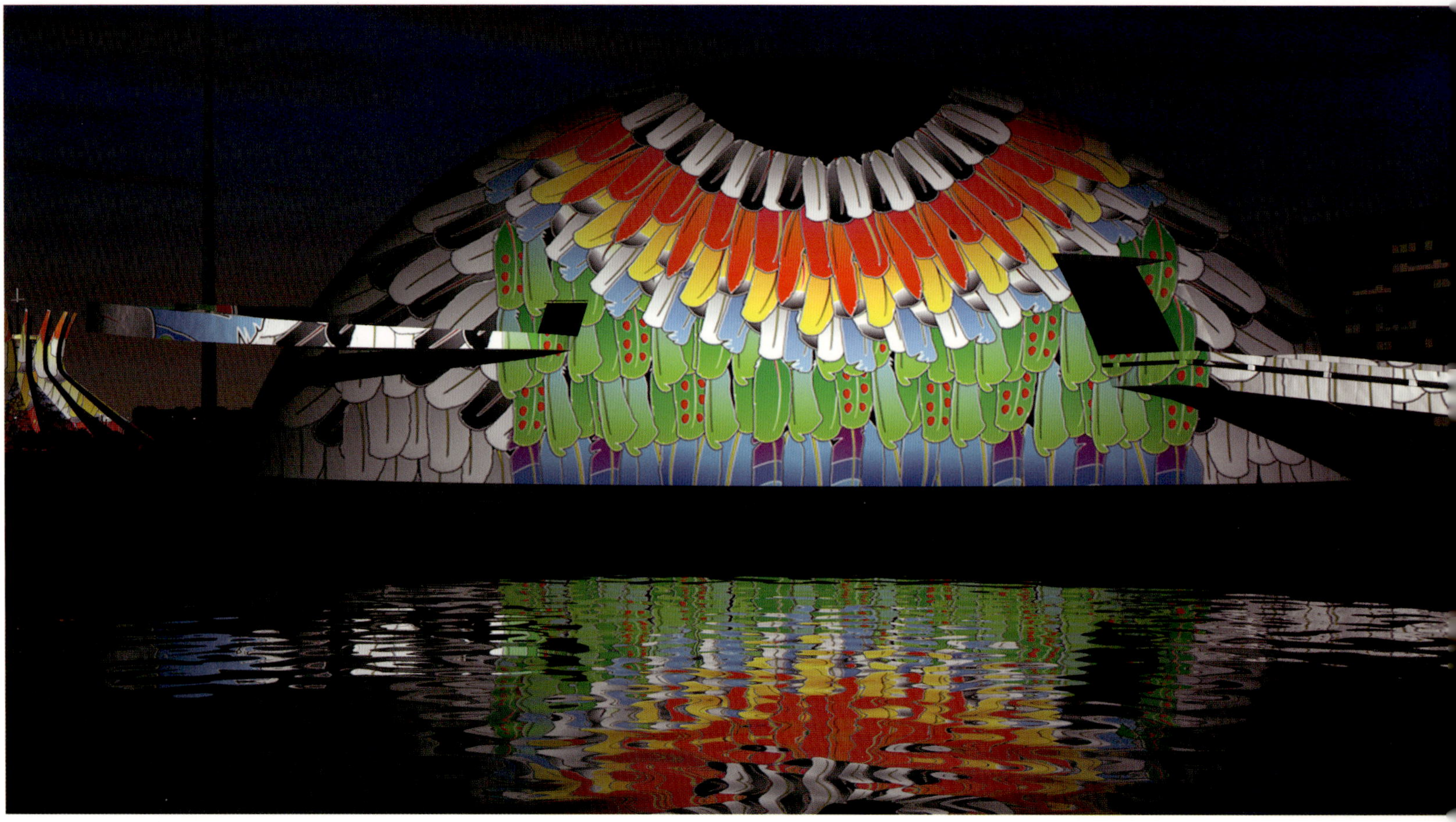

Mankind is being distanced from nature as a result of the intensification of work patterns, compressing of time, information overkill and all kinds of pollution and stress. Dazzled by the accelerated technological achievements, we forget the natural cycles and the aggression we are inflicting on our environment and we are losing basic core values.

JORGE ORTA

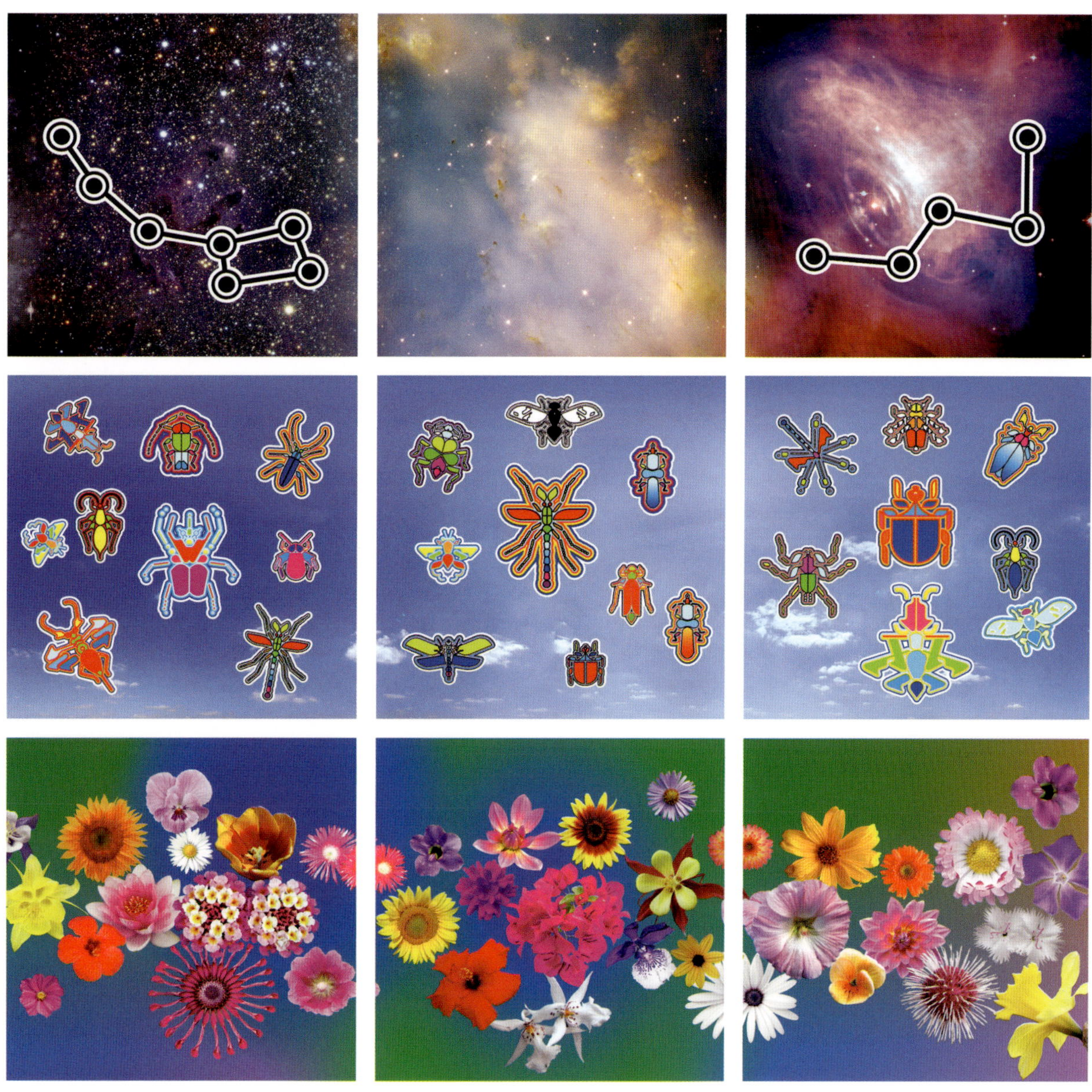

Amazonia, 2009
Laminated Lambda photograph
190 x 190 cm

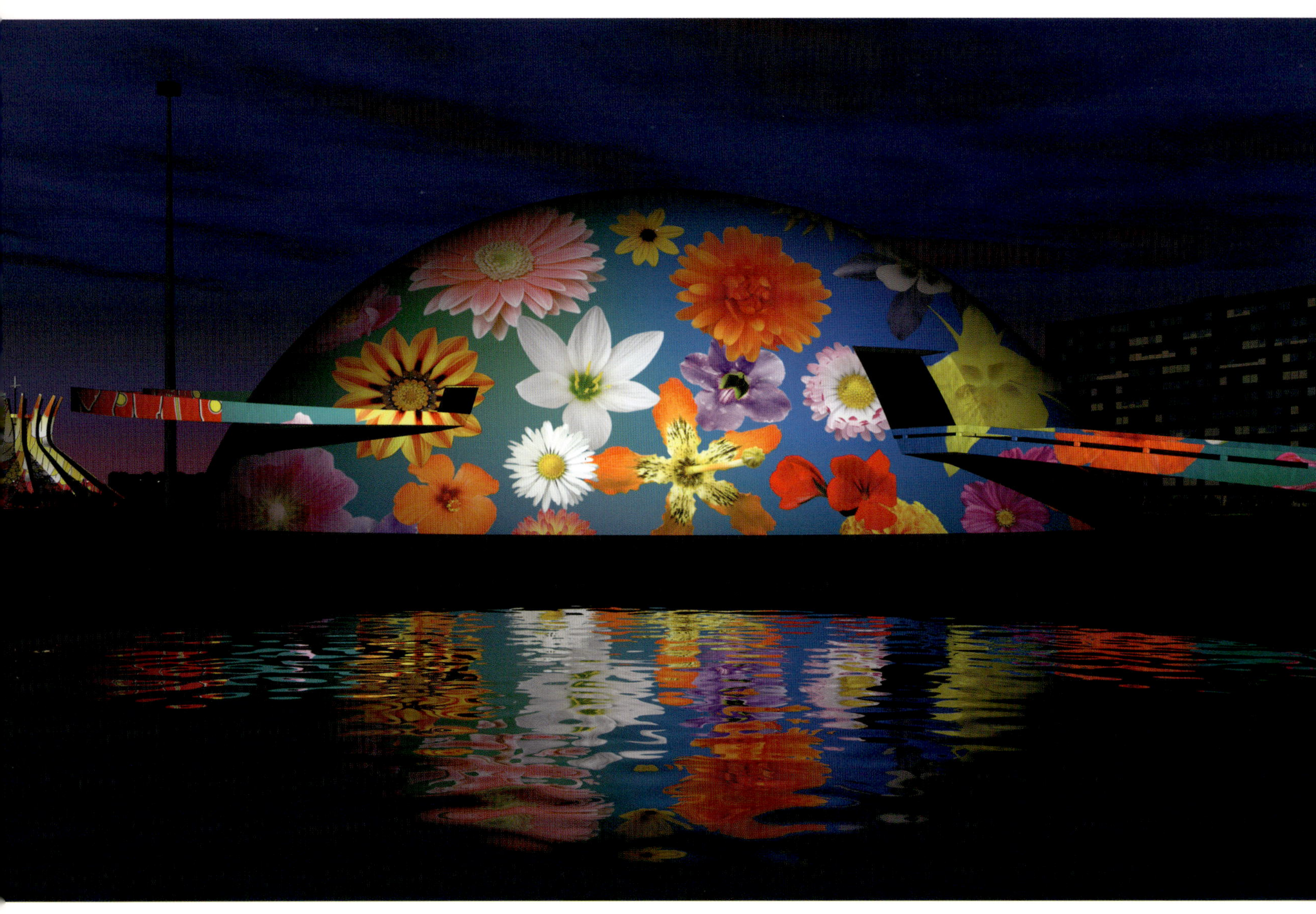

For thousands of years, philosophers have gazed at the stars and known that one thing must exist that is common to and connects the many things within the Universe. Reality cannot be found except in one single source, because of the interconnection of all things with one another.

Gottfried Leibniz

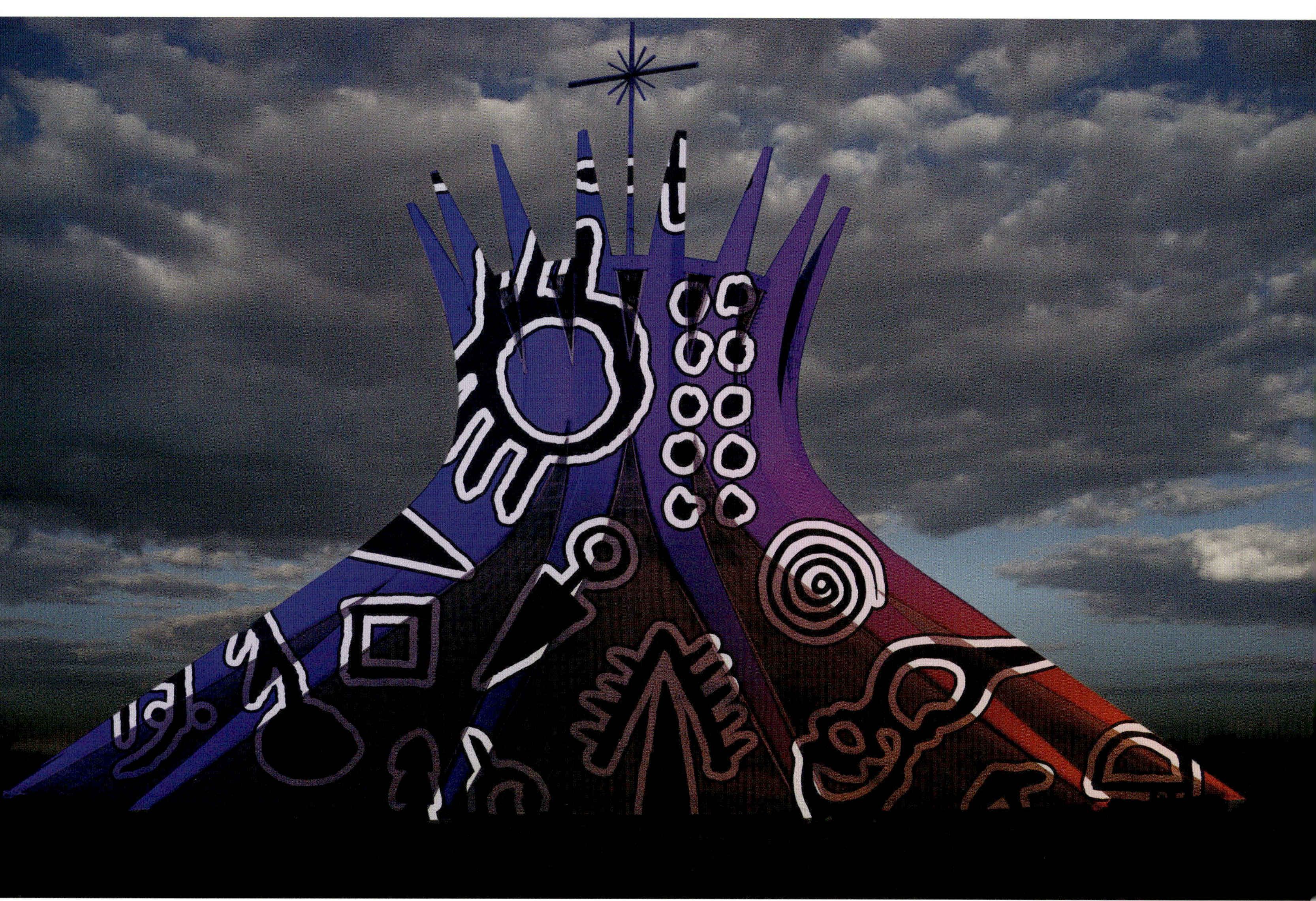

An ecological society is a society that finds the balance between the absolute materialistic and one that would fall into a blissful spirituality.

Nicolas Hulot

BIOGRAPHY

LUCY+JORGE ORTA

studio-orta.com

Lucy Orta was born in 1966 in Sutton Coldfield, United Kingdom. After graduating with an honours degree in fashion-knitwear design from Nottingham Trent University in 1989, Lucy began practicing as a visual artist in Paris in 1991. Her sculptural work investigates the boundaries between the body and architecture, exploring their common social factors, such as communication and identity. Lucy uses the media of sculpture, public intervention, video, and photography to realize her work. Her most emblematic artworks include *Refuge Wear* and *Body Architecture*, 1992–1998, portable, lightweight, and autonomous structures representing issues of survival. *Nexus Architecture*, 1994–2002, is a series of participative interventions in which a variable number of people wear suits connected to each other, shaping modular and collective structures. When recorded in photography and video, these interventions visualise the concept of social links. *Urban Life Guards*, 2004–2008, are wearable objects that reflect on the body as a metaphorical supportive structure.

Lucy's work has been the focus of major survey exhibitions at the Weiner Secession, Austria, 1999; the Contemporary Art Museum of the University of South Florida, for which she received the Andy Warhol Foundation for the Visual Arts Award, 2001; and the Barbican Centre, London, 2005. She is a Professor of Art, Fashion and the Environment at London College of Fashion, University of the Arts London and was the inaugural Rootstein Hopkins Chair at London College of Fashion from 2002–2007. From 2002–2005 was the head of Man and Humanity, a pioneering masters programme that stimulates socially driven and sustainable design, which she cofounded with Li Edelkoort at the Design Academy in Eindhoven in 2002.

Jorge Orta was born in 1953 in Rosario, Argentina. He studied simultaneously at the faculty of fine arts, 1972–1979, and the faculty of architecture, 1973–1980, of the Universidad Nacional de Rosario. Dedicated to transforming the methods and expressions of the dominant art academy, his artistic research explores alternative modes of expression and representation resulting from the specific social and political contexts of Argentina and South America. Jorge became convinced of the social role of art during a period of social injustice and revolutionary violence in Argentina, and his work explores the periphery in terms of expression and audience. Jorge was a pioneer of Video Art, Mail Art, and large-scale public performances in his hometown of Rosario, representing Argentina with *Crónica Gráphica* at the Biennale de Paris in 1982. Interested in interdisciplinary and collective art practices, he founded the research groups Huapi and Ceac to create a bridge between contemporary art and mass audiences, creating public works including *Transcurso Vital*, 1978, *Testigos Blancos*, 1982, *Madera y Trapo*, 1983, *Arte Portable*, 1983, and *Fusion de Sangre Latinoamericana*, 1984. He has published several Manifestos, including: Arte Constructor, Arte Catalizador, and Utopias Fundadoras.

Jorge was a lecturer in the faculty of fine arts of the Universidad Nacional de Rosario and a member of CONICET, the Argentinean national council for scientific research, until 1984, when he received a scholarship from the Ministry of Foreign and European Affairs to pursue a DEA (Diplôme d'études approfondies) at the Sorbonne in Paris. In 1991, a fire tragically destroyed his entire archive of work conducted in Argentina. Parallel to a studio-based practice in Paris, Jorge Orta continued his 1978 light technology artworks and created the first ceramic glass plates for the PAE 2500 (Projector Art Effect), which would allow him to pursue large-scale image projections, called Light Works. From 1991, he created Light Works in mythical sites of architecture of cultural significance across the world, including the Mount Aso volcano, Japan; Cappadocia, Turkey; the Zocòlo, Mexico City; the Gorges du Verdon, France; and the Venetian palaces along the Grand Canal, representing Argentina for the Venice Biennale in 1995. The most exceptional of these Light Works took place in 1992, on a five-week expedition along the Andes mountain range that culminated at the Inca vestiges of Machu Picchu and Sacsayhuamán, to partake in the festival of the Inti Raymi in front of two hundred thousand Peruvian Indians.

Lucy and Jorge created Studio Orta, an interdisciplinary structure for the development of their work, in Paris in 1993. More recently, they restored three historical sites along the Grand Morin river in Marne-la-Vallée, France: the Laiterie (the Dairy) in 2000, and the Moulin de Boissy and the Moulin Sainte-Marie, two former paper mills, in 2007 and 2009, respectively. They relocated their large-scale studios to these former industrial buildings for experimentation and production, as well as workshops, presentation spaces, artist residencies, and a laboratory for artistic and environmental research.

The Ortas' collaborative artwork, which often deals with issues of sustainability, has been the focus of major solo exhibitions, including OrtaWater, held at the Fondazione Bevilacqua La Masa in Venice, 2005, the Museum Boijmans Van Beuningen in Rotterdam, 2006, and the Galleria Continua in Beijing, San Gimignano, and Le Moulin, 2007–2008; Antarctica, held at the Biennial of the End of the World, Ushuaia, and the Antarctic Peninsula, 2007, and the Hangar Bicocca spazio d'arte in Milan, 2008; and Amazonia, held at the Natural History Museum, London, 2010. In 2007, the artists received the Green Leaf Award for artistic excellence with an environmental message, presented by the United Nations Environment Programme in partnership with the Natural World Museum at the Nobel Peace Center in Oslo, Norway.

BIOGRAPHIES OF CONTRIBUTORS

GABRIELLA SALGADO

Gabriela Salgado was born in Buenos Aires, Argentina and has lived in London, United Kingdom since 1995. She studied Philosophy at the Faculty of Philosophy and Literature at the University of Buenos Aires and in 1983 she moved to Barcelona, Spain, where she worked as Director of Exhibitions and International Residencies of Fundació Llorens Artigas in Barcelona. In 1997 Gabriela obtained a Master's Degree in Curating Contemporary Art from the Royal College of Art, London. In 2006 she was appointed Curator of Public Programmes at Tate Modern in London and co-curated the 2nd Thessaloniki Biennale in Greece in 2009.

Since the early 1990s Gabriela Salgado has worked with artists, such as the British sculptor Barry Flanagan, as archivist and curator. She was appointed Curator of the Latin American Art Collection for the University of Essex (UECLAA) from 1999–2005 and has specialised in Latin American contemporary art. She lectures extensively in galleries and museums and has participated as a conference speaker in the 8th and 9th Havana Biennale's in Cuba. She has organised events and conferences for institutions such as the British Council Museum Management seminars in Mexico City and Buenos Aires and the lecture-performance by Mexican artist Guillermo Gómez Peña for the British Museum in London.

Gabriela has curated a number of international exhibitions: León Ferrari: The Architecture of Madness and Arena Mexico at the University of Essex Gallery, United Kingdom, 2002; Alex Gama, Printmaker and Chance Encounters, at Gallery 32, London, 2003; Nostalgia of the Body at Firstsite Gallery, Colchester, 2005–2006; Casa Abierta / Open House in London, 2006; La Octava Región: arte contemporáneo hecho en Oaxaca at the Centro Cultural Recoleta, Buenos Aires in Argentina, 2006 and Humanos Direitos at Galeria EF, São Paulo, Brazil, 2008. In 2005 she organised the project Tucumán Chicano with performance artist and theorist Guillermo Gómez Peña in Tucumán, Argentina and is a member of the multidisciplinary collective La Pocha Nostra, directed by Gómez Peña in San Francisco, California.

JAMES PUTMAN

James Putnam is an independent curator and writer based in London. He founded and was curator of the British Museum's Contemporary Arts and Cultures Programme from 1999–2003 and was formerly a curator of their Egyptian Antiquities Department from 1985–1998. In 1994 he conceived and curated the groundbreaking exhibition Time Machine, which involved juxtaposing works by contemporary artists with ancient sculpture in the British Museum's Egyptian Gallery, and which travelled to the Museo Egizio in Turin, Italy, 1995. His book *Art and Artifact—The Museum as Medium*, 2000 and 2009, surveys the interaction between contemporary artists and the museum.

James Putman was Visiting Scholar in Museum Studies at New York University from 2003–2004 and lectures in Curatorial Studies at Central Saint Martins, University of the Arts London since 2004. He has curated a series of critically acclaimed projects with contemporary artists at the Petrie Museum, University College London and the Freud Museum that have included Sophie Calle, Sarah Lucas, Ellen Gallagher, Noble and Webster and Mat Collishaw. He was curator of Arte all'Arte 9 in Tuscany, Italy, 2005, Associate Curator at the Bowes Museum, County Durham, 2004–2006, and was on the curatorial committee for the Echigo Tsumari Triennial, Japan, 2006. In 2009, he curated Distortion and Library for the 53rd Venice Biennale in Italy and co-curated the inaugural exhibition Mythologies at the Haunch of Venison in London with 45 international artists. Putman is currently a curator for the 2010 Busan Biennale in South Korea.

LUCY+JORGE ORTA CURRICULUM VITAE

SOLO EXHIBITIONS

2010
Amazonia. Natural History Museum, London, United Kingdom
The Gift. Adelaide International 2010: Apart, we are together; Jam Factory, Adelaide, Australia
Lucy Orta. CCANW: Centre for Contemporary Art and the Natural World, United Kingdom
Antarctica. Eté des Arts en Auxois-Morvan, Montbard, France

2009
OrtaWater. Motive Gallery / Vienna Art Fair, Austria
OrtaWater. DSM, Heerlen and Sittard, Holland
70 x 7 The Meal, act XXXI. Sherwell Church Hall, North Hill, Plymouth, United Kingdom
Lucy Orta. Plymouth Arts Centre / Plymouth College of Art & Design, United Kingdom
Light Works—Brasilia em Luz (project). Brasilia, Brazil

2008
Antarctica. Galleria Continua: Le Moulin, Boissy le Châtel, France
Antarctica. Hangar Bicocca spazio d'arte, Milan, Italy
Antarctic Village—13:3. Fries Museum, Leeuwarden, Holland
Antarctic Village—Works in Progress. Motive Gallery, Amsterdam, Holland
70 x 7 The Meal, act XXIX. La Venaria Reale, Turin, Italy
70 x 7 The Meal, act XXVIII. Villa Ephrussi de Rothschild, Cap Ferrat, Monaco
OrtaWater. Expo Zaragoza 2008, Austrian Pavilion, Spain
Body Architecture. The Swedish Museum of Architecture, Stockholm, Sweden
Survival. Fashion Space Gallery, London College of Fashion, United Kingdom

2007
Antarctic Village—No Borders. Galleria Continua: San Gimignano, Italy
Antarctic Village—No Borders. Antarctic Peninsula, Antarctica
Heads or Tails, Tails or Heads. Antarctic Marambio Base, Antarctica
Fallujah—works in progress. Galerie Peter Kilchmann, Zurich, Switzerland
Fallujah. Institute of Contemporary Art / Old Truman Brewery, London, United Kingdom
Fallujah—Casey's Pawns. 11th Prague Quadrennial International Exhibition of Scenography and Theatre Architecture, Czech Republic
Fallujah. Art Forum Berlin / Motive Gallery, Germany
Fallujah—Auszug 01. Context Festival, Hebbel am Ufer, Berlin, Germany
70 x 7 The Meal, act XXVII. Albion Gallery, London, United Kingdom
Nexus Architecture. Tramway, Glasgow, Scotland

2006
OrtaWater. Galleria Continua: Beijing, China
70 x 7 The Meal, act XXV, Open House. Casa Argentina, London, United Kingdom
Selected Works: Lucy+Jorge Orta. Motive Gallery, Amsterdam, Holland
Light Works—Lights on Tampa. Tampa Bay Hotel / University of Tampa, Florida, United States
Light Works—Open House/Casa Abierta. Casa Argentina, London, United Kingdom

2005
Lucy Orta. The Curve, Barbican Centre, London, United Kingdom
Drink Water! 51st Venice Biennale, Fondazione Bevilacqua La Masa, Italy
Water & Works. Museum Boijmans Van Beuningen, Rotterdam, Holland
70 x 7 The Meal, act XXIII—Lunch with Lucy. The Curve, Barbican Centre, London, United Kingdom
70 x 7 The Meal, act XXII. Z33, Hasselt, Belgium
70 x 7 The Meal, act XXI. Pleinmuseum / Centraal Museum, Utrecht, Holland
Totipotent Architecture. Centre for Contemporary Visual Arts, University of Brighton, United Kingdom

2004
Casey's Pawns—Nexus Architecture. Victoria & Albert Museum, London, United Kingdom
Dwelling X. RIBA, London, United Kingdom
Nexus Architecture x 110. Attwood Green, Birmingham, United Kingdom
Light Works—Lille European Cultural Capital 2004. Opera House, Lille, France

2003
70 x 7 The Meal, act XX. UNESCO, Paris, France
Connector Mobile Village. Southeastern Center for Contemporary Art, Winston-Salem, North Carolina, United States
Body Architecture. Lothringer13, Munich, Germany
Dwelling X. Old Market Square, Nottingham, United Kingdom
Collective Dwelling, act IX. Institute for Contemporary Art, Brisbane, Australia
Collective Dwelling, act VIII. Cicignon High School, Fredrikstad, Norway
Light Works—OPÉRA.tion Life Nexus, act IX. 14th World Transplant Games, Place Stanislas, Nancy, France

2002
70 x 7 The Meal, act XIX. Design Academy Eindhoven, Holland
70 x 7 The Meal, act XVII (Enactments of the Self). Sterischer Herbst, Graz, Austria
70 x 7 The Meal, act XVII. Rio Garonne, Toulouse, France
70 x 7 The Meal, act XVI. Ar/ge Kunst Museum Gallery, Waltherplatz, Bolzano, Italy
Connector Body Architecture sector IX. Musée d'Art et d'Histoire de Cholet, France
Connector Mobile Village. Florida Atlantic University Galleries, Boca Raton, Florida, United States
Nexus Architecture x 110. Miami Design District / Art Basel Miami Beach, Miami, Florida, Unites States
Fluid Architecture II workshops. The Dairy, St Siméon, France / Stroom Den Haag, The Hague, Holland
Fluid Architecture I workshops. Drill Hall, Melbourne, Australia
Light Works—OPÉRA.tion Life Nexus, act VIII. Saint-Eustache, Paris, France
The Gift—Life Nexus. TwoTen Gallery, The Wellcome Trust, London, United Kingdom
Borderline. Berlin Ballet: Komische Oper Berlin, Germany / Compagnie Blanca Li: Créteil Maison des Arts, France

2001
70 x 7 The Meal, act XIII. Firstsite gallery, Colchester, United Kingdom
70 x 7 The Meal, act XII. Parc Beauvillé, Amiens, France
70 x 7 The Meal, act XI (They say this is the Place). Antwerp, Belgium
70 x 7 The Meal, act X (Active Ingredients). The American Center for Food Wine and the Arts, Napa Valley, California, Unites States
70 x 7 The Meal, act IX (OPÉRA.tion Life Nexus, act VII). Museum für Angewandte Kunst, Cologne, Germany
70 x 7 The Meal, act V–VII. Casa de Francia / Museo Diego Rivera/ Couvent de la Mercedes, Mexico City, Mexico
Connector Guardian Angel sector VIII. Casa de Francia, Mexico City, Mexico
Connector Mobile Village sector IV. University of South Florida Contemporary Art Museum, Tampa, Florida, Unites States
Light Works—OPÉRA.tion Life Nexus, act VI—Battement des Grands Jours. Palais de Tau / Reims Cathedral, France
Light Works—OPÉRA.tion Nexo Corazòn, act V. Festival del Centro Histórico, El Zocalo, Mexico City, Mexico
The Gift. Firstsite gallery, Colchester, United Kingdom
Arbor Vitae (Making History). Freeport Talke, Staffordshire, United Kingdom

2000
70 x 7 The Meal, act IV. Dieuze, France
70 x 7 The Meal, act III (The Invisible Touch). Kunstraum Innsbruck, Austria
Connector Mobile Village sector VII. Talbot Rice Gallery, Edinburgh, United Kingdom
Connector MacroWear sector VI. Kapelica Gallery, Ljubljana, Slovenia
Connector Mobile Village III. Australian Centre for Contemporary Art, Melbourne, Australia
Connector Mobile Village II. La Cambre E.N.S.A.V., Brussels, Belgium
Connector Mobile Village I. Pitti Immagine, Florence, Italy
The Gift—Life Nexus. Cité des Sciences et de l'Industrie, Parc de la Villette, Paris, France
Light Works—OPÉRA.tion Life Nexus, act IV Millennium. Le Grenier du Siècle / Lieu Unique, Nantes, France
OPERA.tion Life Nexus, act III. Chapiteau Larue Foraine, Paris, France
Light Works—OPERA.tion Life Nexus, act II. Hôpital Robert Giffard, Québec, Canada
Light Works—OPÉRA.tion Life Nexus, act I. Festival Internacional de Arte, Medellin, Colombia
The Gift—Life Nexus. Athens Sculpture Biennale, Greece
The Gift—Life Nexus. Mediterranean seabed, France
Jorge Orta recent works. Galeria El Museo, Bogota, Colombia

1999
HortiRecycling Enterprise, act II. Weiner Secession, Vienna, Austria
Nexus Architecture. Haus der Kulturen der Welt, Berlin, Germany
Nexus Architecture. Passages centre d'art contemporain, Troyes, France
Collective Dwelling, act VII. Fabrica gallery, Brighton, United Kingdom
Urban Life Guards—works in progress. Expofil, Paris, France

1998
Lucy Orta—Urban Armour. Art Gallery of Western Australia, Perth, Australia
Nexus Architecture. Appel d'Air, Paris, France
Nexus Architecture. March Against Child Labour, Lyon, France
Questions from the heart 0023. Espace d'Art Yvonamor Palix, Paris

1997
Collective Dwelling, act II. Le Creux de l'Enfer, Thiers, France
All in One Basket, act I. Galerie du Forum Saint-Eustache, Paris, France
Refuge Wear. East End London, United Kingdom
Commune Communicate (Actions Urbaines). C.P. Metz detention centre, France
Ici et Ailleurs. Le Parvis, Tarbes, France

1996
Modular Architecture. Soirées Nomades, Fondation Cartier pour l'art contemporain, Paris, France
Refuge Wear—Nexus Architecture. Soho Festival, New York
Refuge Wear. Espace d'Art Yvonamor Palix, Paris, France
Light Messenger. Galerie du Dourven Brittany, France

Light Works—Cardinal Cross. Evry Cathedral, France
Light Works—Light Messenger. Coastline of Brittany, France
Light Works—Heart of the Moon. Causseaux Kiln, Limoges, France

1995
Identity + Refuge Act I. Salvation Army Cité de Refuge, Paris, France
Nexus Architecture—Collective Wear x 16. 46th Venice Biennale, Venice, Italy
Light Works—Light Messenger. 46th Venice Biennale, Canal Grande, Venice, Italy
Light Works—Paths of Light. Gorges du Verdon, France
Light Works—Woven Light. Troglodyte villages, Cappadocia, Turkey

1994
Refuge Wear. Montparnasse Station, Paris, France
Nexus Architecture x 8. Cité La Noue, Montreuil, France
Refuge Wear. Louvre / Le Pont des Arts, Paris, France
Refuge Wear. Salvation Army Cité de Refuge, Paris, France
Light Works—Cry from the Earth. Mount Aso, Kyushu, Japan
Light Works—Sacred Light. Chartres Cathedral, France
Light Works—Figures d'Origines. Chapelle de la Salpétrière, Paris, France

1993
Light Works—Light of Stone. Castilla-La Manche, Cuenca, Spain
Light Works—Fire Signs (project). Vesuvius / Institut Français, Naples, Italy
Jorge Orta. Recoleta Cultural Centre, Buenos Aires, Argentina

1992
Light Works—Imprints on the Andes. The Andes Mountain Range, Peru
Light Works—Rive des Amériques. Palais de Tokyo, Paris
Jorge Orta. Center for Art and Communication, Buenos Aires, Argentina
Terre. Galerie Procréart, Paris, France

1991
Light Works—Poème Infographique (Graphic Light Poem). Centre Pompidou, Paris, France
Light Works—Leçons Ténèbres. Basilique de Neuvy Saint Sépulchre, France
Light Works—untitled. Chapelle de la Salpetrière, Paris, France
Jorge Orta. Galería La Kabla, Madrid, Spain
Poussière / Dust. Galerie Paris-Bastille, France

1990–1984
Jorge Orta. Keller-Kinder Gallery, Paris France
Jorge Orta. Frankfurter Buchemesse, Frankfurt Germany
Jorge Orta. Galérie Seul, Brussels, Belgium
Rito y sacrificios. Cloitre des Billettes, Paris, France
Irracional Alatorio. Bernanos Gallery, Paris, France
Sustancia e immaterialidad de signos. Le Pont d'Arcole, Paris
Jorge Orta. Galería Krass, Rosario, Argentina

1984
Fusion de sangre Latinoamericana. Bernardino Rivadavia centro culturel, Rosario, Argentina

1983
Madera y Trapo. Bernardino Rivadavia centro culturel, Rosario, Argentina
Testigos Blancos. Plaza Santa Cruz, Rosario, Argentina

1982
Cronica Grafica. XII Biennale de Paris, France / Bernardino Rivadavia centro culturel, Rosario, Argentina
Jorge Orta. Buonarroti Gallery, Rosario, Argentina

1981
Transcurso Vital. Museu de Arte Contemporanea da Universidade Sao Paulo, São Paulo, Brazil

1978
Transcurso Vital. Plaza Vicene Lopez y Planes, Fisherton, Rosario, Argentina
Jorge Orta. Galería Krass, Rosario, Argentina

1977
Jorge Orta. Galería del Bajo, Rosario, Argentina

1976
Jorge Orta. Galería Dalila Bonomi, Rosario, Argentina

1975
Jorge Orta. Galería Sala de la Pequena Muestra, Rosario, Argentina

1974
Jorge Orta. Galería de Arte Il Duomo, Rosario, Argentina
Jorge Orta. Galería Lirolay, Buenos Aires, Argentina

1973
Jorge Orta. Galería Raquel Real, Rosario, Argentina
Jorge Orta. Galería Krass, Rosario, Argentina
Jorge Orta. Galería Lirolay, Buenos Aires, Argentina
Jorge Orta. Colegio de Graduados de Ciencias Económicas de Rosario, Argentina

GROUP EXHIBITIONS

2010
Urban Life Guard (Eclaircies). Le Quai Angers, France
Antarctic Village—No Borders. MAXXI, Rome, Italy
A New Stance For Tomorrow: Part 3. Sketch, London, United Kingdom
Climate Capsules: Means of Surviving Disaster. Museum für Kunst und Gewerbe, Hamburg, Germany

2009
GSK Contemporary, Earth: Art of a changing world. Royal Academy of Arts, London, United Kingdom
Green Platform: Art Ecology Sustainability. Palazzo Strozzi, Florence, Italy
Dress Code. ISELP, Brussels, Belgium
Pot Luck: Food and Art. The New Art Gallery, Walsall, United Kingdom
Intemperie: Fenomenos Esteticos da Mudanca Climatica e da Antartida. Centro Cultural Oi Futuro, Rio de Janeiro, Brazil
Sur Polar: Arte en Antartida. MUTEC, Mexico City, Mexico
Return to Function. Madison Museum of Contemporary Art, Madison, Wisconsin, United States
Frozen Time: Art from the Antarctic. Stadtgalerie Kiel, Germany
Antarctica World Passport distribution bureau. HEAVEN, 2nd Athens Biennale, P. Faliro Beach, Greece
Retreat. KunstFort Asperen, Acquoy, Holland
Off the Beaten Path: Violence, Women and Art. The Stenersen Museum, Oslo, Norway
(Un)Inhabitable? Art of Extreme Environments. Festival @rt Outsiders 2009, Maison Européenne de la Photographie, Paris, France
A Way Beyond Fashion. Apexart, New York, Unites States
Antarctic Village—Nuit Blanche. FRAC Lorraine, Metz, France
Esthétique des pôles: Le testament des glaces. FRAC Lorraine, Metz, France
Sphères. Galleria Continua: Le Moulin, Boissy le Châtel, France
AntArctica. Haugar Vestfold Kunstmuseum, Tønsberg, Norway
The Spectacle of the Everyday—TAMA project. Xth Biennale de Lyon, Museum of Contemporary Art, Lyon, France

2008
Life Size Utopia. Motive Gallery, Amsterdam, Holland
Poëziezomer Watou 2008. Watou, Belgium
1% Water and our future. Z33, Hasselt, Belgium
Shelter X Survival: Alternative Homes for Fantastic Lives. Hiroshima City Museum of Contemporary Art, Japan
Totipotent Architecture—Skin Deep. KunstFort Asperen, Acquoy, Holland
Sur Polar: Arte en Antártida. MUNTREF Museo de la Universidad Nacional de Tres de Febrero, Buenos Aires, Argentina
Carried Away—Procession in Art. MMKA, Arnhem, Holland

2007
The Politics of Fear. Albion Gallery, London, United Kingdom
OrtaWater—Envisioning Change. Nobel Peace Center, Oslo, Norway
OrtaWater—Environmental Renaissance. City Hall, San Francisco, California, Unites States
OrtaWater—Dans ces eaux là... Château d'Avignon, Saintes Maries de la Mer, France
Urban Life Guard. Galleria Continua: Le Moulin, Boissy le Châtel, France
Antarctic Village—No Borders. 1st Biennial of the End of the World, Ushuaia, Tierra del Fuego, Argentina

2006
Nexus Architecture. 9th Havana Biennale, La Habana Vieja, Cuba
LESS—Alternative Strategies for Living. PAC contemporary art museum, Milano, Italy
This is America! Centraal Museum, Utrecht, Holland
Monument Minimal. Château d'Avignon, Saintes Maries de la Mer, France
Metro Pictures, part two. MoCA, North Miami, Florida, Unites States
Taille Humaine. Orangerie du Sénat, Le Jardin du Luxembourg, Paris, France
Other than Art. G Fine Art Gallery, Washington, DC, United States
Channel. Cupola Gallery, Hillsborough, Sheffield, United Kingdom
The Fashion of Architecture. Center for Architecture, New York, United States
Dark Places. The Santa Monica Museum of Art, California, United States

2005
Contemporaneo Liquido. Franco Soffiantino Gallery, Turin, Italy
Five Rings: Ornaments of Suffering. Fort of Exilles, Piedmont, Italy
Sweet Taboos. Tirana Biennale 3, Tirana, Albania
Fear Gear. Roebling Hall, New York, United States
Pattern Language: Clothing as Communicator. Tufts University Art Gallery, Aidekman Arts Center, Medford, Massachusetts, United States
Fée Maison. La Briqueterie en Bourgogne, Le Creusot, France
Est-Ouest/Nord-Sud: faire habiter l'homme, là encore, autrement. arc-en-reve centre d'architecture, Bordeaux, France
Art-Robe: Women Artists in a Nexus of Art and Fashion. UNESCO, Paris
On Conceptual Clothing. Kirishima Open-Air Museum, Kagoshima, Japan
Biennale de l'urgence en Tchétchénie. Palais de Tokyo, Paris

2004
On Conceptual Clothing. Musashino Art University, Tokyo, Japan
A Grain of Dust A Drop of Water. Gwangju Biennale 2004, South Korea
Totipotent Architecture (Arte all'Arte: Arte Architettura Paesaggio). Associazione Arte Continua, Buonconvento, Italy
The Interventionists: Art in the Social Sphere. MASS MoCA, North Adams, Massachusetts, United States

Flexible 4: Identities. Kunsthallen Brandts Klædefabrik, Odense, Denmark
The Space Between. John Curtin Gallery, Curtin University of Technology, Perth, Australia
Lies and Lust: Art & Fashion. Podewil, Berlin, Germany
Dwelling X. Northern Gallery for Contemporary Art, Sunderland, United Kingdom

2003
Design et Habitats. Centre Georges Pompidou, Paris, France
Flexible. Whitworth Art Gallery, The University of Manchester, United Kingdom
Creuats/Cruzados/Crossed. CCCB, Barcelona, Spain
Armour: The Fortification of Man. KunstFort Asperen, Acquoy, Holland
Nexus Architecture x 50 (Micro Utopias). Art and Architecture Biennale, Valencia, Spain
M.I.U. Mobile Intervention Units (Kaape Helder). Den Helder, Holland
Fashion: The Greatest Show on Earth. Bellevue Art Museum, Bellevue, Washington, United States
Doublures. Musée national des beaux-arts du Québec, Canada

2002
Connector Body Architecture. Laing Art Gallery, Newcastle, United Kingdom
Strike. Wolverhampton Art Gallery, West Midlands, United Kingdom
Somewhere: Places in Refuge. Angel Row Gallery, Nottingham, United Kingdom
Shine. The Lowry, Salford Quays, United Kingdom
Portable Living Spaces. The Fabric Workshop and Museum, Philadelphia, Pennsylvania, United States
Fragilités. Le Printemps de Septembre, Toulouse, France

2001
Mobile Village: Plug In. Westfälisches Landesmuseum für Kunst und Kulturgeschichte, Munster, Germany
Untragbar. Museum für Angewandte Kunst Köln, Cologne, Germany
To the Trade. Diverse Works Art Space, Houston, Texas, United States
Wegziehen. Frauen Museum, Bonn, Germany
Global Tools. Künstlerhaus Wien, Vienna, Austria
M.I.U. (Transforms). G8 Environment Summit, Trieste, Italy

2000
Dynamic City. La Fondation pour l'Architecture, Brussels, Belgium
Air en Forme. Musée des Arts Décoratifs / Vitra Design Museum, Lausanne, Switzerland
Ici On Peut Toucher. Galerie TBN, Rennes, France
Life Nexus Village Fete (Home). Art Gallery of Western Australia, Perth, Australia
Mutations/Modes 1960–2000. Musée Galliera, Paris, France

1999
Body Architecture. Institut Français d'Architecture, Paris, France
Visions of the Body. Museum of Modern Art, Kyoto / Museum of Contemporary Art, Tokyo, Japan
Life Nexus Village Fête (In the Midst of Things). Bournville Village Green, Birmingham, United Kingdom
Collective Dwelling (Design Machine). Kelvingrove Museum, Glasgow, United Kingdom
Model Homes: Explorations in Alternate Living. The Edmonton Art Gallery, Alberta, Canada
Untitled. Ronald Feldman Gallery, New York, United States

1998
Personal Effects: The Collective Unconscious. Museum of Contemporary Art, Sydney, Australia
Addressing the Century: 100 Years of Art and Fashion. The Hayward Gallery, London, United Kingdom
The Campaign Against Living Miserably. The Royal College of Art Galleries, London, United Kingdom
Nexus Architecture. Passage de Retz, Paris, France

1997
Nexus Architecture (Trade Routes: History and Geography). 2nd Johannesburg Biennale, Electric Workshop, South Africa
Produire Créer Collectionner. Musée du Luxembourg, Paris, France
P.S.I. Open. MoMA P.S.I., New York, United States
Bournes Citoyenne (Ici et Maintenant). Parc de la Villette, Paris, France
Touche pour Voir. Le Creux de l'Enfer, Thiers, France

1996
Visual Reports. International Cultural Centre, Antwerp, Belgium
Nexus Architecture (On Route to Mex). Art & Idea, Mexico City, Mexico
Commune Communicate (Actions Urbaines). Casino Luxembourg, Luxembourg
Identity + Refuge Act II (Shopping). Deitch Projects / Salvation Army, New York, United States
L'art du plastique. Ecole Nationale Supérieure des Beaux-Arts, Paris, France
Refuge Wear. Première Vision, Paris, France
Light Works—Via Crucis. Printemps de Septembre, Cahors, France

1995
Survival Kits (On Board). 46th Venice Biennale, Canal Grande, Venice, Italy
Nexus Architecture—Collective Wear x 16. 46th Venice Biennale, Canal Grande, Venice, Italy
Un Sac pour la Rue (Shopping). CAPC Musée d'art contemporain, Bordeaux, France
Identity + Refuge Act I. Salvation Army Cité de Refuge, Paris, France

1994
Ateliers 94. Musée d'art moderne de la ville de Paris, France

1993
Art Fonction Sociale! Salvation Army Cité de Refuge, Paris, France
Body Ware: Habitus. Galerie Anne de Villepoix, Paris, France

1989
Signes Metasociaux. 3rd Havana Biennale, La Habana Vieja, Cuba

1985
1st Art-of-Peace Biennale. Biennale des Friedens, Hamburg, Germany

ACKNOWLEDGEMENTS

2009
BRASILIA EM LUZ—Brasilia, Brazil
Emmanuel Roux (3D rendering) / Anne Loyet & Michelle Robert (Cultures France) / French Embassy in Brazil / Pierre Henry (composer), Isabelle Warnier (studio Son/Re) / Nicola Goretti & Fabio Scrugli (Grupo AG Brasilia) / Nicolas Doerler (artistic director)

2006
LIGHTS ON TAMPA—Tampa, South Florida, United States
Thierry Bal (photography) / Emmanuel Roux (digital design) / The University of Tampa: Dr. Ronald L.Vaughn (president), Deborah Lester, Joanne Steinhardt (artistic coordinator), Santiago Echeverry (workshops) / Tampa City Public Art Program: Robin Nigh (director) Melissa Le Baron (project coordonator) / Gilles Gingras & Louis-Marc Plante (projections)

2006
CASA ABIERTA—Casa Argentina, London, UK
Anna Schori (photography) / Emmanuel Roux (digital design) / Gabriela Salgado (curator) / Argentine Embassy London: Javier Pedrazzini (cultural attaché), Federico Mirré (ambassador) / ETC (projections)

2003–2004
LILLE LIGHTS—Opéra de Lille, Chambre du Commerce et Beffroi, Lille, France
Jean Jean Crance (photography) / Lille 2004: Didier Fusiler (director), Marc Menis (coordination) / Concert: Pierre Henry (composer), Isabelle Warnier (studio Son/Re), Thierry Balasse (sound diffusion) / Jean-Paul Dufour (technical director) / Nicolas Doerler (artistic director) / Charles Carcopino (video projection)

2003
OPERA.tion Life Nexus act IX—Place Stanislas Nancy, France
Jean Jean Crance (photography) / Concert: Pierre Henry (composer), Isabelle Warnier (studio Son/Re), Thierry Balasse (sound diffusion) / Emmanuel Roux (digital design) / Nicolas Doerler (artistic director) / Adeline Cousin (workshop coordinator) / Olivier Coustere (president Trans-Forme) / François Pelissier, (president, Comité Organisateur Local) w/ Henri Blanc (project director) / Maurice Slapak (president World Transplant Games Federation) /

Code of ethics or organ donation:
Michel Dinet (president, Conseil général de Meurthe-et-Moselle) / Laurence Chaupin & Philippe Colson (communication) / Dominique Dautricourt (E.F.G) / A.D.D.O.T.H.

Public sculpture:
André Rossinot (Mayor of Nancy & president, Communauté Urbaine du Grand Nancy) / Joel Huguenin (Vézelize foundry) / Piero Lembo (stone quarry)

2002
OPERA.tion Life Nexus acte VIII—Eglise Saint-Eustache, Paris, France
Jean Jean Crance (photography) / Concert: Simon Stockhausen (composer), Danny Schoeteler (drums), Kalle Kalimar (guitar), Christian Weichner (saxophone) / Yves Roux (lighting) / Emmanuel Roux (digital design) / Nicolas Doerler (artistic director) / Léon Miquel (Contre Jour) / Didier Renaud (projections) / Dominique Dautricourt (E.F.G.),

2001
OPERA.tion Life Nexus act VI—Battement des Grands Jours / Palais de Tau, Reims Cathedral, France
Jean Jean Crance (photography) / Llorenç Barbeur (composer) / Yves Roux & Philippe Desperz (lighting) / Thierry Dumanoir (administrator, Palais du Tau) / Didier Renaud (projections)

2001
NEXO CORAZÓN act V—El Zócalo, Mexico City, Mexico
Mathieu Rousseaux (photography) / Concert: Pierre Henry (composer), Isabelle Warnier (studio Son/Re), Thierry Balasse (sound diffusion) / Roberto Vázquez (director general, Festival del Centro Histórico), Mediha Martínez (public relations) / Jean-Paul Dufour (technical director) / Jean-François Bowen (projections) / Yves Roux (lighting).

2000
OPERA.tion Life Nexus act IV—Millennium—Lieu Unique LU, Nantes, France
Mathieu Rousseaux & Jean Jean Crance (photography) / Jean-Paul Dufour (technical director) / François Bowen (projections) / Yves Roux, Gérôme Billy & Frédérique Peslier (lighting) / Jean Blaise (director, Lieu Unique)

1996
CROSSROADS—Cathédrale d'Évry, France
Mathieu Rousseaux (photography) / Yves Roux & Philippe Martinaud (lighting) / Jean-Paul Dufour (technical director), Père Alain Bobière (general vicar) / Diocese of Évry-Corbeil-Essonnes

1996
LIGHT MESSENGER—Parc du Dourven, Brittany, France
Mathieu Rousseaux (photography) / Frédérique Peslier (lighting) / Galerie du Dourven: Danièle Yvergniaux (director), Didier Lamandé (curator)

1996
VIA CRUCIS—Le cloitre de la Cathédrale Saint-Étienne de Cahors, France
Mathieu Rousseaux (photography) / Frédérique Peslier (lighting), Marie-Thérèse Perrin (director, Festival Printemps de Cahors) / Didier Renaud (projections)

1996
HEART OF THE MOON—Four de Casseaux, Limoges, France
Mathieu Rousseaux (photography) / Frédérique Peslier (lighting) / Didier Renaud (projections) / Colette Billaud (modeling) / Henri-Michel Borderie (curator) / Jean Claude & Lionel Delaygue (directors Royal Limoges) / Paul Blaise (president of culture and Patrimoine, Limousin) / Christian Couty (president, Espace-porcelaine)

1995
LIGHT MESSENGER—Canal Grande, XLVI Biennale di Venezia, Italy
Jorge Glusberg (curator) / Guido Di Tella (Argentine cancillerìa) / Michel Brossard (Philips Lighting) / Hervé Morin & Marie Clerin (photography) / Jean-Paul Dufour (technical director) / Didier Renaud & Jean-François Vowen (projections) / Jérôme de Missolz & Remi Levin (video) / Alessandro del Pra (logistics Venice) / Valerie Ogé / Sophie Vieille / Jean-Michel Place (publisher) / Leila Voight (project associate) / Texts: Norbert Hilaire / Pierre Ponant / Bernard Heidsieck

1995
PATHS OF LIGHT—Gorges du Verdon, France
Mathieu Rousseaux (photography), Jean-Paul Dufour (technical director) / Frédérique Peslier (lighting) / Olivier Hindermeyer (director UCPA)

1995
WOVEN LIGHT—Cappadocia, Turkey
Mathieu Rousseaux (photography), Jean-Paul Dufour (technical director) / Frédérique Peslier (lighting) / UCPA: Olivier Hindermeyer (director), Ameth Diller (coordination), Dragana Ilic (assistant) / Jean-Michel Place (publishing) / Goksin Sipahioglu (Sipa Press)

1994
THE CRY FROM THE EARTH—Mount Aso, Kyushu, Japan
Philippe Fuzeau & Jean-Jean Crance (photography) / Yves Roux (lighting) / François Dussolier (sound) / Emmanuel Roux (digital design) / TV Man Union Japan: Yoko Hatakeyama, Naoto Tanaka, Kazuko Miyazaki / UPIC

1994
SACRED LIGHT—Cathédrale de Chartres, France
Mathieu Rousseaux, Patrice Maurein & Philippe Fuzeau (photography) / Odile Jutten (organist) / Philippe Martinaud & Yves Roux (lighting) / Maïté Vallez Bled (director, Musée de Chartres) / Hélène Violle / Stephan Marinier / Xavier Maignan / Georges Lemoine (Mayor of Chartres) / Alain Erlande-Brandenburg (historian) / chamber of commerce Chartres / Rector of Chartres Cathedral

1993
LIGHT OF STONE—Castille-La Manche, Cuenca, Spain
Fundacion Banesto: Araceli Pere (director), Lola Garrido (curator) / Mathieu Rousseaux & Patrice Morin (photography) / Jean-Paul Dufour (technical director) / Yves Roux (lighting) / Didier Renaud (technician) / Francois Dussolier (sound)

1992
RIVE DES AMÉRIQUES—Trocadéro, Paris, France
Claude Namer (project director) / Philippe Fuzeau & Alain Nozay (photography), Léon Miquel (Contre Jour)

1992
IMPRINTS ON THE ANDES—The Andes Mountain Range, Peru
Claude Namer (project director) / Jean Jean Crance & Philippe Fuzeau (photography) / Claire Seguin (logistics) / Hervé Breuil, Denis Banz & José Huaman (video) / Laurent Aubry & Léon Miquel (Contre Jour) / Eric Palliet (digital design) / Stéphane Marinier (consultant) / Helène Violle (texts) / Vilma Abella (communication) / SIPA Press / Claire Durieux (D.A.I.) / Gladys Moreano (coordination Peru) / Luís Figueroa, Jorge Vignati & Númitor Hidalgo (cinema photography) / Pierre Labbe (French cultural attaché) / Humberto Paredes (Mayor of Comas) / Mario Obando (events director Municipality of Cuzco) / Wilfredo Yepes (anthropologist) / Jean-Pierre Jeremenko (Alliance Française) / Horacio Delgado, Roberto Romero & Juan Ricardo Piroja (Multiservice) / Juan Valdivian (general administrator, Coca Cola Cuzco) / Serge Pey (poet)

1992
POÈME INFOGRAPHIQUE
Palais de Tokyo, Paris
Jouy-enJosas, France
Philippe Fuzeau & Jean Jean Crance (photography) / Léon Miquel (Contre Jour)

1991
POÈME INFOGRAPHIQUE—Georges Pompidou Centre, Paris, France
Jean Jean Crance (photography) / Eric Paillet (digital design) / Stephan Marinier (video), Nils Aziosmanoff (president, Art 3000) / Léon Miquel (Contre Jour)

1991
Leçons Ténèbres—Basilica of Neuvy-Saint-Sépulchre, France
Jean Jean Crance (photography) / Stephan Marinier (curator) / Sylvie Colas (soprano)

BIBLIOGRAPHY

MONOGRAPHS

Pietromarchi, Bartolomeo, ed., *Antarctica*, Milan: Mondadori Electa, 2008.
Orrell, Paula, ed., *Lucy+Jorge Orta Pattern Book: An Introduction to Collaborative Practices*, London: Black Dog Publishing, 2007.
Prince, Nigel, ed., *Lucy+Jorge Orta: Collective Space*, Birmingham: Article Press, 2006.
Williams, Gilda, ed., *Lucy Orta, contemporary artist series*, London: Phaidon Press, 2003.
Smith, Courtney, ed., *Body Architecture*, Munich: Silke Schreiber Verlag, 2003.
Budney, Jen, ed., *Process of Transformation*, Paris: Editions Jean-Michel Place, 1999.
Orta, Lucy, ed., *Refuge Wear*, Paris: Editions Jean-Michel Place, 1996.
Orta, Jorge, ed., *Light Messenger*, Paris: Editions Jean-Michel Place, 1996.
Glusberg, Jorge, ed., *Transparence*, Paris: Editions Jean-Michel Place, 1996.

SOLO EXHIBITIONS CATALOGUES

Perisino, Maria, and Bartolomeo Pietromarchi, eds., *Lucy+Jorge Orta: 70 x 7 The Meal*, Turin: Pocko Editions, 2008.
Guérin, Paul, ed., *OrtaWater, Lucy+Jorge Orta*, Strasbourg: Centre Européen d'Actions Artistiques Contemporaines, 2007.
Holmes, Jonathan and Chris Townsend, *Fallujah*, London: ICA London, 2007.
Cairns, Stephen, and Joanne Entwistle, *Refuge Wear and Nexus Architecture*, Havana: 9th Havana Biennale 2006.
Vettese, Angela, ed., *DrinkWater!*, Pistoia: Gli Ori, 2005.
Hanru, Hou, *HortiRecycling*, Vienna: Weiner Secession, June 1999.
Pettigas, Catherine, ed., *Incandescence*, Paris: Editions Jean-Michel Place, 1998.

GROUP EXHIBITION CATALOGUES

Bureaud, Annick, and Jean-Luc Soret, ed., "Antarctica", in *IN)Habitable? L'art des Environnements Extrêmes*, Paris: Festival @rt Outsiders / Maison Européenne de La Photographie, 2009, p. 24.
Gensini, Valentina, ed., *Green Platform—Through the Platform, Art Ecology Sustainability*, Florence: Centro di Cultura Contemporanea Strozzina Firenze, 2009, pp. 22–29. 112–115.
Kainrath, Peter Paul, "Lucy+Jorge Orta", in *The Delight of Collecting, Works from the Finstral Collection*. Merano: Kunst Merano Arte, 2009, pp. 100–101.
Nyaas-Lyngstad, Tone, ed., *Antarctica*, Tønsberg: Hauger Vestfold Kunstmuseum, 2009, pp. 6–11.
Scardi, Gabi, "TAMA Project Side Effects", in *X Biennale de Lyon*, Dijon: les presses du réel, 2009, pp. 353–354.
Comisso, Francesca, ed., "Lucy Orta, Totipotent Architecture Atoll", in *New Patrons, Contemporary Art, Society and Public Space*, Milan: Silvana Editoriale, 2008, pp. 85–107.
Joly, Eric, "Lucy et Jorge Orta. Le Bureau de délivrance du passeport universel", in *Art Grandeur Nature*, Le Blanc Mesnil: Forum de Blanc Mesnil, 2008.
Matsuoka, Takeshi, ed., *Shelter x Survival: Alternative Homes for Fantastic Lives*, Hiroshima: Hiroshima City Art Museum, 2008, pp. 46–51.
Barruol, Agnès, ed., *Dans ces Eaux là*, Paris: Actes Sud, 2007, pp. 32–37.
Knol, Meta, ed., *This is America*, Herengracht, Amsterdam: JM Meulenhoff, 2006, p. 59.
Scardi, Gabi, ed., "Urban Armor", in *Alternative Living Strategies*, Milan: 5 Continents Editions, 2006, pp. 185–199.
Koike, Kazuko, ed., "Connector", in *On Conceptual Clothing*, Tokyo: Musashino Art University Museum, 2005, pp. 46–51.
Hoos-Fox, Judy, ed., *Pattern language: Clothing as Communicator*, Medford: Tufts University Art Gallery, 2005, p. 8.
Zucca Alessandrelli, Irina. "Lucy Orta", in *Exilles: The Five Rings*, Turin: Umberto Allemandi & Co, 2005, pp. 65–67.
Pinto, Roberto. *Gwangju Biennale, A Grain of Dust a Drop of Water*, Gwangju: South Korea, 2004, pp. 237–239.
Putman, James, "Totipotent Architecture", in *Arte All'Arte: Arte Architettura Paesaggio*, Pistoia: Gli Ori, 2004, pp. 159–179.
Thompson, Nato, ed., *The Interventionists, Trespassing Toward Relevance*, North Adams, MA: Mass MoCA, 2004, pp. 32, 99–100.
De Roden, Peter, ed., "Lucy+Jorge Orta", in *Art from a Natural Source, Kaap Helder*, Den Helder: Kunst en Cultuur Nord-Holland, 2003, pp. 48–49, 94.
Lamoureux, Johanne, ed., *Doublures: Vêtements de l'Art Contemporain*, Québec: Musée national des Beaux-Arts Québec, 2003, pp. 19, 36–37.
Damianovic, Maia, and Sabina Gamper, eds., *To Actuality*, Bolzano: Ar/ge Kunst Galerie Museum, 2002, pp. 46–49.
Beyerle, Tulga, ed., "Collective Wear x 3", in *Global Tools*, Zurich: Kunsthaus Zurich, 2001, p. 145.
Cappellazo, Amy, and Margaret Miller, eds., "70 x 7 The Meal", in *Active Ingredients*, Napa, CA: Copia—The American Center for Wine Food and the Arts, 2001.
Heinzelmann, Markus, ed., *Untragbar*, Ostfildern: Hatje Cantz / Museum für Angewandte Kunst Köln, 2001, pp. 20–21.
Heinzelmann, Markus, ed., *Plug In*, Münster: Westfälisches Landesmuseum für Kunst und Kulturgeschichte, 2001, pp. 140–141.
Pinto, Roberto, and Emanuela De Cecco, eds., *Transforms*, Trieste: CCNI 2001, pp. 19–29.
Koop, Stuart, and Vikki Mc Innes, eds., *Red*, Melbourne: Australian Centre for Contemporary Art, 2000, p. 51.
Prince, Nigel, and Gavin Wade, eds., "Life Nexus Village", in *the Midst of Things*, Birmingham: August Media Ltd, 2000, pp. 60–61.
Smith, Trevor, ed., *Home: an archaeology of the social link*, Perth: Art Gallery of Western Australia, 2000.
Kohmoto, Shinji, ed., *Visions of the Body: Fashion or Invisible Corset*, Kyoto: The National Museum of Modern Art and Tokyo: Museum of Contemporary Art, 1999, pp. 160–163.
Wollen, Peter, ed., *Addressing the Century*, London: The Hayward Gallery, 1998.
McDonald, Ewen, ed., *Personal Effects*, Sydney: Museum of Contemporary Art, 1998.
Lacloche, Francis, ed., "Lucy Orta, Dans le Même Panier", in *Carnet d'un mécène*, Paris: Caisse des Dépôts et Consignations, 1997, pp. 43–49.
Jammet, Yves, ed., "Lucy Orta, Bornes Citoyennes", in *Ici et maintenant*, Paris: APSV, Parc de la Vilette, 1996, pp. 73–75.
Sans, Jérôme, ed., "Identity + Refuge", in *Shopping*, New York: Time Out, 4 September, 1996, p. 11.
Sans, Jérôme, ed., *On Board log book*, Venice, 1995.
Sans, Jérôme, ed., "Un Sac Pour La Rue", in *Shopping*, Bordeaux: *CAPC Magazine*, 9 September, 1995.
Pagé, Suzanne, and Béatrice Parent, eds., *Ateliers 94*, Paris: Musée d'art moderne de la ville de Paris, 1994.
Piguet, Philippe, ed., "Vêtements Refuges", Seine Saint Denis: Fond départemental d'art contemporain, Département de Seine Saint Denis, 1994, p. 80.
Ardenne, Paul, and Denis Lebaillif, eds., *Art Fonction Sociale!*, Paris: Cité du Refuge Paris, 1993.

BOOKS, MAGAZINES, JOURNALS

2010

Girault, Marie. "Lucy et Jorge Orta, Poètes Engagés", *Artension*, vol. 99, January/February 2010, pp. 30–34.
Fluck, Apolline. "Vêtements véhicules, Lucy+Jorge Orta", *Azimuts Revue de design*, vol. 34, Spring 2010, pp. 8–23.
Gowronski, Alex. "Between Art and Action", *Contemporary Visual Art + Culture Broadsheet*, vol. 39, March 2010, pp. 49–52.

2009

Barbero, Luca Massimo, and Elena Ciresola, eds., "Lucy+Jorge Orta", in *Index 2*, Venice: Marsilio, 2009, pp. 98–105.
Berk, Anne, "Hoopvolle Kunst van Studio Orta", *Financieel Dagblad no 1*, 10 January 2009.
Carbonaro, Simonetta, "If only we wanted to", *The Hub, focus on research. London College of Fashion*, Issue 6, February 2009, pp. 19–20.
Chavez, Juan David, ed., *Habitarte: la mirada crítica desde el espacio escultórico contemporáneo hacia la arquitectura doméstica actual*, Medellín: Consejo Profesional Nacional de Arquitectura y sus Profesiones Auxiliares: Universidad de Antioquia, Facultad de Artes, 2009.
Hambly, Vivienne, "Into the Amazon's Earth", *Sublime*, Issue 17 October 2009, pp. 13–20.
Jocks, Heinz-Norbert, "Kelider Machen Identitaten", in *Dressed! Art en Vogue*, Ruppichteroth, Germany: Kunstforum International, 2009, pp. 164–175.
Lamunière, Simon, ed., "Antarctic Village—No Borders Lucy+Jorge Orta)", in *Utopics: Systems and Landmarks*, Zurich, Switzerland: JRP Rigier, 2009, p. 21.
Klanten, Robert, and Lukas Feireiss, eds., *Spacecraft 2: More Fleeting Architecture and Hideouts*, Berlin: Gestalten, 2009.
Orta, Lucy, ed., *Mapping the Invisible, EU-Roma Gypsies*. London: Black Dog Publishing, 2009, pp. 134–137, 140–143.
Papastergiadis, Nikos, "Lucy Orta: The artist as enabler", *Art & Australia*, vol. 47, no. 2, Summer 2009, pp. 240–241.

2008

"Antarctica", *Urban*, vol. 21, April 2008, pp. 21–26.
"Antarctica: Viaggio al Confini del Mondo", *Elle Décor*, Issue 19, May 2008, p. 626.
Perra, Daniele. "Design on Ice", *BOX*, June 2008, pp. 36–51.
Capelli, Pia, "All'Hangar Bicocca, Da Oggi a Milano la grande mostra di Lucy+Jorge", *Libero*, 2 April 2008, pp. 28–29.
Capelli, Pia. "All'Hangar Bicocca gli Orta", *Arte*, 3–9 April 2008, pp. 50–51.
Casati, Marta, "Lucy+Jorge Orta", *EspoArte*, April–May 2008, pp. 79–85.
Chiodi, Stefano, "Visionari del Pronto Soccorso", *Specchio. La Stampa*, May 2008, pp. 104–106.
Pratesi, Ludovico, "Dal Polo Sud la mostra glaciale che affronta temi scottanti", *Il Venderedi di Republica*, 28 March 2008, p. 97.
Di Genova, Arianna, "Antartide, il continente dell'utopia no borders", *Visioni*, 3 April 2008.
Echavarria, Pilar, "Life Nexus Village et Refuge Wear", in *Architecture Portative: Environnements imprévisibles*, Barcelona: Links Books, 2008, pp. 182–185.
"Antarctica ai confini del mondo", *Gd'A*, May 2008, pp. 98–99.

Grassi, Manuela, "Antartide formato Bicocca", *Panorama*, 28 March 2008, pp. 202–204.
Monem, Nadine, ed., *Contemporary Textiles: The Fabric of Fine Art*, London: Black Dog Publishing, 2008, pp. 27, 144–147.
Irace, Fulvio, ed., *Casa per Tutti: Abitare la Citta Globale*, Milan: Mondadori Electa, 2008, p. 160.
Legrenzi, Susanna, "Un Nuovo Mondo Venuto dal Freddo", *Corriere Della Serra*, 15 March 2008, pp. 240–244.
Mammi, Alessandra, "Red Carpet. Colloquio con Lucy e Jorge Orta", *L'Espresso*, 13 March 2008, p. 157.
Meneguzzo, Marco, "Gli Orta in Antartide, l'ultima terra senza confini nazionalistici", *Avvenire*, 8 April 2008, p. 26.
Mirenzi, Franco, "Lucy+Jorge Orta, Antarctica", *OFArch*, June 2008, p. 16.
Mostafavi, Mohsen, "Architecture's Inside", in "What about the inside", *Harvard Design Magazine*, vol. 29, Fall 2008, p. 107.
Moralto, Rossella, "Lucy+Jorge Orta", *Arte e Critica*, vol. 55, June–August 2008, p. 94.
Moretti, Silvia, "La Globalizzazione fra i Ghiacci", *Insideart*, April 2008, pp. 30–31.
Naidoo, Ravi, "A Better Future by Design Art Fashion and Social Consciousness", *Design Indaba*, 2008, pp. 7–15.
Orta, Jorge, "The Antarctica Project", in *Urban Climate Change Crossroads*, New York: Urban Design Lab, 2008, pp. 123–128.
Perra, Daniele, "Beyond Borders", in *Progetto e Percorsi—BOX*, Summer 2008, p. 36.
Perra, Daniele, "Installazioni Nomadi, Antartico alla Bicocca", *Luna*, April 2008, p. 78.
Pirovano, Stefano, "Vernissage in Antartide", *Casamica*, February 2008, p. 62.
Rovesti, Fabrizio, "Lucy e Jorge: La fine del mondo dall'Antartide alla Bicocca", *Prealpina*, 13 April 2008, p. 34.
Rowena, Liu, "Lucy+Jorge Orta, Antarctica Hangar Bicocca Milan", *IW Magazine*, July/August 2008, pp. 88–91.
Tamburi, Laura, "Lucy+Jorge Orta, La missione libertaria dell'arte", *New Age*, May 2008, pp. 72–75.
Zambianchi, Ivana, "Installazioni/ai confini del mondo", *Brava Casa*, May 2008, p. 61.

2007
Bannet, Alma, "Lucy Orta il cibo avanzato", *Velvet*, August 2007, p. 157.
Bigi, Daniela, "Antarctica: An Emblematic Village", *Arte e Critica*, vol. 53, December 2007, pp. 60–65.
Harris, Gareth, "Antarctic Village", *The Art Newspaper*, vol. 172, no. 180, 2007, p. 6.
Bubmann, Klaus, "Lucy Orta", in *Plug-in*. Amsterdam: Einst und Mobilitat, 2007.
Lagroue, Bruno, "Nouvelle vie pour le Moulin de Boissy", *Le Briard Coulommiers*, 19 October 2007, p. 10.
Moreno, Shonquis, "Antarctic Village", *Surface Magazine*, vol. 66, no. 180, 2007, p. 70.
Peña, Ann Mari, "Antarctic Village—No Borders", *The Hub, Diversifying Fashion. London College of Fashion*, July 2007, pp. 14–18.
Perlez, Jane, "Fallujah: An Assault in Iraq", *New York Times*, 29 May 2007.
Mandrini, Riccarda, "Antarctica", *Vogue Italia*, December 2007, p. 58.
Virilio, Paul, "Interview with Lucy Orta", in *Design and Art: Documents of Contemporary Art*, London: Whitechapel Press; Cambridge, MA: MIT Press, 2007, pp. 122–123.

2006
Doswald, Christoph, ed., *Double-Face: The Story about Fashion and Art from Mohammed to Warhol*, Zurich: JRP Ringer, 2006, pp. 170–171.
Drummond, Diana, "Lucy Orta", in *Textile Art for Our Time*, Oxford: Berg Publishers, 2006, pp. 208–213.
Hanisch, Ruth, *Absolutely Fabulous! Architecture for Fashion*. Munich: Prestel Verlag, 2006, p. 138.
Hemmings, Jessica, and Marilyn Murphy, "Adorned in Ideas", *Fiber Arts*, vol. 32, no. 4 2006, pp. 40–41.
Kaufman, David and Christian Schwalbach, "Body of Work", *Departures*, Autumn 2006, p. 114.
MJM, "Retablir le lien social", in *Inspirations*, Paris: Maison & Objet, 2006, pp. 34–35.
Pinto, Roberto, "Lucy Orta", in *The Power of Fashion: About Design and Meaning*, Brooklyn, New York: Terra Press Publishing and Arnhem: ArtEZ Press, 2006, pp. 322–325.
Thackara, Davina, "Lucy Orta", *Contemporary* 21, no. 87, 2006, pp. 58–61.
Teunisson, José, ed., In *The Power of Fashion: About Design and Meaning*. Arnhem, The Netherlands: ArtEZ Press, 2006.

2005
Antonelli, Paola, ed., *Safe: Design Takes On Risk*, New York: Museum of Modern Art, 2005, p. 11.
Beckers, Macribe, "Positief Design", *Elle Wonen*, no. 98, March 2005, pp. 36–37.
Braddock, Sarah, and Marie O'Mahony, *Techno Textiles: Revolutionary Fabrics for Fashion and Design*, London: Thames & Hudson, 2005, pp. 175-176.
Cooke, Rachel, "Be Prepared", *Observer*, 11 September 2005, p. 6.
Croci, Valentina, "Lucy Orta", *Ottagono*, June 2005, pp. 21–22.
Di Marzio, Mimmo, "La Biennale nel sogno dell'acqua", *Il Giornale*, 20 June 2005, p. 23.
Hains, Bruce, "Gwangju Biennale", *Frieze* no. 89, 2005, pp. 127–129.
Melhuish, Clare, "Lucy Orta", in *Home Cultures 2*, Oxford: Berg Publishers, 2005, pp. 221–227.
Morozzi, Cristina, "Vestito da Abitare", *Amica* no. 39, 2005, pp. 104–107.
Putnam, James, "No labels", *Art Review*, vol. LVI, September 2005, pp. 60–65.
Roots, Frank, *Cabins: Dens and Bolt Houses*, Paris: Fitway Publishing, 2005.
Schofield, John, *Combat Archaeology: Material Culture and Modern Conflict*, London: Duckworth Publishers, 2005.
Smith, Courtney, and Sean Topham, eds., *Xtreme Fashion*, Munich: Prestel Verlag, 2005, pp. 150–152.
Townsend, Chris, "Lucy Orta: Art, Fashion, Mobility", *Art & Architecture Journal*, vol. 62, Summer 2005, pp. 37–39.
Von Fichern, Sigrid, "Ein Kleid, Ein Haus", *Vogue Deutsch*, Apri, 2005, pp. 162–164.
Von Naso, Rudiger, "Gesellschaftsspiele", *Madame*, May 2005, p. 68.
"Transgressing Fashion", *Crudelia*, no. 23, 2005, pp. 10–11

2004
Apfelbaum, Sue, "Social Fabric: Lucy Orta", *res 7*, no. 4, 2004, p. 22.
Barano, Claudia, "La visibilita degli invisibili", *Activa Fashion Design Management*, vol. 39, 2004, pp. 108–115.
Becker, Jack, "Recent Projects", *Public Art Review*, Fall-Winter 2004, p. 48.
Caretta, Enrica, "Meglio Condividere", *Marie-Claire Italia*, vol. 5, 2004, pp. 161–166.
Conekin, Becky, "Orta's Current Collaboration", *The Hub, Research Publication. London College of Fashion*, November 2004, pp. 55–57.
Coomer, Martin, "Showgirls", *Elle UK*, September 2004, p. 105.
Baqué, Dominique, ed., *Pour un Nouvel Art Politique*, Paris: Flammarion, 2004, pp. 100, 112, 127–137.
Gabrielli, Paolo, "Art as Fashion", *Art Review* 54, September 2003, pp. 50–55.
Gockel, Cornelia, "Lucy Orta: Body Architecture", in *Garbage Art*, Ruppichteroth: Kunstforum International, 2004, pp. 353–354
Laurence, Dreyfus, "70 x 7: la comida", in *Deguste*, Paris: CulturesFrance, 2004, p. 98.
Long, Kieran, "Nexus Architecture", *Icon*, October 2004, pp. 186–87.
Pawson, John, and Lucy Orta, "To be minimalist... or maximalist", *The Guardian*, 19 April 2004, pp. 4–5.
Phillips, Ian, "Worlds Apart", *The Independent*, 3 April 2004, pp. 46–47.
Saltzman, Andrea, *El cuerpo Disenado Sobre la forma en el proyecto de la vestimenta*, Buenos Aires, Argentina: Editorial Paidos SAICF, 2004, p. 73.
Tevi, Alice, "Lucy Che Salva il Mondo", *La Repubblica delle Donne*, 11 September 2004, pp. 68–72.
Thompson, Henrietta, "Chalayan versus Orta", *Blueprint*, vol. 219, May 2004, pp. 128–129.
Thompson, Henrietta, "Home Is Where The Art Is", *Blueprint*, vol. 217, March 2004, pp. 86.
Topham, Sean, ed., *Move House*. Munich: Prestel Verlag, 2004, pp. 52–55.
Quinn, Bradley, "Body Architecture", *Selvedge*, Issue 01, July/August 2004, pp. 52–55.
Vettese, Angela, "Lucy e ombre", *Vernissage*, vol. 52, September 2004, p. 3.
Von Naso, Rudiger, "Charakter Zeigen!", *Madame*, February 2004, pp. 72–75.
Willemin, Veronique, ed., "Les Vêtements Refuges et Nexus Architecture", *Maison Mobile*, Paris: Collection Anarchitecture, 2004, pp. 114–117.
Cuenca la luz en el paisaje, La Fondacion Cultural Banesto, 2004, pp. 18–23

2003
Bick, Emily, "Techno Fashion", *Contemporary* no. 51, 2003, pp. 66–68.
Evans, Caroline, ed., *Fashion at the edge: spectacle, modernity and deathliness*, New Haven, CT: Yale University Press, 2003, p. 236.
Fossati, Maddalena, "Insieme si può", *Marie Claire Italia*, no. 5, May 2003, p. 166.
Goetz, Joachim, "Das Bedurfnis nach Schutz, Geborgenheit und Gemeinsamkei", *TDK*, 24 September 2003.
Hermann, Alice, "Il faut avoir une esthetique et un statement, l'un ne fonctionne pas sans l'autre", Paris: Stiletto Edition, 2003, p. 112.
Hoffmann, Justin, "Lucy Orta", *Kunst-Bulletin* no. 11, November 2003.
Mulholland, Neil, "All You Need to Know", *Frieze*, Issue 73, March 2003, pp. 91–92.
Paolo, Gabrielle, "Art as Fashion", *Art Review*, vol. LIV, September 2003, pp. 54–59.
Quinn, Bradley, ed., *The Fashion of Architecture*, Oxford: Berg Publishers, 2003, pp. 151–180.
Van den Hoven, Geerit, "En Zorgouldig Vormgegem Utopia", *Uit & Kunst*, 30 October 2003, p. 4.
White, Lisa, "Lucy Orta: Mobile Intervention Unit IV", *View On Colour*, Issue 24, June 2003, pp. 34–35.

2002
Altena, Arie, "Over de gastvrijheid van kunst", *Metropolis*, no. 5, October 2002, pp. 51–53.
Bokern, Anneke, "Lucy Orta, Fluid Architecture", *Bauwelt* no. 35, September 2002.
Bolton, Andrew, ed., "Interview with Lucy Orta", in *The Super Modern Wardrobe*, London: V&A publications, 2002, pp. 130–139.
Boucault, Vincent, "Lucy Orta habille le monde de ses Vêtements Refuges", *Le Monde*, 17 June 2002.
Budney, Jen, and Adrian Blackwell, eds., *Unboxed: Engagements in Social Space*, Ottawa, ONT: G-101 Publications, 2005, pp. 52–65.
Braddock, Sarah, and Marie O'Mahony, eds., *Sport Tech Sportswear: Revolutionary Fabrics*, London: Thames & Hudson, 2002, pp. 48, 61, 68, 72, 76, 84.
De Martrin, Maia, "Sans rêves il n'y a pas de projets", *Art Actuel*, no. 19, March 2002, pp. 56–59.
A, A, "Urban Armor", *Dwell*, vol. 3, San Francisco, December 2002, p. 80.

Price, Matt, "Somewhere, Places of Refuge in Art and Life", *[a-n] For Artists*, November 2002, p. 6.
Haagsma, Lotte, "Beschermende kleding als symbol", *Tubelight* no. 2, September 2002, pp. 19–20.
Quinn, Bradley, ed., *Techno Fashion*. Oxford: Berg Publishers, 2002, pp. 19–26.
Van Driel, Anne, "Solidair regenjack", *De, volkskrant Amsterdam*, 25 July 2002, pp. 8–9.
Hamaide, Chantal, "Le village mobile de Lucy Orta", *Intramuros*, June/July 2002.
Virilio, Paul, "Un habitat exorbitant", *Architecture d'Aujourd'hui*, no. 328, June 2002, pp. 112–119.
Smith, Courtney, and Sean Topham, eds., *Xtreme Houses*, Munich: Prestel, 2002, pp. 112–115.
Sozanski, Edward J, "Art in the bag", *The Philadelphia Inquirer*, 3 January 2002.
Such, Robert, "Out of the Woods", *Blueprint*, no. 194, April 2002, pp. 72–74.

2001
Berwick, Carly, "Clothes Encounters", *ART News* 100, November 2001.
Bralic, John, "Corporeal Limits", *Monument*, June/July 2001, pp. 74–77.
Comte, Béatrice, "Le Zocalo de Mexico—L'Oeuvre d'un soir", *Le Figaro Magazine*, 27 April 2001, pp. 96–98.
Ishiguro, Tomoko, "Creating a future from, voluntary social action", *Axis Japan*, vol. 90, January 2001, pp. 89–93.
Jiménez Flores, Maricruz, "Connector Gardien", *Cronica Mexico City*, 31 March 2001, p. 29.
Jeffett, William, "Lucy Orta", *New York Arts*, no. 12, December 2001, p. 9.
López, Raúl, "Corazones Ángeles Clausuran el FCH", *Cultura*, 2 April 2001, p. 4.
López, Raúl Sergio, "Diseñan luces sobre la Catedral", *Cultura*, 27 March 2001.
Marger, Ann-Mary, "Lucy Orta: Fashioning Change Through Art", *St Petersburg Times, Sunday Arts*, 18 November 2001.
Muchnic, Suzanne, "Eat, drink and be cultural", *Los Angeles Times*, 25 November 2001, pp. 83–85.
Neradil, Barbara, "The art of connection", *The Oracle Tampa*, 21 November 2001.
Noé, Paola, "Transforms", *Tema Celeste*, March 2001.
Poncet, Emmanuel, "L'art à l'école", *Beaux Art Magazine*, October 2001, p. 156.
Posca, Claudia, "Plug-in: Einheit und Mobiliat", *Kunstforum International*, no. 156, 2001, pp. 391–393.
Rodríguez, Gómez, "Fiesta de luz en Catedral", *Cultura*, 27 March 2001, p. 30.
Schulze, Karin, "Zwischen Qual und Lust", *Financial Times Deutschland*, 17 July 2001.
Socha, Miles, "The Great Unworn", *Women's Wear Daily*, vol. 182, 7 August 2001.
Wright N, Bruce, "Fabric Interventions", *Public Arts Review*, vol. 12, 2001, pp. 11–14.
White, Lisa, "Hortirecycling", *View On Colour*, Issue 18, 2001, pp. 26–27.

2000
Aberle, Marion, "Wohnkleider und Hosenzelte für die Nomaden des 21 Jahrhunderts", *Frankfurter Allgemeine*, 15 January 2000.
Bartolotti, Paola, "Le umane tribu rivestite da Lucy", *Corriere di Firenze*, 12 January 2000.
Escolano, Véronique, "Fermeture du Grenier: LU se projette", *Loire-Atlantique*, 2 January 2000, p. 22.
Gallagher, Bryan, "Portable Habitat", *B-guided SCP*, 2000, pp. 40–43.
Hernández, Juan, "El arte debe ser elemento fundamental de la transformación social: Jorge Orta", *Unomásuno*, 11 December 2000, p. 36.
Hill, Peter, "Deconstructing Deconstruction", *Art Monthly Australia*, no. 130, June 2000, pp. 13–14.
Hufschlag, Inge, "Im Overall das Wohnen wagen", *Handelsblatt Düsseldorf*, 18 January 2000.
Leprun, Sylviane, "Le temps du risque: La création comme enterprise", in *Le Risque en Art*, Paris: Editions Klincksieck, 2000.
Piccinini, Laura, "Trovare Casa in un Vestito", *Amica*, no. 8, February 2000, pp. 226–227.
Reid, Chris, "It's in your head, Outside inside", *Space Time*. 2000, pp. 52–55.
Rota, Nelda, "A Firenze in Mostra l'Uomo Oggetto", *Il Secolo XIX*, 16 January 2000, p. 16.
Ruiz Salcines, Mauricio, "El Arte, proceso de transformación social", *El Dìa*, 30 November 2000, p. 24.
Taroni, Francesca, "La nuova estetica delle relazioni tra open-air buffets e banchetti senza fine", *Casa Vogue Italy*, October 2000, p. 70.
Tommasini, Cristina Maria, "Body Architectures, Survival Clothes", *Domus*, March 2000, p. 74.
Vargas, Angel, "Jorge Orta realiza proyectos compremetidos con individuo y sociedad", *La Journada*, April 2000, p. 5.
Virilio, Paul, "Un habitat exorbitant", *Architecture d'Aujourd'hui*, no. 328, June 2000, pp. 112–113.
Warr, Tracey, and Amelia Jones, eds., *The Artist's Body*, London: Phaidon Press, 2000, pp. 187, 284, 287

1999
Borchhardt-Birbaumer, Brigitte, "Soziale und strukturale Strategien", *Wiener Zeitung*, 16 July 1999.
Braunstein, Chloe, "G-Y'm", *Architecture d'Aujourd'hui*, no. 328, 1999.
Chelotti, Chiara, "Lucy Transformation for Multiples Architecture Modulari", *L'Uomo Vogue*, 1999, pp. 136–143.
Fitoussi, Brigitte, "Robe 'n' Nobel", *Numéro*, no. 8, November 1999, p. 50.
Goldberg, Roselee, ed., *Performance, l'art en action*, London: Thames & Hudson, 1999, p. 58.
Harmel, Françoise, "Process of Transformation", *Architecture d'Aujourd'hui*, no. 225, March 1999, p. 6.
Hirvensalo, Virve, "Wrap around shelter", *Frame*, vol. 2, 1999, p. 21.
Hofleitner, Johanna, "Landwirtschaft & das Kleinstadtische", *Schaufenster Die Presse*, 25 June 1999.
Morozzi, Cristina, "L'Art à Porter", *Intramuros*, no. 73, October/November 1999, pp. 24–25.
Miller, Margaret, "Body Architecture", *The Tampa Tribune*, 28 February 1999.
Milani, Joanne, "Artist weaves activism into unorthodox garments", *The Tampa Tribune*, 21 February 1999.
Müller, Florence, ed., "Collective Survival Sack", in *Art & Mode*, Paris: Editions Assouline/Thames & Hudson, 1999, p. 66.
Morozzi, Cristina, "Vestito da Abitare", *Amica* no. 39, September 1999, pp. 104–107.
Pignalosa, María-Cristina, "Jorge Orta abre el círculo del arte", *VEA*, 15 June 1999.
Szabo, Julia, "Wear House", *I-D*, vol. 46, May 1999, pp. 58–63.
"Arte que transforma", *El Espectador*, 8 June 1999, pp. 6–9.

1998
Budney, Jen, "Who's it for? 2nd Johannesburg Biennale", *Third Text*, no. 42, February 1998, pp. 88–94.
Charland, Denis, "La route du coeur 1998/1999/2000", in *Le Sabord*, Trois Rivières, QUE: Edition Le Sabord, 1998, pp. 6–19.
Crosling, John, "Body Architecture", *Architectural Review*, no. 65, spring 1998, p. 98.
De Santis, Sophie, "Les formes de Lucy Orta", *Figaroscope*, 13–19 May 1998.
Diawara, Manthia, "Moving Company: 2nd Johannesburg Biennale", *Artforum International*, March 1998, pp. 86–89.
Eshun, Kodwo, "Refuge Wear", *ID Magazine*, no. 179, September 1998, p. 106.
Farina, Fernando, "Una mujer colombiana tambien es una especie en extencion", *La Capital*, 13 December 1998, p. 8.
Goldberg, Roselee, ed., *Performance live art since the 60's*, London: Thames & Hudson, 1998, p. 58.
Heartney, Eleanor, "Mapping the Postcolonial", *Art in America*, no. 6, June 1998, p. 51.
Quick, Harriet, "Refuge Wear", *Frank*, October 1998, pp. 74–75.
Sanders, Mark, "Lucy Orta", *Blueprint*, no. 150 May 1998, p. 34.
Sumpter, Helen, "Art Couture", *The Big Issue London*, 27 April 1998.
Woehl, Annick, "L'artiste-araignée", *La Colmar*, 14 November 1998, p. 48.
Zaya, Octavio and Paul Virilio, "Nexus Architecture", *Atlantica* no. 19, 1998, pp. 74–81.
Yann, C, "La Street Life de Lucy Orta", *Jalouse*, no. 8, March 1998.

1997
Ardenne, Paul, ed., *L'Age Contemporain*, Paris: Editions du Regard, 1997, pp. 200, 339.
David, Catherine and Paul Virilio, eds., "The Dark Spot of Art", in *Documenta Documents 1*, Ostfildern: Cantz, 1997, p. 50.
Dikeou, Devon, "Survival Kit", *Zing Magazine*, 1997.
Orta, Jorge, "Antartique 2000", *Effet de Lieu—3e imperial*, 1997, pp. 39–46.
Orta, Lucy, "From the nest to the web", *View Point*, 1997, pp. 116–124.
Gooding, Mel, "Jorge Orta with Lucy Orta signs-light", in *Public:Art:Space*, 1997, p. 52.
Guillaume, Valérie, "Architectures Corporelles", *Art Press*, no. spécial 18, 1997, pp. 84–85.
Restany, Pierre, "La drammatizzazione del vincolo sociale", *Domus*, no. 793, May 1997, pp. 102–103.
Morozzi, Cristina, "Wearing vs. Inhabiting", *Intramuros*, no. 73, 1997, p. 25.
Quick, Harriet, "Lucy Orta: la mode dans la rue", *Vogues Hommes International*, no. 2, 1997, pp. 154–155.
Virilio, Paul, "Les scaphandres urbains", in *Le Sabord*, Trois Rivières, QUE: Edition Le Sabord, 1997, pp. 24–25.
Virilio, Paul, "Urban Armor", *Dazed & Confused*, no. 29, March 1997, pp. 72–79.
Zugazagoitia, Julian, *Misteri della Presenza, magia della luce*, Spoleto: Spoleto Festival, 1997, pp. 24–27.

1996
Bamberger, Nicole, *Lucy Orta, Kits de Survie*, Paris: Jardin des Modes, 1996, p. 8.
Coleman, David, "In Soho, Art and Fashion are on the outs", *The New York Times*, 15 September 1996.
J-F, J, "Jorge Orta allume le four des Casseaux", *L'Echo du Centre*, 4 September 1996.
D, P, "Premier rendez-vous sous la lune au four des Casseaux", *Le Populaire*, 13 July 1996.
Polegato, Lino, "Commune Communicate", *Flux News Liege*, no. 10, August 1996, p. 3.
Piguet, Philippe, "Architectures Corporelles", *L'Oeil*, no. 478, January 1996, p. 10.

1995
Cabasset, Patrick, "Lucy Orta", *Vogue France*, no. 754, March 1995, p. 85.
Dellinger, Jade, "Lucy Orta", *Zing Magazine*, Autumn 1995.
De Vandière, Anne, "Éthique dans l'esthétique", *Avenue*, no. 1, 1995, pp. 53–55.
Glusberg, Jorge, "Orta, un argentino en Venecia", *Artes Visuales*, 6 June 1995, p. 4.
Orta, Jorge, "La peinture luminographique", *Revue International de l'Eclairage*, March 1995, pp. 96–99.
Painchaud, Rita, and Charland, Denis, "Porteur de lumière", *Le Sabord*, Autumn 1995, pp. 4–12.
Siegle, Jean-Dominique, "Des top models à l'Armée du Salut", *Beaux Arts Magazine*, 1995, p. 20.
Mohal, Anna, "Der Kunstler als Dandy", *Atelier 1*, 1995.

1994
Boutoulle, Myriam, "Après les falaises de Cuenca, il va tagger la cathédrale de Chartres", VSD, 8 September 1994, pp. 84–87.
Boutoulle, Myriam, "Jorge Orta illumine Chartres", *Beaux Arts Magazine*, September 1994, p. 20.
Boudaud, Michel, "Lumiéres d'exception sur la cathédrale de Chartres", *Le Chartre*, 1994, p. 2.
Fayolle, Claire, "Vêtement Refuge", *Archicrée* no. 260, Autumn 1994, p. 26.
Gabrion, Isabelle, "Du Machu Picchu à Chartres, une même lumière", *La République*, 12 August 1994.
Gauville, Hervé, "Tremplin pour débutants", *Libération* no. 42, 9 November 1994.
Piguet, Philippe, "Cité de Refuge", *La Croix*, 7 November 1994.
Pittolo, Véronique, "Les petits endroits pour le corps", *Beaux Arts Magazine*, 1994, p. 129.
"Chartres celebrates its 800th birthday in light", *The European*, September 1994, p. 4.
Roussillat, Jean-Claude, "Chartres: symphonie de lumières sur la cathédrale", *La République*, 18 September 1994, p. 5.
Sissons, Saskia, "Technicolour extravaganza leaves Chartres spellbound", *The European*, 23–29 September 1994, p. 3.

1993
A, A,"'La luz en el paisaje'ofrecerá una imagen irrepetible de Cuenca", *Cuenca*, 24 September 1993, p. 7.
A, A, "Noche mágica en la Hoz del Huécar", *Cuenca*, 26 August 1993, p.6.
Ergino, Nathalie, "Living Room", *Documents*, no. 2 February 1993, pp. 24–26.
Hemmings, Jessica, "Political Art", *Fiberarts USA*, January 1993.
Lebenglik, Fabián, "El color que cayó del cielo", *Plastica*, 19 January 1993, p. 12.
Marot, Laurent, "Le Machu Picchu à l'heure du XXIème siècle", *Perù*, 30 April 1993, p. 26.
Montanaro, Hugo, "Claude Namer y Jorge Orta", *Art Nexus*, 1993, pp. 146–147.

1992
Bruzzone, Andres, "Fuego Sobre Machu Picchu", *Descubrir*, November 1992, pp. 17–20.
Dupoint, Juliette, "E improvisamente sul machu picchu", *Corriere della Sera*, 11 September 1992, pp. 41–47.
Jacquot, Didier, "Une éclatante leçon de ténèbres", *La Nouvelle République du Centre-Ouest*, 12 April 1992.
Mongibeaux, Jean-François, "Feux sur Machu Picchu" *Le Figaro magazine*, 11 July 1992, pp. 38–42.
Nale, Eduardo, "Un argentino proyectó enormes signos sobre Machu Picchu", *La Maga*, 9 December 1992, p. 28.
Silva-Santisteban, Rocio, "Huellas en los Andes", *Somos Cronicas*, May 1992, p. 41.
"Fiesta: Oiticica et Orta", *Muséart*, July–August 1992, p. 130.
Videla, Albino Dieguez, "A la iluminación por el arte", *La Prensa*, 29 November 1992.

1991
Mackey, Jorge, "Cuando el arte encuentra su razón de ser", *La Capital*, 19 May 1991.

1983
"Una nueva forma de arte 'para ponerse'", *Democracia del litoral*, 13 December 1993, p. 23.

1981
"Artista purificador de sus propias busquedas", *Rosario*, 19 April 1981.

1975
Miércoles, Nicolas, "Oleos y xilografias de Jorge Ignacio Orta acabada muestra de un estilo y una obsession", *El Norte*, August 1975.

Black Dog Publishing Limited
10A Acton Street
London
WC1X 9NG

T. +44 (0)207 713 5097
F. +44 (0)207 713 8682
E. info@blackdogonline.com

All opinions expressed within this publication are those of the author and not necessarily of the publisher.

Edited by Lucy Orta
Designed by Ellen Gögler

British Library Cataloguing-in-Publication Data.
A CIP record for this book is available from the British Library.

ISBN 978 1 907317 04 0

Black Dog Publishing is an environmentally responsible company. *Lucy+Jorge Orta: Light Works* is printed on FSC accredited paper.

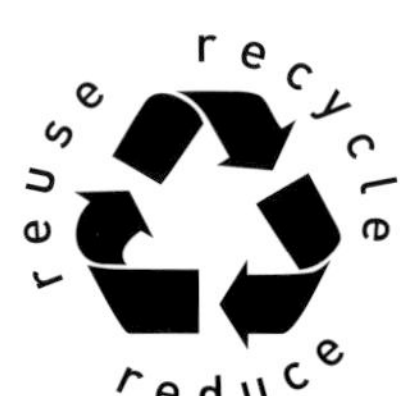

architecture art design
fashion history photography
theory and things

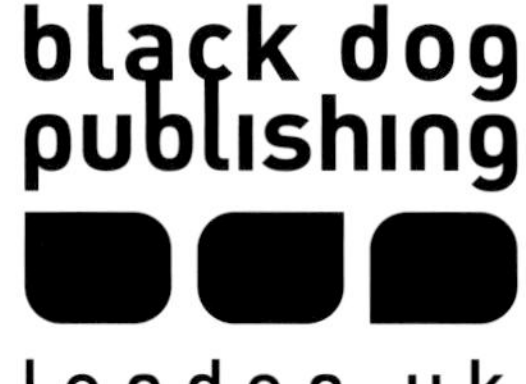

www.blackdogonline.com